SAILING YACHT DESIGN

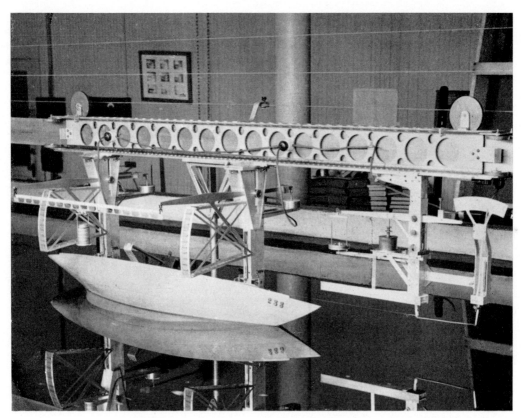

1. A model being tested in the Stevens Tank, Hoboken, U.S.A.

Sailing Yacht Design

THIRD EDITION

BY

Douglas Phillips-Birt

A.M.R.I.N.A.

Adlard Coles Ltd   London

Granada Publishing Limited
First published in Great Britain 1951 by Adlard Coles Ltd
3 Upper James Street London W1R 4BP
Frogmore St Albans Hertfordshire AL2 2NF

Second edition 1966
Second impression second edition 1969
Third impression second edition 1971
Fourth impression second edition 1972
Third edition 1976

ISBN 0 229 11563 2
Printed in Great Britain by
Fletcher & Son Ltd, Norwich

Contents

List of Diagrams

List of Plates

Acknowledgements

My thanks are due to many people. Some of the material in this book appeared originally in the *Yachting Monthly* and *Yachting World*, and to their editors Maurice Griffiths and Bernard Hayman, and likewise to Iliffe Books, Ltd., the publishers of *Yachting World Annual*, which was edited by myself, I am grateful for permission to reproduce. A larger part of the chapter on Rating Rules was originally delivered as a paper before the Royal Institution of Naval Architects in London, and to the Institution I owe thanks for permission to republish the paper and the discussion following it, which appears as Appendix 8. Appendix 9 is reprinted by kind permission of the Offshore Rating Council.

For allowing me to publish their designs I am grateful to James McGruer, A. Mason (U.S.A.), Arthur Robb, F. B. R. Brown, John Alden (U.S.A.), Abeking and Rasmussen, J. Laurent Giles and Partners, while Ian Proctor was good enough to let me use the sectional drawings and basic scantlings of his range of light alloy masts. To Robert Clark I owe a rigging list and to Alan Buchanan a full building specification, both excellent examples of their kind.

In the acknowledgements to the first edition, of which this book is an expanded and considerably rewritten version, I mentioned that the origin of the work was a series of articles published in *Yachts and Yachting* shortly after the war, and portions of these articles remain in the present text. At that time I was helped by the British Shipbuilding Research Association with books from their library usually loaned to members only. Since then, a period on the Advisory Committee for Yacht Research has led me to appreciate the extreme poverty of fundamental scientific knowledge of sailing yacht design and the essentially *ad hoc* character of most design methods—of which this book is a witness. I confess to scepticism as to whether practising yacht architects have yet been much assisted by the offerings of purer science.

Certainly we should remember what Jack Laurent Giles once said in a lecture: "Beware of him who claims knowledge of yacht design, for we know only about the rudiments—the rest is conjecture." My final acknowledgement should be to my friends the designers for the inspiration of their work.

Preface

WHEN this book was first published the International Offshore Rule was still under discussion, and both its ultimate form and even whether a common rating rule throughout the world for offshore racing yachts would become a reality, were matters of uncertainty. Now the rule has been in use internationally and a Mark III version has appeared, which is published in full in Appendix Nine.

That it is a rule of forbidding aspect has become widely appreciated. In attempting to do so much it has become tied into knots of equations the character of which may make pure mathematicians wince. Certainly yacht architects may despair of ever seeing the ultimate boat through the thickets of symbols. Sir David Mackworth has made a detailed quantitive study of the rule, and has contributed Appendix Ten, in which he describes computer methods of analysis and draws some conclusions. The span of a designer's lifetime not having increased at the same rate as the complexity of rules, the computer would now seem to have become an essential tool for the designer of offshore racing yachts.

The I.O.R. rule has, so far as hull measurements and formula are concerned, the basic structure of the old R.O.R.C. rule, but with a number of additions. The observations made on the latter rule in Chapter Nine have been retained; also Appendix Eight, which in so far as it concerns the now defunct R.O.R.C. rule, is a useful introduction to Appendices Nine and Ten.

The radical changes in keel profiles that have occurred and proved acceptable in even large yachts of ocean going type will be evident from a comparison of Fig. 28B and Fig. 35. To what extent designs of this type are attributable to the fact that measurement rules — even the I.O.R. — do not assess wetted surface is uncertain. In fact, the reduction on wetted surface achieved by the fin-keel and independent rudder configuration may not always be considerable, and this design, which has now become the conventional, does appear to have merits apart from considerations purely of rating. But directional stability has certainly been reduced. Efforts to preserve it to an adequate degree have been partly responsible for the fitting of rudder skegs and tabs on the fin-keel. These return some of the wetted surface that had been eliminated by adopting the fin and independent rudder form, and bring it back in a more offensive form, since the frictional coefficients for these shorter appendages are higher than those for an unbroken full keel.

It will be noticed that in Fig. 28B, right hand design, the rudder is hung on a skeg raked forward from the bottom, and the trim tab on the fin is similarly angled. This feature has been shown in the model testing tanks to be advantageous in terms of lower resistance for a given rudder angle. Whether the effects of small appendages can be accurately reproduced in the tank is open to question, owing to the different frictional régime in which the model operates compared with the full scale craft. But this feature of skeg design is worthy of note and is becoming more common.

The reliability of modern mechanisms has made the "lifting keel" practicable, though to what degree it can become widely acceptable other than in advanced racers is doubtful. By "lifting keel" is meant one that may be withdrawn wholly inside the hull, together with its load of ballast; which differentiates it from the centreboard, which has no sensible effect on stability due to weight. When the latter is fully lifted, there still remains the partial or stub keel, containing the ballast, as an appendage to the canoe body. The lifting keel, when lowered, is able to carry the centre of gravity of the ballast to a depth perhaps greater than that in a fixed deep keel yacht.

The lifting keel has long been an ideal. It has always been irking that in order to win the fine gift of weatherliness in a deep draught yacht, it is necessary also to drag the keel and ballast through the water when the wind frees and lateral area and stability diminish in importance. The lifting keel has obvious advantages. Also several objections apart from cost. Should the keel jam when raised, the stability is much reduced, and the canoe body with no lateral plane whatever would be a cripple when worked to windward. Clearly, this could lead to a dangerous position at sea.

It has been claimed that one advantage of drawing the keel up into the hull is that the prismatic coefficient of the hull is thereby increased, with great advantage at the higher sailing speeds compared even with a conventional centreboard yacht with its partial keel containing the ballast, which cannot of course be retracted. It is believed that this is a misreading of the significance of the prismatic coefficient (see page 64 et seq.) and that no advantage accrues on this score.

While developments in keel configurations and rig have been the remarkable feature of late years, only the bustle stern marks any vital development in hull form. The effect of this is to produce a lower wave making resistance at the higher speeds, and this *is* indeed a prismatic effect. Such discontinuities in the absolute fairness of hull lines are well-known features of naval architecture. The bulbous bow has become familiar today in steamships. The possibilities of the bulbous stern were recognised about a quarter of a century ago, but no advantage could be taken of this in propeller driven ships owing to its effect on the wake stream. This objection not applying under sail, the bulbous stern, or bustle, has become a valuable feature of hull form.

It is now well recognised that most of the more practical questions about the hull form of sailing yachts have to be answered empirically in the model testing tank. It is worth noting that Frederik Henrik Chapman was using models some 200 years ago to develop the hulls of sailing vessels. A reprint of Chapman's famous *Architectura Navalis Mercatoria* (1768) — a folio of superb ship plans and drawings — formerly, I believe, available only in a German edition, has just been produced by the publishers of this book.

In this Third edition, the opportunity is taken to add, in Appendix Nine, the amendments to the International Offshore Rule, the incorporation of which produces Mark III.

CHAPTER ONE

Introductory Note

THE ideal designer of sailing yachts is a magnificent creature who is at once a hydro-dynamist, an aerodynamist, an engineer, a practical boatbuilder, an experienced seaman under sail, and an artist. The last qualification is nebulous and unteachable, but it is no less than the cement holding together the other qualifications and making them serviceable.

For the capital problem in the design of a sailing yacht is the multiplicity of the factors involved, which make it impossible to rationalise the activity and reduce it, except in the broadest terms, into a system that may be applied by rule. It used to be said that Best Boat = Best Hull + Best Rig. Research has now shown that this was a convenient over-simplification and the equation must be rewritten Best Boat = Best (Hull + Rig) Combination. This adds yet further to the tumult of variables through which an architect has to find his way partly by faith in his star, by a sense of direction that is instinctive rather than rational.

FOUR BASIC DEFINITIONS It is necessary at the outset to become familiar with the fundamental definitions given below:

Displacement. A floating body displaces a weight of liquid equal to its own weight. A yacht which weighs 10 tons makes a hole in the sea which would contain 10 tons of water were the yacht not occupying it. If a model yacht weighing 40 lb. is lowered into a full bath, 40 lb. of water will overflow. It should be added that a yacht of 10 tons Thames Measurement rarely displaces this weight, but usually appreciably less, and there is no connection between the two measurements.

To calculate the displacement of a yacht, the volume of her immersed body has to be found. This may be done from the hull lines, using certain rules which were first applied to this work in the eighteenth century. They were described by Vice-Admiral Frederik Chapman, the father of naval architecture and a competent man of letters also, in his *Treatise on Shipbuilding* published in 1775. The method in use today is little changed. Having calculated the displacement from the drawings, it is then known that the yacht must weigh this amount if it is to float at the assumed waterline.

Centre of Buoyancy. Buoyancy, therefore, is equal to weight, the upthrust of the one balancing the downthrust of the other. Buoyancy acts on all parts of the submerged hull, but just as the distributed weight of a solid body may be assumed to be concentrated at the point where the body balances—the centre of gravity—so buoyancy may be regarded as a single force acting through the centre of buoyancy. The centre is situated at the C.G. of a solid form having the shape of the vessel's underwater body. It is the C.G. of a block of ice so shaped as to fill the hole which a yacht makes in the water. In fact, the centre of buoyancy was originally called the centre of gravity of the displacement.

Centre of Gravity. This is the point where the many components of a vessel's weight

16

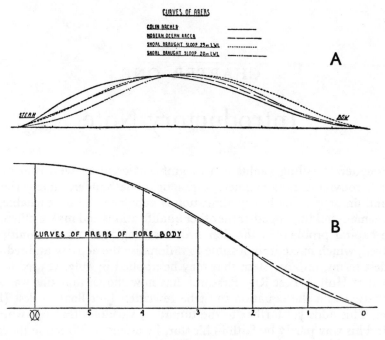

CURVES OF AREAS

COLIN ARCHER ⸻

MODERN OCEAN RACER ⸻

SHOAL DRAUGHT SLOOP 29ft LWL ⋯⋯⋯⋯

SHOAL DRAUGHT SLOOP 20ft LWL ⸺ ⸺

A

STERN   BOW

CURVES OF AREAS OF FORE BODY

B

Fig. 1. *Curves of areas*

may be assumed to be concentrated. Since the hull of a yacht is approximately symmetrical about its central plane, the centre of buoyancy is in this plane, and if the yacht is to float without a list, the C.G. must be in the plane also. Heavy weights on one side must be balanced by equally heavy ones on the other.

The same applies to fore and aft trim. If a yacht is to float at the waterline shown on her drawings, not only must her weight be equal to that of the water which, according to the drawings, will be displaced at that waterline, but the longitudinal C.G. must fall in the same fore and aft line as the C.B. If the actual C.G. is aft or forward of the C.B. shown, the yacht will sink by the stern or head in order to bring the C.B. into line with the C.G.

Curve of Areas. The waterline length of a yacht is usually divided, for purposes of design, into ten equal parts by eleven ordinates, at each of which is drawn a transverse section. If the underwater area of each section is measured and then put through Simpson's rule, the displacement may be found. If the section areas are plotted, to a convenient linear scale, along equally spaced ordinates at right angles to a line representing the waterline length, a curve drawn through the points is a curve of areas. Fig. 1 shows the curves for three yachts, together with one curve which was once mistakenly assumed to be an ideal shape. The curve of areas gives a picture of the way in which the displacement is disposed along the length of the hull. A full-ended yacht will have a full-ended curve; one with fine ends will show a more tapering curve. It will be seen that the 29-ft. shoal draught sloop is full-ended, while the smaller one is less so. The ocean racer is the finest of the three forward, but aft she has as full a body as either of the others.

The curve of areas has many uses in the course of design.

2. The *Jullinar*, showing the reduced wetted surface and the excess of water-line length over measured length (Science Museum).

3. The *America*, with fine lines in the fore and after bodies (Science Museum).

4. The *Volunteer*, of the "compromise" American type, with less beam and more draught than earlier yachts (Science Museum).

5. The *Mosquito*, designed according to Scott Russell's wave line theory in 1848 (Science Museum).

CHAPTER TWO

The Progress of Yacht Design

DURING the centuries when the sailing ship dominated the seas, little was known of the science of hull form. The modelling of a ship's hull remained, throughout the ages of sail, a matter of instinct and guess handicapped periodically by misleading theories; and the sun which set on the last of the Viking galleys had seen a ship as well-shaped for speed as the one which rose on the first yachts of Victoria's reign. In rig there had been some progress; in habitability the *Waterwitch* of 1832, built by Joseph White of Cowes, was an advance on the longship of Lief Ericsson. But Joseph White and the remote Viking ship-wright would have found themselves speaking the same language and unable to answer the same questions, in any discussion on the hull shape of their creations (Fig. 2).

A knowledge of the science which governs hull design grew up with the steamship. By the time it had reached any significant bulk, the sailing ship had ceased to be of any great naval or commercial value. But it had become a thing of pleasure, and the new science which was growing up with power ships was applied to sailing yachts. A knowledge of the basic facts of design was thus gained, but because the separate problem of the sailing yacht was not studied apart from the steamship, even the new race of educated designers, which grew out of the shipwright-designers of an earlier generation, still owed their success mainly to sound instinct and artistic inspiration.

*　　*　　*

In Falconer's *Navalis Architecturalis* there is a plate showing an elevation plan of a sailing ship, and superimposed upon its underwater body is a fish. This may not have been the dawn of the cod's head and mackerel's tail theory of hull design, but it is a striking and authoritative support for the idea which still guided the shape of the first yachts over a hundred years later. "The Arts are very much helped," said William Sutherland in the *Shipwright's Assistant* of 1700, "by observing how nature displays herself in forming of creatures suitably to their various actions in the several elements."

To find an analogy between the action of a fish and that of a ship was easy, and equally so was it to overlook the essential difference between a body moving totally immersed in a fluid and one such as a ship travelling on the surface and introducing thereby totally different considerations. The young designer of a later day, who was rumoured to have measured the immersed cross-section areas of the duck destined for his Sunday luncheon was observing nature to better effect than his forerunners who concentrated on the displacement distribution of many different breeds of fish.

It was the fish form which dominated in the shape of the smaller naval vessels in the early nineteenth century, and the first yachts in both England and America imitated the navy and the pilot boats, though they usually had lighter scantlings. Yachting in its modern from is the product of Victorian prosperity, and prior to 1837 there were probably

B

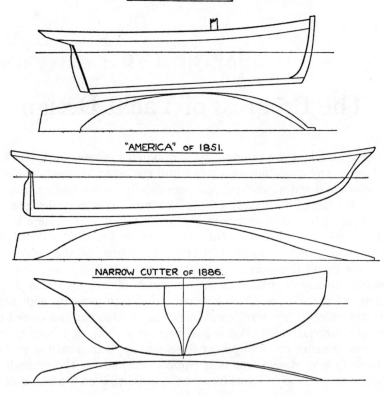

FIG. 2. *Round bow, hollow bow and plank-on-edge types*

not a hundred yachts in existence of more than 20 tons. There was little progress in the sport until after the Crimean War. The yachts which developed then were of about three to three and a half beams to their length, high-sided, and rather crank as a result of the popular "round as an apple" midship section combined with all inside ballast. The greatest beam was a little ahead of admidships, and the bows were full and round, the angle of entrance at the waterline being about 30 degrees. The buttock lines were steep forward, but had a beautifully smooth, gentle sweep along the after-body, which designers today sometimes manage to embody in hulls having a waterline form much superior to that of the early yachts. The volumes of the fore- and after-bodies were about equal, the centre of buoyancy being amidships. The bluff bows were bad in a seaway, and the ships were slow, though reputably fairly dry—probably on account of their slowness.

The system of design at this time, and for the next forty years, was the carving of a wood block model to a shape that pleased the eye. On completion, the model was sawn into sections, from which the offsets were measured. Or sometimes, as a refinement of this procedure, the block was made from a number of planks dowelled together, and which were separated on completion of the carving, when they gave the shape of the yacht's waterlines in plan. The shapes were then transferred to paper by running a pencil round the curve of each plank in turn, the lines being thus reconstructed on paper. But the majority of design work never entered the paper stage. This precluded all but the most elementary calculations. Many of the rule-of-thumb designers were unable to calculate displacement, or sometimes even to define the meaning of it.

* * *

Yacht design in the U.S.A. was at this time probably superior in technique to that prac-tised in Britain. It was partly attributable to the fact that American yachting was founded not by landsmen turning to the sea for a sport and pastime, but chiefly by men who had made money in shipping, and who often themselves were shipmasters. They tended to prefer the work of experienced designers of big ships to the efforts of the small boatbuilder. There remains from the late eighteenth and early nineteenth centuries enough evidence in surviving drawings to show not only a high state of draughtsmanship, but also of excellent technical acquirements in marine architecture. The calculation of displacement and centre of buoyancy, even of stability, was common, and so was the use of the C.E. and C.L.R.; also a recognition of the approximate nature of their conventionally assumed positions—in which respect we are only a little wiser today.

Models were used, however, to offset an important deficiency in draughtsmanship. This was the lack of knowledge of the buttock line projection. The importance of a smooth, clean delivery of water along the after-body of the hull was recognised, as it was by English shipwrights; but without buttock lines this could not be checked on a drawing. So, for the fairing of the run and after-body, either a model had to be used, or alterations made on the mould and ribands when the hull was in frame.

Thus the model and drawings might be used in collaboration. But, curiously, a decline in the standards of American design occurred. The model, instead of remaining an accept-able adjunct of intelligent design, developed into a means simply of whittling hull shapes. By 1850, British and American design appear to have been equally bad in technique, and remained so for a couple of decades.

Those interested in the development of scientific design were keen to decry the model carving method of developing hull lines. In Britain, P. R. Marett, in his famous *Yacht Building*—a pioneer work—wrote: "The great want of scientific principle in the construc-tion of yachts must be evident to anyone who has given the matter any consideration . . ." and described the model method as a "pernicious influence." Perhaps he overstated his case in the flush of rebellion against rule-of-thumb methods. Today we look back rather more leniently on the carvers of models, knowing that all designers are in a big measure instinctive modellers. Steers, the *America*'s designer, not only used the model but also sometimes adjusted the lines of his craft when they were in frame, having the ribands removed, and the moulds pared down here, padded out there, until the shape satisfied his eye.

A quarter of a century or more after Steers had polished the shape of the *America* in this way the great American architect of his day, Carey Smith, was adopting the same technique, spending hours in the mould loft, or in the building shed, fairing the hull lines with a shipwright. He also used models, prepared oversize from an initial set of lines, which he worked down to a shape that pleased his eye. This, it should be remembered, was a highly qualified American designer who had been influenced by Marett, whose first yacht, the *Vindex* of 1870, had been laughed at as a "paper boat" because she had been drawn not whittled, and who later designed *Vanitie* which was to serve as a trial horse to the first *Endeavour* prior to the 1934 America's Cup series. There is nothing fundamentally objectionable in the use of models during the process of design. Models do not necessarily produce bad design; but in the fifties of the last century they had done so.

The "want of scientific principle," so evident at that time, was not so much a matter of technique, but of the lack of knowledge behind it. It was not until the results were known of William Froude's enquiry into the nature of ship resistance, which was begun in 1867, that any rational approach to the subject of yacht design could be made. Froude developed the technique of model tank testing, and it was from model experiments that a sound knowledge of the principles of hull form was gained. They were to be the guides of Watson, Fife, Nicholson, and their followers.

*   *   *

But prior to Froude's work there had been many tentative and often confusing theories developed, as efforts were made to learn some better solution to the secret of the form of least resistance than that offered by the fish theory.

Models were used in the attempts to elucidate the problem. As early as 1763 it had been decided that the resistance of a ship varied as the square of the speed, a singularly close approximation to the truth for the speeds at which sailing ships move; and even this knowledge has been partly anticipated in the previous century. Further experiments, made in 1775 by towing models, extended this knowledge and showed that at higher speeds the resistance increased at a greater rate than the square of the speed. Such conclusions were true to the facts established a century later. The exact nature of the resistance encountered by a ship was still unknown, and it is this which is of value to the practising designer. It was guessed, and rightly, that the shape and area of the midship had an important influence on resistance. This partial truth was extended to the definite untruth that the resistance of a yacht was equal to that of a flat board having the shape and area of the midship section, and towed through the water with the flat surface leading. This idea was commonly held until the middle of the nineteenth century.

The fact that a major portion of a yacht's total resistance was due to surface friction was not sufficiently well understood to have any practical effect on design until the late nineteenth century. "I had the advantage," wrote G. L. Watson, " . . . of specially early access to Professor Froude's investigations, and cut [away the wetted surface of the 5-ton *Clotilde*] in a somewhat timid fashion, though sufficient for her at that time to be compared to a cart-wheel, with the accompanying prediction that she might run on land but would never sail in salt water." But this was nearly eighty years later.

The most detailed research prior to Froude into the resistance of ships was that done by Vice-Admiral Frederik Chapman and it is of interest to note that eighty years later, in an edition of *Yachts and Yacht Building*, Marett still expressed great faith in Chapman's work and especially in a geometrical system of designing devised by him.

Chapman was the first to realise the fact, which today is a fundamental of naval architecture, that the way in which the bulk of the hull is disposed fore and aft has a big influence on resistance. As a result of experiments with models, and the analysis of the lines of many ships, he showed that the ideal distribution varies with different types, but it was the cod's head and mackerel's tail form which he generally favoured.

Chapman tried to find a law governing the distribution of the displacement. For a range of designs, he divided the area of each section by a constant, which was the breadth at the midship section, and he plotted the quotients along perpendiculars set off from a base-line. He found that the curve through the points frequently resembled a parabola in successful ships. Working back from this, he produced a series of formulae from which, having decided on the leading features and dimensions of a design, the sectional areas might be calculated. If, in drawing a design, the areas thus found were adhered to, the displacement and position of the centre of buoyancy did not need subsequent calculation, both features being predetermined in the original calculations. It was, as Marett said, an "elegant principle" and he showed some attractive yacht designs of his period based upon it.

*   *   *

In 1851 the *America* sailed to England, and by her success caused English yachtsmen, and the more educated of the builders, to consider what was wrong with the shapes of their yachts. Amongst them was John Fincham, a Master Shipwright of Portsmouth Dockyard. Twenty-five years earlier he had criticised the yachts of the Royal Yacht Squadron, and had suggested that a scientific examination of yacht shapes should be made by taking off the lines of existing yachts and examining their elements. The secrecy in which builders held their models made this impossible—some years later Hunt's Universal Yacht List regretted that builders were not keener to publish details of their yachts—but with the *America*'s success Fincham again urged his views.

In hull shape the *America* (Fig. 2) was the antithesis of the English yacht's "fish form." Her fore-body was long and her after-body short; the angle of entrance at the waterline was only 17 degrees, and there were 7 in. of hollow in the run of the bow. Her greatest beam was well aft of amidships, and her centre of buoyancy 4 ft. aft of this point. The *America* was the new idea in yacht design, and she was to influence the shape of yachts for the rest of the century, and to some extent even up to the present day. But she was the great advertiser of an idea rather than its originator. The *Mosquito*, built in England in 1848, had been given a long, hollow-lined bow, but the yacht was not successful, and the experiment received little notice. Even earlier, in 1826, the *Menai* had been built for that indefatigable experimenter T. Assheton Smith, with a long hollow bow which gained the yacht all the obliquity which yachting writers so often gave to the unusual. But the *Menai*, like the *Mosquito* twenty-two years later, made no converts.

During these years Scott Russell was propounding his wave-line theory of design which had the effect of producing a shape of hull similar to that of the *Mosquito* and the *America*. The theory behind the system was ingenious but fallacious. It specified fixed lengths for the fore- and after-bodies, the former being 60 per cent of the length, whilst the shape of the waterlines, all of which were to be of the same nature, were to be in the form of a mathematical curve representing the distribution of water in a sea-wave. The effect on hull shape was to produce a long hollow-lined bow and a short, full stern. The schooner *Titania*, of 100 tons, was built to test Russell's ideas, but she was not successful, probably because of her defects aloft. It is an interesting fact that this yacht did not fully conform to the theory which she was built to test, but few yachts ever did so with precision owing to the exaggerated shape produced by the stereotyped curves.

It has never been explained how George Steers, the *America*'s designer, came to adopt the long, hollow-bow model of hull, which was as much a reversal of the current practice in America as it was in England. The *America* was not his first design of this shape, the

Mary Taylor having preceded her; and it seems likely that Steers had heard of Russell's theory and was guided by it. The success of the hollow-bow yachts in the U.S.A. led to the reconstruction of many older craft of bluff-bow vintage, the fore-bodies being lengthened and their curvatures flattened.

The same thing happened in England. A large part of the English yachting fleet was virtually rebuilt, the apple bows being removed and the yachts lengthened with long, knife-like bows. And there is no doubt that as a result faster and better yachts were often produced, but the fine bows cannot receive all the credit. The apparent superiority of the fine bows was partly due to the lengthening of the hull which resulted, though at this time the importance of length for speed was not fully realised. And much of the real talent in Steer's work was not realised—the perfect harmony of the fore- and after-bodies, the smoothly flowing curves and the beautiful proportions and balance. The *America* was steered with a tiny tiller, and Lord de Blaquiere, who subsequently owned her, wrote: ". . . I steered her when going seven knots close hauled and in some Bay of Naples swell, standing to leeward of the tiller and pressing against it with my little finger only."

Scott Russell's wave-line theory produced hulls of unreasonable fullness aft and fineness forward, and as a result of the lengthening of the bows, the proportions of many yachts became bad. The perfect balance of the *America* was lost for many decades. The fish-form theory did not die; from time to time it was resurrected, and for a number of years after the appearance of the hollow bow Mr. Fincham insisted that good behaviour at sea was the result of having the centre of buoyancy ahead of amidships. But the blending of the fine and full bows to produce harmonious and balanced hulls of today was not to occur for many decades.

In 1852, Lord Robert Montague's *Treatise on Shipbuilding, Including Yachts* appeared, and at about the same time Marett's book was first published. Marett favoured the fine bow, so lately arrived at the time when he wrote, but he strongly criticised the stereotyping of form produced by Scott Russell's wave-line theory. His book was an excellently reasoned approach to yacht design. He sought to rationalise the intuitive knowledge of form which had made the shape of so many successful yachts, and hence to arrive at the general laws which govern proportions and type. The greater part of the book consisted of the most careful and detailed analyses of many successful yachts, and though today the work is of historical interest only, for a long time it was the standard guide to the art of yacht design.

It is particularly interesting to see that Marett studied the shape of the heeled waterlines. Today, in one of the latest works on naval architecture, the section which deals with yachts suggests that the shape of the heeled waterlines is the surest test of hull balance. Marett also stresses that ". . . unless the several centres of gravity maintain the same relative positions after inclination, the constructor's care in designing the vessel is rendered nearly useless." The phraseology is unfamiliar, but this insistence that a yacht should maintain her fore and aft trim on heeling is one of the usually important conditions of a balanced hull.

The years between 1860 and 1890 saw English yachts becoming progressively narrower (Fig. 2), reaching a climax in such craft as the *Oona*, which had more than six beams in her waterline length.* This evolution in form was not the result of any knowledge of hull design, though it was partly due to developments in construction

* See also page 51.

methods. The narrowing of yachts was due to the tonnage laws, with their excessively heavy tax on beam, which allowed yachts to be made larger and heavier, and hence able to carry more sail area, provided that beam was reduced to compensate for the greater length. Thus the 5-tonners grew in length from about 25 ft. to 34 ft., in displacement from 6 tons to 12 tons, and in sail area from about 700 sq. ft. to over 1,000 sq. ft. And the price for the greater dimensions was paid in beam, which in the smaller boat would have been about 7 ft. 3 in., and in the larger was 5 ft. 6 in. Adequate stability for the huge sail spreads of the long narrow boats was made possible by the development of the out-side lead keel attached by keel bolts—perhaps the most significant of all constructional developments in yacht design, and for a long time resolutely distrusted.

Thus design became a matter of how to apply more brute force to propulsion, not how to reduce the resistance which had to be propelled.

Whilst in England this lack of knowledge was not productive of actually dangerous yachts, craft were produced in the U.S.A. between 1860 and 1880 which were unfit for serious sailing. As W. P. Stephens has said: "The capsizing of small open boats and yachts, even when attended by fatal results, was too common to attract much notice; and the larger yachts came in for a full share of very narrow escapes and an occasional disaster . . ."

In England, ignorance of the laws of naval architecture was ameliorated by the fundamentally stable type of yacht encouraged by the tonnage laws and the rating rules derived from them. Even when the extremes of narrowness represented by such yachts as the *Oona* had been reached, stability was ensured by the great draught and weight of keel; such yachts heeled rapidly to a big angle and then became very stiff; capsizing was impossible since at no angle of heel did these lead-mines lose their righting moment.

In the U.S.A. the shoal draught centreboard yacht, than which no type demands more knowledgeable design, became the dominant type, and gradually displaced the deeper draught keel yachts such as the *America*. Thus it came about that whilst on one side of the Atlantic yachts yearly became narrower and deeper, on the other they became broader and shallower. Two national types were born, each of which is still reflected in the modern practice in design. The laws of stability were not understood, ballast was wholly internal, and yachts of remarkable beam and shallowness, having much initial stiffness but a small range of stability, dominated the American yachting scene. The greatest of the disasters which occurred was that to the *Mohawk* in 1876, a schooner of 140 ft. in length and drawing only 6 ft., which was lost when lying at anchor with her sails set. She was struck by a squall coming off the high hills of Staten Island, and capsized, drowning her owner and his guests.

But still, several years later, there was no conviction that the deep draught, heavily ballasted British type was the right one. When two such yachts threatened to challenge for the *America*'s Cup in 1885, two authoritative American opinions were unflattering: "I have doubt that the English yachts will get here. . . . I think an Atlantic passage will jerk the sticks out of them," wrote one. "The ability of modern British racing yachts to live at sea is yet problematical," wrote another. "The attempt to sail over here, except in the finest weather, would be dangerous, rash and foolhardy in my opinion; for these deep, sharp, lead-loaded sailing machines have no reserve buoyancy, and when pressed they must pound . . . you will not see any of these diving-bells over here yet awhile."

*   *   *

The opposed types of yacht existing on each side of the Atlantic led to fierce competition when the two met, and to equally fierce battles in the press conducted by such writers of prowess as W. P. Stephens, Captains McKay and Coffin, and C. P. Kunhardt. And the winning side, as in most battles of lasting significance, was the one which favoured a compromise between extremes.

The two types became merged into one which was beamier than the English planks on edge, deeper than the American skimming dishes, and with outside ballast. This evolution of form was largely due to the work of amateurs who studied design and raised it to drawing-table status. It may be noted that Edward Burgess, the father of Starling, both of whom may be said to have made a profession out of designing America's Cup defenders, was himself an amateur, who turned to his hobby for a livelihood when his family's fortunes failed.

The evolution of the compromise between the two extremes occupied many years. The seamarks of progress are such yachts as the *Vindex* of 1871, which was narrower and deeper than the current skimming dishes; the *Mischief* of ten years later, which was wider and shallower than the English craft, but had an outside keel; and the first Burgess Cup defender, *Puritan*, which was of moderate proportions, and though with a centreboard had 48 tons of lead on the keel. With the appearance of the English *Thistle* (Fig. 3), which was one of the beamiest and shallowest English yachts for many years, the extremes had met.

But even today tradition, working in its mysterious way, partly accounts for the tendency towards narrowness in the average English yacht, and for the big beam of the average American one.

*　　　*　　　*

In 1877, Colin Archer had advanced his wave-form theory. Archer was an artist and a designer of distinction, but the only interest in his theory today is the fact that for over half a century—until, in fact, only a little short of the present day—its influence was powerful. Yet it cannot be justified, and on the whole its effect on design was bad.

Archer adopted Scott Russell's wave-form curve, but specified that it should be the curve of areas, and not any particular curve in the hull's shape, which should conform to it. Archer stated that the curve of areas of the fore-body should be a curve of versed sines, and that of the after-body a trochoid; the fore-body should occupy 0·6 of the water-line length, and the after-body 0·4. The hull lines were thus not stereotyped, but simply the progression of the displacement along the length. Widely varying shapes of hull might show the same progression.

The nature of the Colin Archer curve is shown in Fig. 1 (p. 16) compared with those of some modern yachts. The type of yacht encouraged had a long lean fore-body and a bustle aft; it was a bad form, but fortunately it was rarely rigidly adhered to. Even those designers who were expansive enough to show the curves of areas of their designs superimposed upon the Archer ideal, as Albert Strange and many others used to do, were not ashamed to show appreciable divergence from the ideal.

In the U.S.A., Carey Smith was influenced by Colin Archer and guided in his design practice by the standard ideal curve shown in Fig. 1. Edward Burgess followed the theory, though the curves of areas that he adopted were not precisely those of Colin Archer, but modified in the light of the area curves of his own or other American craft whose success had been proved. Used in this manner the curve of areas was an excellent guide to hull form; but the curves adopted by Burgess were close enough to that indicated in Fig. 1 to throw the centre of buoyancy well aft and produced fine-lined bows in association with full sterns.

*   *   *

William Froude was a keen yachtsman, but his research work was done in the cause of the big steam ships, and applied only indirectly to sailing craft. In 1875 he published the results of his first experiments, and it was these of which G. L. Watson had received prior information. Froude showed that the total resistance of a ship came from three main sources, of which the two most important were skin-friction and wave-making. For the practical yacht architect the most important result of his work was the demonstration that skin-friction accounted for most of the resistance of a yacht at low and moderate speeds.

Froude was not only a scientist; he was a populariser of the best sort and, like other members of his talented family, he wrote good English; hence his work gained wide recognition quickly in the more general circles of practical designing.

It was at this time that he developed the laws connecting the behaviour of a ship with its model built to any scale, the lack of which had handicapped early investigators such as Chapman. Froude was the first person to tank-test the model of a yacht. Though he and his son developed the technique for testing models of power ships so fully that there is little essential change in it today, it was not until 1932, and in the U.S.A., that Professor K. S. M. Davidson extended the method to cover the very different motion of sailing craft. Between the days of Froude and Davidson models of yachts were occasionally tank-tested, but the results gave no confidence to designers.

The new knowledge of surface friction opened the way for the second revolution in design. This was the reduction of wetted surface, which progressed until the long, straight keels common until 1877 had been replaced by the triangular underwater profile entirely modern in appearance. The model yacht had arrived.

The famous *Jullinar*, designed by an amateur, was the first yacht in which wetted surface was drastically reduced; in place of the deep forefoot and long keel, she was cut away forward and aft, and the length of straight keel was less than half that of the waterline. The yacht was designed to have a long waterline on a short measured length, the sternpost which formed one end of the length measurement being placed forward of the end of the waterline. *Jullinar* embodied the two primary principles of fast yacht design—small wetted surface and great length—the one reducing skin-friction and the other wave-making. She had other important qualities. Chief amongst them was the beautiful fairness of the hull lines, and the perfect balance of the hull.

In order to achieve the maximum length on the waterline Bentall devised a heavy canoe stern, which is less surprising today than it was when the accepted form was the wide, long counter. *Jullinar*'s stern was firmly based in the logic of her design; the clipper bow is less easy to place. The straight stem of yachts contemporary with her would have been suitable for Bentall's purpose, and the interesting fact was brought to light in 1955, when a complete set of working drawings of this yacht were found, that an earlier, provisional design, dated a year before *Jullinar*'s drawings, had the same stern and run of profile as *Jullinar*, but the conventional straight stem. Bentall later developed the clipper bow, suggested to him perhaps by the American yachts of the day, and this made the daring and seldom repeated combination of clipper bow and canoe stern.

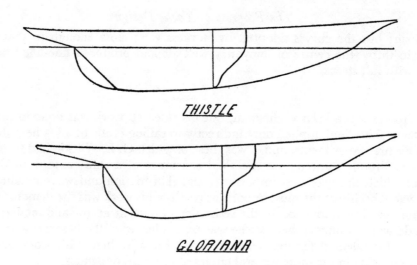

FIG. 3. *The emergence of the modern shape*

Jullinar was followed five years later by the 10-ton *Evolution*, also from Bentall's board. She was a brilliant failure. Brilliant because she embodied the third principle of fast yacht design, which is the separation of the hull into a canoe body and an appendage keel. It is the secret of efficiency to windward, and in our time all yachts follow the principle except the tubbiest of cruisers. She was a failure because, built under the tonnage rule then in force, her beam was reduced to an extent which precluded adequate stability.

In the America's Cup challenger *Thistle* (Fig. 3) Watson reduced wetted surface. She still had more of it than a modern yacht of similar size, but the amount proved inadequate, and she sagged away to leeward when sailing on the wind. This was because the keel section, unlike *Evolution*'s, was thick and shallow—hardly separated from the body of the hull—hence unable to develop the fin action which produces lateral resistance. The tucked-in garboard and deep keel, which are the necessary adjuncts of the cutaway profile, had not been properly developed.

This Herreshoff did in the *Gloriana* in 1890 (Fig. 3). In this yacht the forefoot was completely eliminated, and the forward endings of the waterlines were full, convex curves. The midship section was of the S-form now so familiar, with narrow garboards and a keel of slender and efficient section. Herreshoff rightly conceived that the blunter form of entrance caused by the lack of forefoot need be no disadvantage, and the yacht was spectacularly successful, though condemned by all the most expert yachting writers of her day.

Gloriana's success was enough nearly to kill the class to which she belonged; but, as so often, there was a failure to recognise the crucial features of her design. The importance of the bow overhang was overestimated, and that of the hull form from which it grew was unappreciated for a while. The fact, however, that she was painted white—an unusual colour for an American yacht at this date—was not missed, and a number of yachts were repainted in this colour with the hope of increasing their speeds.

Gloriana's importance as a seamark in the development of yacht design extended beyond her hull shape to the engineering details of her construction and rigging. Prior to her new appearance a designer's work was chiefly the provision of a lines drawing and a sail plan. Both construction and rigging details tended to follow established practices that might safely be left to the builder. Herreshoff was at this time primarily an engineer, and in his approach to design he remained one during his brilliant years in sail that followed *Gloriana*. This yacht had carefully planned steel framing and double-skin planking, and she was lighter and with a higher ballast ratio than her contemporaries. Her rigging was superior in design, lighter and stronger. As Professor George Owen said of *Gloriana* nearly half a century after her appearance, she "exemplified more than any of her predecessors, the importance of scientific engineering in racing yachts."

In 1893 the *Britannia* appeared with the new spoon bow which was roundly abused. The small difference between the shape of *Britannia* and that of the J-class yachts with which she raced in her last seasons, some of which were designed forty years after her, shows that in hull form the modern yacht had arrived with the *Britannia*. The next striking developments in yacht design were the changes in rig which followed the 1914–18 War. But the progress in hull form which occurred during the *Britannia*'s life, though not obvious to the uninitiated, was as significant as anything which had gone before.

*   *   *

The development of the Bermudan rig was the result of aerodynamic studies which, applied to yachts, showed that length of luff was more important for windward efficiency than length along the foot. Where designers in the past had crowded more sail on their yachts by lengthening the booms, thereby increasing the area with the least deleterious effect on stability, later designers limited the sail area and improved its effectiveness by adding to the height of the sail plan. This desire to improve the efficiency of the sail area was due partly to the International and Universal rating rules. It was no longer possible for a designer to give a yacht as much sail as the stability would allow; it became necessary to get as much drive as possible from a strictly limited area. And coinciding with this period of development was the post-1918 need to reduce large crews on the score of expense.

Aerodynamics gave a new understanding to the art of sailing. The aerofoil function of a sail was perceived, and this led to the development of the most efficient aerodynamic shape which was possible within the limits set by masts and canvas. At first these limits were very restricting. The evolution of the Bermudan rig to its present state is mainly the story of how masting and rigging was devised to withstand the stresses of tall, narrow sail plans. A Bermudan mast today may have its centre of gravity at twice the height above the waterline of one of the old, gaff-rigged yachts with fidded topmasts. Were the mast of similar, solid construction it would be twice as heavy and have four times the heeling moment of the old mast. Before the high triangular sail became practicable it was necessary to devise masts which were at once stronger and lighter. It became primarily a problem of staying. For many years it was considered, and rightly, that the Bermudan rig was unfitted for serious seagoing.

The Marconi mast, in which the lower mast, topmast and topsail yard were combined in one spar, was the first mechanical step towards the Bermudan rig, though it was made simply with the object of reducing the weight aloft in gaff-rigged craft. By 1902 some racing yachts had discarded the fidded topmast, the topmast being socketed into the mainmast.

In 1912, Nicholson designed *Istria,* in which the topsail yard also became part of the mast. Gaffs became more highly peaked and topsails narrower, until the canvas aft of the mast, though still comprising a mainsail and a topsail, became almost triangular in shape.

The next step, to the Bermudan mainsail, was made after the 1914–18 War, the pioneer work being done in Scandinavia and England. During the 1924 racing season in the 12-Metre class the Bermudan-rigged yachts were clearly superior to their gaff-rigged opponents, and the greater driving power of the triangular sail was established. But the luff-foot ratio of mainsails was still low, little more than 1 : 1, and the progress from this to mainsails of two, two-and-a-half and even more than three to one, is the result of constructional developments. Primarily it is due to the mast track. It allowed designers to attach stays to the mast at any height they wished, and thus made it possible for tall, light masts to be held upright.

* * *

The quality of balance, which makes a yacht docile and at all times under complete control, has been sought with varying degrees of success during the history of yacht design. Together with speed and seaworthiness, it has been regarded as an ideal of design always to be aimed at, though not understood sufficiently well always to be achieved. The quality was unexplained and a little mysterious; the well-balanced yacht was a tribute to the flair of her designer, showing that he had learned something of the almost human nature of a ship under sail, which might be docile or wilful, well-mannered or unpredictably capricious.

In the late nineteenth and early twentieth centuries many yachts were dangerously unbalanced. In strong, reaching winds it was not uncommon for them to run wild. An unbalanced yacht is not unknown today. In spite of much study, balance under sail has not yielded all its secrets. But it is now possible to ensure, in the design stage, a reasonable degree of good balance; this represents striking progress in the art of design. The system was useful, but as it omitted many important elements in the problem, it alone was unable to produce balanced yachts.

The better understanding of hull and sail balance which we have today owes much to the work of model yachtsmen. Racing models until shortly before the Second World War were usually steered with the Braine steering gear, which is not in operation when beating to windward, and the essential quality in a model was the ability to keep a steady course to windward with the helm locked amidships. The fact that a breed of models was produced capable of doing this, and at a time when yachtsmen were still labouring at the tillers and wheels of extremely unbalanced yachts, indicates the successful attention which was paid to the subject by model yachtsmen. Their theory may be criticised, but their results were impeccable, and the modern type of well-balanced yacht owes much to the model.

Between the two wars, and simultaneously with the progress towards well-balanced yachts, and tall narrow sail plans giving greater drive per square foot of area, was the steady though slow trend towards lighter displacement which is continuing today. Displacement, like balance, is considered more technically elsewhere; for the present it is enough to observe that very slowly, and in the face of strong after-guard actions, the virtues of light displacement have been recognised, together with the fact that weight and seaworthiness are not synonymous, but may be antithetical. Now we regard as moderation in design displacements 20 per cent lighter than would have been considered desirable a few decades ago for serious offshore work.

Meanwhile, a development in the technique of design was occurring comparable with, though less general than, the earlier progress from pine block and chisel to drawing-board and pencil. This was the use of models in a testing tank, and was actually only an extension of a technique which already had been used in power ship design for over half a century.

*   *   *

Tank-testing has not revolutionised yacht design, and no outstanding trend in design may be attributed directly to the technique. But it has become a tool of such value to the designer that Charles Nicholson was prepared to say in 1946 that "it is quite useless for us to hope to compete successfully in Anglo-American class racing before our designs can be properly tank-tested." The subsequent results of international racing have confirmed this statement.

The testing tank is not able to design a yacht, and the initial conception must still come from the designer. But a model in a tank can tell him more of the merits and defects of the shape he has chosen that can the full-size yacht. From a designer's point of view, a season's racing results are difficult evidence from which to judge the merits of any particular feature of design. There are so many factors involved in yacht-racing as a sport, and particularly in ocean-racing, which are irrelevant to the racing yacht considered purely as an effective machine. It is often an impossible feat for a designer to see where he has been right, where wrong; false deductions are easily made. The testing tank removes all irrelevant features, and allows hull shape to be studied in isolation and with the precision of a scientific experiment. It can do more than simply compare the abilities of different designs; it allows a systematised programme of research into the basic problems of yacht design to be undertaken.

The technique for tank-testing sailing models was due to the late Professor K. S. M. Davidson, whose work, begun in 1932, has been done at the Stevens' Tank, Hoboken, U.S.A. Since the war it has been undertaken at several places in Britain, including at the National Physical Laboratory, and on a considerable commercial basis by Saunders-Roe (Westland Aircraft, Ltd.) of Cowes. The technique appeared to have received a bad setback at the time of *Sceptre*'s débâcle in the 1960 series of America's Cup races. In fact, this event proved nothing about tank-testing that was not already appreciated by those who used the system with success in the U.S.A. Nor was responsible opinion in Britain shocked, and never has there been so much tank-testing in Britain of sailing craft than since the 1960 America's Cup races. It is appreciated that the tank is a smooth water test able to measure speed made good to windward in smooth water, and even in this has to rely on a series of suppositions, including sail force coefficients, of doubtful validity. Also, as Saunders-Roe discovered, the standard of accuracy in the average yacht drawings and the calculations based on them of such vital features as centre of buoyancy and gravity were not sufficiently high to assure the fairness of comparisons between designs made in the tank, and that ordinary yacht drawing office calculations must be re-worked before the results are applied to tests.

CHAPTER THREE

Speed and Resistance

THE source of a sailing yacht's power is the wind, and in harnessing it a complex system of counteracting forces becomes established which, when the yacht is in steady motion—changing neither speed, course nor angle of heel—becomes a system in equilibrium. It is illustrated in Figs. 4 and 5, which show the fundamentals of the sailing problem. Frequent reference will be made to Figs. 4 and 5 throughout this book.

It may be noted here that purists regard a problem as one of statics whenever there is the condition of equilibrium, even though motion may be involved, dynamics entering only when the system becomes out of equilibrium. Since the conditions under sail are ever-varying and the equilibrium illustrated in Figs. 4 and 5 exists only momentarily, the sailing-problem, even to the purist, is one of dynamics.

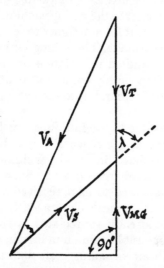

FIG. 4. *Vector diagram of windward sailing*

The conditions illustrated show the yacht close-hauled, the true wind being about 45 degrees off the bow. The action of the wind on the sails produces a force which may be resolved into two components, one a driving force along the line of motion and the other a lateral force at right angles to it. From Fig. 5 it will be seen that when close-hauled the latter is much the larger (see also Table 9, p. 81, which gives representative numerical values for the drive and lateral, or drift, forces for various points of sailing).

To resist the lateral air force the hull and keel produce a lateral water force which is the product of an angle of leeway or yaw. This is considered at greater length in Chapter Six. The lateral air force and the water force produced by hull and keel are equal when a

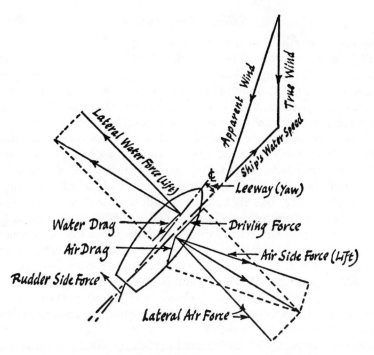

FIG. 5. *Forces involved when sailing to windward*

state of steady motion exists and form a couple with, in Fig. 5, a windward turning moment. Hence, partially, the weather helm shown.

The relatively small driving force produces motion, which in turn produces water drag as a result of the yaw angle and the various other sources of resistance which this chapter considers. The driving force and the water drag, each parallel to the line of motion, form another couple, which also, in the circumstances illustrated, has a windward turning moment. Equilibrium, which is the condition necessary for a steady course being maintained, is established by the rudder, thus enabling a balance to be produced between the whole complex of forces.

The design of a sailing yacht is fundamentally a matter of producing a vessel in which the system of forces illustrated in Fig. 5 is most favourable to good performance, while the yacht herself provides at the same time any accommodation required and the necessary degree of seaworthiness and amenability to control under a wide variety of conditions.

SPEED The resistance of a yacht varies with her speed and increases very rapidly with it. Where normal displacement vessels are concerned, by which is meant those unable to achieve planing action as a result of dynamic lift, speed is a function of length and the practicable maximum speeds of such craft are in the ratio of the square roots of their sailing lengths. This is a basic fact of hydrodynamics and will be more clearly understood later.

From it is derived the speed-length ratio, which provides a criterion for comparing vessels of different sizes, or for that matter comparing yachts with their own model to any scale. The speed-length ratio is conveniently expressed as the speed of the vessel in knots divided by the square root of the waterline length in feet, and is commonly written in the form $V/\sqrt{L}$ (colloquially vee-on-root-L). Its significance may be appreciated when we say that if a yacht and a model of the yacht are run at similar speed-length ratios (e.g. a 36-ft. waterline yacht at 6 knots and a 4-ft. waterline model of her at 2 knots) the pattern of the wave-throw of yacht and model will be of identical forms.

The optimum, low resistance, form of hull is partly determined by the speed-length ratio, and varies considerably between $V/\sqrt{L}$ values of 0·5 and 1·5. As a result there can unfortunately be no ideal form for a sailing yacht, whose speed depends on the wind of the moment. Design may sometimes be governed by the object of achieving good light or heavy weather performance; but even in the broadest sense this will not usually be practicable, except occasionally in inshore class racers designed for a particular locality.

The highest speeds attained when sailing to windward in smooth water rarely exceed $V/\sqrt{L} = 1$, and in a seaway a ratio of 0·8 is not slow. During summer months in North Europe weather statistics show that light winds are more common than is usually apparent, and a high proportion of sailing time is spent at $V/\sqrt{L}$ values of below 0·6. In a wind of 6–9 m.p.h., for example, the J-class yacht *Ranger* averaged 5·3 knots over a distance of 15 miles dead to windward—a $V/\sqrt{L}$ value of 0·57. In winds of Force 3 smaller craft may average about $V/\sqrt{L} = 0\cdot6$–$0\cdot7$.

In practice, the highest speeds are made in reaching winds, but under the ideal conditions of strong winds and smooth water they will rarely exceed $V/\sqrt{L} = 1\cdot5$, and such an average will not be maintained for long. We are concerned purely with single-hulled vessels for the moment. One of the highest speeds of the *Satanita*, which with her length of 93 ft. 6 in. on the waterline was the fastest cutter ever built, was *17* knots, giving a $V/\sqrt{L}$ value of 1·5. *Britannia* averaged 12·5 knots ($V/\sqrt{L} = 1\cdot3$) on the last lap of the Channel race in 1866, and this was one of her greatest achievements. Modern, smaller ocean-racers when driven exceptionally hard have averaged $V/\sqrt{L} = 1\cdot6$ for periods of one to two hours, but the speeds are exceptional.

In theory, the highest speeds are attainable when running before the wind, but this is not so in practice. The vector subtraction of boat and wind speed when running produces a lower driving component of the wind force than when reaching, and in spite of the fact that under the latter circumstances there is a wasted lateral component of the wind's force, a driving force is obtained exceeding any that is practicable when the wind is aft. For example, in a wind of 15 knots a driving force of 1·05 lb./sq. ft. may be achieved with a true wind on the beam and a boat's speed of 5 knots. With the same boat speed and wind strength the maximum driving force attainable from the wind dead astern would be 0·7 lb., or 66 per cent of that when reaching. In stronger winds the disparity between the two driving forces would be reduced. Theoretically the driving force with the wind astern would eventually exceed that possible in reaching conditions, owing to the boat speed increasing at a very much slower rate than the wind speed; but by the time this state is reached the wind strength and seaway would have reduced the situation to chaos.

The conditions of coastal sailing—which, of course, include much offshore racing—entail a high proportion of time being spent hauling to windward, and hence of speeds usually lower than $V/\sqrt{L} = $ unity. A high proportion of time reaching and running will also be spent at speeds in this region of the speed range. The figures indicate the relatively low speeds for which sailing hulls have to be designed.

6. A 12-Metre model being run in the tank of Westland Aircraft, Ltd.,
Saunders-Roe Division (Westland Aircraft, Ltd.).

7. Tank test model. The studs on the forebody are to induce turbulence in the boundary layer (Westland Aircraft, Ltd.).

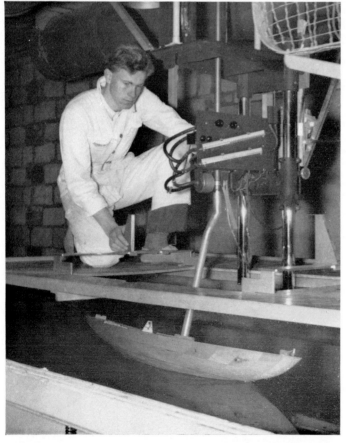

8. A model in position under the dynamometer at the beginning of a run (Westland Aircraft, Ltd.).

The modest average speeds under sail have been little increased during the years of scientific design, and the orthodox yacht, which obtains a high proportion of her ultimate stability from ballast is hydrodynamically incapable of any exceptional further development. Stability is directly proportional to the displacement for given values of the righting levers. But resistance at the higher sailing speeds is also nearly proportional to the displacement. The fact that, under sail, the driving force that may be applied is a function of the stability, which varies at much the same rate and in the same direction as the resistance, raises a situation like that of Zeno's problem of Achilles and the tortoise, but without its fallacy. Really high-speed sailing necessitates stability without the weight of ballast, and hence double hulls or outriggers.

Some examples of recorded high speeds under sail by yachts appear in Tables 1, 2a and 2b below.

Table 1 gives figures for five well-known and fast yachts sailing four points off the wind, and it will be seen that, with *Ranger*'s exception, the figures give ratios of about one. The 4½ knots of the little *Vigilant*, owned and sailed by Uffa Fox, produces a slightly lower proportionate speed than the 7 knots of the larger *Nina*. *Dorade* at 6·2 knots is sailing at a speed corresponding with *Landfall*'s 8 knots, and all these craft are making exceptionally good time to windward, and one which they will not often reach. *Ranger*'s figure produces a more normal value, giving a speed-length ratio of 0·57, and even then she is sailing nearly as fast as the average wind strength. We may say that, beating to windward, a yacht is sailing fast to exceed a speed-length ratio of 0·6, and she will spend much of her time below this figure.

Off the wind higher speeds prevail, but it will be seen from Table 2a that a ratio of 1·5 is rarely exceeded. It will be observed that 7·9 knots for *Svaap* corresponds to the 17 knots of the huge *Satanita*, which, I think, was the highest speed the latter ever reached. They are all exceptional speeds, and we may say that under the best conditions of wind and sea—a strong wind and a calm sea—speeds which give a ratio of 1·5 are rarely reached by sailing craft, which are doing well if they reach a ratio of one.

One abnormal speed is shown: that of an English International 14-ft. dinghy. The Fourteens plane, their hull lines being more like those of power-craft than sailing yachts, and under these conditions they do not fall within the category of displacement craft; i.e. vessels which, at all speeds, are supported by the force of buoyancy. A vessel when planing has the dynamical support of her speed, and normal ballasted yachts cannot achieve this, being unable to stand the wind which would be required to produce such a speed.

The ratios shown are all calculated from the waterline lengths of the yachts concerned, and, since the sailing length in each case is slightly greater, the ratios should be correspondingly lower. We may say that, for all-round performance, fast yachts should be designed to offer least resistance at speed length ratios of less than unity. They will not often exceed this.

Some further record of high speeds may be recorded. Robert Clark has noted as two examples of outstanding speeds under sail that of 26·3 ft. waterline *Naiande* which in the 1949 season maintained a speed giving a $V/\sqrt{L}$ value of 1·67 for three hours, and the 31-ft. waterline *Corinna* which, in 1946, held $V/\sqrt{L} = 1·63$ for one hour. A 32-ft. waterline sloop made the passage from St. Tropez to Cannes, a distance of 24 miles, in 3 hours, giving an average $V/\sqrt{L}$ value of 1·4. The same yacht made the longer passage from Ajaccio (Corsica) to St. Tropez—132 miles—in 19 hours. Here $V/\sqrt{L} = 1·25$, which is a high

TABLE I
SPEEDS CLOSE-HAULED
Four Points Off Wind

Yacht	Type	Length W.L.	Speed	V/√L	Remarks
Vigilant	22 sq. metre	25 ft. 6 in.	4–5 knots	0·90	In heavy sea
Dorade	Ocean-racer	37 ft. 3 in.	6·2 knots	1·02	—
Nina	Ocean-racer (Schooner)	50 ft.	7 knots	0·99	—
Landfall	Ocean-racer (Schooner)	60 ft.	8 knots	1·03	—
Ranger	J-class	87 ft.	5·3 knots	0·57	Dead to windward for 15 miles in 6–9 m.p.h. wind

TABLE 2a
SPEEDS WITH COMMANDING WINDS

Yacht	Type	Length W.L.	Speed	V/√L	Remarks
Fourteen feet International Dinghy			9 knots	2·41	Reaching in high wind and planing
Svaap	Ocean Voyager	27 ft. 5 in.	7·9 knots	1·5	Recorded in *Deep Water and Shoal*
Brilliant	Ocean-racer	49 ft.	9·7 knots	0·72	Average of 24 hrs. run crossing Atlantic 1933. 230 miles sailed
Lintie	6-Metre	22 ft. 6 in.	7 knots	1·5	Sailing double-reefed from Cowes to Burnham
Astra	23-Metre	60 ft.	10·7 knots	1·38	
Britannia	Cutter	86 ft. 9 in.	12·5 knots	1·3	Last lap of Channel race, 1866. One of her highest recorded speeds
Satanita	Large Cutter (also Yawl)	93 ft. 6 in.	17 knots	1·5	Broad reach in strong wind
Sappho	Schooner	121 ft.	13·1 knots	1·2	Day's run Sandyhook–Queenstown trip, 1869. Log says: "Fresh breeze, very smooth, sea like a lake."

TABLE 2b*

Yacht	*Aikane*	*Ondine*	*Tern IV*	*Atlantic*	*Clipper*
Date	1961	1963	1926	1905	1850s
Sailing length (feet)	46	49	52	160	225
Day's run (nautical miles)	306	248	214	340	370
Average speed (knots)	12·7	10·3	9·0	14·1	16·5
Relative speed	1·88	1·46	1·25	1·15	1·10

* The lengths recorded in Table 2b alone are an estimate of sailing length, exceeding the length waterline by amounts judged on the basis of the profile and sections of the vessels' overhangs. *Aikane* is a catamaran.

average to maintain under sail for so long a period. All the above yachts were of moderately heavy displacement.

All the speeds given above are, of course, speeds through the water. Both from the point of view of design and performance at sea, when sailing on the wind it is speed made good to windward (V_{mg}) that is of primary importance, and this is determined by a vector triangle combining the yacht's speed through the water (V_s) and the angle between the course and the true wind. This is illustrated in Fig. 4 which is basically the triangle illustrated at the top of Fig. 5 with the addition of speed made good to windward.

RESISTANCE AND SPEED The motion of a yacht under sail is retarded by five sources of resistance, and it is one object of an architect to reduce these to the minimum possible. The total resistance is composed of (i) Frictional resistance; (ii) Wave-making resistance; (iii) Induced drag; (iv) Eddy-making resistance; (v) Air resistance. These will be considered in turn, but first we should examine the variation of the total resistance with the speed.

The total resistance of a sailing yacht is, for its size, very high. Surface friction is considerable because of the big area of keel which has to be added to that of the canoe body; whilst wave-making resistance is also in excess of power craft of similar dimensions, a sailing craft having a length-displacement ratio sometimes three to four times as great in order to gain sail carrying power by dead weight of keel. The angle of heel of a yacht also adds to the resistance. Table 3 gives resistance figures, measured heeled and upright, for the yacht *Campanula*, resistance being expressed in tons per ton of displacement, and it will be seen that the increase on heeling is about 10 per cent. It is for these reasons the speeds of yachts under sail cannot be high, and are usually decidedly low. (See also Fig. 6.)

Table 3 also reveals the rapid increase in total resistance with speed. Within the small range of figures shown, an increase in speed from 4 to 6 knots, or 50 per cent, has raised the resistance by 249 per cent. This rapid growth of resistance with speed is a fundamental feature of the subject. It is more vividly revealed in the gathering steepness of the curve in

36

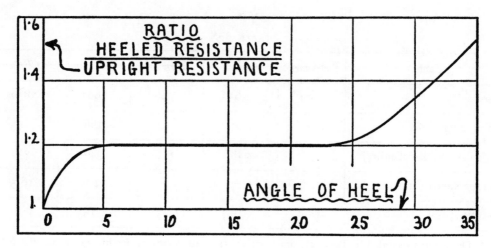

FIG. 6. *Increase of resistance with heel*

TABLE 3
RESISTANCE HEELED AND UPRIGHT. YACHT *Campanula*

Expressed in Terms: $\dfrac{\text{Resistance in Tons}}{\text{Displacement in Tons}} \times 100$

Speed (knots)	4	5	6
$V/\dfrac{V}{\sqrt{L}}$	0·82	1·02	1·23
R/D (Upright)	0·46	0·87	1·62
R/D (Heeled)	0·51	0·96	1·78

Fig. 7, which is that of total resistance of a 6-Metre, the figures written along the curve being speed-length ratios. The comparatively gentle gradient of the curve below 0·8 may be compared with its steepness from this point onwards, and especially the very steep rise after 1·2.

At what rate does the total resistance grow as the speed rises? Up to a speed-length ratio of between 0·6 and 0·8 it increases as the square of the speed, which means that a 60-ft. yacht moving at 4 knots encounters four times the resistance that she met at 2 knots. By the time a speed-length ratio of one is reached, resistance varies about as the fourth power of the speed. A point of interest, though not of great practical value where normal sailing craft are concerned, is that after a certain speed-length ratio has been reached, the rate of increase of resistance begins to drop again until a point is reached when it is once more increasing only as the square of the speed. The maximum ratio for displacement craft, however, may be accepted as 1·5, so they cannot make use of this fact.

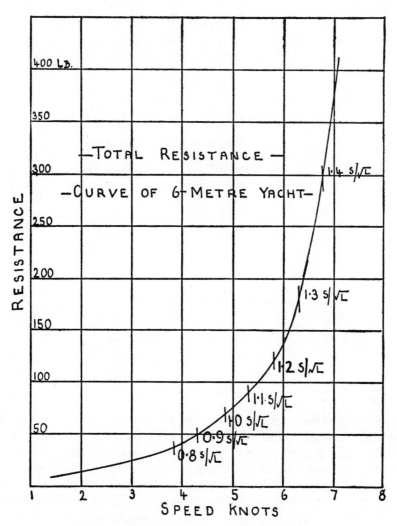

Fig. 7. *Total resistance curve of a 6-Metre yacht*

But it is significant for dinghies and twin-hulled or hydrofoil craft. Once planing has begun, the resistance of such craft becomes again mainly frictional, and a small increase in driving power will increase the speed at a greater rate than before planing started.

Not only does the total resistance increase rapidly with speed but its proportionate composition changes greatly as the speed increases. For the moment we will confine our attention to the two main sources of resistance, friction and wave-making.

Table 4 shows the proportions which the two main resistances bear to one another at various speed-length ratios in a very light displacement yacht. Even at a speed-length ratio of 0·8 75 per cent of the total resistance is frictional. At a ratio of 1·1 the two are about equal, and after this the wave-making gains in influence rapidly. (Friction is increasing also, but wave-making is doing so more rapidly.) By the time a speed-length ratio of 1·4 has been attained friction has a proportion of only 17 per cent of the total.

TABLE 4

PROPORTIONATE COMPOSITION
TOTAL RESISTANCE LIGHT DISPLACEMENT YACHT

$\dfrac{V}{\sqrt{L}}$	Proportions of Total Resistance	
	Skin Friction	Wave-making
	per cent	*per cent*
0·8	75	25
0·9	70	30
1·0	65	35
1·1	51	49
1·2	37	63
1·3	26	74
1·4	17	83

The curve in Fig. 8 presents a truer picture of these proportions in a yacht of more average form. Skin friction, whilst still predominating by a big margin at the lower and moderate speeds, does not bear quite so large a proportion of the total resistance; and as the speed grows, wave-making becomes the biggest source of resistance earlier. Thus, at a speed-length ratio of 0·4 wave-making accounts for about one quarter of the total, at 0·7 for a third, and at 1·0 for about three-fifths of the total. This is the effect of heavier displacement hulls with their smaller wetted surface but larger wave disturbance.

It will be evident, from the analysis of yachts' speeds, that under normal conditions skin friction is the predominant resistance whatever the shape of hull. In his book, *The Common Sense of Yacht Design*, Francis Herreshoff stresses this point and goes so far as to say that the gradual reduction of wetted surface is the most important development in yacht design during the past century.

SURFACE FRICTION So far as surface friction is concerned, we may say that today we are in possession of most of the answers and that it is simply a matter of applying them intelligently to each case. This may be a rather too complacent attitude to take, for the subject, studied deeply, leads to many complexities; but from the point of view of the yacht designer and the yachtsman wishing to grasp the essentials of resistance, only a small part of the vast volume of data available is of practical value. The most important source of resistance it certainly is, but its reduction presents the designer with a much simpler problem than does the reduction of wave-making, since the factors involved are common to all sizes and speed-length ratios.

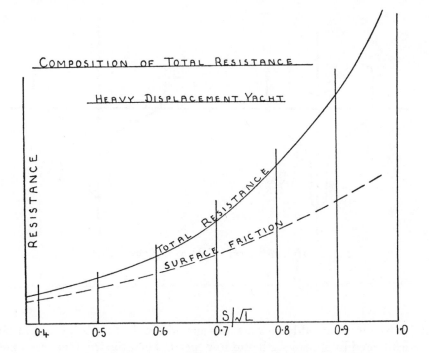

FIG. 8. *Composition of total resistance—heavy displacement yacht*

The amount of wetted surface friction encountered by a yacht depends on four factors: (1) Area of surface; (ii) Length of surface; (iii) Roughness of surface; and (iv) Speed. The first of these is almost common sense although friction between a liquid and a solid differs in this respect from that between two solids, when the amount is independent of the areas in contact.

The area of wetted surface of sailing yachts is considerable in spite of their cut-away keels—virtually fin keels—and is more than that of the *America* and others of her period. Cruising yachts, with their tendency towards the hollow midship section and deep keel, also have more surface than those of, say, half a century ago, when the hulls were fuller and there was little in the way of a fin keel. An interesting example of the deleterious effect of wetted surface was seen when the Scandinavian-born 30 sq. Metres used to race with the 6-Metres. A comparison of their midship sections is shown in Fig. 9(*a*) and (*b*). The Thirties had only three-quarters of the sail area of the Sixes and less than two-thirds of the displacement, but their wetted surface was greater. In good sailing winds, when wave-making becomes of importance, the Thirties, in spite of their smaller sail area, used to walk away from the Sixes; in moderate and light winds the Sixes did the walking away.*

The frictional wake is the body of water set in motion, as a result of friction, by a vessel's passage through it. Frictional resistance is the result of shearing forces in the water of this wake. The water inside the wake moves at varying speeds, ranging from that of the ship next to the hull itself, to a motionless state at the outer edge of the wake. The water

* See page 58.

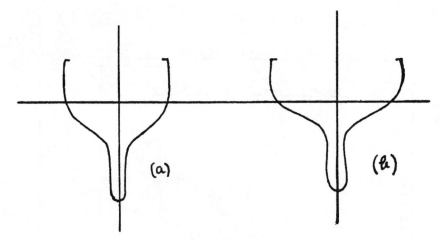

FIG. 9. *Midship sections—6-Metre and 30 sq. Metre*

in this band is usually in an eddying state, but sometimes the flow is smooth, or laminar, a condition encouraged by short length and low speed. Then the frictional resistance varies only directly as the speed, and there is reason to believe that laminar flow sometimes exists along the bows of short-keeled yachts. It is an area of low resistance. But if turbulent flow is the régime prevailing it is the leading edge that has the greatest resistance and the deep draught, short keel boat suffers more than old-fashioned types (Fig. 10(*a*) and (*b*)).

A long yacht experiences less frictional resistance per square foot of wetted surface than one shorter, and the criterion affecting the ratio of the two resistances—assuming the same quality of surface in either case—is the Reynolds number, which naval architects define as VL/v where V is the speed of the surface, L its length in the direction of motion and v the coefficient of kinematic viscosity. For our purpose we need to go further into the origin and validity of this criterion, which I considered in my *Naval Architecture of Small Craft*. It has the inconvenience that the divisor is tiny—about 0·000013 in ordinary sea water—and the Reynolds number correspondingly enormous.

At a Reynolds number of ten million the frictional coefficient for turbulent flow is 0.003 and for laminar 0·0004, and since the frictional resistance under conditions of wholly turbulent or wholly laminar conditions is proportional to this coefficient, the reward for even small areas of laminar flow over the planking of a yacht is obviously considerable. But under most conditions it is unlikely to be achieved. For example, at 2 knots in an 18-ft. boat in very calm water, useful areas of laminarity may be accepted; in a 25-ft. boat at 4 knots it is unlikely.

WAVE-MAKING George Watson, after describing the details of his perfect yacht, amongst whose features was a gold or platinum keel, added as an afterthought: "But by that date I hope we won't care for sailing in such a sluggish element as water."

Sluggish! The word fits the case as aptly as the lines of a Watson yacht fitted the sea. It is difficult to move quickly through water owing to the amount of energy wasted in pushing it aside; and it is the waves created by yachts in motion which cause the low limit

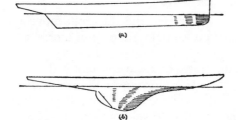

(A)

(b)

FIG. 10. *Long and short keels*

of their maximum speed. When sailing at the speed-length ratio of o·8, 25 to 40 per cent of the resistance is due to wave-making, the exact proportion depending on the form and displacement of the yacht. At a $V/\sqrt{L}$ value of one the proportion rises to between 50 and 60 per cent, whilst at a ratio of 1·4 over 80 per cent of the total resistance is due to the waves generated. The effect of waves swamps even the rapidly increasing frictional resistance (Fig. 8).

On being set in motion, a floating body creates a wave system around itself which is the product of complex changes of pressure beneath the surface of the water. The water pressure on the submerged surface of the hull varies from point to point, the nature and amount of the variation depending on the speed and shape of the yacht. The pressure distribution over ships' hulls at varying speeds has been analysed, and it is possible, for

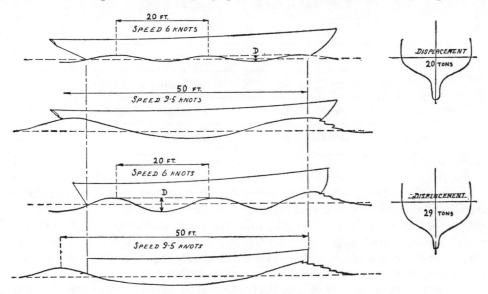

FIG. 11. *Speed and wave formation*

certain restricted shapes of hull, to calculate the amount of the wave-making resistance. But even for power-driven ships the method is not generally applicable, and designers are driven to model testing tanks to measure the quantity by experiment. The more complicated motion of a sailing yacht prohibits calculation.

The total wave system of a yacht consists of three separate ones, the most important of which is a transverse system which shows itself as a series of crests along the length of the hull. The wave movement travels with the hull (Fig. 11). At low speeds the crests will hardly be visible; as the speed rises the waves deepen and the crests move apart, until, at the yacht's maximum speed, she is carried on a single wave, with a crest at the bow and another slightly aft of the stern.

The distance between the crests of the transverse wave system is the truest indication of a yacht's speed at a given moment, for she is moving at the speed of the waves she creates. The speed of the type of wave system we are considering is governed by the distance between crests, and waves of equal lengths, travel at the same speed (see Table 5). As the yacht moves faster, the crests of the transverse wave system become farther apart. The power necessary to produce the waves increases in the same proportion as their lengths, and simultaneously the depth of the system becomes greater, which again increases the energy involved in sustaining the system. Thus, the faster a yacht moves, the greater becomes the resistance she meets due to her own wave-making, and eventually there comes a time when she is sailing at full career on a single wave length. She is supported at bow and stern on a crest, and there is a deep hollow amidships. Her speed-length ratio at this point will be between 1·3 and 1·4. This condition is shown in the second sketch in Fig. 11.

TABLE 5

Length of Wave	Speed in Knots
0 ft. 6½ in.	1 knot
5 ft. 0 in.	3 knots
20 ft. 0 in.	6 knots
80 ft. 0 in.	12 knots
200 ft. 0 in.	19 knots

The beneficial effect of length on speed will be apparent: and it will further be observed that the length in question is that which a yacht is able to use when sailing. Overhangs, by adding to the sailing length, raise the maximum potential speed of a yacht.* The craft without overhangs in the fourth sketch of Fig. 11 will need more energy to produce a 50-ft. wave system, other things being equal, than that in the second drawing. Her maximum potential speed will, for this reason, be less.

It is because of the ability of long yachts to make long waves that the craft produced by rating rules always tend to get longer as the rule grows older. In the J-class the 80-ft. L.W.L. *Enterprise* and 80·75-ft. *Shamrock V* were followed by the 83-ft. *Endeavour I*, and later by the 86-ft. *Endeavour II* and *Ranger*. Francis Herreshoff, in producing the 86-ft. *Whirlwind* in the same year as *Enterprise*, unquestionably showed greater foresight, in this respect, than the other designers. The same trend was seen in the 6-Metre class. The

* I am aware that this statement may be questioned, and that the primary value of overhangs may be regarded as the greater stability they provide (see page 272). But practical experience does indicate that their length-producing function is important.

original yachts, of about $21\frac{1}{2}$ ft. on the waterline, stretched to $23\frac{3}{4}$ ft., and it is to be noticed that the increase in length had to be attended, according to rule, by a slight decrease in sail area and an increase of some 20 per cent in displacement. A greater weight has had to be propelled by less power. Such is the sacrifice which advantageously may be paid for additional length.

But it is not only the length of waves which affects resistance; the depth of system is also involved, a deep wave needing more energy to sustain it than a shallow one. The energy needed to produce a wave varies about as the square of its depth; thus one wave twice the height of another needs four times the energy to keep it in motion at the same speed. It is, therefore, desirable for a yacht to produce not simply a long wave system, but a shallow one also, and whilst the ability to achieve the former depends on length, the latter is governed by the shape of the hull and its displacement.

Large displacement-length or beam-length ratios produce deep wave systems; the rolling quarter waves of the heavy yachts are well known. When reasons of accommodation or the demands of a rating rule force a designer to adopt heavy displacement, it is essential that the other wave-producing element of beam should be reduced to redress the balance. This occurred in the 6-Metre class, where the beam shrank from an average of 7 ft. to 6 ft., and would have been lower had this not been the least allowed by rule. Such a yacht, shown in Fig. 11, third sketch, is sailing at the same speed as her lighter sister, and hence the equal spacing of the wave crests; but in order to achieve the same speed she will need considerably more wind.

In light to moderate displacement yachts, beam need not be a resistful feature. The beamy hull of moderate displacement narrows appreciably on heeling, and this combined with her greater stiffness at small angles of heel makes beam a feature which should not be stinted.

The depth of the quarter wave is sensitive to the run of the buttock lines in the after-body. Steeply rising or curving buttocks, caused by a body which is too deep for its length, produce a heavy quarter wave. If the stern of a yacht is unduly pinched, and the greatest depth of the buttock lines is amidships, buttocks of this bad character will result. The buttocks of racing dinghies, with their greatest depth at about 33 per cent of their length from the bow, and having a long, flat sweep from their lowest point to the stern, are well formed for speed, but it is a shape which conflicts, in larger yachts, with other essential qualities. The principle of the "long, clean run," though rather over-exercised by yachting journalists discussing design, should always be remembered.

RESISTANCE AND HEEL   When a yacht heels and loses the symmetry and fairness of her upright lines an increase in resistance ensues. The shape of the hull under these conditions may be examined by means of heeled waterlines, and perhaps as usefully with heeled buttock lines, when it will be seen that the upright curves may assume unfair shapes. The increase of resistance becomes sudden and steep once the lee rail is immersed.

Fig. 6 (p. 36), based on the data of the *Gimcrack* tests, shows the augmentation of resistance due to heel in the case of a yacht having moderate displacement and good length of overhangs. There is an initial increase of 20 per cent in the first 5 degrees of heel. Thereafter no further augmentation occurs until the rail is immersed, when the resistance grows rapidly and amounts at 35 degrees to 60 per cent more than the upright resistance.

The lack of increase in resistance between heel angles of 5–25 degrees may be attributed to the overhangs of the yacht, which allow a progressive lengthening in the waterline of the yacht and hence longer sailing lines, which offset the greater resistance of the

TABLE 6

GENERAL MAXIMUM SPEEDS OF DISPLACEMENT YACHTS

Length ft.	Knots	Time per Mile mins.	secs.
9	3·75	16	0
16	5·00	12	0
25	6·25	9	36
36	7·50	8	0
41	8·00	7	30
49	8·75	6	51
64	10·00	6	0
81	11·25	5	20
100	12·50	4	48
121	13·75	4	21
144	15·00	4	0

The above speeds may be exceeded, but only in exceptional circumstances.

heeled form. This is one of the several advantages of reasonable overhanging length in sailing yachts. Without overhangs the resistance would increase steadily with the angle of heel.

INDUCED DRAG   Induced drag may be defined as the increase in resistance due to heel and yaw angle.* The effect of yaw angle on performance is dealt with more fully in Chapter Six. For the moment it is sufficient to say that drag inevitably occurs when the hydrofoil, which is the keel, produces the lift that balances the lateral component of the wind force and prevents leeway (Fig. 5). Apart from this source of resistance, due purely to the keel's hydrofoil action, there is the further augmentation of resistance caused by the angle of obliquity at which the hull, like the keel, moves through the water once an angle of yaw is established.

The keel drag is due to the total force developed by the keel being turned through a small angle from the normal to its chord, so that a component of the force acts in opposition

* Resistance due to heel and yaw may be separated and treated apart, but since both arise concurrently in a sailing yacht they may be considered as a combined source of resistance.

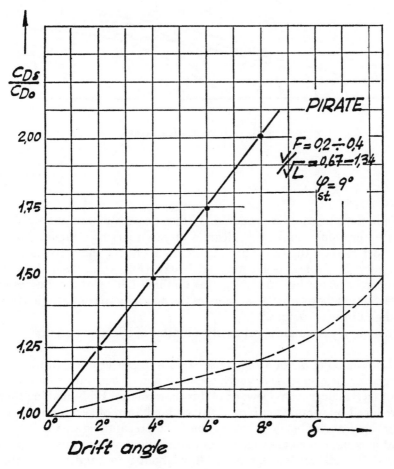

FIG. 12. *Effects of yaw angle*

to the motion. The angle is the result of three influences which in aerodynamic terms are known as (*a*) Profile drag, (*b*) Form drag, (*c*) Wave drag. The first consists mainly of the frictional resistance of the keel's surface, augmented by flow effects produced by its curved shape. Form drag is the result of the limited depth of the keel (draught) which allows interference between the low and high pressure systems, respectively to windward and leeward, appearing in the form of a downward flow and vortices under the keel. Wave drag is a similar action occurring round the keel and at its after-edge. The separation of form and wave drag is a matter of complex aerodynamic theory which can have little practical application to the sailing design problem at present.

Induced drag, in sailing nomenclature, is the sum of all keel and hull drags resulting from sailing at an angle of yaw, and which when sailing with the wind forward of the beam and well heeled may produce, at any speed, an addition to the upright resistance of perhaps 40 per cent. The greater part of this increased resistance is due to yaw. This may be seen in figures derived from tank tests. At 25 degrees of heel and zero yaw the

46

FIG. 13. *Fine and full sterns*

resistance of the model was 97·5 grammes. With 2 degrees of yaw the resistance was increased to 112·5 grammes, and at 4½ degrees of yaw to 142 grammes. The latter is an increase of 45 per cent on the resistance at this angle of heel and zero yaw. Further data has been provided by Professors Kempf and Nutku (Fig. 12), which show that for one 14 ft. centreboard sharpie hull the drag was doubled between yaw angles of zero and 8 degrees. The fact, as they said, ". . . indicates the necessity to confine ourselves to smaller drift [yaw] angles in new designs."

The reduction of yaw angle is primarily a matter of effective keel design.

EDDIES Eddy-making is not a big consideration in power craft, but in sailing yachts it may be larger for two reasons. A yacht spends much of her time sailing not where she is pointing but several degrees to leeward of this (yaw angle). Eddy-making there must be, though it is reduced by rounded curves, a streamlined form of keel, and the avoidance of any corners or sharp angles below the waterline. Such precautions are rarely neglected, but recently I was looking at a smaller cruiser of admirable design in other respects in which the fore-edge of the keel was left flat, a width of about 6 in., and this was blended into the fore and aft run of the keel by a sharp radius.

No less serious as a source of eddy-making is a propeller aperture with its inevitably blunt sternpost and the disturbance the hole in the lateral area introduces into the water flow aft. A locked propeller, discussed later, may be the biggest source of eddy-making of all.

It is sometimes claimed that full waterline aft, demonstrated by the pecked, or in a minor degree by the chain dotted lines in Fig. 13, introduce more eddy-making than the finer stern illustrated by the full line. But this is unlikely. Eddy-making is more liable to be caused by excessive steepness of the buttock lines in the stern than by fullness of the waterlines.

AIR RESISTANCE Air resistance is a very small proportion of the total but may still be enough to account for a difference of a few seconds per mile between two yachts, which may amount to the difference between a race won or lost.

Recent decades of developments in design have progressively led to reductions in windage aloft from spars and rigging, and the modern masthead sloop sets its canvas area more economically in terms of air-resistance than any earlier vessels. But simultaneously there has been a continuous increase in the wind-resistance of hulls.

In a paper read before the Royal Institution of Naval Architects in 1961, H. M. Barkla presented a new and revealing ratio:

$$\frac{\text{Area of hull between sheer and waterline}}{\text{Area of sail with largest headsail set}}$$

Some of the values of the ratio presented by Barkla are:

Satanita (large cutter of 1892)	0·067
Weetamoe (J-class sloop of 1930)	0·084
I.Y.R.U. 6-Metre class boat	0·121
International Dragon class boat	0·164
Tomis (International 8-Metre cruiser-racer)	0·172
Yachting World Seahorse (small ocean-racer)	0·208
Vale of York (Laurent Giles modern cruiser)	0·209
Orthops (Clark designed ocean-racer)	0·212

Even if *Satanita* be excluded and we consider a 6-Metre class boat, which had long overhangs and freeboard that in immediate post-war years was considered moderately high, we still find that her ratio is 0·121 compared with the 0·212 of the contemporary offshore racer, and the ratio of the latter is three times that of *Satanita*. It is suggested by Barkla that 50 per cent of the windage resistance when sailing to windward is due to the air-resistance *of the hull alone.**

It is a tribute to other features of design that the modern yacht is able to exceed the performance to windward of the older boats with much lower hull windage ratios. Perhaps we have now reached a time when having come to appreciate the virtues of fairly high freeboard we should recall again the merits of low windage. It is one of the many small factors that contribute to the highest performance.

The above ratios take into account only the area of the hull's topsides. Though when heeled the coachroof, deckhouse and similar superstructures will be partially masked by the hull, their windage area in many modern yachts may be a considerable additional item.

---

* In his book *The Sailing Yacht* Juan Baader gives a calculation for the wind resistance of a Dragon. At a speed of 4 knots his figures show that of the total calculated wind resistance, 45 per cent is due to the hull, which we should note has low freeboard and an insignificant cabin top. He further shows that at this speed the hull frictional and wind resistances are *almost equal* and that the latter *exceeds the wave plus induced resistance by 15 per cent*! This suggests how under-estimated the importance of wind resistance may be in design studies.

CHAPTER FOUR

The Midship Section

A YACHTSMAN once bought a yacht which he did not care much for in any other way simply because he fell in love with her midship section, and George Watson said of him that he hadn't paid much for the boat herself but the price had been stiff just for the part of it he liked.

This might suggest a subtle denigration of the importance of midship sections, which Watson never intended. Also, the yachtsman concerned no doubt cared for more about the boat than just the midship section as he viewed her hauled-out. He must have, for the whole character of a boat is permeated by her midship section. It is like fate. It cannot be overcome; its domination may be twisted a little this way or that, but its mastery remains supreme. Which suggests how appropriate is that old term for the midship section—master section.

The midship section exerts its dominating influence in two ways. Firstly, it is the principal factor determining the displacement of a hull in relation to its length, and this is the fundamental characteristic of any yacht. It is a fairly close approximation to the truth to say that with equal waterline lengths the displacement of two hulls will be in proportion to the areas of their midship sections. Thus, if we assume that Sections 13 and 14 in Fig. 14 are respectively used as the basis of two 30-ft. waterline designs, their displacements will be approximately equal, the areas of the two midship sections being the same though they differ in shape. This assumes that the keel profiles of the two boats are not radically dissimilar.

The second influence of the midship section is due to its effect on the shape of all the other sections from bow to stern. It is true that with certain hull forms, notably in modern yachts with considerable beam or short ends, architects may contrive to make a wide departure from the shape amidships in the sections at bow and stern. An extreme earlier example of this may be seen in the typical old pilot cutter or Brixham trawler form, in 18 (Fig. 14), the deep, full midship section being run out to narrow V-bow sections and wide Y-stern sections. But usually, in the interests of harmonious design, and in the belief that there may be some hydrodynamic advantage in the practice, the sections of sailing yacht hulls from amidships out to the bow and stern usually maintain closely the characteristic shape of the midship section, the end sections making parallel curves within the master section. A draughtsman's skill is sometimes judged on his ability to maintain this similarity of character in shape throughout the length of the hull (Fig. 15, p. 54).

All the midship sections illustrated in Fig. 14 have been drawn proportional to a 30-ft. waterline hull to make direct comparison easier. Many of the sections illustrated are those of actual yachts which are appreciably larger or smaller than this length; but that need not invalidate comparisons. Midship sectional shapes, while being the crucial arbiter of the form of a sailing yacht, are independent of its size. Section 13, for example, that of

9. Full-bodied type of hull of moderate beam and draught giving little wetted surface and small depth of fin.

10. *Myth of Malham*, earliest of the light displacement snub-ended, high freeboard, R.O.R.C. rule type of offshore racing yacht.

11. (*Right*) I.Y.R.U. 6-Metre class sailing on a single wave-length, with a crest at bow and stern. Speed is between six and seven knots at this point.

12. A stern view of the wave-making of 6-Metres sailing at a similar speed to that of Plate 11.

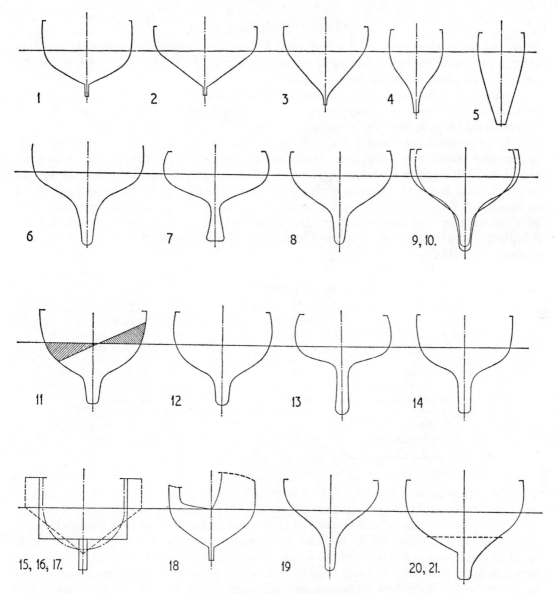

FIG. 14. *Comparative midship sections*

the 33-ft. waterline offshore racer *Myth of Malham,* has been used in yachts of more than 80 ft. on the waterline and in half-decked dayboats of less than 20 ft. Section 19 is that of a 24-ft. waterline *Tumlaren;* it closely resembles that of the great 93-ft. waterline cutter *Satanita* which had a 91-ft. mainboom and more than 10,000 sq. ft. of sail area. Section 6, that of *Britannia,* is found today in many cruiser-racers of 25–35 ft. on the waterline. Section 1 has been used in sailing freighters exceeding 100 ft. length and in heavy rowing-boats. We may be thankful, however, that Section 5, belonging to the 32-ft. waterline

D

Oona, has never been adopted for any craft appreciably larger or smaller. It was bad enough just once; though it has to be confessed that sections only a little less perverted were once common in several sizes of yacht.

Before going further into the nuances of usual midship section shapes, it may be as well to examine a few basic geometrical forms, each of which, incidentally, has been used for actual midship sections. So consider the three superimposed midship sections shown in 15, 16, 17 respectively—triangular, rectangular and semicircular form so far as their underwater bodies are concerned. These are the three generic shapes from which all actual midship sections are formed. They have been drawn to be of equal areas and attached to each is a keel appendage giving the same draught to the three sections. Being of equal area they are strictly comparable and we may assume they will produce hulls of approximately the same displacement when used for a common waterline length. Adopting our selected 30-ft. waterline length, the dimensions of the three hulls will be as shown in Table 7.

TABLE 7

	Triangle	Rectangle	Semicircle
Beam	12 ft.	9 ft.	8 ft. 4 in.
Draught	6 ft.	6 ft.	6 ft.
Displacement	10 tons	10 tons	10 tons
Wetted surface (proportion)	18·5	21	16·5

If we consider the elements of these three generic midship sections certain principles will be revealed applicable to all other shapes of midship section, whether curved in form or not. It will be evident immediately that the triangular section is a straightforward modern chine hull with keel, of the kind that has been successfully used lately in many small cruiser classes and some offshore racers. The rectangular section is that of the sailing barge, still *just* with us, and no inconsiderable sailing performer, including to windward in smooth water. Both these forms are approximated to closely in round bilge craft. The section of the *America* type (2) is almost precisely triangular, so high and hard is the bilge, and many modern light displacement yachts with high bilges and flat floors resemble the triangular shape in their underwater body (Sections 8 and 13, for example). The third basic type, the semicircular, is very common, and was commoner, in narrow, heavy displacement yachts, though the semicircularity may have been disguised by the reverse turn of full garboards (12). All possible midship sections incline towards one or other of the three basic types illustrated in 15, 16, 17.

From the Table above it will be evident that the primary advantage of the semicircular type of midship section is the low wetted surface. The semicircular sectioned hull is able to contain a given amount of displacement within the minimum of wetted surface, and this is its prime value. It is the reason why racing eights have semicircular sections.

On the other hand, the section, on account of its small beam, lacks stiffness. The stiffest section of the three is the triangular, with 12 ft. of beam compared with 8 ft. 4 in. of the semicircular for the same displacement. The triangular section lies about midway between the rectangle and the semicircle in wetted surface. A curved section based on a compromise between the triangle and the semicircle is a common yacht form. In these three shapes, with their various proportions of beam, hull depth and wetted surface, but all producing the same displacement, we find the fundamental characteristics of all midship sections.

It will be evident that the rectangle, or any curved approximation to it, tends to lack depth, and may in certain sizes give insufficient headroom. The triangular tends, however, to restrict breadth of cabin sole, which in small craft may be inconvenient. In these respects the semicircular section is the happy compromise.

In Section 1 we see the character of midship section once common in the mass of sailing craft which worked round our coast—fishermen, pilot boats, freight carriers, small naval craft—the traditional little ship midship section as evolved in our waters, with a depth equal to about half the beam and fairly low and easy bilges. All ballast was internal. Yachts were like the working craft, for yacht architecture had not yet set its own course towards the surprising results that were later to be achieved. Section 1 is that of a yacht built in 1822, but a century later this archetypal section was still found in sailing trawlers, pilot boats and yachts based on the working craft.

In America, and dating back to days before the Civil War, a type of midship section unknown in Europe had been evolved (Section 2) with a virtually triangular underwater body and high, hard bilges. This section was one element in a new type of hull form devised in the New World where speed under sail became an ideal pursued with an intensity unknown in Europe. The hulls were fine-ended (known as "sharp") and the midship section, with considerable breadth in relation to its immersed area, was of a stiff, easily driven form. That shown in Section 2 is the midship section of the *America* which won the cup that has been causing trouble ever since.

An English yacht, built in the same year, the *Volante* from Wivenhoe (Section 3) suggests the course in British yacht design. Under the influence of a measurement rule which taxed beam heavily but depth not at all, the proportion of the latter to the former has increased compared with the archetypal section, and in this section we see yacht architecture beginning to set its own course. Working craft are load-carriers in some form or another; yachts are not. It was thus practicable to reduce the bulkiness of the latter's midship sections and produce a steep floored, high bilge form triangular, like the American in underwater shape, but of much greater draught and less beam—a section aptly known as "pegtop." Ballast was still all inside.

It was the gradual adoption of outside ballast, enabling degrees of stability to be achieved hitherto unobtainable, in combination with a series of yacht measurement rules that murdered beam but allowed designers to have as much draught as they cared to take, which led to the extraordinary progression in yacht design indicated in Sections 3, 4, 5, and already outlined in Chapter Two. Early yachts with the pegtop section might have had about $3\frac{1}{2}$ beams in their waterline length. During a period of ten-odd years the L.W.L.-beam ratio increased to four, to five and finally to more than six when, in 1886, the incredible *Oona* appeared (Section 5) with a beam of 5 ft. 6 in. on a waterline of 34 ft. and some 70 per cent of her weight in a board based lead keel. Even had she not been lost with all hands including her designer, *Oona* was too much even for the phlegmatic British yachtsmen, who had been accepting with remarkable calm the amazing shapes that yachts were assuming.

An entirely new measurement rule was devised which produced, mercifully, entirely different results, an early example of which was the celebrated *Britannia* (6). Between the *Oona* of 1886 and the *Britannia* of 1893 we seem to move from antiquated quaintness to perfect modernity. *Britannia*'s midship section, scaled to a 30-ft. waterline, would produce an admirable hull; and indeed James McGruer in a number of his fine modern cruising yachts uses midship sections scarcely distinguishable from *Britannia*'s having the same high and fairly hard bilge, the flat floors and the full, easily turned garboards.

The new rule allowed the development of what we may regard as the "modern" yacht form, in which the midship section consists in varying degrees, of two distinct portions—a canoe body providing the floatation, and an appendage keel giving lateral resistance. Under the rule hull form subsequently evolved into the skimming-dish types of hull, which is not always desirable. Section 7 shows the midship section of *Shamrock III* of 90 ft. on the waterline. She was not built to this particular rule, but was strongly influenced by some earlier large yachts which were. In our own day the dish or champagne glass section, in combination with high freeboard, has produced the contemporary light displacement ocean-racing yachts, of which *Myth of Malham* was a forerunner. The obviously close relationship between Sections 7 and 13 is obvious, despite the differences in size of the two yachts. Section 8 is that of the first *Endeavour*, a beautiful compromise between the semicircular and the triangular but with pronounced tumblehome. This type was the product of a later rule intended to encourage more fullness of body than the skimming-dish type without eliminating the salient keel.

At this point we might conveniently think about tumblehome—that is, the sloping inboard of the topsides so that the maximum beam lies at a point below the deck level. Section 7 is an extreme example of tumblehome; it is moderate in Section 8 and just perceptible in Section 6.

One important result of tumblehome is a reduction in the area and hence the weight of the deck. In view of the deck's height, particularly in modern high freeboard yachts, this may be of appreciable benefit to stiffness. With the pronounced tumblehome indicated in Section 7 the saving may amount to 8–10 per cent in deck weight. A second advantage is that tumblehome keeps the deck edge and rail clear of the water until a bigger angle of heel is reached. The considerable tumblehome shown in Section 7 may make a difference of 5 degrees in the angle of heel at which the rail dips compared with a section having slightly flared topsides. The resistance curve of any yacht shows an abrupt rise the moment the deck edge becomes buried, owing as we have seen to the sudden alteration in immersed hull shape. There is a further consideration that rigging screws and all the clutter of chainplates and fittings near the deck edge are then dragged through the water. In the smaller, lighter craft, inshore racers and half-deckers in which water swilling about the deck may get below, tumblehome may be very valuable. Even in the largest yachts it is adopted, as in *Endeavour* (8), to keep the covering board and fittings dry for as long as possible.

A further advantage is more obscure. When a yacht heels she tends to lift bodily in the water, for the volume of the topsides immersed to leeward would otherwise be greater than that lifted out of the water on the weather side, and this as we and Archimedes know, would be contrary to the law governing the displacement of floating bodies. Hence the hull lifts to equalise the in- and out-wedges, as the shaded areas in Section 11 are called. This lifting process, if excessive, may be deleterious to performance, a matter dealt with in Chapter Eight.

Tumblehome has the disadvantage of reducing the sheeting base available on deck for headsails and often entails having outboard chocks to carry the sheet tracks—these, of course, being within the maximum beam though outside the deck rail. Tumblehome also has an unhappy aesthetic effect often not appreciated. It causes harsh highlights to be thrown on to the topsides. Since tumblehome is usually carried through all the sections abaft amidships and out to the stern, this band of crude light produces an ugly line of ungraduated shadow in the quarters. The soft, graduated shadow produced by slight flare (Section 11) along the topsides is an element of grace in a hull, as Fife knew and other architects since.

Following round a midship section, down from the topsides, we come next to that crucial feature of shape, the turn of the bilge. It is the most influential feature of a midship section once the beam has been selected; it largely determines the hull depth and displacement. Sections 13 and 14 are of quite different types. They have much the same beam and identical draught, but 14 has about 50 per cent more displacement than 13 owing to a relatively slack bilge.

The superimposed sections in 9 and 10 are both of the same displacement, but one section has a higher, harder bilge, and more beam, and is of a stiffer character. But it is important not to be misled over the relationship between stiffness and hardness of bilge. A bilge may be made hard simply by having tumblehome introduced above it, or soft if run off into flared topsides. Sections 11 and 12 have identical underwater bodies and waterline beams, but owing to flared topsides 11 has no discernible turn of bilge, which in 12 is clearly evident though not sharp. Section 11 looks the weaker, yet in fact it is more stiff than 12 owing to its greater maximum beam.

Less crucial than the turn of the bilge, the curve of the garboards is still an important feature in a midship section's shape. Originally garboards had no curve (Sections 1 and 2) and swept garboards in the modern manner were the outcome of external lead keels (Section 4); though they virtually disappeared when the plank on edge season was at its height, and narrow U-shaped sections plunged to their load loaded depths (Section 5). Curved garboards came into prominence with the beamier, shallower hulls produced by the length and sail area rule of 1888—and have been with us ever since.

Essentially the garboards are simply the reverse curves linking the more or less flat-sided keel with the more or less rounded body of the hull. Two extreme forms of garboard are illustrated in 20 and 21. Down to the level of the pecked line the sections are identical; but below it the one to the left has been run into an angular garboard, that to the right has a full garboard that blurs the distinction between the keel and canoe body. One effect of fullness of garboard is to give simultaneously an increase in displacement and a reduction in wetted surface. The section to the right has appreciably the greater displacement but it is contained within an envelope of smaller wetted surface; below the pecked line this section has 10 per cent less surface than that with an angular garboard.

This suggests one value of full garboards—they provide a way of adding to the displacement at a low cost in resistance. Firstly, the added displacement being low down where the hull is narrow is likely to be less resistful than were it obtained by greater beam

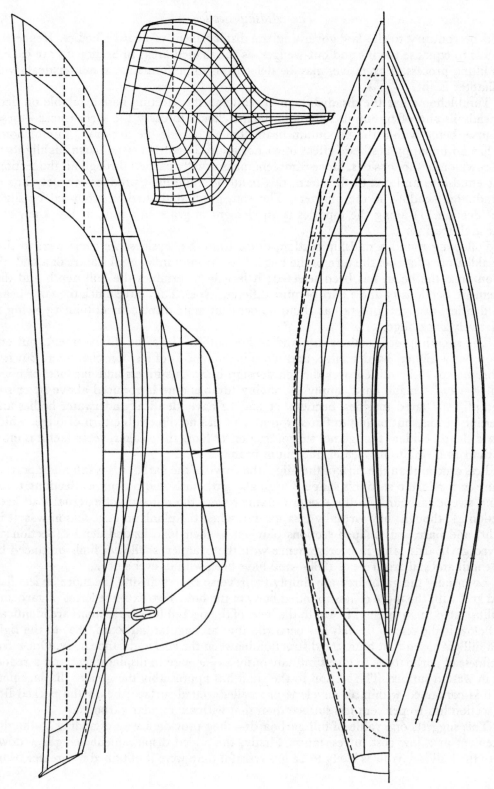

FIG. 15. Mindy designed by F. B. R. Brown. L.O.A. 36 ft. L.W.L. 27·5 ft. Beam 9 ft.

or a fuller bilge, while the reduction of wetted surface is of great advantage in light airs. Many fast light wind boats have had full garboards, and it is a device that has often been resorted to by designers of rated class boats in which a certain minimum displacement is stipulated by rule.

There is another advantage to slack garboards, which is that they may allow a reasonable breadth of cabin sole to be obtained in a hull where otherwise it would be deficient. This will be evident from the *Tumlaren* type of sections in 18. With the tight garboards more usual in light displacement craft (Sections 7 and 13) either headroom or sole breadth may be unduly restricted in a small hull; but the slack garboard of the *Tumlaren* obviates this.

CHAPTER FIVE

Hull Form and Type

THE question of type will presumably exercise yachtsmen until they sail the seas no more. There can be no complete answer because so much depends on circumstances; whilst even if precisely the same circumstances are envisaged, there is still no single, ideal boat to suit them. But the widely different ideals advanced are often the result of confusion as to what purposes a yacht is to serve.

Thus Conor O'Brien once used to propagate, in his forceful prose, opinions which were based on common sense born of experience, and yet which never influenced the design of yachts generally because they applied to conditions not met by most yachtsmen. Only the minority are ocean wanderers. For this work we may accept the fairly heavy displacement, long keel yacht, able to look after herself in bad weather when handled by a small crew, and having a rig in which strength and the ability to make the most of free winds are of more importance than speed and weatherliness.

But the average yachtsman spends the majority of his time in coastal waters, when it is speed and weatherliness, the attributes of the racing yachts, which are of most value. The yacht capable of "going anywhere" is inclined to get nowhere when coastal cruising, and she will probably make a better job of crossing an ocean than of dodging down Channel in English summer weather. In coastal waters the ability to go to windward means safety and to go fast brings peace of mind. Combined with speed and weatherliness the cruiser needs good accommodation and, in our own time, the sort of hull which will handle well on a moderate sail area.

DIMENSIONS AND PROPORTIONS The data which a designer will keep of his own completed designs, and of the fittings and rigging specifications of yachts which he knows well, will be very detailed. But for blocking out a design more general information is needed, and applying to a big range of yachts. It is here that the general data book is of value. It should include the leading dimensions, and certain important ratios known. The information collected should be such as may be obtained from small scale and published drawings, for if large-scale plans are needed to derive the particulars, the time and trouble spent in finding them will reduce the range of data collected. The more complicated coefficients are not worth the labour of the calculations involved.

The information collected is best kept in a loose-leaf book laid out in the way shown in Fig. 16. It will be seen that the data shown is easily found and collected. It includes the six leading hull dimensions, the sail area, and four useful ratios. The length/beam and length/draught ratios are calculated by dividing the waterline length by the beam and draught respectively. A narrow yacht will thus have a big L/B ratio; one of deep draught a small L/Dr ratio. The shoal-draught type is characterised by small L/B and large L/Dr ratios. The displacement-length ratio is of particular interest. Care must be taken

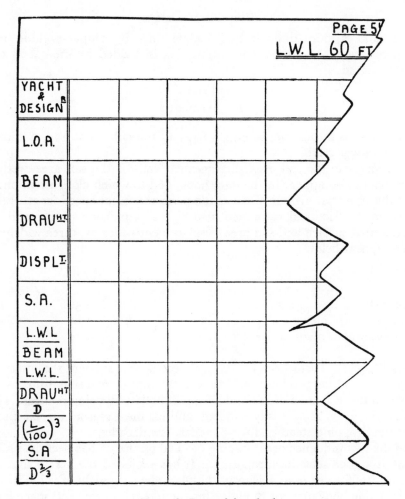

FIG. 16. *Page of data book*

in calculating it, since it compares a cubic measurement with a linear one. The displacement is divided by one-hundredth of the length cubed, displacement being measured in tons.* The constant of 100 is used in order to keep the ratio in manageable figures, and it will range between about 200 for light displacement yachts to 500 for heavy.

A consistent method of measuring sail area must be used for the data book, and though there are arguments for assessing it as the maximum area of actual working canvas, including the largest working Genoa but excluding, in a yawl or ketch, mizzen staysails, it will be found most generally satisfactory to measure sail area as that of mainsail plus 100 per cent foretriangle plus mizzen, if there is one.

The three ratios together form a neat commentary on the proportions and type of any yacht, and provide a means for comparison with other craft not necessarily of the same size. With a slide rule they may be worked out in a few minutes. The sail area/

* Appendix Two.

displacement ratio is more difficult to calculate since it compares cubic and square measures. In this case, the sail area in square feet is divided by the cubed root of the displacement squared.

$$\frac{\text{Sail Area}}{(\text{Displacement})^{\frac{2}{3}}}$$

If the displacement is 8 tons, the square is 64, and the cube root is 4. A slide rule will again give the answer readily.*

Complementary to the sail area/displacement ratio is the sail area/wetted surface ratio, which should also appear in the data book, and to which close attention should be paid as it is the principal arbiter of a yacht's performance at speed-length ratios below about 0·8, when the frictional resistance is so high a proportion of the total. Values of the sail area/wetted surface and sail area/displacement ratios for three widely dissimilar types of yacht appear below.

	S.A./W.S.	*S.A./ Displacement*$^{\frac{2}{3}}$
Six-metre	2·50	180
Thirty square metre	1·65	165
Heavy displacement cruiser	2·10	147

DISPLACEMENT Displacement has in recent years been the most discussed element of design, and for good reason. Moderately light displacement means lower first cost, the wood in the hull, area of sail and weight of ballast all being reduced. The upkeep is cheaper and the yacht more easily handled, and for these reasons displacement/length ratios have been dropping steadily during the last few decades.

Perhaps the best influence ocean-racing has had on design has been its proof of light displacement as a good seagoing proposition. It has exploded the heresy that heavy displacement is in itself a virtue in a seaway. Displacement is partly of value in so far as it is needed to provide buoyancy for the full construction and outfit, and space for comfortable accommodation. Space is now obtainable in very light hulls, but for deep-water cruising moderately heavy displacement is needed to carry the necessary stores and gear. And it is needed too in some less ambitious cruisers. Light displacement is a virtue only so long as it remains light; the light displacement yacht floating below her marks has the worst of both worlds.

Light displacement produces a bigger boat for a given weight, and a faster boat for a given sail area; if a chosen amount of displacement is spread over a long waterline the result will be a roomier boat and one of greater potential speed than if the same displacement is concentrated into a shorter waterline. But the price per ton displacement of the lighter boat will be higher. Each ton yields more in accommodation and sailing power but costs more in cash.

Today, light displacement offshore craft have displacement/length ratios of as little as 208. To obtain low displacement ratios whilst retaining the high ballast ratio necessary for good performance, scantlings and outfit have to be reduced, and the former means greater expense. Below a certain displacement ratio, therefore, a price has to be paid in

* Appendix Three.

cash or comfort, below deck, and we may place this ratio at about 340 which may be compared with the 310 of the I.Y.R.U. classes. If the price is paid in comfort, however, and spartan standards are accepted below deck, a displacement/length ratio of as low as 250 may produce a relatively cheap yacht.

It must be kept in mind, as an advantage of heavier displacement, that if one yacht has twice the displacement and the same waterplane area as another she receives the same disturbing effect from a rough sea and has about twice the resistance to the disturbance, so that other things being equal she has very much smaller motions in roll, pitch and heave.

The curves in Fig. 17 are a guide to displacements for various lengths of yacht. The top curve labelled "cruiser" represents good moderate practice in modern types of cruiser-racer, and the values are somewhat below those acceptable in the years before the Second World War. The lowest curve represents really light displacement suitable for craft in which constructional and accommodation weights have been reduced to the minimum. The middle line, derived from the displacement allowances of the old I.Y.R.U. rule, to which the 12-Metres are still built,* means fairly light displacement for sailing yachts with full accommodation and seagoing equipment.

THE FORE AND AFT SHAPE OF THE HULL   The chief influence on wave-making resistance is the fore and aft form of the hull, the optimum shape of which varies with the speed-length ratio. In the design of power-propelled craft this enables the hull shape to be suited to a predetermined speed, and allows the form to be adapted to the most economical performance at the point in the speed range that will be most used in service. Under sail this is impracticable. Appreciable latitude in fore and aft shape is possible without any significant loss in the average performance over the wider range of speed-length ratios at which sailing is done. Design is to this extent simplified. Also, hull shape *per se* has its importance reduced on points of sailing when the wind produces any appreciable lateral component of force and an important arbiter of performance becomes the ability of the hull to develop efficiently a hydrodynamic force opposed to it; and this is little affected by hull shape. Again, under sail, the driving force that can be effectively employed is governed by the stability, which in turn is influenced by the fore and aft lines; and it may be advantageous to produce a more resistful yet stiffer hull. The relative freedom permissible in the choice of the fore and aft lines of a sailing yacht is one reason why amateurs may design them successfully, but would fail with a power vessel.

Three generic types of sailing hull have been adopted in sailing yachts, distinguished by the way in which the displacement is disposed fore and aft. In the cod's head and mackerel's tail shape, found today in modified form only, the bulk of the hull is in the forebody, the bluff bow tapering into a long, fine-lined after-body. The reverse of the cod's head type is the wedge, which has a long, lean forebody and full stern. Fig. 18(*a*) and (*b*) are moderate examples of this type, though without any undue fullness aft. It is the type indicated in the Colin Archer curve of areas in Fig. 1. The third type lies between the two above; it is almost symmetrical in shape, and this is the name by which it is conveniently known. In the symmetrical form the volumes of the displacement forward and aft of amidships are almost equal, and the symmetry is readily visible in the run of the waterlines and diagonals. Two clear examples of the type are in Fig. 18(*c*) and (*d*).

* See Chapter Nine.

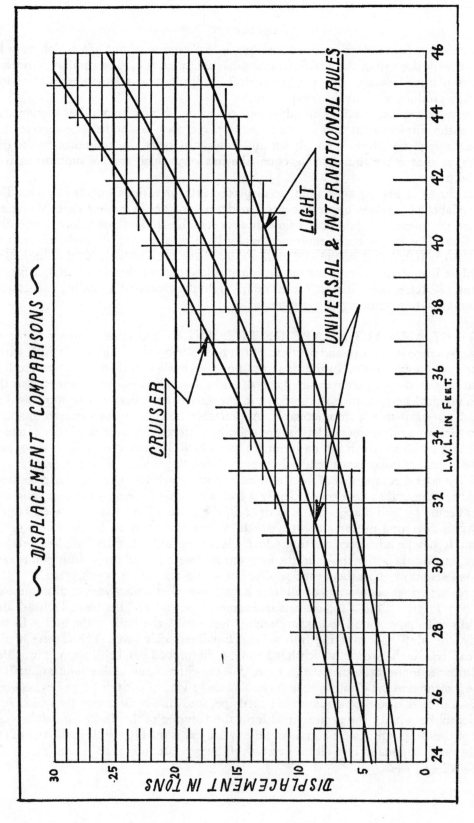

Fig. 17. *Typical displacement values for three groups*

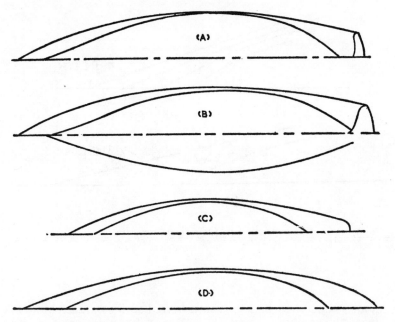

FIG. 18. *Comparison of shapes*—Nina, Landfall, Amoukura, Evenlode

The three forms are reflected in the shape of their curves of areas, and the considerable variation that may exist in these within the range of normal yacht types is suggested in the curves of Fig. 1. In the wedge form of hull the longitudinal centre of buoyancy will be well abaft of amidships, at about 0·56 L.W.L. In the symmetrical form it will lie close to amidships, at 0·51–0·52 L.W.L., though the volume of the keel may draw

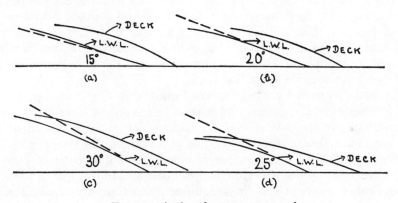

FIG. 19. *Angles of entrance compared*

the C.B. of the complete yacht abaft of this. In the cod's head type the C.B. will be at or even forward of amidships.

The resistance qualities of the three generic types of hull are shown in the curves of

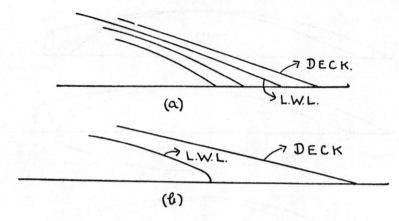

FIG. 20. *Snubbed forward waterlines*

Fig. 21. The models concerned had the same wetted surface areas. Model A was of the cod's head and mackerel's tail type with the longitudinal centre of buoyancy at 43·88 per cent of the waterline length from the bow; Model B was symmetrical about amidships; and Model C was of the wedge form with the C.B. at 56·12 per cent. Fig. 21 shows the resistances of these models plotted against speed-length ratios. Up to a ratio of slightly below 0·5 the full-bow shape gives the least resistance, the fine bow has the greatest, whilst between the two lies the symmetrical form, but closer to Model A than B. At a ratio of 0·5 there is an indeterminate region where there is nothing to choose between any of the models, but by the time a speed-length ratio of 0·6 has been reached the order of efficiency has been reversed. The cod's head type has the greatest resistance, the fine bow model the lowest, and again between the two, but with a bias towards the smaller resistance, comes the symmetrical hull. Between the ratios of 0·6 and a shade below 1·0 this order is maintained, but it will be noticed that the resistance of wedge form increases more rapidly than that of the symmetrical one, until at a ratio of 1·0 the two curves cross and the resistance of the symmetrical hull becomes the least of the three, remaining thus over the range of speeds practicable for sailing craft.

It will be seen that over a range of speeds from about $V/\sqrt{L} = 0.45$–1.0 the wedge form of hull is superior to the others, and beyond this is only a little inferior to the symmetrical form at speeds up to $V/\sqrt{L} = 1.4$. Below $V/\sqrt{L}$ there is a slight advantage in the cod's head form. There is justification on this evidence for the form of hull having the after-body appreciably fuller than the fore-body, and the centre of buoyancy from 3 to 5 per cent or more of the waterline length abaft amidships. But in view of the importance, from other points of view in design (see pages 109–115) of a hull that approximates to the symmetrical form, it is convenient to find that the wedge form may be modified in the direction of a closer degree of symmetry without serious increase of resistance at normal sailing speeds.

It may be seen in Fig. 21 that there are humps in the resistance curves, and that in places the resistance seems to be getting smaller as the speed increases. For the sake of simplicity the speed-length ratio has been plotted against a quantity labelled "Resistance,"

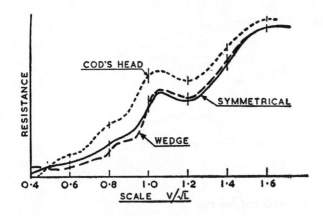

F<small>IG</small>. 21. *Curves of total resistance*

but this actually is a resistance constant found by dividing the resistance by the product of the speed squared and the displacement to the power of two-thirds. If an increase in speed is accompanied by a small increment in resistance only, the value of the constant may become smaller in spite of the slightly greater resistance.

In the present day there has been a trend in design back towards the cod's head form—*Sceptre* had many predecessors—and the high degree of favour that it was shown in the past may be accounted partly to its good light wind performance. But from the point of view purely of resistance modern hydrodynamic evidence shows no reason for adopting the shape, except for some collateral advantages it may have. A deckline with its greatest beam forward of amidships, and a waterline that is boldly full forward, with more than usual of the volume of the displacement disposed immediately below the water-line in the vicinity of the mast, provide buoyancy and power forward that appear peculiar-ly advantageous when carrying a hard-sheeted Genoa. The advantages of this form of hull, which Charles A. Nicholson has adopted with success in his designs, indicate the many diverse features that may influence the hull form of sailing yachts.

PITCHING Whatever may be said in favour of the full bow and fine stern form of hull, on the above scores or on those of balance on the helm (Chapter Eight) the form of hull is definitely suspect of a liability to excessive pitching, and no form of behaviour is more detrimental than this to speed to windward. Once heavy pitching begins a boat has to be sailed freer, which reduces speed made good to windward (V_{mg}), and heels farther, which lowers the speed through the water (V_s). It was not only *Sceptre* amongst British inshore racing yachts whose poor performance has been attributed to an excessive ten-dency to pitch, and in offshore sailing the fault is no less damaging.

Heavy pitching is likely to occur as soon as the pitching period of a yacht matches or comes close to the period of encounter with the waves. Sailing at approximately 45 degrees to a seaway at usual speeds there is a likelihood for pitching periods to be similar to the encounter periods, and the instinctive cure for this (for little data are available for the calculation of the respective periods) adopted by designers is to shorten the pitching periods of their yachts by the maximum possible concentration of weights fore and aft, carried even to the extent of stowing the cable near amidships. By this means it is hoped

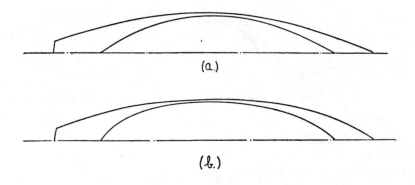

(a.)

(b.)

FIG. 22. *Fine ends and full ends*

to keep pitching periods well below the point of synchronisation with wave periods, This can be the only justification for the sometimes apparently excessive enthusiasm shown for keeping weights out of the ends of sailing yachts. In most sailing yachts with 40–45 per cent ballast ratios the fore and aft weights are already extremely concentrated.

Apart from adjustments in pitching period, pitching may be materially reduced by modifications in hull form. Pitching is excited by the bow and damped by the stern. Hence the full bow, with considerable buoyancy and lifting surface, produces high exciting forces, and if this is matched by a narrow stern with little buoyancy and hence able to produce only slight damping effect, the pitching may become fierce. For the damping of pitch there are clear arguments in favour of the more typically American form of hull, with relatively narrow, well-veed sections forward and fairly wide hard-bilged sections aft, especially in yachts intended mainly for racing offshore rather than round the buoys in relatively sheltered waters (Fig. 27).

PRISMATIC COEFFICIENT When running or broad reaching without any considerable degrees of heel or yaw, the relative fullness or fineness of the ends of the hull has an important effect upon the wave-making resistance.

The convenient criterion of the fore and aft fullness of a hull is the prismatic co-efficient (C_p). It is the ratio of the volume of the displacement to a prism having the area of the immersed midship section and the length of the load waterline. Geometrically it may be expressed as the proportion between the area contained within the curve of areas (Fig. 1) and a circumscribing rectangle. The prismatic coefficient is simply a convenient numerical means of defining and recording the fullness of the ends of a hull in relation to the middle body, an index of the quickness with which the fore and aft lines swing about amidships. *This being so, the keel should not be included in the calculation.** *The keel*, especially modern fin keels *are* strictly appendages to a canoe body, whose shape the prismatic is intended to define. In Figs. 22 and 23 full and fine ended yachts are compared. In the former (*a*) has a smaller prismatic coefficient than (*b*). Fig. 23 shows two load waterlines, B producing a higher coefficient than A.

* Despite the dogmatic statement made in the latest edition of Skene's *Elements of Yacht Design.*

13. *Westward of Clynder* designed by James McGruer, a 30 ft. waterline fast cruising yacht uninfluenced by any measurement rule, but exemplifying the increase in beam of modern English yachts.

14. A fine afterbody and well-veed stern sections in a design by Robert Clark (John I. Thornycroft & Co., Ltd.).

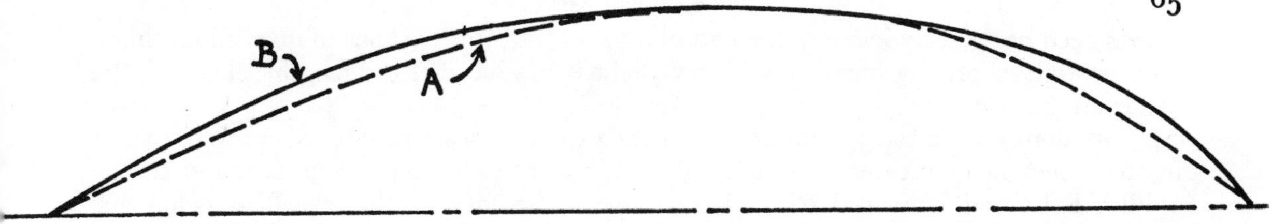

FIG. 23. *Load waterlines suitable for high (B) and low (A) prismatic coefficients*

For the various speed-length ratios there are optimum prismatic coefficients, and the correct coefficient for the speed concerned materially lowers the resistance at that speed. The sailing yacht architects' problem is to decide which speed-length ratio to use as the criterion. Optimum prismatics are given in Table 8:

TABLE 8

$V/\sqrt{L}$	*Prismatic Coefficient*
0·6	0·53
0·8	0·53
1·0	0·525
1·1	0·54
1·2	0·58
1·3	0·62

At speeds below $V/\sqrt{L} = 1\cdot0$ the optimum prismatic remains pretty steadily at 0·53–0·52, and since a sailing yacht spends much of her life moving at speeds below this value the low prismatic may be acceptable. Many successful yachts, however, have prismatic coefficients of 0·54 or a little more, suiting speeds of ratio 1·1–1·15. Such hulls have a distinct advantage when reaching and running under brisk conditions. A higher than optimum prismatic at the lower speeds is a less serious disadvantage than it might seem, as at the lower speeds the wave-making resistance, which is the fraction of the total affected by the prismatic, is relatively small. It is better to have too high a prismatic at low speeds than too low a prismatic at high speeds. Furthermore, under sail the bigger prismatic, with the fuller ended hull entailed, gives a higher metacentre and greater sail carrying power.*

LENGTH AND SHAPE OF THE ENDS Cruisers, unlike racers, do not need overhangs to gain unmeasured length. Three considerations govern the length of the ends: (i) expense, (ii) behaviour at sea, (iii) the all-inboard rig. Overhangs formed by easy

* See Chapter Seven.

E

curves need not greatly increase the cost of a yacht, but it is cheaper to do without them, and for a given price a bigger and faster yacht is produced if the length is kept on the waterline.

Opinions on the right amount of overhang to go to sea with moved for many years in the direction of greater length, until even the considerable amounts found in the old I.Y.R.U. and Universal Rule classes have found favour. The excellent behaviour of the J-class *Yankee* on her Atlantic crossing in 1935 gave support to such views, and in yachts of this class the total overhanging length was about 50 per cent of the waterline. That of the average 12-Metre is about 60 per cent. Here, certainly, is a veering of ideas since the time when Claud Worth, after drawing out the bow of *Tern IV*, which was 48 ft. on the waterline, into an overhang of 4 ft. said it was as far as he thought it wise to go in a seagoing cruiser.

Claud Worth was certainly cautious in his estimate; unless economy is to the forefront, a reasonable amount of overhang is advantageous in the purest of cruisers, and a total length of one-third of the waterline is a reasonable figure for craft of normal displacement. The amount should be equally divided between bow and stern. Considerations of balance dictate this, and equally so does behaviour at sea. Overhangs give reserve of buoyancy, promoting dryness and allowing a ship to lift easily and drop gently, whereas the old straight-stemmers were notorious divers – a feature generally accentuated by an excess of buoyancy in the counter, which still further depressed the bow. It is so reasonable to make the reserve of buoyancy equal at either end, or if unequal, to put the excess into the bow, which has to do the shouldering of the sea, that the reason why designers persisted for so long in putting more buoyancy aft is difficult to explain. The good behaviour of yachts which have a well-shaped transom, and a bow overhang of perhaps three times the length of that aft, is well known. An aesthetic point to remember is that the stern overhang tends to look longer than that forward owing to the lower freeboard, and yachts with springy sheers and equal overhangs at either end will appear to have more out of the water aft than forward.

Overhangs of more than one-third of the waterline length may sometimes be needed to keep the rig all inboard. There is certainly no justification, other than economy or unfortunate rule influence, for having shorter overhangs augmented by bowsprits and bumpkins. There is discomfort in even a short bowsprit when changing headsails, and though the disadvantage of a bumpkin is not so serious, there is an unpleasing lack of balance when the latter is fitted alone.

It is probably most logical to relate the length of the overhangs to the displacement. A heavy displacement yacht needs more overhang than a light craft. Sundry influences in the past led to the association of light displacement and long ends, heavy displacement and short ends, and the result was that whilst already buoyant and "floaty" boats had more spare buoyancy than needed hanging on the ends, the heavy ships with their tendency to plunge have insufficient to support them. So long as the rig can be kept inboard the overhang length of light displacement hulls may advantageously be reduced to one-quarter or even one-fifth of the waterline length. Perhaps the *Myth of Malham*'s most important contribution to the art of design lay in her demonstration of the effectiveness of short ends and light weight, and numerous yachts have followed her example since 1940.

In section the overhangs of a cruiser should be well lifted and full-U sections must

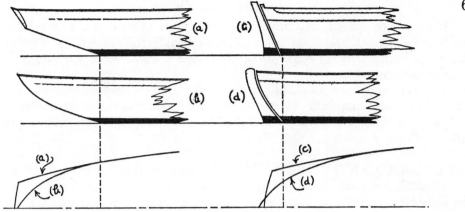

FIG. 24. *Four types of stern*

be avoided. If a waterline drawn at 25 degrees of heel shows that any considerable area of the section at the aft waterline ending becomes immersed, it reveals that the stern is too full and will drag up a nasty stern wave, besides upsetting the balance on the helm. It is also impossible to draw bow sections of reasonable shape which will match a full stern in reserve of buoyancy.

The type of stern combining the greatest number of advantages is probably the orthodox counter, of moderate width at the arch board and well-V'd in section Fig. 24(*a*). It is most important that the width should not be excessive, but there is a temptation to make it so when trying to gain space on deck aft, and room for a quarter berth below. The canoe stern, perhaps the most aesthetically satisfying of all, is not so good for speed,

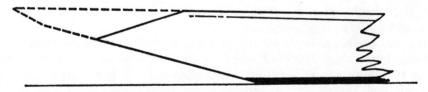

FIG. 25. *The retroussé stern designed to save weight*

and reduces the space aft, but it ideally matches the bow volumetrically. A common idea that the canoe stern has the quality of parting heavy following or quartering seas would not seem to have the slightest foundation. A transom end on a yacht with a full after-body creates a big drag as it dips into a sea, which greatly augments the height of the stern wave, whilst it lacks the buoyancy to lift to the commotion which it has created. But a light, well-lifted transom, terminating a finely drawn after-body, can be excellent at sea and delightfully sightly in harbour. Apart, however, from the fact of having the rudder hangings in sight and accessible for repair, the transom has no advantages over a correctly drawn counter, though infinitely better than a bad one (Fig. 24(*b*) (*c*) and (*d*)).

We may say, indeed, that any of the usual types of stern can be excellent in a seaway if well designed, and there is probably more difference between the behaviour of a well and a badly designed stern of the same type than between any two well-designed sterns of different types.

The sections at the bow should also be well V'd. This does not mean weak shoulders and lack of breadth on deck, but rather that the volume of the overhangs is not carried too low, as in the full-U shape, which slam heavily and put a tremendous strain on the hull.

FREEBOARD AND SHEER   There are many yachts designed in the last century whose hull shapes could be little improved today. Only their low freeboard dates them. The higher freeboard now generally to be found is one of the most rational improvements in design during the last forty years.

An example will illustrate the trend. The 24-ton *Eilun*, designed by Mylne in 1902, and the winner in the R.O.R.C. big class in the 1946 season, has a minimum freeboard of 2·5 ft. on a waterline length of 38 ft. Today the freeboard on such a length would be about 3·2 ft., an addition of 28 per cent.

The advantages of high freeboard may be summarised as: (i) Greater range of stability; (ii) Lower resistance due to the lee rail being kept clear of the water; (iii) A drier deck at sea; (iv) More space below deck. Against these advantages must be set: (i) greater windage, and (ii) slightly higher C.G.

The amount of the freeboard is closely related to the curve of the sheer, and no line which is drawn in the course of design is so far beyond rational analysis as the sheerline. Let it be confessed that the logical sheer is nearly straight. A heavily sprung sheerline means that there is too much freeboard at the ends or too little amidships, or both. The freeboard at the stem must be enough to prevent the yacht from ducking her bow too readily. But the worst seas come aboard at amidships on the windward side, whilst it is the height at this point to leeward which determines how soon the lee rail becomes immersed. High freeboard amidships is a blessing at sea, and it can be achieved only by excessive height at the ends or a flat sheer.

Yet it is undeniable that the beauty of a yacht depends more on her sheer than on any other line in the ship. The craft which catch the eye in a crowded moorings, those which leave the impression of beautiful conceptions beautifully executed, generally have lively curves in their sheerlines. The artist in every designer makes him wish to draw such curves, and apparently all creators of ships have fallen for the temptation, back to the remotest times when ships, sheerlines and architects together get lost in the mists of antiquity. To achieve this, the stem must be slightly higher and the minimum freeboard slightly lower than pure reason dictates. Particularly is this necessary in short-ended yachts, which look like logs on the water if their sheer is inadequate. The *Gauntlets*, though not an extreme example, suffer a little from this aesthetic defect—which is an advantage to them in every other way. In longer-ended yachts the sheer may be flattened in harmony with the straighter stem and counter, and it is sometimes of advantage to draw out the ends simply to harmonise with a flatter sheer.

The form of the sheer is partly fixed when the amounts of the freeboard at bow and stern, and at the lowest point, are decided. But a great number of curves may be passed through three widely spaced points, even when a stiff spline is used, and though two yachts may vary little in their amounts of sheer, the natures of the curves may be widely different. From the great variety of bold sheerlines which may be drawn—there is little room for differentiation in the flatter variety—two board shapes may be detected. In one, the position of minimum freeboard is well aft, the curve of the rail from the stern to the lowest point has little hollow in it, and from this point to the stern there is little lift in the line. In the other, the lowest point is farther forward, the sheer is formed by an altogether hollower curve, and it has more lift aft. The latter we still associate with Fife. The former is more modern, and accounts for the apparently drooping stern seen in so many contemporary yachts.

The hogged or reverse sheerline is now common and in the smaller light displacement yachts is functional, but even Laurent Giles, who once described it as "the new look which seems to slide across the paper before ever the boat has taken the water," has failed to blend it into a new form of yacht beauty. Reverse sheers are obviously to be accepted on their merits, but it seems that they can no more provoke a sense of grace than a bowler on a businessman. The sheerline that is straight, drawn with a straight-edge, appears hogged in practice, and in practice too appears to have neither less nor more aesthetic merits than the reverse curved line. Sheer and freeboard are discussed in relation to accommodation in Chapter Twelve.

SHOAL DRAUGHT Shoal draught yachts present a rather more difficult problem in design than do those of deep draught, and chiefly in the matter of gauging the quantities of beam and displacement which should be combined with the chosen length and draught. Stability must be ensured, but it has to be done on less draught and generally less displacement than in the deep draught type. Shoal draught is usually adopted purely for its advantages when estuary and inshore sailing, but there are those with great experience of shallow draught yachts in deep waters who consider their behaviour superior in many ways to the deeper vessels. The records of Henry Howard's famous ketch *Alice*, of 44 ft. L.W.L. and 4 ft. draught, and of many other craft support this view.

Shoal-draught yachts may be placed in two classes. Firstly, there is the type, un-uncommon in England except in the smallest sizes, having no outside ballast, and relying wholly on beam and inside ballast for stability, and on the centreboard for sailing. Secondly, there is what may be called the semi-keel type, originally developed in the U.S.A. in an effort to combine the advantages of the English deep-draught yachts with the American shoal centreboarders. The average English shoal-draught yacht is of this type, having less draught than the normal, but with an appreciable area of flat keel surface and most of the ballast outside. The first class, of which *Alice* was an example, suffer from the disability, which Maurice Griffiths has stressed, of being unable to sail when the board is housed; should it jam, the yachts are helpless. Those in the second class will sail reasonably, even to windward, with the board raised. Modern centreboarders tend to lie close to the lower curve in Fig. 26.

When blocking out the dimensions of shallow-draught yachts, a reliable collection of data relating to successful craft of the same size is needed. The amount by which the proportions will vary from the normal type depends on the shallowness of the draught chosen, and if it is to be only slightly reduced, the other proportions may be similar to those of an average deep-draught yacht. The loss in stability caused by the higher keel may be compensated by less sail area, for the hull will be more easily driven. The following

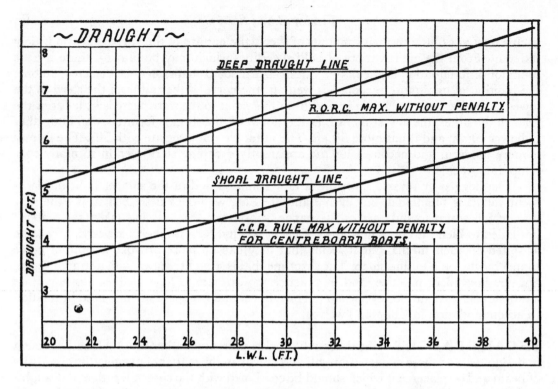

FIG. 26. *Draught comparisons, using old R.O.R.C. and C.C.A. rule standards as basis*

comparison of two designs by the same architect, one deep-draught, the other shoal, are closely alike except for their draughts and ballast keel weights:

					8-ton Sloop	7½-ton Estuary Sloop
L.O.A.	..	..	..	..	34 ft.	34 ft. 7 in.
L.W.L.	..	..	..	..	24 ft.	24 ft. 2 in.
Beam	..	..	..	..	8 ft. 2 in.	8 ft. 6 in.
Draught (Hull)	..	..	..	..	5 ft. 3 in.	4 ft.
Draught (C.B.)	..	..	..	..	—	6 ft.
Displacement	..	..	..	..	6·36 tons	6·26 tons
Outside Keel	..	..	..	..	2·75 tons	2·30 tons
Sail Area	..	..	..	..	500 sq. ft.	420 sq. ft.

A problem in shoal-draught design is the accommodation of the ballast keel. If the draught is reduced, but the fullness of body maintained, there is insufficient depth of keel to take the required volume of metal, and the balance has to be placed inside. The above 7½-tonner is thus forced to carry 11½ cwt. internally. Obviously, lead keels are of particular advantage in these circumstances.

As shoal-draught becomes more extreme, so the beam must be increased and a flatter section adopted. Below is a comparison of a small shoal-draught cruiser by the Dutch yachtsman and architect Baron van Hoevell, and the tabloid designed by Nigel Warington Smyth for his own use.

					Normal	*Shoal*
L.O.A.	..	..	..	..	30 ft. 7 in.	29 ft. 6 in.
L.W.L.	..	..	..	..	22 ft.	21 ft. 8 in.
Beam	..	..	..	..	8 ft. 3 in.	9 ft. 2 in.
Draught (Hull)	..	..	..	..	5 ft. 2 in.	3 ft. 3 in.
Displacement	..	..	..	..	4·7 tons	4·1 tons
Outside Keel	..	..	..	..	1·75 tons	1·5 tons
Sail Area	..	..	..	..	375 sq. ft.	375 sq. ft.

The relative merits of hulls verging towards the wedge or the symmetrical shapes may still be open to discussion, but where the really beamy shoal-draught type of yacht is concerned there is no doubt that performance depends on adopting the wedge shape, with very fine forebody, full after-body and the longitudinal centre of buoyancy and the greatest beam at about 58 per cent L.W.L. from amidships. The much advertised and successful *Finisterre* class of boat are of this type, with a small angle of entrance at the water-line and extremely full stern. Another example of the type, less extreme but still pronounced, appears in Fig. 27, which shows a 25 ft. 5 in. L.W.L. centreboard sloop by the American architect A. Mason. Note the fineness forward and fullness aft of the underwater body. The penalty for such a shape is a temperamental boat harder to sail at her best than one of narrower and more symmetrical form. Beamy, shallow, wedge-shaped boats may be very fast, but they are fickle; narrower more symmetrical boats may be fast too and have more phlegmatic habits.

Centreboarders designed with a serious view to high performance have, with the board lowered, greater draught than the deep-keel yacht and a more effective lateral area; hence their success. But such boards entail great expense and considerable mechanical complications.

A particularly difficult matter in shoal-draught design is the placing of the centreboard, and little guidance can be given. To justify vagueness, it may be added that the late Starling Burgess once said he did not know how to place a centreboard; and in a majority of designs it will be found that the accommodation layout has as much influence as sailing considerations.

If the centreboard is placed too near the bow the C.L.R. will move forward when the board is lowered, producing weather helm; if too far aft, lee helm may result. But the average shoal-draught hull, which is generally of slightly unbalanced hull form, is not easily induced to carry lee helm, and if the board is too far forward the weather helm can become vicious. In one case, where the hull balance was reasonably good, though not perfect, and the board was placed so that its leading edge left the hull at 0·41 per cent of the waterline length from forward, vicious weather helm was produced. But if the hull is of perfectly balanced shape, the ideal is to place the centreboard so that its C.W.P. falls vertically below that of the hull alone. The orthodox C.L.R. is not a good guide in this case, and an approximate position of the C.W.P. must be used. We may assume this position to be between 40 and 45 per cent of the L.W.L. from forward. The C.W.P. of the board, which may be accepted as being at the C.G. of its immersed shape, should therefore

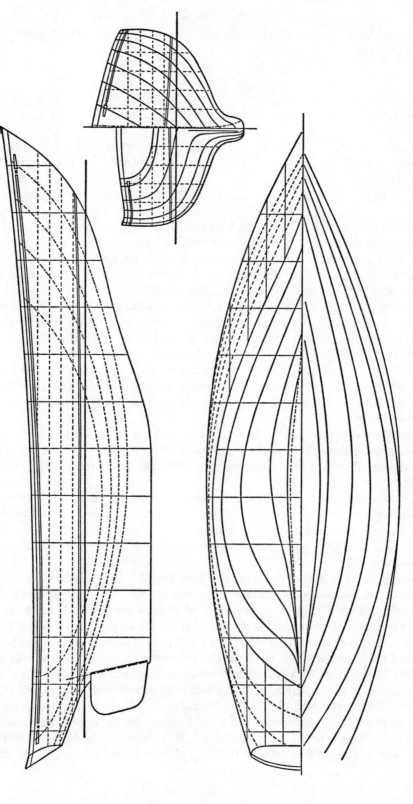

FIG. 27. *American centreboard cruising sloop by A. Mason, showing extreme pear form of underwater body. L.O.A. 34 ft. 2 in. L.W.L. 25 ft. 5 in. Beam 10 ft. 6 in. Draught (ex-centreboard) 3 ft. 9 in.*

be at about 0·45 L.W.L. This assumes, of course, that the placing of the sail plan over the hull is such that the yacht is balanced with the board raised. Actually, since the hull is rarely perfectly balanced, it is usually necessary to place the board farther aft than specified above, and it will be found that if the board is placed at between 0·5 and 0·6 L.W.L. balance with the board down will be satisfactory.

The problem of placing centreboards is nowadays solved sometimes by using boards in tandem, a main one near amidships, with an auxiliary aft. This, at the expense of mechanical complication, not only allows good balance to be established to windward, but gives a most valuable means of steadying the ship when sailing downwind, the auxiliary board aft being ideally placed for this purpose.

A similar principle has lately been used by Illingworth and Primrose to steady the steering downwind of short but deep-keel light displacement yachts, which are liable to run wild when reaching or running. Under these conditions a dagger board is lowered through the cockpit sole right aft.

TWIN KEELS Much of the history of small craft is concerned with the efforts of designers and builders to mitigate as effectively as possible the unfortunate hydrodynamic fact that boats tend to sail better to windward when they have keels far deeper than is convenient. For deep draught is in all other respects the curse of the mariner. Sometimes it is impossible for him to accept it at all if his boats are to serve their purpose. So during the centuries of sail, the coastal craft of Holland, the bloodstream of the country's economy, depended upon the leeboard. By means of these side keels which might be raised and lowered the working craft of Holland worked in the estuaries and coastal waters which lie so thinly over the continental shelf of that locality.

We may begin with the over-simplification that what we now call twin keels are in effect fixed leeboards. They are a means of attaining the same end without the mechanical complication of hoisting and lowering, and also with less liability to damage and with higher efficiency. Unlike the leeboard, the twin-keel arrangement is an upstart in small-boat design. The leeboard, like the dike and the windmill, was one of the basic elements in the Dutch way of life. Twin keels have no distinguished lineage, and the earliest record of them appears to be no more than eighty years old. Their development in their contemporary form began in the 1920s. The pioneer was Lord Riverdale, then the Hon. R. A. Balfour, who in 1923–4 produced the first twin-keel *Bluebird*, a small craft with an overall length of 25 ft. She was widely criticised at the time, but is still operating happily in Holland. In the early thirties he began designing a bigger *Bluebird*, which came out in 1939, 48 ft. overall, 39 ft. on the waterline, with twin keels and rudders. In her an important technical step was taken in that her keels were not parallel to the centreline. This yacht has now cruised more than 50,000 miles offshore.

A few years earlier Lord Riverdale's work in the first *Bluebird* had been extended by Robert Clark, then at the beginning of his professional career, who produced for C. E. Foster the 25 ft. overall twin-keel *Buttercup*. She drew 2·5 ft. of water when upright and the keels were parallel to the centreline. Here we may well note the practical advantages of twin-keel yachts:

1. Light draught—as a deep-keel yacht *Buttercup* might have had a draught of 5 ft., while the second *Bluebird of Thorne*, which on a waterline length of 39 ft. drew 4·75 ft. as a deep-keel yacht, might have had a draught of 7·5–8 ft.

2. The ability to take ground upright, whether it is hard or soft, and hence to be suitable for moorings where grounding occurs on every tide.
3. A twin-keel yacht draws more water heeled than when upright.

The second *Bluebird of Thorne*, with an upright draught of 4·75 ft. drew a maximum of 6·5 ft. when heeled. Thus, when a twin-keeler touches bottom and abruptly swings upright she automatically frees herself, and the helmsman has a chance of getting clear of the shoal water—the reverse of what occurs with the deep-keel yacht, which when losing way on touching digs herself more firmly then ever into the bottom.

It was these practical advantages which accounted for the surge of interest in twin-keel boats which has been a characteristic of yachting since the war. The scarcity and expense of deep-water moorings and the increasingly crowded state of the popular yachting centres gave a new importance to craft able to use the less-frequented estuaries. Hence there were some twenty-six classes of small twin-keel boats in the Boat Show a few years ago, and it is claimed that there are more than 3,000 of such craft afloat in our waters. It should be noted that they are all small craft, often of chine form for amateur construction; they are intended for economical yachting under conditions which at present make this more and more difficult.

It will be obvious that the new *Bluebird of Thorne* (Fig. 28) as also her immediate predecessor, though to a lesser degree, does not fall into the above category. There is nothing economical about her. She is a large yacht, coming into Class 1 R.O.R.C. in waterline length, and her owner has variously described her as "a high-performance cruising machine" and "a flat-out twin-keeled yacht"; and Arthur Robb has called her "a twin-keel cruising or ocean-racing yacht of relatively large size."

These descriptions outline the requirements with which Lord Riverdale approached Arthur Robb, providing the considerable amount of data that he already had collected on twin-keel craft. The design which produced this latest *Bluebird* is the collaborative work of an experienced yachtsman with a specialised interest in this type of yacht, and an architect of wide experience who retains a devotion to detail and technique which the successful yacht designer may lose in the process of filling the demands for his work.

The contemporary popularity of twin-keel yachts has been due to economic factors. Twin-keel design for the thousands has inevitably precluded scientific research into the potentialities of this type of sailing hull. It is a sad but obvious fact that biggish yachts and the money behind them can provide more technical data than small boats designed to satisfy the needs of the moment. It is possible (but not certain) that twin-keel yachts may prove able to sail as well as deep-keel boats with a draught 80 per cent greater, and also have all the practical advantages of light draught. *Twin keels may prove to be the most exciting breakthrough in sailing design that has occurred since the Bermudan rig.* It is even possible to believe that though twin keels began to be considered only as a practical alternative to the deep-draught vessel when it was essential to have shallow draught, it might occur that they are superior under any circumstances, regardless of limitations on draught.

If so the recognition of the fact may be due to the third *Bluebird of Thorne.*

The twin-keel question has occupied many people's attention apart from those wanting to provide economical cruisers. A series of tank tests made by Saunders Roe (Westland Aircraft) in the Isle of Wight, financed by Dr. A. Lamont of Philadelphia, produced data that have not been published. *Bluebird of Thorne*'s tests were made in the

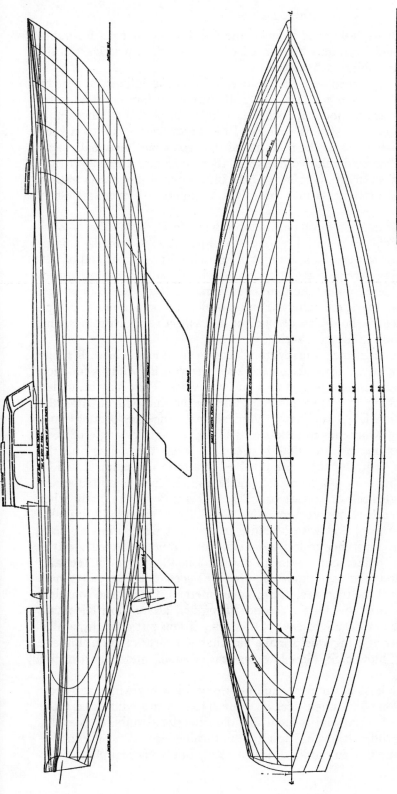

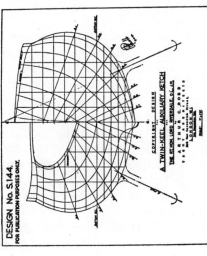

FIG. 28. Lines of twin-keel yacht Bluebird of Thorne by Arthur Robb. L.O.A. 50 ft. L.W.L. 40 ft. Beam 12 ft. Draught (upright) 5·33 ft. Displacement 16 tons

same tank, and again, and for equally good reasons, the full data are not yet for publication. But some tentative conclusions may be reached which may place twin keels in the van of further development in sailing-yacht design.

The tank tests were first concerned with the basic hull. Robb was influenced here by one of his own most successful offshore racers, the 32-ft. waterline *Uomie*, which is recognised by all who know her as the model of docile behaviour and perfect balance under all conditions. The special and critical tests concerned the appendages—the twin keels and twin skegs and rudders—for it is in the minutiae of the profile and sectional shapes of these members, their angling and relative positions, that good performance in such boats depends. It is through these hydrodynamic studies, impossible without tank testing, that the performance of twin-keel yachts may be raised to superiority over single-keel craft.

It will be evident that twin keels must unavoidably be of low aspect ratio. We associate aerofoil and hydrofoil efficiency with high aspect ratios; hence the dinghy's deep, narrow centreboard, the importance of deep draught in normal sailing yachts and of tall, narrow Bermudan rigs. During recent years attention has been centred on low aspect ratio aerofoils owing to flying developments, and much information has been accumulated that has been valuable in the maritime sphere. For example, the non-retractable type of roll-damping fins owe much to the design of efficient low aspect ratio hydrofoils, and these are precisely what is required for twin keels.

Twin keels allow certain refinements in hydrofoil design impracticable with single keels. They may be of asymmetrical form, since each keel performs its primary function on one tack only—the starboard fin on the port tack and vice versa. They may be angled to the centreline, thus establishing a yaw angle without turning the hull with it. Also, the lee keel when in full operation is approximately vertical and hence performing more efficiently than the single keel which has to produce its lift at the yacht's angle of heel. Then there are subtle interactions in water flow between the keels themselves and the keels and the skegs. Complex hydrodynamics are involved in all the above, but it will be evident that there is a possibility of raising twin keels and skegs to hydrodynamic superiority over the deep-draught single keel; or at least equality. If this is done, the many other practical advantages of twin keels represent pure gain. We shall have won light draught, facility for taking the ground level and with absolute security, as well as having keels with a superior fin action, i.e. resistance to leeway angle. But it must be noted that the latter effect is the outcome of refinements in design and that small changes in keel and skeg profile, section, angling and relative positions can produce big changes in performance.

Several other advantages of the twin-keel design have emerged. One is the considerable directionable stability of the type. Of the second *Bluebird of Thorne* Lord Riverdale wrote twenty years ago: "The critic might say: 'Of course, if you put enough parallel fins underneath, nothing short of a tug would make her change course rapidly.' But she did come about satisfactorily, blow high, blow low, big seas or small, under short or full canvas."

This directional stability is of particular value in strong following winds and seas, conditions when even fairly long-keel single-keel craft are liable to run wild—and those with narrow and deep fin keels very wild indeed. But the directional stability does not bring with it the equipoise of difficult turning and a large turning circle; and the rudder action is efficient partly because the lee rudder operates nearly in the vertical plane.

An adventitious advantage of twin keels appears to be a resistance to pitching which they create presumably due to flow effects over the weather side keel operating nearly horizontally and producing forces in a vertical plane. It is not possible here to deal with the flow patterns that may exist along the bottom as a result of the angle of the twin keels and their interaction, but clearly they produce pressure systems under the hull that must be markedly different from those of a single-keel vessel, and which may be directed beneficially. The damping of pitch and the reduction of the fierce plunging to which small craft are prone in many seaways are a substantial benefit to speed under such conditions, apart from comfort. A further contribution to sailing efficiency offered by twin keels is an augmentation of dynamic stability, for when heeled what is immersed of the weather keel produces lift directed downwards in the vertical plane—a righting moment acting on the yacht.

The performance of twin-keel boats under power should not be forgotten. It is a characteristic of the contemporary auxiliary sailing yacht, even of the purer offshore racing breed, to have high engine power installed. Where 1 b.h.p. per ton displacement was once considered enough and 2 verging on excessive, today 3 b.h.p. per ton is usual and more not uncommon. *Bluebird of Thorne* is in the general trend with 3·4 b.h.p. per ton of displacement. Such liberal mechanical power is something to be deployed effectively; yet this is handicapped by the nature of the single-keel sailing yacht whose hull is not well adapted to mechanical propulsion and whose propeller often has to work under paralysing circumstances. The twin-keel sailing yacht is a promising motor-boat. The propeller operates in water clear of any major hull disturbance and the hull itself is of a good form for propulsion by engine. Here, again, we come across an adventitious advantage of twin keels. They appear to have a beneficial action on the longitudinal wave system which is such a powerful influence on the build-up of resistance as speed is increased. The testing-tank predictions indicated that the yacht would have a speed of 9·3 knots when using 50 e.h.p. (say 100 b.h.p.). The speed was realised on trials, and for a displacement of 16 tons this would be creditable for a pure motor yacht. It is also worth noting that the fierce rolling which is the bugbear of the yacht under power alone will be sensibly reduced by the twin keels, which under these conditions become unusually efficient deep-bilge keels.

It is perhaps surprising that the *Bluebirds of Thorne* have been developed by an owner (he is Commodore of the Royal Cruising Club) whose primary dedication is to deep-water sailing. The advantages of shoal draught, of course, are always with the cruising yachtsman who, however much ocean he covers, comes back to the coast usually where the amenities of the yachting centre are not available and deep-water anchorages, slipping and such facilities are absent. We have been concerned above with twin-keel yachts in general, with particular reference to the work of Arthur Robb and Lord Riverdale on this latest of the *Bluebirds*.

Apart from the keels, she may be examined in the drawings simply as a highly developed cruising yacht in which pure sailing performance has been a fundamental consideration. The rig, with its wishbone main and semi-wishbone mizzen, is the owner's design, and based on the experience of the former *Bluebird*. The layout of the yacht is instructive and suggests that comfort may be achieved today in a 40-ft. waterline hull of very moderate displacement so long as the multitude of sails and hands required in offshore racing need not be accommodated.

THE VEE-BOTTOM HULL   The chine hull has a long history behind it, particularly in the U.S.A., where the ability of the type under sail was first demonstrated. It
has always had advantages for amateur construction, and with the development of marine
plywood it has gained a further value, being the shape of hull best suited to this form of
construction. The combination of chine hull and plywood planking is one of the most
promising developments in modern design, and in spite of the high price of plywood
provides a cheaper means of professional construction than the planked hull.

It is a platitude of general naval architecture that the vee-bottom hull, under power,
is inferior to the round form at speeds less than those at which a degree of planing is
present. Under sail the same is to be expected; but the paucity of systemised testing of
vee-bottom hulls under the full range of sailing conditions has made opinion of their
ability a matter of individual guesswork. It is likely that to windward the disadvantages
of their hull form may be mitigated to some extent by the beneficial effect of the chine
angle itself in producing a certain amount of lateral resistance.

The report of the Turkish Shipbuilding Research Institute by Professors G. Kemph
and A. Natku entitled *Model Tests with Sail Boat Pirate* provides some necessary data, which
confirms the opinions generally held of the chine hull amongst naval architects. The report
showed that the vee-bottom boat *Pirate* was inferior to the two round-bottom hulls considered at angles of heel up to 30 degrees, yaw angles of 0°–6°, and speeds up to $V/\sqrt{L} =$
1·2. Thus, at $V/\sqrt{L} = 0.95$ the respective resistance coefficients of the vee and one of the
round hulls (the America's Cup Defender *Ranger*) was 2·5 and 2·9, and at $V/\sqrt{L} = 1·1$,
2·3 and 2·6, the resistance coefficient being

$$\frac{\Delta^{\frac{2}{3}} \times V^2}{R}.*$$

* Δ = weight of displacement.

At $V/\sqrt{L} = 1·2$ the chine hull gained the superiority. Another comparison showed that
at $V/\sqrt{L} = 0·8$—a common sailing speed—the resistance coefficients of the chine boat
and another round hull (the 5-metre *Trial*) were 1·07 and 1·7, giving a resistance lower
by nearly one-third for the latter, and by a greater amount at lower speeds.

The comparisons in the report were derived from boats of widely different sizes
and types but reduced to a common size for the tests. The chine hull was the most favourable of her kind for low resistance, with very light displacement-length ratio—a half
that of the J-boat—whilst the round bilge boats were of relatively full form. The
chine boat also had a higher keel efficiency, which throws the onus for inferiority on the
type of hull. It is reasonable to assume that the fuller-bodied, seagoing chine hull would
have registered a higher resistance coefficient, and would not have been superior to the
round hulls even at appreciably higher than a $V/\sqrt{L}$ of 1·2. The latter feature showed
itself when the light displacement chine boat was assumed to be the same length as the
J-boat tested. It is significant that so favourable a vee-bottom form should have been
markedly inferior to the round hull up to this speed ratio when of the same length and
half the displacement-length coefficient.

For good performance in vee-bottom sailing craft moderate to light displacement
appears to be essential. The fore and aft camber of the chine should be as slight as possible,
and there appears to be a distinct advantage if the chine has no immersion amidships

at the datum waterline. In seagoing craft with accommodation it is necessary to have chine immersion amidships to gain the necessary displacement, but again, excessive fore and aft rocker is to be avoided. Only slight warping in the plane of the bottom aft of amidships is desirable, and excessive beam is to be avoided.

When a chine hull is designed with light displacement, fairly narrow beam, flat fore and aft run of chine line, and an efficient keel, the type has proved able to surmount its natural disadvantages and compete with the round form. But where internal space and heavier displacement are required, it is inevitably much inferior.

THE PLANING HULL The ability of a sailing yacht to plane depends on her having sufficiently light weight combined with big driving power, and on a shape of hull capable of developing hydrodynamic lift at high speeds. Much nonsense is talked by the technically unqualified about planing, and it was a desirable corrective to this when J. Laurent Giles said once: "No sailing boat can plane." This is too sweeping; but planing is not occurring most of the times when helmsmen claim that it is, and it has never been achieved in a ballasted sailing craft, since dead weight of keel precludes a high enough power-weight ratio being obtained.

A criterion by which the potentialities, so far as hull shape is concerned, for planing may be judged has been devised by a writer in *Sail*. It gives a criterion of hydrodynamic lift, which apart from power applied is chiefly a function of the displacement and the load waterplane area. A narrow yacht will not plane under conditions when a broader, flatter craft of equal weight and sail area will do so. The formula is:

$$\frac{\text{Displacement (lb.)}}{\text{L.W.L. plane (sq. ft.)} \times \text{(Length W.L.)}}$$

Values range between 4·0 for a 6-Metre and 0·82 for a Canoe, with the International 14-ft. and National 12-ft. classes lying between them at 1·22 and 1·47 respectively. We may expect some degree of planing up to about 1·5, provided there is enough power.

The planing hulls developed in England are characterised by short, deep-chested fore-bodies having the point of greatest depth at about one-third of the length from forward, and long runs with very flat buttocks. This shape of hull is not necessary for planing, and many craft capable of doing so are of a more symmetrical form. The deep-chested hull, if sailed upright, will produce less wave-resistance owing to the flat after-body, but such a shape of hull is not satisfactory when it cannot be held upright by the lever arm of the crew as movable ballast.

Planing may be defined as the condition existing when a proportion of the weight of the boat is carried by an upward pressure created by her motion on the flat or nearly flat areas of the bottom. The boat is no longer supported mainly by buoyancy (though there is always some residual buoyant support) but by a force generated through speed.

The object of planing does not lie, as so often is supposed, in the above reduction of displacement, for the process of derived dynamic lift entails producing drag which off-sets any gain in the lower wave-making resistance that results from the reduced displacement. It is the reduction of wetted surface that is sought; hence the value of spray strips and chines in racing dinghies.

No appreciable degree of planing occurs until the speed-length ratio exceeds about

2·5, which entails speeds of $8\frac{1}{4}$, $9\frac{1}{2}$ and 10 knots respectively for dinghies of 12, 14 and 16 ft. Reliable reports indicate that 14 ft. International class dinghies reach about 11 knots at a maximum speed, though as much as 14 knots has been claimed by experienced helmsmen. Even the lower speed would allow an appreciable degree of planing to exist.

The condition of planing is often mistakenly assumed to exist when a boat just passes beyond the phase of riding on a wave length exactly equal to her own length, when the speed-length ratio is 1·34 and owing to the big wave-making resistance the speed-power curve is beginning to rise almost vertically. This is the condition reached by the 6-Metre in Fig. 7 at a speed of $6\frac{1}{2}$ knots. So heavy a boat cannot be pushed beyond this speed; but the lighter, unballasted boat may. If there is enough power available in relation to weight, and the stern lines of the boat are suitable for minimising the height of the stern wave, she may be carried over the hump in the wave-making resistance curve, after which resistance increases at a much slower rate. The curve begins to flatten at speeds beyond about $V/\sqrt{L} = 1\cdot5$.

As a result of the smaller rate of increase in wave-resistance with speed, it follows that a small increment in wind speed or fractional better trimming of the sheets will produce a bigger increase in speed than hitherto. The boat will appear to surge forward, to be lifted, to skim. It may be shown that to increase the speed of a 10 ft. dinghy from 3·8 knots to 4·4 knots (the latter speed giving $V/\sqrt{L} = 1\cdot4$) the wind pressure must be increased from 0·2 lb./sq. ft. to 0·55 lb./sq. ft., or by 75 per cent. But once over the hump, to increase speed from 6·3 knots to 6·9 knots the wind pressure need be raised only from 1 lb./sq. ft. to 1·05 lb./sq. ft., a matter of 5 per cent. Yet this still has nothing to do with planing. The boat is simply behaving like a fast displacement craft.

The conventional ballasted seagoing yacht is unable to harness power beyond that provided by about 100 sq. ft. of canvas per ton. For speeds in the region of $V/\sqrt{L} = 2\cdot0$ some 400 sq. ft. per ton may be required, which can be carried when weight is reduced by eliminating ballast and the loss of stability entailed is offset by the movable ballast of the crew in dinghies, or by the use of twin hulls or outriggers.

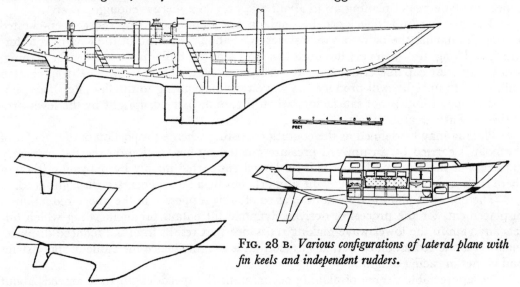

Fig. 28 b. *Various configurations of lateral plane with fin keels and independent rudders.*

15. A narrow counter but buoyant stern by Robert Clark.

16. *Drumbeat*, 40 ft. waterline, designed by Ray Hunt, an example of the American type of beamy, shoal-draught centre-board yacht with no salient keel.

17. (*Below*) *Drumbeat* racing (Beken and Son).

CHAPTER SIX

The Keel

THE keel has four purposes: (i) It produces most of the hydrofoil action needed to resist the lateral component of the wind force (this is a statement that needs modification in the case of full-bodied boats with little salient keel); (ii) It influences the steering and handling qualities; (iii) It provides accommodation and lever for the ballast; (iv) It supports the boat when on the ground.

THE ELEMENTS OF KEEL ACTION When sailing with the wind anywhere forward of dead astern there is a component of the wind strength (labelled lateral air force in Fig. 5) acting at right angles to the boat and tending to produce broadside drift. It is the function of the keel to resist this. The side or drift force is strongest under close-hauled conditions, when it may be about three times the driving force; that is, the component of the wind force propelling the ship is less than one-third of that trying to drive her broadside. With the true wind on the beam, the two components are approximately equal. With the true wind 135 degrees off the bow the driving force is some four times that of the drift force, and with the wind astern the drift force disappears. The above relationships are shown in Table 9, in which ratios of the drive and drift forces are shown for four points of sailing.

TABLE 9

Angle of True Wind from Bow (degrees)	45	90	135	180
Driving Force	28	62	58	40
Drift Force	80	66	15	0

Note.—The above figures were calculated for a wind speed of 15 knots and a boat's speed of 5 knots.

The function of the keel is to resist the drift force, in which it is helped to a greater or lesser extent by the body of the hull. The boat assumes (Fig. 5) an angle of yaw or leeway (the former term is preferable owing to the more general use of the word leeway to mean drift to leeward) and the keel becomes a hydrofoil producing lift appropriate to its angle of incidence, at the price of unavoidable additional resistance. The latter comes, firstly, from the angle of obliquity at which the keel is forced through the water; secondly, from the increased wave-making resistance of the hull itself under these conditions (see induced drag, page 44).

The efficiency of a keel lies partially in its ability to produce the necessary lift or resistance to broadside drift, at a reasonably small angle of yaw. The chief factors governing this are firstly the aspect ratio of the keel, which is mainly governed by draught, and, secondly, the fore and aft sectional shape of the keel. The area of the keel also plays its part. A deep, narrow keel, found at its most extreme in the centreboard of a racing dinghy, produces the necessary lift at a high value per unit of area, but the area being small the angle of yaw has to be large. Since the lift-drag ratio of a given keel may not vary much over a big range of yaw angles, this big angle would be immaterial but for the hull above the keel. When the hull is that of a normal displacement yacht, and particularly if this is a relatively beamy centreboarder, the big increase in the wave-making resistance of the hull as the yaw angle increases becomes serious.

We must consider for a moment how the aspect ratio of a keel should be defined. Efforts have been made to link the lift and drag forces measured from tests with model keels of various aspect ratios with the aerodynamic data derived from the much more numerous measurements made on aeroplane wings. The conclusion reached is that the aspect ratio of a keel may most reasonably be expressed as

$$\frac{1 \cdot 7 \times (\text{draught})^2}{(\text{Lateral Area Below W.L.})}$$

The constant $1 \cdot 7$ is empirical. The fact that the salient keel has the hull above it, reduces the interference between the low and high pressure sides of the keel, but its degree of efficacy in this respect is uncertain and also varies with the speed. It has in addition to be appreciated that the underwater lateral area is a vague criterion since part of this area, as projected on paper, is composed of the more or less flat keel and part of the more or less rounded hull, and the proportions of the one to the other varies widely with different types of boat. Where an extremely heavy displacement boat is concerned, there may be little salient keel. In the lightest types of hull, however, the majority of the underwater lateral area may lie in the fin.

The precise form in which aspect ratio should be expressed is more important to research workers than designers; but it will be obvious that if satisfactory correlation between keel and aircraft wing data can be established a mass of valuable information from the aerodynamic sphere will become applicable to yacht design.

Were the resistance and performance of a sailing yacht dependent solely on the keel, the problem of sail would be more readily systemised and calculable from first principles, but the complex interaction of hull and keel prohibits this. As H. M. Barkla, M.A., B.SC., has aptly said: "In its barest essentials a yacht consists of an aerofoil producing the required forward thrust, but also an unwanted lateral thrust; the keel takes up this lateral thrust at the cost of extra drag; a floatation device supports the whole at the cost of considerable resistance, and provides stability to meet the capsizing moment of the rig . . ."

Keel action is simply illustrated in Figs. 29 and 30. When running before the wind there is no lateral component of the wind force, and no yaw angle (Fig. 29(*a*)). When sailing to windward (*b*) an angle of yaw established itself which is sufficient to produce a lateral water force equal to the lateral wind force, whilst the yacht meanwhile sails along the pecked line XP.

This action is shown in Fig. 30(*a*). If a flat plate, or a streamlined body, is held in a stream of water flowing in the direction S—that is at a small angle to the fore and aft line of the body—a force approximately at right angles to the body will be developed,

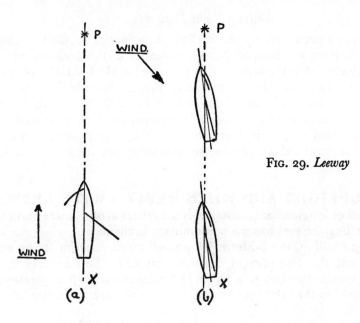

FIG. 29. *Leeway*

and it will tend to move in the direction F. If the body itself is moved obliquely through still water a similar effect is produced, and there will be a force tending to move the body about at right angles to its line of motion. We may call this force "Lift." But the price

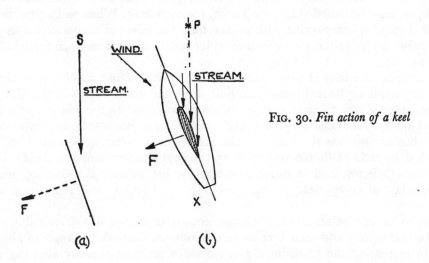

FIG. 30. *Fin action of a keel*

for obtaining lift is a measure of head-resistance, or drag, and the efficiency of a fin is the amount by which the lift exceeds the drag. The lift-drag ratio is the fraction:

$$\frac{\text{Lift}}{\text{Drag.}}$$

The resultant force produced by the keel is proportional to CAV^2, where C is a coefficient that depends on the hydrodynamic properties of the keel—chiefly its aspect ratio and sectional shape—A is the area, and V the speed of the boat. C and A are within the designer's control. The variations in speed mean that no fixed keel can be ideal under all conditions. In certain circumstances the area is excessive for the lateral force needed; then sails such as the Genoa, which produce a big lateral force, may be used effectively; but boats whose keel action is inefficient have to lower these early owing to their inability to produce the necessary lateral water force to counteract the air force at a sufficiently moderate yaw angle.

RESISTANCE UPRIGHT AND WHEN HEELED WITH LEEWAY The simple straight-ahead or longitudinal resistance is the criterion of a power hull's efficiency. But for windward sailing the keel has the predominant influence.

During a season's sailing, the 6-Metre *Jill* proved much superior to the newer boat *Jack* except when running. The upright resistance curve of the slower boat, however, showed lower values than the faster, a fact which accounted for her greater speed off the wind, but showed too that the upright resistance is no sure indication of windward ability.

Neither, however, is the longitudinal heeled resistance, which though greater than the upright does not account for the complex action of the keel when the yacht is both heeled *and* making leeway. Fig 31 shows the resistance of a 6-Metre at various angles of heel, and with allowance made for the lateral force causing the heel. It thus differs from the longitudinal heeled resistance, and exceeds it considerably. The additional resistance caused by leeway, which when sailing to windward is about three times that caused by heeling alone, may be called (Chapter Three) induced drag. When sailing to windward, the hull of a yacht is comparable with an aerofoil. The effect of an aerofoil is to produce fin action, and the fin action we have to consider is that of the keel when forced obliquely through the water.

The comparative tests of two other 6-Metres, *Westward* and *Ripples*, show the action of leeway is producing lateral resistance. Both were successful yachts in the U.S.A., and the former visited English waters in 1934. *Westward* was good on the wind; *Ripples* excelled before it. Tank tests revealed that the upright resistance of *Westward* was greater than that of *Ripples*, but so also was the heeled resistance when no account was made of leeway. But the lift-drag ratio of *Ripples* was some 25 per cent smaller than *Westward*'s. Her keel was of lower efficiency, and in order to create the lift, or lateral resistance, needed to balance the lateral component of the wind force, she had to sail at a bigger angle of yaw.

It has to be appreciated that a bigger leeway angle is not objectionable in itself, but is so in that it may add considerably to the induced drag. A big angle of obliquity is effective in increasing the lift from a given area of fin, and thereby allowing a fin of smaller area to be used. In a hull such as a racing dinghy's this is of advantage. When a hull of greater bulk is attached to the fin, however, the added resistance due to the oblique motion of the hull itself may counteract the greater lift-drag ratio of the keel. On the other hand, greater speed to windward may sometimes result from allowing a slightly greater leeway angle—by narrowing the keel, for example, keeping draught constant, and reducing the wetted surface.

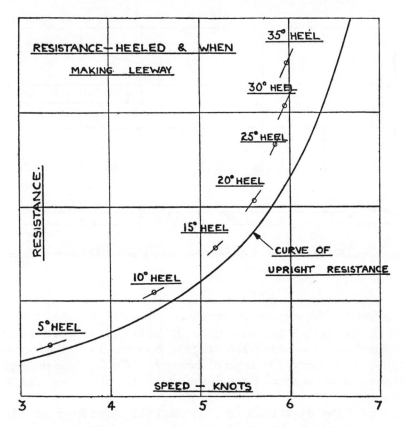

FIG. 31. *The effect of heel and leeway angle on resistance*

THE LATERAL PROFILE OF THE KEEL Efficiency to windward is the result of a high lift-drag ratio in the hull-keel combination, and this is mainly a matter of designing a salient keel. The more nearly a keel approaches a true fin which is an appendage to the canoe body, the greater its effectiveness will be. In the full-bodied cruiser, the fin action has to be developed chiefly by the hull, which is a poor shape for this purpose. This is one more argument for the light displacement hull which, apart from the low resistance of the hull itself, allows big depth of keel on a moderate draught.

A deep, short keel gives a high aspect ratio. The beneficial effect of aspect ratio is shown in Fig. 32. The curve applies to rectangular plates, the aspect ratio being the height divided by the breadth. It will be seen that the lift-drag ratio increases rapidly in the range of aspect ratios between a half and three. It continues to increase beyond this, but more slowly; the increase between three and ten is only slightly more than that between one and three. Draught, within limits, is therefore the most important element in windward ability.

Usually the draught is limited by rule or other practical considerations. Fig. 26 shows the maximum draughts allowed without penalty under the R.O.R.C. rule, and also a shoal-draught line indicating generally minimum practicable draughts unless a

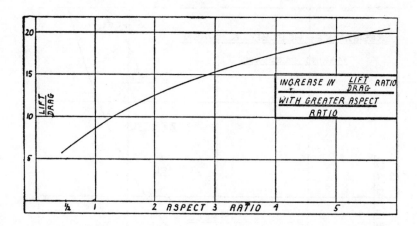

FIG. 32. *Increase in lift/drag ratio with greater aspect ratio*

centreboard is fitted. Having given the maximum allowable draught, it is the length of the keel which is most easily made the variable. If the draught is kept constant, length of keel may be varied within a considerable range without much affecting the value of the lift. But length of keel reduces the angle of leeway or obliquity. The price paid is more frictional resistance and the speed through the water (V_s) will be reduced, though V_{mg} may be improved.

Keels are fins of low aspect ratio. In this respect they differ from the sails, which are fins operating in air, and have an aspect ratio of 6 or more in modern sail plans. Typical keel profiles, with their aspect ratios, are shown in Fig. 33 and from the values of the ratios an idea may be gained of the relative efficiencies of the keels considered purely as hydrofoils.*

The semi-elliptical keel profile exemplified in (d) and (e) may be slightly more efficient, for a given aspect ratio and section, than the trapezoidal profiles of (b), (c) and (f). It was the greater efficiency of this profile which accounted for the elliptical wings of the Spitfires, and keels of this shape are comparable ellipses but of much smaller aspect ratio. But the greater efficiency of this shape over the trapezoidal keel, tapering at the bottom to about half its width at the top, is very slight, and the advantages in the other respects might seem to give the favourable balance to the keel profile bounded by more or less straight lines.

A characteristic of most sailing yachts from Olin Stephens' office, however, is the complete elimination of the toe in keel profiles, and the adoption of the triangular form of (b), which this architect is assured from numerous tank tests gives the best results.†

Fig. 33(d) is the keel with the highest ratio shown. The next highest, that of (c), could be made greater by simply reducing the length of the keel. This would upset the ballast distribution and lower the stability, but neglecting this consideration what would

* Aspect ratios illustrated in Fig. 32 have been worked from the keel areas only, as shown shaded, omitting the body of the hull, and calculated by $\dfrac{(Depth\ of\ keel)^2}{Area\ of\ keel}$. They therefore differ from aspect ratios obtained as explained above.

† Within the last year or so Olin Stephens has been adopting the trapezoidal form with toe.

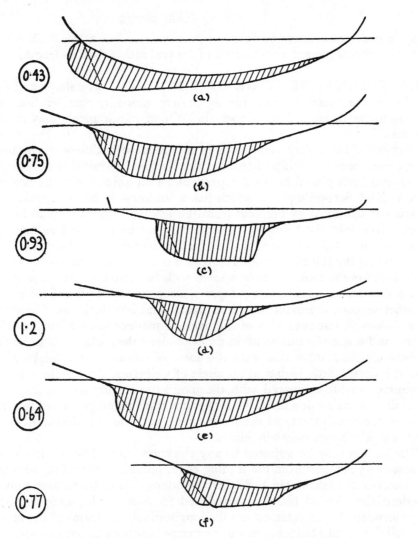

FIG. 33. *Lateral profiles and aspect ratios*

be the effect on fin efficiency? The amount of lateral resistance would be little affected by the reduction, but the leeway angle needed to produce any required amount of lateral resistance would be increased. The angle of yaw at which the hull and keel would be forced through the water would be greater, and hence the resistance created by the hull itself increased whilst the frictional drag of the shorter keel would be less.

In the case of a light displacement hull, such as (*d*), the latter gain may more than offset the greater resistance of the hull. But if the hull is of heavy displacement, the drag it causes at the greater angles of yaw will make the longer keel profitable. Length of keel may therefore be related to the displacement. A heavy hull is best suited with a longer keel which will keep down the yaw angle; a light hull may be allowed to sail with greater leeway in order to reduce the keel's wetted surface. But at all times when practicable it is more profitable to add to the depth of the keel rather than its length.

LONGITUDINAL SECTION OF THE KEEL　The shape and thickness of the keel's longitudinal section should ideally be determined by considerations of high lift and low drag under its conditions of operation. Other requirements may modify the choice somewhat.

Numerous laboratory tests have been made with different symmetrical aerofoil sections, and recent tank experiments at the National Physical Laboratory, Teddington, with various keels placed beneath a particular hull have shown the beneficial effects of the N.A.C.A.* Section 63–006, which has a thickness to breadth ratio of 0·06 and the maximum thickness at 35 per cent from the leading edge. It should be noted that the rudder, faired into the sternpost of a yacht, may be regarded as part of the aerofoil section, and included in its breadth (i.e. the length of the keel plus rudder and any depth) in determining the thickness ratio. The results obtained with this N.A.C.A. section under a yacht's hull in the tank are in agreement with the aerofoil data—a point of significance —which shows at angles of up to 7 degrees, a superiority of lift and lower drag compared with other sections of similar form but greater and less thickness. The thickness ratio of 0·06 is, however, less than that of the average modern yacht's keel, which may be 0·08 or more, and is usefully this width in order to allow the ballast keel to be disposed lower. Aerodynamic data show that with this form of section and a thickness ratio of 0·012 the drag is only a little higher at an angle of 5 degrees, though there is a more distinct disadvantage in lift compared with the 0·06 ratio section at this angle. The lift-drag ratio of the thicker section has to be set against the advantage gained in stability through the lower centre of gravity of the ballast keel, and this is a decision that probably the testing tank alone can rationally make.

The section may be adjusted to any thickness ratio. The form, with its maximum thickness at 35 per cent from the leading edge, provides less volume forward than many of the excessively blunt-nosed keels that are adopted in order to surmount the difficulty, in modern short-keeled boats with reduced forefoot, of disposing the ballast keel far enough forward. In the rated classes the longitudinal keel forms of the latest boats show great variation, with a tendency towards extreme bluntness in certain cases, and in others a relatively pointed form. The present trend, in class boats and ocean-racers, is for a maximum thickness in the region of 30–35 per cent from forward and an easing of the curve at the leading edge, and this is in accordance with aerodynamic data. Hydrodynamic requirements alone might indicate a further reduction in the fullness of the keel forward, but it is doubtful if this would be noticably profitable.

The laminar flow keel has been sought in recent years, without any evidence of success, which is not surprising. It requires a sharp entrance to the keel with the maximum thickness well aft, and much has been tried in several yachts, of which the *Myth of Malham* was the forerunner. A sufficient degree of laminar flow to be effective seems unlikely to be achieved in practice.

Problems involved in the hull-keel relationship are amongst the most subtle that face a designer, and the least tractable to handle at the drawing-table. Does it pay to thicken the keel section, thereby placing more of the displacement in the keel, and hence allowing

* American National Advisory Committee for Aeronautics.

a shallower body and flatter buttocks—also more stability—or is it better to have a more slender keel and a fuller hull? This is a problem presented in all rated classes and in unclassed yachts also. And again it is answerable only by tank-testing. The data which might be derived from a methodical series of tank tests, similar to those done on the resistance of power vessels, would be of value; but in this matter of the reciprocal influence of hull and keel, the ideal combination would apply only to one type of boat, and probably to one wind strength only. Individual testing would seem to be the only sure method.

Tiny differences in performance affect racing results, and the minutiae of design can be tested only by racing or a testing tank. The ability of one boat to lie half a point closer to the wind than another means a tenth of a mile gained to windward for every mile sailed. And this half point may be the result of some small feature of keel design, the effect of which cannot be assessed from purely theoretical reasoning or careful drawing-table work.

THE RUDDER Under sail, the rudder must be considered not only as the means of altering or holding course, but also as an agency for increasing the fin action of the hull and keel. For this purpose, between 2 and 3 degrees of weather helm produce the best results, the effect of it being to increase the amount of lift derived from a given leeway angle. The Dutch 5-Metre *Trial*, which was tested in the Wageningen tank, Holland, had a deeply immersed rectangular rudder designed with a section which, with the rudder at 3 degrees, formed a fair continuation of the keel's curvature on the windward side. The value of this small amount of weather helm, which was learned at the Hoboken tank in the U.S.A. and subsequently confirmed at Wageningen, will be evident from the earlier consideration of keel lift and drag. With weather helm the lift of the rudder is in the same direction as that of the keel and augments it; with lee helm it opposes the keel's lift. It increases the resistance rapidly. The advantage of weather helm is lost, however, at relatively small rudder angles. Four degrees of weather helm entail a higher resistance than a central rudder; but only 2 degrees of lee helm are more harmful than 6 degrees of weather helm.

The size of the rudder is most logically connected with the lateral area, which is the chief element in directional stability. Fig. 34 gives values of the ratio:

$$\frac{\text{Area of lateral plane}}{\text{Rudder area}}$$

As with other representatives of the fin family, high aspect ratio is desirable in rudders, but choice in this matter will be fettered by the draught and the protection of the keel when aground. The aspect ratio of rudders

$$\frac{\text{Depth}^2}{\text{Area}}$$

will be found to range between about 2 and 3·8 for efficient shapes. Shoal-draught boats may be forced to have rudders of aspect ratio unity or less. Apart from the lowering of the lift-drag entailed, the breadth needed in shallow rudders to obtain the necessary area throws the centre of pressure of the rudder farther abaft the rudder post and increases, for a given turning force, the moment, and hence the weight in the helm.

In craft large and small a rudder hung independently of the main fin on a skeg is

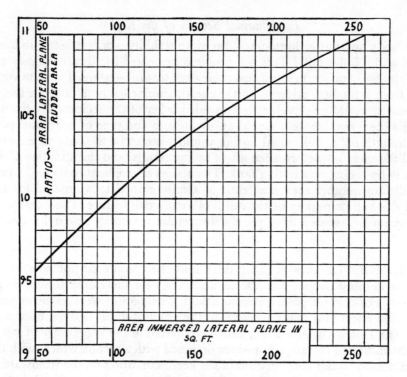

FIG. 34. *Rudder area*

now common. This is an evolution from the earlier spade rudder, hung with no skeg ahead of it—a type that is still often adopted. The advantage of the skeg is its ability to increase the lift coefficient of a given area and shape of rudder and to raise the angle at which stalling occurs. The stalling of the rudder may account for many of the cases when fin boats with spade rudders have become uncontrollable; and it is to be noted that the stall tends to come at a lower angle with the higher aspect ratio rudders. Spade rudders are saved from their own defects to some extent by their usually low aspect ratio, adopted to reduce the bending moment in the rudder post. With independently hung rudders the skeg, which increases the strength of the rudder hangings, protects the rudder to some degree, and increases its hydrodynamic efficiency, is an obvious correlative.

Experiments have shown that for a given total area of rudder and skeg, up to 25 per cent of the area may be disposed in a fixed skeg ahead of the rudder without materially lessening the lift coefficient of the rudder-skeg combination. That is, a rudder of only 75 per cent of the area of a spade rudder, and with a correspondingly smaller moment arm of its centre of pressure, need be turned by the helm.

Rudder action is affected by the rake of the sternpost. The latter may be raked up to 45 degrees in the interests of reducing wetted surface; but when helm is applied at a big angle of heel the turning force is then appreciably less, the rake reducing the component of the rudder force doing useful work. Heavy weather helm may then result. A rake of 30 degrees, allowing a smaller rudder area and rudder angle, appears to offset the slightly greater wetted surface, and ensures more certain control.

STEERING, STEADINESS AND HEAVING-TO Directional stability, or steadiness on course, is partly the result of a keel having a high resistance to turning, in view of which in the past long keels have been favoured as a seaworthy feature. The accepted view of a quarter a century ago was that of Commander E. G. Martin in *Deep Water Cruising*: "All practical yachtsmen know the special advantages gained by designing a yacht with a straight keel and a good grip of water at the bow are steadiness upon the helm under all conditions, and reliability when hove-to." Again, "In one other respect I think the long-keeled ship with a good forefoot has an immense advantage over the other. When a vessel is hove-to in a really heavy sea she will heave her bow a long way out of the water as she breasts each wave . . . The bow of the yacht which throws her whole forebody clear of the water as she scends is blown off."

The steadiness conferred by length of keel may equally be regarded as insensitive steering. It produces slow turning and considerable lethargy in stays. Fortunately the erratic behaviour common in the older types of boat when given short keels was due partly to their rigs, whose centres of effort were too far forward when placed over a hull with reduced forefoot. The correction of the balance between main and head canvas allows the sensitive steering provided by a fairly short keel to be combined with the steadiness once considered to be inseparable from a deep forefoot.

In modern yacht design the concern is chiefly with short and very short keels, and with fin keels with independent skegs. The excessive length of keel and depth of forefoot once regarded as an essential of seaworthiness may be treated as a confusion of cause and effect in the analysis of seaworthiness.

Unfortunately, the precise effect of keel length on steadiness, and the amount of sacrifice in steadiness—or directional stability—that results from very short keels cannot be readily assessed. The relatively long keel provides a boat that is easier to steer, and needing a less sensitive touch when on the wind; but the resistance to turning entails greater effort being applied at the helm when yawing in a beam or quartering sea. In spite of the greater resistance to yawing offered by the longer keel, this alone does not always compensate for the greater effort in the helm of overcoming the inertia of the long keel once yawing has started, and broaching-to is more likely to occur in a long than a moderately short keel boat. It has to be confessed that data is lacking, however, on much in connection with directional stability. Fig. 35 shows a variety of modern keel profiles.

The early departures from the long keel in seagoing craft took the form of the triangular profile of Fig. 35(*a*). The elimination of the toe of the keel was considered to have merit on the basis of a theory, having no hydrodynamic justification that can be discovered, that a boat in following and quartering seas tended to pivot and turn on the toe. Most modern keels of moderate length have reverted to the trapezoidal form of lateral area (Fig. 35(*b*) and (*d*)) common in the older boats, but of increased depth and aspect ratio.

It should be possible, in theory, to obtain the steadiness of a relatively long keel by means of a short, salient, fin-keel, and an independent skeg well aft carrying the rudder. A number of modern yachts of light and moderately heavy displacement, and of sizes up to 30 ft. on the waterline, have been given this configuration of keel. The lighter boats of this type have proved to be wild in steering in heavy quartering seas; but how much of this is to be attributed to keel form, how much to speed and light displacement, is uncertain. Theoretically, it seems likely that the independently hung skeg and rudder is not

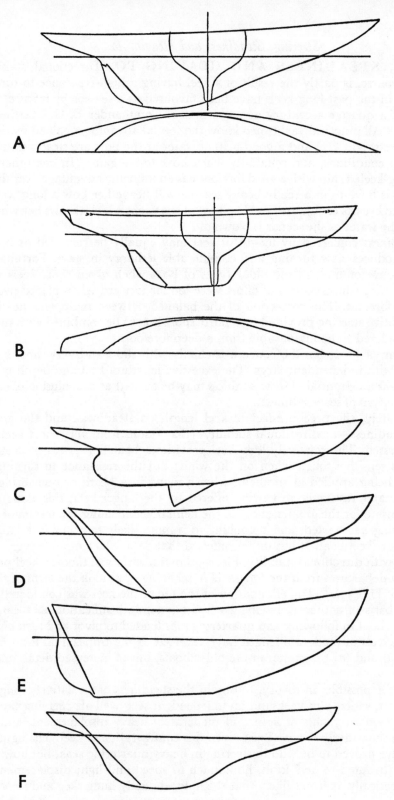

FIG. 35. *Various configurations of lateral plane*

to blame, and that this may be as steady, with the right balance between keel and sail centres, as any other, and with several collateral advantages.

The modern, short-keeled and well balanced yacht may be hove-to under mainsail and headsail in a moderate sea-way, lying five to six points off the wind. When hove-to under sail the keel is in the stalled condition, owing to the very large leeway angle; and then the effectiveness of the keel depends on area rather than aspect ratio. The leeward drift with a long keel is likely to be less, and the ability of a boat to look after herself, without falling off and gathering speed when alone with the helm locked, is improved. Under these conditions, and these alone it seems, length of keel is justifiable.

The issue is complicated today by the modern technique of handling that has been evolved through ocean-racing, in which a boat continues sailing in winds up to Force 8, beyond which it has been found best to heave-to under bare poles. For one thing, in these stronger winds canvas is unlikely to stand; for another, the leeward drift under these conditions does not appear to be considerable. Much of the lore of heaving-to was evolved in days when yachtsmen hove-to at Force 6 or 7, and streamed a sea anchor in Force 8.

The general conclusion from the point of view of design that may be reached today is that yachts which are not to be sailed through moderate gale conditions, and in which heaving-to is likely to be a common manoeuvre, should not have an extremely short keel or a fin keel with independently hung skeg and rudder. But nothing indicates the necessity for the very long keel that was once considered essential in deep-water craft.

A lateral plane composed of a narrow fin keel providing most of the lateral area and carrying the ballast, associated with a rudder placed well aft and hung on its own, or having an area of skeg ahead of it, has now become most familiar. Four examples are illustrated, in Fig. 28 B.

The fin and independent rudder, confined until recent years to small and light displacement yachts, has been found to be effective in larger craft and ones with a high displacement-length ratio. The steering qualities of this type of keel configuration often prove to be as good as those of full keel boats, one reason for which may be the greater efficiency of the rudder.

That there is still enough area in these cut-away profiles to generate the necessary water side force may be attributed to (i) the efficiency of modern sail plans, which give a smaller lateral component of air force, this being partly due to the use of terylene; (ii) the high lift-drag ratio of the small keel area, resulting from its high aspect ratio and effective longitudinal sections.

Assisting (ii) may be a flap or tab forming the trailing area of the fin-keel. Setting this at an angle of weather helm increases the lift-drag ratio of the fin while simultaneously lowering the drag of the main rudder. Sometimes there is a linkage between the main rudder and the trimming tab of the fin; more usually the tab angle is applied independently, allowing a more versatile system of fine adjustment.

In Fig. 28 B (b) it will be seen that there is a tiny skeg ahead of, but separate from, the rudder. This may help to smooth the flow of water over the rudder and to add a very little lateral area in an effective position, well aft. The advantages of a full depth skeg ahead of the rudder, as in the Alan Gurney design (Fig. 28 B (a) and also in (d)) have been discussed (page 90).

Something approaching a break-through in keel design has been occurring in the last few years, and now some form of the fin and independent rudder configuration appears to have proved the inevitable answer to yachts built under existing rating rules (including the forthcoming rule of the Royal Ocean Racing Club) none of which include wetted surface area as a factor in measurement. Even in craft unaffected by measurement rules, the fin and skeg has shown itself to be suitable, as in *Sir Thomas Lipton* designed by Robert Clark, winner of the Singlehanded Transatlantic race in 1968. This yacht proved remarkably steady on the helm despite the shortness of the fin keel.

Little can be said to assist the designer in determining the position of the fin keel under the canoe body. The range of choice is restricted by the necessary position of the ballast keel's C.G., which in turn is affected by the sectional and profile shapes of the fin. Except in so far as it influences the position of the C.G., the profile shape of the fin does not appear to be of critical importance, and there appears to be little to choose between the curved leading edge (Fig. 35 C (c)) or the profile more closely resembling a trapezoid or parallelogram; though the latter forms are better for the disposal of the ballast. The angle of the leading edge should not be steeper than about 45 degrees.

CHAPTER SEVEN

Stability and Ballast

WHEN a yacht is upright, the resultant forces of buoyancy and gravity act at the middle line of the ship, and through their respective centres (Fig. 36A). But on heeling slightly, the forces swing out of line transversely, and form a couple which tries to right the yacht (Fig. 36B). Owing to the altered shape of the hull under water, the C.B. swings to leeward, whilst the C.G., being fixed by the construction and ballast weights, remains where it was on the centreline, and swings with it. The horizontal distance between the two forces is the arm of the righting couple, or the righting lever; this is conventionally known as GZ but is marked as X in Figs. 37 and 42. If, owing to the shape of the hull or a high C.G., an angle of heel is reached when the C.B. lies to windward of the C.G., then the couple has a capsizing moment. In modern, ballasted yachts there is usually plenty of positive stability left at 90 degrees of heel, while the capsizing angle may be 130 degrees or more, this giving the ability to recover rapidly from a knock-down blow. Even shoal-draught boats, with a draught of less than one-ninth of their waterline length, can have plenty of stability at 90 degrees if correctly shaped and ballasted. But a long range of stability does not necessarily produce stiffness within the range of useful sailing angles, and it is this quality which is particularly desirable in small and medium-sized yachts. Large craft are a slightly different problem.

The righting lever changes in length with the angle of heel, at first being small, then increasing to a maximum at from 40 to 80 degrees, depending on the shape and ballasting of the hull, and finally getting smaller again until it becomes an upsetting lever. If the length of the righting lever, GZ, in feet, is multiplied by the displacement, in tons, the product is the righting moment in tons/feet, and this is the true measure of stability. It can be equated with the heeling moment produced by the sail plan in any given strength of wind.

It will be seen that a yacht of light displacement may have righting levers at certain angles of heel which are greater than those of a heavy displacement craft, but the righting moment, or power to carry sail, will be smaller owing to the lesser displacement. Heavy displacement gives the ability to carry sail, but at the price of a hull which needs more sail to drive it—a vicious circle—and the quality to be sought is stability combined with as little additional resistance as possible.

If the lengths of the righting levers are plotted in graph form against the respective angles of heel, the result is a curve of righting levers, and stability moments may be plotted in the same way. But the production of such curves is a long job, and their value for yacht work is slight. Except in cases of very large yachts or ones of exceptional form, stability calculations are rarely made, experience and comparison with similar yachts being the usual guide. To produce the curves, the transverse position of the heeled C.B. has to be found for a number of different angles of heel, which is laborious work, whilst the vertical

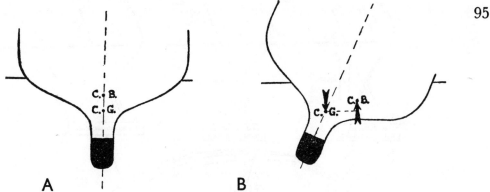

FIG. 36. *The righting couple*

position of the C.G. must also be known. It is a point of interest that though stability calculations are made on the assumption of a waveless waterline, tank tests have indicated that the results achieved are not as far from the truth as might be imagined. A long-ended craft sailing at high speed has the support of wave crests to leeward, under the bow and counter, which add to her stability; but there is also the deep hollow amidships on the leeward side, and it appears that the flat waterline used for calculations functions as a satisfactory mean for the highly irregular one existing in practice. Uffa Fox has recorded that the calculations made by John Samuel White's when they were building *Wishbone* agreed well with her behaviour in practice, when wind strengths were measured with an anemometer.

It has also to be appreciated that, for stability purposes, the effective angle of heel is the angle of the prevailing wave slope and not to the natural vertical. If, in a beam sea with 30 degrees of heel, a wave of 30 degrees slope passes under the hull the momentary angle of heel will be 60 degrees. Furthermore, the wave formation may produce for a brief period a reduction in the yacht's displacement, and hence in her righting moment, as she rolls or pitches. Thus, after an offshore gale, when the wind has dropped appreciably but has left behind a considerable sea still running, a yacht is unable to carry the amount of canvas that the wind strength might seem to justify.

Once the sail area has been decided, the angle of heel which will be produced in any chosen wind strength may be approximately calculated; or, alternatively, the sail area which will allow the required degree of stiffness may be found. But it is a calculation which is rarely made, though a striking case of its use occurred when the America's Cup defender *Enterprise* was designed. Her stability was calculated and adjusted so that she might sail at her most suitable angle of heel in the wind strengths which meteorological records showed to be expected during September over the Cup course off Rhode Island. The relationship between stability and resistance is a problem of yacht design which is not fully understood, though tank tests may in time elucidate it. Since resistance increases with stability, whilst the power to carry sail does so also, but probably not at the same rate, there must be some ideal combination of sail area and stability to suit a given set of conditions. It was this that the *Enterprise*'s designer sought to find, and the work has

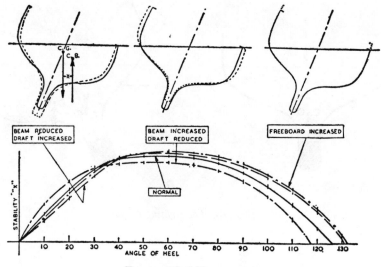

FIG. 37. *Stability curves*

been carried forward in recent America's Cup research with 12-Metres. It is a problem of interest mainly in the racing classes, for in cruisers and ocean-racers the amount of sail area has to be governed by more practical considerations.

Usually, however, it is for comparative purposes that stability curves are of most use, for they are able to show the influence of beam, draught, displacement, freeboard and ballast ratio on stability. It is more important to appreciate the general effect of these features than to calculate the numerical values for a single design. This is the use to which we shall now put stability curves.

THE POWER TO CARRY SAIL Stability depends, firstly, on a low C.G., which is the result of great weight or low placing of the ballast keel; and, secondly, on a shape of hull which allows the C.B. to swing well off to leeward on heeling, this being encouraged by big beam and high freeboard. Since the total stability is the product of the righting arm and the displacement, in comparing the relative stabilities of different shapes the yachts considered must be of equal displacement.

Fig. 37 shows the effect on stability of altering the beam, draught and freeboard of a design in which the displacement and ballast-ratio are kept constant. The curve labelled "Normal" is that of a cruiser-racer, designed with one eye on the R.O.R.C. rule, having 40 per cent of her displacement in the keel, a little trimming ballast, and less than the maximum allowed draught. Her stability increases up to an angle of 60 degrees, and she still has the power to right herself from an angle of 120 degrees. Suppose the beam were reduced and the draught increased. The curve is now less steep at the outset, indicating a more tender ship, but at 35 degrees it crosses the "Normal," and from henceforward it gives more stability. The angle of vanishing stability is raised from 125 to 132 degrees. Narrow, heavily ballasted yachts have stability of this nature—tender at the outset but growing rapidly with the angle of heel.

18. "Open" layout in a 28 ft. 6 in. waterline ocean racing yacht by Robert Clark.
19. The same yacht looking aft. Note that the navigation space is amidships.

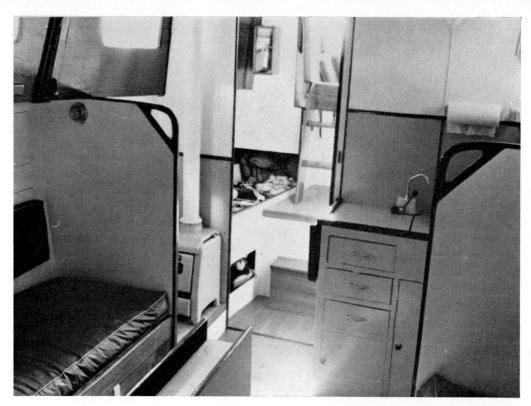

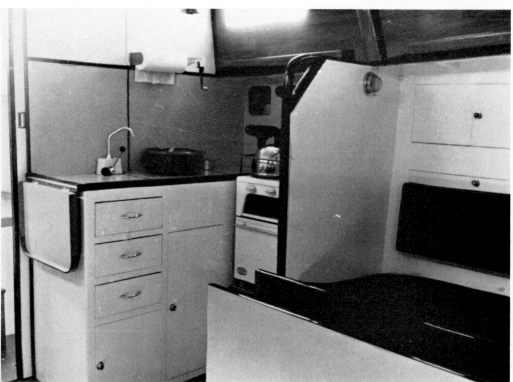

20 & 21. Port and starboard sides of cabin looking aft in the C. R. Holman-designed *Fargo*.

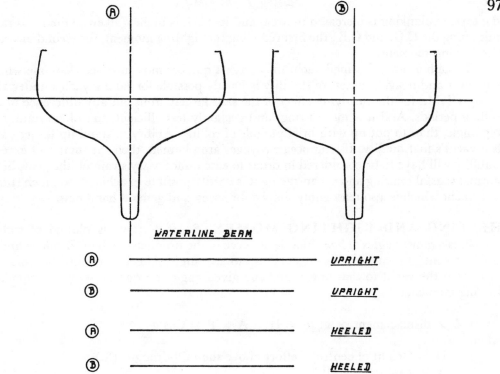

WATERLINE BEAM

Ⓐ ———————————— UPRIGHT

Ⓑ ———————————— UPRIGHT

Ⓐ ———————————— HEELED

Ⓑ ———————————— HEELED

FIG. 38. *Effect of midship section shape on heeled waterline beam*

In this example the effect of increasing the draught is to lower the C.G., which causes a lengthening of the righting lever; but the influence of this is not enough, at the smaller angles, to compensate for the narrower hull, which does not allow so big a leeward movement of the C.B. On heeling further the effect of the smaller beam is lessened—it will be found that the waterline beam of a narrow and deep hull tends to increase on heeling, and that of a beamy shallow hull to decrease—and that of the lower C.G. is increased. Thus the stability becomes more than that of the "Normal" (Fig. 37).

If, now, the beam of the "Normal" is increased and the draught reduced, the curve becomes steeper at the outset and at all good sailing angles, but it falls away below the "Normal" once the deck edge is immersed. This shallower type of hull allows a bigger lateral movement of the C.B. at the smaller angles, but the effect is lost once the weather bilge is lifted out of the water, whilst the smaller draught causes a higher C.G. The diminishing asset of beam is illustrated in Fig. 38. Upright, the waterline beam of section A exceeds that of section B. Once the two sections are heeled to the covering board their waterline beams are equal, which is an indication of their change in comparative stabilities.

If freeboard is added to the "Normal's" beam and draught, the stability is much improved at the bigger angles. Freeboard is of value when a yacht is hard pressed, though it causes a reduction in stability at smaller angles. The deck and its weights are raised;

G

the topside planking is increased in area, and its C.G. is higher; likewise the rig is raised, this lifting the C.G. and C.E., the first reducing the righting moment, the second increasing the heeling moment.

Though a broad-beamed yacht may have a quicker motion at sea than one which is narrower and heavier, excess of stability is hardly possible for sailing yachts under about 25 tons T.M., for the steadying effect of the sails largely irons out any difference in their rolling periods. And it is more tiring, and certainly less efficient, to sail constantly at a big angle, than to put up with brief periods of rolling. Ability to stand up to her canvas is a yacht's first quality. If long ocean voyages are planned, then the matter of excessive stability will have to be considered in order to ease unnecessary strain on the gear, but for normal coastal cruising and ocean-racing it is hardly possible to achieve too much stiffness in a yacht which is also reasonably shaped for speed and general handiness.

HEELING AND RIGHTING MOMENTS If a curve is plotted of righting moments against angles of heel (that is, a curve of the products of the GZ values and the displacement), the area under the curve up to any angle of heel represents the work done in heeling the yacht to that angle. For any given angle the righting moment equals the heeling moment:

$$\text{GZ} \times \text{displacement} \times 2240 = H \times A \times P \times \text{Cos}^2\theta$$

where:

H = Height of centre of effort above the mid-draught (ft.)
A = Sail area (sq. ft.)
P = Wind pressure (lb./sq. ft.)
θ = Angle of heel.

In the above equation $\cos^2\theta$ allows for the diminution of effective sail area with heel and also for the loss in the length of the lever H of the heeling moment.

Wind pressures for various speeds and Beaufort numbers are as below:

Average Wind Speed (m.p.h.)	Pressure (1 lb./sq. ft.)
2	0·01
5	0·08
9	0·28
14	0·67
19	1·31
24	2·30
30	3·60
37	5·40
44	7·70

Once the heeled positions of the centre of buoyancy have been found and the vertical centre of gravity, the angle of heel for a given wind pressure may be calculated from the above expression. To make the calculation for one angle alone, that chosen being the maximum effective sailing angle, provides instructive data on the yacht's power to carry sail, and it is possible that had this work been done many tender yachts in existence would have been modified in the design stage.

THE METACENTRE AND STABILITY AT SMALL ANGLES This is usually considered initially in studies of stability, but sailing conditions, and also the routine of yacht design, give prior importance to the general effect of proportions upon stiffness over the range of useful sailing angles. Then the stability for the maximum sailing angle may be checked as above. By using the metacentre a quicker and easier comparative check on stiffness may be made.

At very small angles of heel the metacentre is at the point of intersection of the centre-line and the vertical through the heeled centre of buoyancy. At larger angles it is still in the line of this vertical, but it may be above or below the intersection with the centreline depending on the stability characteristics of the vessel.

Mathematically, the metacentre is at a distance above the centre of buoyancy equal to the moment of inertia of the waterline plane (heeled or upright) about its longitudinal axis, divided by the volume of the displacement. The beamy, shallow type of hull is characterised by a high metacentre when upright, but one which falls rapidly on heeling, the narrow and deep hull by an initially low metacentre which rises on heeling. The intersection of the vertical through the heeled centre of buoyancy and the upright centreline is the point above which the centre of gravity cannot be raised without causing instability.

For the smaller angles of heel, before the metacentre has moved from the intersection of the upright centreline and the line of the buoyancy's upthrust, it follows from plane geometry that $GM = GZ \times \sin \theta$. The metacentre at these smaller angles is readily calculable. It is also possible to determine fairly easily, by means of an inclining experiment on the completed yacht, the vertical position of the centre of gravity. By this means GM is found for a small angle, and hence GZ. A criterion may then be established that provides a standard of comparison between various yachts, and with an adequate collection of data on existing boats, allows the effect of design alterations to be assessed in the drawing-board stage. The method is used in the drawing office of Messrs. G. L. Watson, and variations of it in other offices.

For the small angles cos angle of heel may be taken as unity. Then, using the same symbols as formerly,

$$H \times A \times P = G.M. \times \sin \theta \times \text{displacement} \times 2240$$

The right-hand side of this expression is a stability criterion suitable for comparing the relative stiffness or tenderness of various yachts. It is unable to give information of the range of stability, or of comparative stabilities at large angles. Stiffness, however, is such an important quality under sail that a ready means of assessing it is valuable.

A STUDY OF STABILITY CURVES Full stability curves for two yachts, produced by the office of G. L. Watson, are shown in Figs. 39 and 40. The former is of a 20-ton cruising yacht of moderate type, without extreme draught or high ballast ratio, and it will be seen that she retains positive stability at an angle exceeding 120 degrees, whilst the G.Z. righting lever is at its maximum when the yacht is on her beam ends. It should be noted that in these two analyses it is righting levers, not righting moments, that are plotted against the angles of heel.

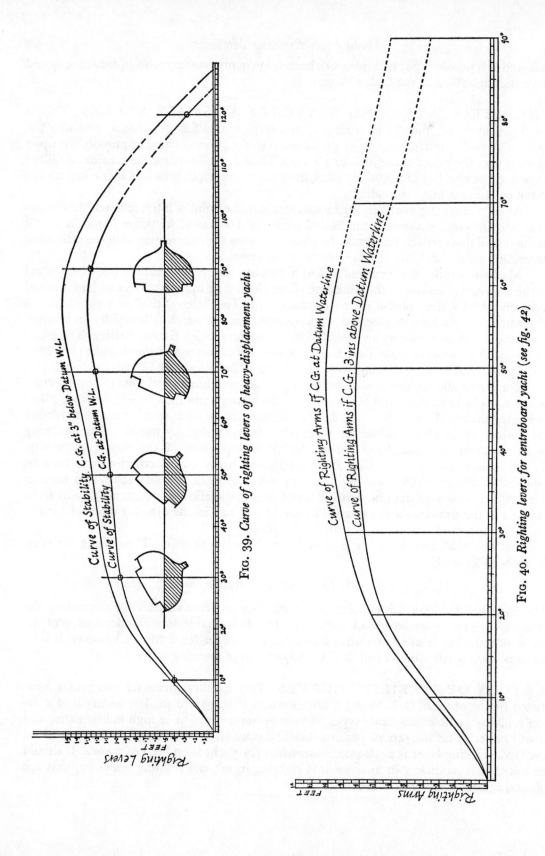

FIG. 39. Curve of righting levers of heavy-displacement yacht

Curve of Stability. C.G. at 3" below Datum W.L.

Curve of Stability. C.G. at Datum W.L.

Curve of Stability

Righting Levers

FEET

Curve of Righting Arms if C.G. at Datum Waterline

Curve of Righting Arms if C.G. 3 ins above Datum Waterline

FIG. 40. Righting levers for centreboard yacht (see fig. 42)

Righting Arms

FEET

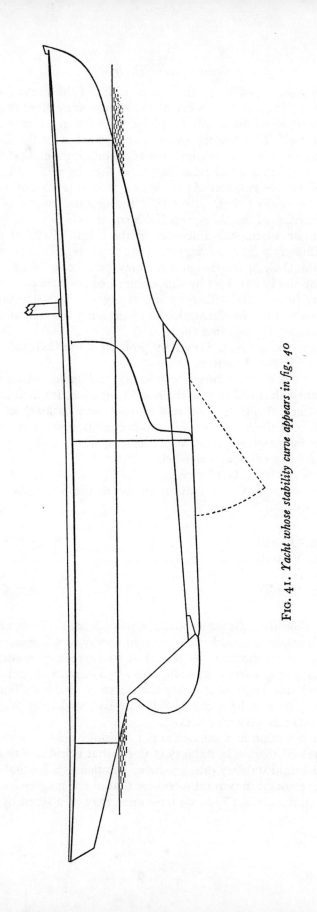

FIG. 41. *Yacht whose stability curve appears in fig. 40*

Two curves are shown, in Fig. 39, for two positions of the yacht's vertical centre of gravity separated by 3 in., the one being at the datum waterline, the other below it. Such a change in position might be produced by a reduction in internal ballast in the interests of increased load. The general tendency in a yacht is for the C.G. to rise in the course of years, owing to the height at which the accumulating weights are usually added. It will be seen that the effect of a difference of 3 in. in the height of the C.G. is slight until the bigger angles of heel are reached. At 10 degrees it is insignificant, but at 30 degrees substantial. It will be evident that, where G is the original centre of gravity and G_i the new position, the effect of the change on GZ is equal to $G_iG \times \sin \theta$ (angle of heel). If we assume G_iG to be 10 in., the difference in the length of GZ at various angles of heel will be approximately 7 in. at 44 degrees, 4 in. at 24 degrees, 2 in. at 11 degrees.

A lowering of the C.G. in the design stage may be accomplished by increasing the draught and lowering the ballast keel by this amount, or by increasing the weight of the keel. The latter may be affected either by increasing the ballast ratio, in which case the total displacement will not be changed, or by increasing the weight of metal carried, and also the displacement, by the same amount.

The effect of such changes on the resultant position of the C.G. may be found by the methods described in Chapter Fourteen.

It will be clear that a stability curve, such as that in Fig. 39, is based on assumptions of perfect watertightness that will not be realised in practice. Implicit in the curve is the supposition that hatches, skylights, coachroof scuttles, and cockpit, let no water below deck when the sea is over the coachroof. Since this condition will not be achieved, there is importance in the long righting lever at 90 degrees, which will provide a margin for stability losses due to free surface of water below deck.

These limitations are more vividly suggested in Fig. 40, the curve of righting levers of the 18-ft. dayboat class by G. L. Watson known as the Salcombe Saints (Fig. 41). Details of the boats are:

Length Overall	..	..	..	..	24 ft. 6 in.
Length Waterline	..	..	..	..	18 ft. 0 in.
Beam	..	..	..	..	6 ft. 0 in.
Draught (hull)	..	..	..	..	2 ft. 6 in.

It is a class of shallow draught centreboard boats with ballast keels, and it is of interest to see that the boats retain a considerable lever in theory at 90 degrees, though unlike the yacht in Fig. 39 the maximum lever occurs at 50 degrees, or 30 degrees sooner. In practice the boats have long narrow cockpits, and at 50 degrees of heel begin to fill over the coaming. Beyond this angle of stability the curve is obviously fictitious; but it is instructive to observe that such light draught, lightly ballasted craft might have positive stability to their beam ends were they decked.

To achieve this condition in a shoal-draught cruising yacht with its higher weights, beam has to be increased to gain in stability of form what is lost due to the high C.G. of the keel. The higher initial stability thus produced compensates for that lost in the small depth of C.G., but it remains important to ensure that at the greater angles of heel there is no sudden loss of form stability. This, we have seen, may be assured by good freeboard.

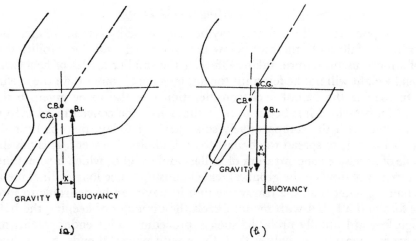

FIG. 42. *Stability due to weight and to shape*

STABILITY AND BALLAST We may regard the ballast keel as the expensive portion of stability, for whilst the shape of the hull will not, within reason, affect the cost, the lightness of hull construction necessary for a high ballast ratio, the amount of lead, and the large sail area which a heavily ballasted hull can carry, all cost money.

Stability of weight is essential if a yacht is to be uncapsizable. But the effect of mere weight is not as powerful as may be imagined. Fig 42(a) shows a narrow, heavily ballasted yacht heeled, the stability arm being represented by the distance X, which is GZ. The pecked line passing through the upright C.B. divides X into two portions, that to the left being stability due to weight, and that to the right being due to shape. It will be seen that the latter is the larger, and in all yachts of normal shape the stability due to shape is the major portion.

In cruising yachts, the C.G. ranges from slightly above to slightly below the water-line, depending on how near to the cruiser-racer a yacht approaches. The situation is then that shown in Fig. 42(b) where the C.G. is above the C.B. From Fig. 42(a) and (b) it may be apparent that additions to the ballast will not have such a big proportionate effect on the stability as might be imagined. In a certain design a reduction of 12 per cent was made in all hull weights—excluding rig. The saved weight was added to the keel, and the resulting increase in righting moment was 3½ per cent, at 30 degrees of heel. That is, GZ was increased by this amount. This skinning out of the construction work would have made the ship expensive to build and considerably less strong.

It may be guessed from this that the effect of using iron rather than lead for the keel will not be as deleterious as sometimes is imagined. Iron is slightly over two-thirds of the weight of lead, and it is usually not practicable to thicken an iron keel sufficiently to bring the C.G. as low as that of a lead keel. The proportion of stability lost by substituting iron for lead will vary with different yachts, but will always be slight. In one worked example the stability loss was 4 per cent where the yacht was of deep draught and with 40 per cent of her weight in the keel. In this example the C.G. of the iron keel was 4 in. higher than that of the lead, and the C.G. of the yacht was raised by 2 in. Such a loss is small, and the important point to realise is that it may be made good by very small increases in the beam, freeboard or fullness of the hull below the waterline. And the stability thus derived will be of a more useful nature, taking effect at the smaller angles of heel, whilst that of additional weight will not be felt until the angle of heel is more than the useful sailing angle.

In placing the ballast keel, consideration has also to be given to the fore and aft motion. In principle, it is better to have the ballast too concentrated than too spread fore and aft; but with the comparatively short keels of today, there is little danger of a designer being able to spread the ballast to an undesirable extent. It is possible that a fetish is made of excessive concentration of ballast and weights, which is sometimes even carried to the extent of stowing the ground tackle amidships. The longitudinal metacentric height is so much greater than the transverse that it may even be desirable to spread the ballast more fore and aft; but with modern keels the difficulty of keeping the ballast weight far enough forward usually prohibits such a procedure. Fine-ended yachts may reasonably have more concentrated ballast than those with powerful ends, but a sluggish lift to the bow is more likely to be due to lack of buoyancy forward than to excess of weight.

STABILITY OF FORM AND WEIGHT   The division of stability into two parts, one due to form and the other to weight, has already been observed (Fig. 42). One of the most subtle problems of design, which can be no more than stated, is the question of what proportion these two kinds of stability should bear to one another to suit a given set of conditions. As the late Dr. J. F. Allan said in his paper on "Yacht Testing" before the Royal Institution of Naval Architects: "Changes in stability can be made by both variations in form and distribution of weight, and since the two variations are most unlikely to produce the same effect, it is desirable to investigate these separately. ... A limited series of tests with a particular yacht form would give a valuable guide to the effect of these independent changes in the C.G. position on close-hauled performance. ... The changes in stability produced by variation in form are probably far more important, since they affect not only the initial stability to a greater extent, but also the range of stability."

The ratio between the stability due to weight and the total stability increases with the ballast ratio, and it is possible that for any given ratio there is a certain ideal proportion of form to weight stability. An important secret of performance to windward may be locked up within this question of the proportions of the two kinds of stability, but no general guidance in the matter is possible.

STABILITY AND SIZE   A big yacht is inherently stiffer than a small one. If all the linear dimensions of a yacht are doubled, the stability is increased sixteen times—that is, as the fourth power of the scale—this being the result of doubling the righting lever and increasing displacement eight-fold (i.e. two-cubed). Conversely, if size is reduced, the stability is diminished by the fourth power of the scale. If the linear dimensions are halved, the stability will become one-sixteenth of what it was. But the heeling moment, which depends, for a given weight of wind, on the sail area and the height of the centre of effort, varies only as the cube of the scale. The yacht, which we assumed to be altered in scale so as to have sixteen times the stability, will only have eight times the heeling moment if the sail area is raised in proportion. She will be altogether stiffer, and able to stand more wind or more sail. But if the scale is reduced so that the linear dimensions are halved, which

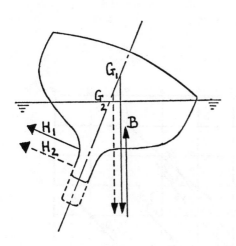

Fig. 43. *Greater heeling effect due to increased draught*

reduces the stability to one-sixteenth of what it was, the heeling moment will be only one-eighth of its previous amount, and the yacht will be too tender to carry her canvas.

Hence the smaller a yacht is the sturdier she must be. The proportions of beam to length and displacement to length must be higher for a 25-ft. waterline boat than for one of 60-ft. It is the inherent lack of stability in small yachts which necessitates the coarsening of the hull lines, and in the smallest cruisers stability becomes the chief problem and the most important influence on hull shape.

DYNAMICAL STABILITY The above analysis of stability has not included one aspect of the subject that affects sailing craft in a complex way; which is the changes in stability occurring when the yacht is sailing and developing, through her keel and underwater body, the necessary lateral water force to resist the lateral wind force.

This force acts through the C.L.R. whose position is at some distance below the waterline, the distance depending chiefly on the draught. If the draught is increased and hence the ballast keel lowered the statical stability, as considered above, will be increased, but the C.L.R. is also lowered and hence, too, the heeling moment of the lateral water force (H_2) whose action on the keel is to push it towards the surface (Fig. 43). As a result the shallower boat with the smaller statical stability may heel less than the deeper when sailing. This is indicated in Fig. 44(a) and (b) produced from tests carried out by Professor Ata Nutku in Istanbul in 1960. The curves in (a) show a deep draught hull, those in (b) the same hull and weight of ballast, but with a shallower keel. Angles of heel are plotted on a base of speed for various angles of yaw—the delta values marked on the curves.

Consider a speed of 1·5 metres per second and a yaw angle of 4 degrees. It will be seen from Fig. 44(a) that the deeper draught boat then heels to 19 degrees; under similar conditions of speed and yaw the shallower boat heels to only 11 degrees. At 2·5 metres per second and zero yaw the deeper hull heels to 25 degrees, the shallower to $27\frac{1}{2}$ degrees. The first result is due to the fact that with 4 degrees of yaw the lateral water force is considerable; at zero yaw it is slight, and the effect of the deeper draught and lower C.G. predominates.

This effect of dynamical stability will account for many disappointments experienced

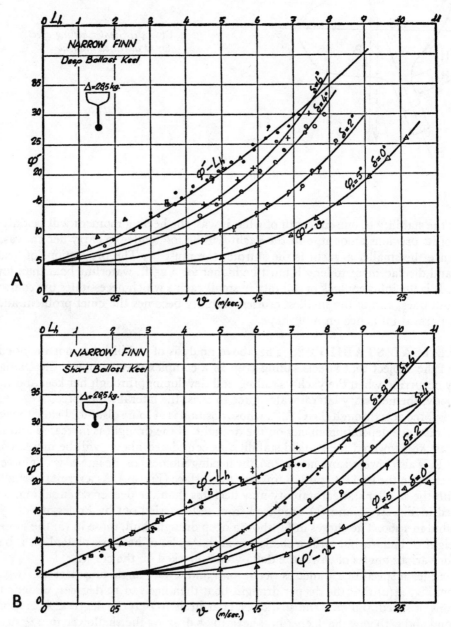

FIG. 44. *Effect of draught on heel (A = Deep ballast keel. B = Short ballast keel)*

over the stiffness of a yacht. A yacht may be given generous beam to ensure stiffness but when this is associated with the big maximum draught allowed under the R.O.R.C. rule the result may not be so stiff a boat as expected.

There is a further point that should be noted from Fig. 44(*a*) and (*b*)—namely, that there is a lateral water force even when the angle of yaw (delta) is zero. This must be accounted to the fact that though the relatively flat keel may have little influence at zero yaw, the heeled hull forms a hydrofoil developing lift due to its asymmetry and regardless of its lack of yaw.

The fact that the deeper hull heels more does not mean that for any particular set of conditions it is the inferior performer. Being deeper the keel has a greater aspect ratio and hence is able to develop the required lateral water force at a smaller angle of yaw. Her speed made good to windward, despite the greater angle of heel and the additional frictional resistance of the deeper keel, may then be the superior. But when sailing freer the shallower hull gains the advantage.

CHAPTER EIGHT

Balance

BALANCE in its broadest sense is that complex of qualities that makes a boat always docile and under the complete control of the helm. Speed may be achieved without balance, but under the full range of seagoing conditions balance is likely to assist speed by virtue of the ease of handling that it confers.

Balance in a narrower sense means lightness on the helm under all reasonable conditions of speed and heel. The well-balanced yacht sails to windward with a few degrees of weather helm only, and even when hard-pressed is light to handle. She is not acutely sensitive to changes of canvas, and does not carry lee helm except momentarily perhaps in light winds. When sailing free the amount of weather helm increases with the wind, but never becomes excessive.

Certain aspects of balance may be treated for convenience as a hydrostatic problem. This applies particularly to the hull form. A yacht that radically changes her fore and aft trim on heeling and "bores" (i.e. goes down by the head) will tend to gripe, her new, heeled axis of advance producing this effect; and the prevention of boring is partially a matter of hull form (*vide infra*). But the problem, even here, is partly hydrodynamic, though hydrostatic methods may be sufficient to confirm that the hull alone will not have vicious steering effects under way. The other vital aspects of balance, which chiefly concern the placing of the rig over the hull and the keel beneath it, offer themselves to no simple, hydrostatic solution, and the designer is faced with a complex of shifting forces the control of which cannot be systemised at the drawing-table.

THE SHIFTING FORCES Balance under sail depends partly on the relationship between two sets of wind and water forces which act on a yacht when sailing, and also upon the shape of the hull. The first of the wind and water forces is the component of the wind strength parallel to the centreline, which drives the yacht forward. It will lie off the centreline by varying amounts depending on heel, and on whether the sails are hardened in for windward work, or started for freer winds. Balancing this force is the amount of the hull's straight-ahead resistance, and the two forces form a couple.

Secondly, there is the component of the wind's force square to the centreline, which produces leeway, and this makes another couple with the equal force of the lateral resistance of the hull and keel. The latter force acts through the centre of lateral resistance (C.L.R.) the fore and aft position of which is adjusted by the rudder action. The latter allows, for any condition of speed, heel, and trim of sails, the following equation to be satisfied—wind force square to the centreline multiplied by the fore and aft distance between this and C.L.R. equals wind force parallel to the centreline multiplied by the transverse distance between the line of action of this force and the fore and aft resistance. This is the equation expressing balance under conditions of steady motion. Since it is desirable that it should be satisfied without excessive rudder action, the initial location and any subsequent movements of the C.L.R. when under way are seen to be of fundamental importance in hull balance.

THE CENTRE OF LATERAL RESISTANCE   Traditionally, the C.L.R. has been assumed to lie at the geometric centre of the underwater profile, though in fact this point has no definite relation either to the initial position of the true C.L.R. or its subsequent positions when heeled and making leeway. It has been suggested (K. C. Barnaby, Parsons Memorial Lecture, 1950) that this geometric centre might be named C.L.A. (centroid of lateral area) to avoid confusion with the true centre. In the following pages C.L.R. always means the true and not the geometric centre.

So far as the keel alone is concerned theory is able to provide quantitative data on the position of the C.L.R., derived from the information on symmetrical aerofoils. So long as the thickness-length ratio of the keel is not less than 0·06 and the keel is of streamline form with its maximum thickness at about 30–35 per cent from the leading edge, the C.L.R. remains fixed at about 26 per cent from the leading edge, for angles of incidence up to more than 20 degrees, which is far in excess of useful yaw angles. The normal keel profile is trapezoidal rather than rectangular, and a close approximation to the C.L.R. is obtainable by dividing the lateral area of the keel into a number of horizontal parallel strips, assuming the C.L.R. for each strip to be at 20 per cent from the leading edge, and then combining these separate centres as for a C.G. calculation.

The convenient fact that the C.L.R. is fairly accurately calculable and also fixed when the keel alone is considered becomes of less value when we consider the hull and keel in combination. The disturbing effect of the hull, with probably in addition certain wave-making influences due to the displacement of the fin itself, produces a slight forward movement of the C.L.R. at medium angles of heel and yaw, followed by a considerable movement aft at leeway angles of 4–5 degrees and bigger angles of heel. But simultaneously with increasing heel, there is a growing separation between the component of the wind's strength parallel to the centreline and the yacht's straight-ahead resistance. This produces a turning tendency contrary to the former which usually offsets the lee helm that would otherwise follow from the sternwards shift of the C.L.R.

The following table, based on experiments at the Stevens Experimental Towing Tank, Hoboken, shows for four yachts—the first three of ocean-racing type—the relationship between angle of heel, yaw angle, centre of pressure, and speed. With the obscure exception of *Baruna* at 10 degrees of heel, the yaw angle increases with heel and speed, and the centre of pressure (or C.L.R.) moves aft in all cases, after its slight initial forward movement, through a range of 5–10 per cent of the waterline length.

CENTRE OF EFFORT   As for the C.L.R., the C.E. is conventionally assumed to be a centroid—in this case the geometric centre of the sail plan. But the actual C.E. is yet more variable in position than the C.L.R., being affected by the trim of the sails on different points and the reciprocal influence of the sails.

Considering first the windward condition: the C.E. may then be accepted to be about 20 per cent of the sail's mean width abaft the luff of the sail, and by combining these positions for each sail—usually we have a mainsail and jib only to consider—the C.E. of the plan may be obtained.

TABLE 10

	Angle of Heel	Yaw Angle	C.P. aft of Bow W.L. end as per cent W.L.	Speed Knots
Baruna	10	5·0°	37·6	6·4
L.W.L. 50 ft.	20	3·4°	37·5	8·0
△ 39·4 tons	30	4·5°	43·0	8·4
Stormy Weather	10	3·7°	35·1	5·8
L.W.L. 40·25 ft.	20	4·1°	34·8	7·2
△ 18·86	30	5·25°	40·6	7·5
Edlu II	10	2·6°	38·8	6·3
L.W.L. 48 ft.	20	3·2°	36·6	7·9
△ 34·18 tons	30	4·2	48·9	8·2
15 ft. half-decker	10	3·5°	34·0	3·5
△ 1·125 tons	20	4·0°	32·1	4·4
	30	5·4°	40·3	4·6

When C.E.s and C.L.R.s are derived by the conventional centroid method, it is the practice to arrange that the C.E. so derived lies a little ahead of the C.L.R., the amount being known as "lead." Lead in modern sloops varies between 4–8 per cent, and the conventional guide in placing a sail plan above a hull is to provide an amount of lead that experience, preferably of similar designs of known performance, shows to provide a satisfactory hull-sail balance. But if the closer approximations to C.E. and C.L.R. described above are employed, it will be found that the positions of the centres are probably reversed, the C.L.R. lying ahead of the C.E., and these are the more likely dispositions of the actual centres when sailing.

Once the sheets are started, the C.E. swings off to leeward causing, as we have seen above, a considerable separation between the air driving force and the water resistance, and this makes a windward turning couple.

HULL SHAPE AND BALANCE The shape of the hull itself may introduce hydraulic side pressures that affect balance on the helm. In the past certain purely geometric or hydrostatic theories of balance have concentrated on the hull aspect of the problem to the exclusion of others, and over-emphasised its importance. The flighty behaviour that we have observed, of the other wind and water forces that influence balance, and the difficulty of bringing them under certain design control, has also encouraged the focusing of attention on hull shape, which is more readily systemised. Its influence is important but not predominant.

If a model of a balanced hull—either of power or sail variety—is ballasted to a certain angle of heel and set in motion, and is then allowed to run without any external forces acting on it other than the ordinary water resistances which will eventually bring it to rest, the model will follow a straight course whilst slowing down. An unbalanced model will describe a curve. It should be noticed that there can be no question here of any turning effect due to the wind; we are not dealing for the moment with sailing hulls, but simply with craft floating at an angle and being given motion straight ahead. Any alteration in course must be due to some effect of hull form.

Shortly before the war, the Hon. R. A. Balfour made some experiments along the above lines with models from which he later developed his twin-keeled 36-ft. L.W.L. yawl *Bluebird of Thorne*. The first model was unbalanced and the other balanced, and they were towed at reasonable scale speeds and then released. Mr. Balfour reported: "The unbalanced model invariably pursued a curved path whilst slowing down . . . Under similar conditions the balanced model invariably pursued a straight course in continuance of its centreline."*

One result of a yacht's angle of heel is an altered distribution of water pressure over the heeled surface. Since this surface is asymmetrically disposed about the upright fore and aft plane of the hull, there may when in motion be an unbalanced pressure component capable of altering the course. Again, the distribution of wetted surface is now asymmetrical also, and the frictional moment will have a component out of line with the direction of motion. Both effects are probably small compared with the misarranged volume of the displacement and its rudder action, and it is in the symmetrical arrangement of this volume that the secret of hull balance would seem to lie.

This was stressed by Mr. K. C. Barnaby, o.b.e., m.i.n.a., in his contribution to the discussion which followed a paper by the late Rear-Admiral Alfred Turner on the metacentric shelf theory of hull balance read before the Institution of Naval Architects. Mr. Barnaby questioned the rolling theory on which the shelf is based, but considered that the alignment of the forces of buoyancy, which the shelf is concerned with, tended to produce a straight-running hull. But he attributed the success to a different cause. "If we look," he said, "at the effect of misarranged *volume* of displacement on directional stability, we do get very definite horizontal forces. When we have a bad metacentric shelf we have winged-out displacement on one side or other of a line passing through the C.B. and parallel to the vessel's centreline (and to the desired course). This is equivalent to turning a portion of the vessel into a bow or stern rudder with a small inclination to the centreline."

Hull balance, in fact, is primarily a matter of producing a shape of hull that on heeling immerses approximately equal volumes of the topsides at the fore and aft ends. An innately straight-running hull is balanced in the geometrical sense of the word, the waterlines and diagonals balancing about amidships and having a similar type of curvature throughout the fore- and after-bodies. This character of hull is indicated in Fig. 15, p. 54.

A particularly significant line is the bilge diagonal. More than any other single line in a yacht's drawings, this diagonal is revealing of hull shape, and there is a system of drafting hull lines in which the bilge diagonal is one of the first lines to be drawn. The bilge diagonal of a balanced yacht will be found to have its point of greatest breadth near 55 per cent of its length from forward, or only a little aft of it, and the line will curve symmetrically about this point for more than 50 per cent of its length.

* *Yachting Monthly*, Vol. 79, page 268. See also Chapter Five, page 75.

112

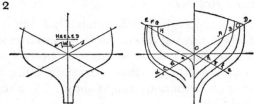

FIG. 45. *Heeled waterlines*

HEELED WATERLINES The shape of the heeled hull, and an indication of whether it is likely to produce undesirable steering effects, may be seen by plotting heeled waterlines. This is an approximate, visual test.

The plotting of a heeled waterline is a similar process to that of drawing the normal waterlines shown in the hull lines of a yacht; the waterline is simply struck at an angle across the body plan. Though designers sometimes make their tests for hull balance at small angles of heel only, it is best to draw the heeled waterline at the maximum efficient sailing angle, which is when the lee rail is a few inches clear of the water—an angle of between 25 and 30 degrees for most yachts. If the balance is satisfactory at this angle, it will not be wrong at the intermediate angles, but the inverse is not always true.

Fig. 45 shows a sketch body plan, eight sections only being drawn for clarity, with a heeled waterline struck across it. To draw the heeled curve, a straight line is drawn to represent the fore and aft centreline, with the section spacing marked along it, and the leeward side of the heeled waterline is found by plotting the distances OA, OB, OC, OD, OE, etc., out from the straight line at their appropriate section numbers, and striking a curve through the points. It is convenient to plot the leeward side below the straight line and the windward side above it. To plot the windward side the distances Oa, Ob, Oc, Od, Oe, etc., are laid off in a similar way. It may be seen that when, as in the sketch body plan, part of the section at the aft waterline ending becomes immersed on heeling, the heeled waterline will not return to the centreline at this end, but will lie to leeward of it.

The heeled waterline will not be symmetrical about the centreline, but will be fuller to leeward than to windward. The significance of its curve lies in the harmony, or lack of it, between its forward and aft ends, and particularly the ends to leeward. Fig 46(*a*) shows the curve of a geometrically perfectly balanced hull—that of an ocean-racer. There is no change in her fore and aft trim on heeling. The same balance is revealed in its heeled waterline. The curve of this line, both on the windward and leeward sides, is harmonious and approaches the symmetrical. The axis of the heeled shape will be parallel with the upright centreline.

Lack of balance is most clearly shown by the curve of the heeled waterline to leeward at its aft end. Fig 46(*b*) shows the heeled waterline of a 22 ft. waterline yawl—a typical example of a once common shape. She carried considerable weather helm, though this was mitigated in practice by sailing with the mizzen sheet started and the staysail hardened. The fore end of the heeled waterline to leeward is lean, whilst aft there is a pronounced bump, a fullness, quite out of harmony with the fore end. In badly unbalanced craft this fullness is very pronounced, and the shape will be emphasised if another heeled waterline slightly below the L.W.L. is drawn. In the case of the balanced hull the lower waterline will be found to be as harmonious as the L.W.L. Fig 46(*b*) shows the tortuous shape of this

22. (*Above*) Cabin arrangement with pilot berths on either side (Trevor Davies, A.R.P.S.).

23. (*Below*) Spaciousness in a wide beam American yacht by Philip L. Rhodes.

24. A saloon in natural wood by John Alden.

25. The same as Plate 24 looking forward (R. G. Lock).

26 & 27. Lavatory and fo'c's'le arrangement by Camper and Nicholson.

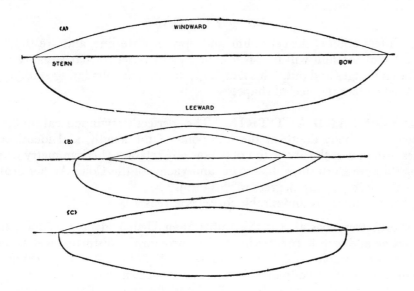

FIG. 46. *Balanced and unbalanced heeled waterlines*

lower waterline in an unbalanced hull: it will not always show the bulge of the L.W.L. itself, but may fall into an unfair hollow as shown. It will often be found that in unbalanced hulls, whilst the waterline itself is fuller aft than forward, both on its windward and leeward sides, the lower waterline to leeward may be finer aft than forward. On the windward side it will have the same excess of fullness aft as the L.W.L. The heeled hull, in fact, will seem twisted, and the axis of its shape will not be parallel with the yacht's course.

The essential feature for balance, then, is that the curvature of the heeled waterlines' fore and aft ends should be of the same character: fullness at one end must be matched by fullness at the other, or slackness in the curves matched by slackness. Fig. 46(c) shows the heeled waterline of a long-ended scow type. The aft, leeward end of the heeled waterline shows a bump, but this is matched by a similar fullness forward, and the yacht is perfectly balanced: the fullness at the ends is caused by the immersion of the long overhangs, and so long as the ends are in harmony, balance will be maintained.

Abrupt, unmatched changes of curvature at the ends of the hull indicate, in fact, areas where winged-out displacement may produce pressure changes that can result in steering effects. To be sure of the curvature of the waterlines' extremities, it is best, when plotting heeled waterlines, to take an intermediate section between that at the aft waterline ending and the one next forward; this is assuming there to be the usual ten sections in the waterline length, though if it is more closely divided this may not be necessary. Particularly where the nature of the curve changes quickly and unfairly, as may the lower heeled waterline of an unbalanced hull, is the intermediate section needed; with widely spaced sections the unfairness in the waterline will not be so apparent, and may even be missed.

It should perhaps be mentioned that the heeled waterlines (Fig. 45) are drawn

H

through the intersection of the centreline and upright waterline, and are thus unrealistic to the extent that the hull will lift on heeling in still water so that equality is produced between the in wedges and out. This fact, important when calculating stability, is not of significance when judging heeled shape.

HEELED FORE AND AFT TRIM The perfectly symmetrical hull, with the greatest beam and body depth at the mid-point of the length, and identical fore and after-bodies, would pass the above test of balance by retaining her symmetry when heeled. The Viking ships, modern ships' life-boats, and yachts of the Colin Archer Scandinavian type approximate in varying degrees to this form.

Complete symmetry is undesirable for several reasons.

(i) In short, steep coastal seas, V- rather than U-shaped bow sections, fine at the waterline and well flared, perhaps slice through the disturbed water more easily. This is a debatable idea, but one so generally held that it must carry weight. It means that the fore-body must be more finely drawn than the after-body.

(ii) In smaller craft the concentration of weights aft—the auxiliary, the crew in the cockpits, fuel tanks—demands reasonable fullness in the quarters. Also, such fullness gives space on deck and below, where it may be needed for a quarter berth. Stability is slightly increased by a full waterline aft.

(iii) Fairly flat buttock lines are needed to avoid eddies at the stern and an easy delivery back to the surface of the displaced water.

(iv) Very beamy craft, with a L.W.L./beam ratio of less than about 2·75, must have relatively fine fore-bodies if an acceptably slender angle of entrance is to be drawn out of the breadth amidships; but it is impracticable to draw a fine after-body for such a craft without producing a pot-bellied model of hull subject to extreme pressure changes under the water producing steering effects.

The balanced hull may depart widely from symmetry so long as the topsides which are immersed on heeling do not alter too severely the fore and aft trim in the process. A simple visual test of this was devised by Denys A. Rayner and later adopted by Captain Christian Blom of the Royal Norwegian Navy, who applied it to power-propelled ships (*Sea Speed and Steering*, read before the Institution of Naval Architects in April 1949). Its merit is the vivid impression it provides of the action of the in- and out-wedges on heeling.

To make this analysis heeled waterlines are drawn as hitherto across the body plan. The object is now to measure the difference in the areas of the in- and out-wedges at each section. In the case of small-scale designs this is best done by placing transparent squared paper, divided into inches and tenths, over the sections, and counting the number of squares contained in each wedge. The actual areas are not required, simply the proportions, so it is sufficient to record the number of squares without regard to scale. An alternative method is to consider each wedge as a triangle, which it so nearly is, and to find its area by the ordinary mathematical rule.

Fig. 47(*b*) shows three of the sections from the body plan of the Lowestoft drifter in (*a*). Look first at Section 10, which is the transom. Here there is no out-wedge since, when the hull is upright, none of the transom is immersed. Therefore, all we have to do is record the area of X. At Section 9 subtract area A, the out-wedge, from B, the area of the in-wedge. Notice the large difference. At Section 3 subtract C and D, and here

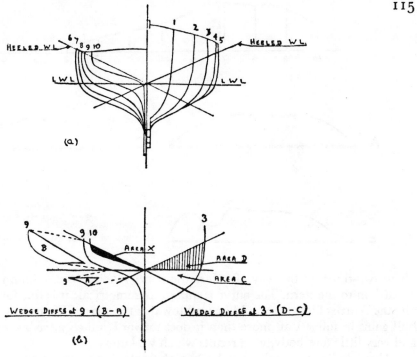

FIG. 47. *Sections of Lowestoft drifter*

the difference will be found to be less pronounced. Working thus through the body plan, numbers for each section are obtained which are proportional to the additional area immersed on heeling. If the results are plotted as a curve, it will reveal the change in the distribution of the displacement on heeling.

The easiest way to plot the values of the wedge differences at each section is to calculate what percentage each is of the greatest wedge difference. It does not matter to what scale the results are plotted, but it if is desired to make the curves of a number of yachts and to use them for comparative purposes, uniformity is desirable. Suppose the base-line is made 12 in. long. This must be divided into the same number of equal parts as is the waterline by the sections in the body plan—in the present case ten. Now take the greatest wedge difference; this will usually come about amidships or somewhat aft of this point in badly balanced craft. We are going to plot the wedge differences vertically at each section along this line; the greatest difference we shall make 2 in., which will be found to be a convenient scale, and the others will be in proportion to this. Thus, where the wedge difference is 50 per cent of the greatest difference, it will be represented by a line 1 in. high. Obtain a spot at each section marked on the 12 in. line and draw a curve through them. It will not always be a fair curve, and frequently it will have bumps and hollows in it; it will be necessary to draw it freehand.

Fig. 48 is the curve for the Lowestoft drifter. What does the curve tell us about the vessel? It will be seen that at the bow it forms a fine and gently rising curve up to a point

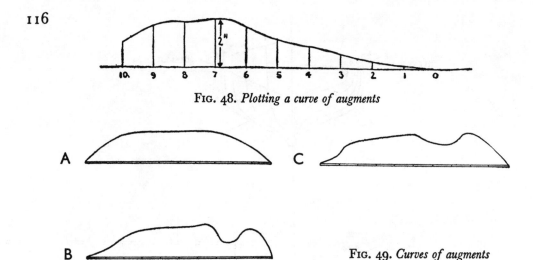

FIG. 48. *Plotting a curve of augments*

FIG. 49. *Curves of augments*

about two-thirds of the way aft. Here the curve reaches its maximum and the fullness is carried on to the stern. The curve is quite unsymmetrical; it is fine forward and very full aft; the centre of its area would be well towards the stern. This means that on heeling the hull gains in fullness aft more than it does forward; much after-body is being immersed and very little fore-body, with results which we know.

Good balance is indicated by the character of curve shown in Fig. 49(*a*). It is parallel, or nearly so, to the base-line for most of its length, and the ends have a similar character. This indicates that the fore- and after-bodies are in harmony, and the wedge differences at bow and stern more or less equal. Once again it is the symmetry of the line which is important. Sometimes there will be humps and hollows in the curve, as in Fig. 49(*b*) and (*c*), both of which are from yachts which balance well in practice. It will be seen that the volume of the topsides immersed aft in these two yachts is not greatly different from the amount forward. The curves, though irregular, do not have the lack of harmony of Fig. 48.

So long as the general run of the curve indicates that the yacht will not change trim badly on heeling, unfairness would seem to be of little importance, though Mr. Rayner, to whom I suggested this, replied in the *Yachting Monthly*: "I find that the curves of yachts from the boards of the great masters of the art have neither bumps nor dips . . ." But whatever the importance of such irregularities for indicating lack of fairness in the hull lines, they are not of importance when judging balance. It is possible that the curves, if executed with great accuracy (though if this is needed the most important advantage of the system, which is simplicity, would be lost), may be used to indicate places where the fairness of the hull lines could be improved. Thus the hollows shown may be the result of tumblehome in the quarters which has not been blended properly; the line of greatest beam in the way of the tumblehome may have been allowed to droop until parallel with the waterline instead of following the upward sweep of the sheer.

The similarity of the two curves in Fig. 49(*b*) and (*c*) is interesting. They are based on yachts from the board of the same designer, and though they are of different size and type, the influence of the same hand would seem to be indicated in the like nature of the curves.

HULL, FIN AND SAIL The above analysis of the balance problem is able to provide little more definite guides than the pointers provided by a knowledge of the couples formed by the fore and aft and transverse resolutions of wind and water forces acting on a yacht when sailing, and the various factors that influence their amounts, together with means of examining whether there may be steering effects inherent in the hull form.

It may simply be added that, in general, the narrow sailing hull is more easily balanced than the beamy type. For reasons that have been discussed, it is necessary, when shaping a beamy hull, to avoid an excessive degree of fineness aft and no less so an undue amount of fullness forward. In broad-beam yachts an approach to the wedge form of hull has to be made if speed and weatherliness are to be assured, and this is liable to endanger balance.

Also, once a yacht is in motion a complex series of pressure patterns occurs under the water, and variations and sudden changes in these, capable of disturbing balance by altering the equilibrium of the two wind and water force couples, are likely to be bigger round the more violently curved form of a beamy boat than one with the more gentle curvatures produced by narrow beam.

CHAPTER NINE

Rating Rules—Hull and Rig Considerations

WITH the exception of the last section of this chapter, on the rule governing the International 12-Metre Class, the following notes on yacht measurement originally appeared as a paper read by the author before the Royal Institution of Naval Architects in London. The 12-Metre rule has been added owing to its revived importance.

A most valuable discussion, which followed the paper, is published as Appendix 8, in which a number of the leading racing yacht designers and rule-makers advance their views, and which also includes much of general interest in sailing yacht design.

CONTEMPORARY EUROPEAN YACHT MEASUREMENT RULES

(a) International 5·5-Metre Class rule.
(b) International 7, 8, 9, 10·5, and 12-Metre Cruiser Racer Classes rule.
(c) Royal Ocean Racing Club rule.

The basic structures of the above rules appear below under their appropriate headings. Only the leading features that are discussed in this paper are given; the full texts, as they appear in the respective handbooks, occupy about seventy printed pages.

Rule (a) governs one class only, and the boats concerned are small, half-decked, inshore racers of about 22 ft. on the waterline and displacing between 1·5–2·0 tons. This has been one of the Olympic Games yachting classes on the last two occasions.

Rule (b) governs five classes. In all cases rating approximates to the waterline length of the yachts. The rule was formulated to produce yachts capable of racing together, within each class over inshore courses, without time allowance, and to be fit also to cruise, or to race offshore under the time allowance conditions of the Royal Ocean Racing Club.

Rule (c) is, in the words of its preamble, to encourage "... the design and building of yachts in which speed and seaworthiness are combined, without favouring any particular type." Whereas, under Rules (a) and (b), yachts of each class are of equal rating and race without time allowance, under (c) ratings may be unequal and the differences corrected by handicap based on time allowance.

THE OBJECTS OF YACHT MEASUREMENT RULES   Yacht measurement

rules began with no other object than of assessing size, in terms of tonnage or rating, the figure obtained being treated as an index of speed potentiality from which time allowance for racing might be calculated. This, in principle, is the system still retained in Rule (c) above. An extension of this method was the establishment of "classes" comprising yachts of equal measurement under the chosen system. In either case rules inevitably began to influence the shape of yachts. They became the forcing house of design; and the progress of sailing yacht architecture has been for part of its time the wayward and often eccentric changes in design produced by unforeseen mathematical quirks in the measurement rule in force. As such they were often irrelevant to any true technical progress; but also the genuine architectural advances that did occur were the direct, if unanticipated, by-product of experiments encouraged by the evasion of measurement systems.

Most of the notable developments in yacht architecture were the product of faulty rules that for a moment in their history allowed profitable experiments in design to be made. One such was Dixon Kemp's Length and Sail Area rule, given to this Institution in his paper in 1887, and which six years later was to produce the *Britannia* for the Prince of Wales. This yacht set the stamp of the one classical form of beauty that yacht architecture has raised. Yet the rule, of the rudimentary form:

$$\frac{\text{Length Waterline} \times \text{Sail Area}}{6,000} = \text{Rating}$$

and with few safeguarding restrictions, was wide open to the abuse that it very shortly received. A result of this was the study of yacht rating by R. E. Froude, the formulation of his Linear Rule of 1896, and later his First International rule, described in his paper before this Institution in 1906, which set the pattern of all the European International rules until 1939.

With the fuller appreciation that naval architects have today of the influence of measurement on design, tightly formulated rules with numerous safeguarding clauses have appeared, intended to produce a chosen type of yacht and giving freedom to the architect only within the close limits of the type. The "type" producing European rules are (*a*) and (*b*) above, and with their closely meshed network of safeguards and restrictions no great variation in design is likely to be produced by them. This discourages eccentricity, but unavoidably also inhibits development.

Rule (*c*) attempts to give designers absolute freedom in the selection of type, and by the skilful balancing of the speed factors to produce boats that, however different, have much the same speed potentialities if their ratings are equal. This rule is for oceangoing racing yachts, which to some extent simplifies rather than complicates rule-making; for extreme and eccentric features of design, in hull or rig, which might find their way into an inshore racing yacht, are likely to be prohibited by the sea itself in those that go offshore in all weathers.

THE ELEMENTS OF MEASUREMENT RULES There are three elements of which measurement rules must be composed. Firstly, the two speed-producing factors:

(*a*) Length;
(*b*) Sail area;
 and, thirdly, the speed-stopping factor, which is usually accepted as
(*c*) Displacement.

(*a*) and (*b*) need little elaboration, at least of their principle, beyond noting that the length concerned must be (unlike in the Dixon Kemp rule) the effective sailing length, which differs from both the waterline length at rest and the length overall by amounts that depend on the character, in profile and section, of the ends of the hull. The logical outcome of a waterline length measurement is, of course, a swim-ended barge able to perhaps double its measured waterline length on heeling. The extreme scow type of racing yacht, found until lately on the Canadian lake of St. Louis, is of this type.

The displacement factor may seem self-evident, especially in view of the fact that useful speeds under sail tend to be in the region of $V/\sqrt{L} = 0.7-1.1$, when resistance is acutely sensitive to displacement, and in the upper part of the range, almost directly proportional to it. However, although this is the view explicit in rules (*a*) and (*b*) and implicit in (*c*) which does not directly measure displacement, it is not perhaps, a perfect interpretation of the facts of sailing hydrodynamics.

BASIC FORMULAE OF CONTEMPORARY RULES

International 5.5 Metre Class. The basic formula is:

$$\frac{L \times S^{\frac{1}{2}}}{12\,V^{\frac{1}{3}}} + \frac{L + S^{\frac{1}{2}}}{4} = \text{not more than 5.5 m. or 18.04 ft. where measurements are in}$$

linear, square and cubic metres, or the corresponding feet.

The formula is shown graphically in Fig. 50.

The rule is thus composed of two additive portions, the first of which with the heavily weighted $V^{\frac{1}{3}}$ in the denominator, encourages a full-bodied boat with heavy displacement; the second, containing only length and sail area, providing a bias towards the lightest boat possible. The two parts originally formed separate American rating rules. Their union by the late Major Malden Heckstall-Smith produced a formula that attempts to maintain a balance between the heavy boat and the light, the under-canvassed boat and the over-canvassed.

It will be seen from Fig. 50 that the equation produces straight line variations between L, S and V, and that 3 in. of length costs approximately 7 sq. ft. of sail area, whilst 64 lb. of displacement receives a bonus of about 2 sq. ft. of sail area. Without associated restrictions a rule such as this would produce too great a diversity between its three elements, allowing one-weather or one-locality boats to appear; so the flexibility of the formula is stiffened by restrictions to check extreme developments. The principle of these affecting hull design are:

(*a*) Maximum V = 2 m³ or 70.62 ft³
(*b*) Minimum V = 1.7 m³ or 60.27 ft³
(*c*) Maximum S = 29 m² or 312.0 ft²
(*d*) Minimum S = 26.5 m² or 285.0 ft²

The maximum value of L is controlled automatically by the maximum value of V and the minimum of S, and the range of possible rated lengths appears in Fig. 50.

Two further important limits on hull dimensions that do not appear themselves in the formula are:

(*f*) Minimum beam—1.9 m. or 6.23 ft.
(*g*) Maximum draught—1.35 m. or 4.43 ft.

This rule offers the designer a simpler problem, at least mathematically, than either of the others considered below, in which the influence of the variables cannot be reduced to simple relationships. But even the straightforward mathematical problem set here has no ready drawing-board solution. The following measured dimensions will produce a 5·5 Metre:

TABLE II

	L	V	S
(a)	26·75	70	286
(b)	26·00	61	286
(c)	26·00	70	306
(d)	25·00	60	311

A general conclusion indicated by the past experience of rating rules is that where an increase in length may be obtained without any considerable cost in sail area, it is advantageous, even if an appreciable increase in displacement is entailed. For reasons suggested below heavy displacement may not, *per se*, be the harsh penalty suggested by the rule, which gives it the hearty benefit of a coefficient of 12 in the denominator. On the other hand, the definite pattern emerging from past rating rules may be upset in the present case where measured sail area is more heavily penalised than formerly, and boats tend to be under-canvassed in light winds.

A reasonable line of development under this rule would seem to be the adoption of the maximum displacement (disposing it as economically as possible in terms of wetted surface) and to balance L and S so that the resulting boat is not under-canvassed. One feels a preference, for example, for dimensions (c) above rather than (b), for 9 cu. ft. of displacement cleverly disposed is perhaps a small price to pay for an additional 20 sq. ft. of sail area. Dimensions (a) and (d) are respectively those of a heavy and a light weather boat; but the heavy sacrifice of length in (d) would certainly be felt in average British sailing conditions.

For draught, the maximum allowed is a natural minimum owing to the value of aspect ratio in the keel, no compensation being offered under the rule for less than the maximum. Optimum beam to suit given dimensions is less easy to decide. The great value under sail of a steeply rising stability curve in the useful range of sailing angles (up to about 25 degrees of heel) places a premium on stability of form; but when racing to windward in a seaway beam does appear to increase resistance more than calm water resistance tests indicate. Moreover, tank tests with 5·5 Metres made in Italy by Professor Alfrio Di Bella showed, in the results that he sent to me, only a very slight increase in resistance with angles of heel up to 30 degrees; indeed, some of the models showed, according to his curves, a progressive *decrease* in resistance with heel, but this I think was due to errors of judgement in the fairing of the test spots. It seems likely that for yachts able to increase their length sufficiently on heeling, the effect of heel on resistance is slight—and this was found to be so in Dr. Davidson's *Gimcrack* experiments. Excessive heel, however, also reduces the effective sail area and lowers the drive coefficient of the

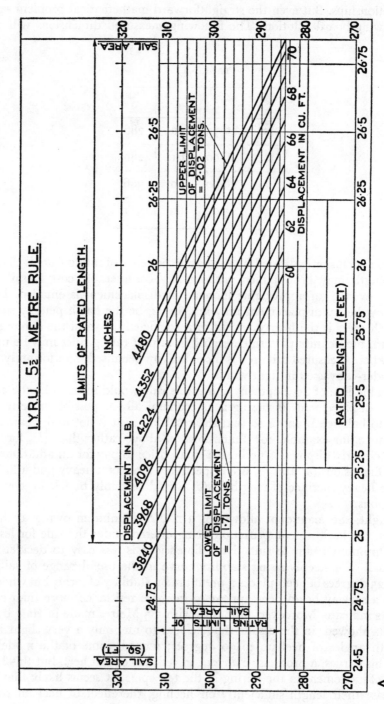

I.Y.R.U. $5\frac{1}{2}$ - METRE RULE.

LIMITS OF RATED LENGTH.

A

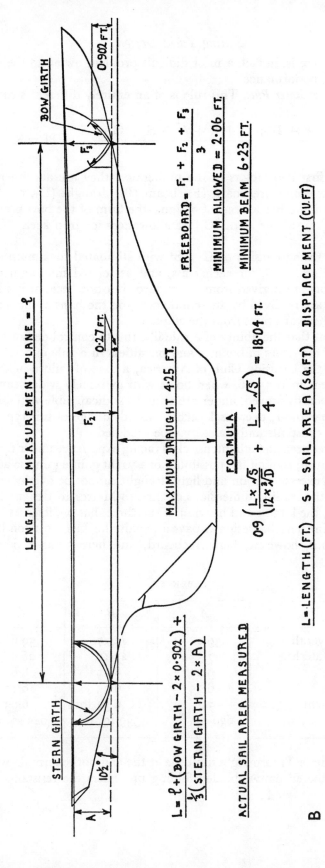

BOW GIRTH

0.902 FT.

$$\text{FREEBOARD} = \frac{F_1 + F_2 + F_3}{3}$$

MINIMUM ALLOWED = 2.06 FT.

MINIMUM BEAM 6.23 FT.

LENGTH AT MEASUREMENT PLANE = ℓ

F_3

0.27 FT.

F_2

MAXIMUM DRAUGHT 4.25 FT.

FORMULA

$$0.9 \left(\frac{L \times \sqrt{S}}{12 \times \sqrt[3]{D}} + \frac{L + \sqrt{S}}{4} \right) = 18.04 \text{ FT.}$$

L = LENGTH (FT.) S = SAIL AREA (SQ.FT) DISPLACEMENT (CU.FT)

FIG. 50. (A & B) *Elements of I.Y.R.U. 5·5-Metre class rule*

STERN GIRTH

10½°

$$L = \ell + (\text{BOW GIRTH} - 2 \times 0.902) + \frac{1}{3}(\text{STERN GIRTH} - 2 \times A)$$

ACTUAL SAIL AREA MEASURED

A

B

rig. The choice of beam is, in fact, a most difficult problem owing to the devious effects of stability on sailing performance.

International Cruiser-Racer Rule. This rule is of an entirely different structure from the above:

$$\frac{L + S^{\frac{1}{2}} - F + B + D + P + A + H + C - K}{2} \times Pf = \text{Rating}$$

Except for the first two factors in the numerator, they are all either "normal" or "base" quantities governing freeboard (F), beam (B), draught (D), displacement (P); or coefficients governing other aspects of design—the form of the bow profile (A), of the underwater profile (H), of the stern (C), or allowances for iron keels (K) and type of propeller fitted (Pf).

Fundamentally rating consists of $L + S^{\frac{1}{2}}$ with stipulated maximum and minimum values of the waterline length for each class, and associated minimum displacements. The next seven factors are derived from a standard, but not necessarily ideal, hull, and penalties or bonuses are received by an actual yacht, on the basis of the scales laid down in accordance with her variations from the standard.

It will be evident that the ability of a rule like this to control design depends on the nicest adjustment of the scales of bonuses and penalties. In a rule of similar structure to this, the formula of the Cruising Club of America, a case of failure in this adjustment became glaringly clear in 1955–56, when boats with extremely wide beam and shallow draught with centreboards proved, under rating and handicap, able virtually to eliminate the competition of narrower, deep-keel yachts. An advantage of this type of rule is the ease with which the constants and scales may be modified.

There has not yet been enough intense class racing experience under the rule to reveal any flaws in its structure; though the possibility of a yacht gaining undue advantage from the bonuses given to excessive beam and light draught cannot be overlooked.

Table 12 gives the leading dimensions of three 8-Metres to designs by Mr. James McGruer. Design A, the largest and heaviest of the three, has 0·5 ft. in excess of the base beam for her waterline length. Design C pays a penalty for being 0·1 ton below the base displacement; she has, however, high freeboard, and here gains a bonus. Design A appears in Fig. 51.

TABLE 12

	A	*B*	*C*
Length Overall	39·0	42·17	39·6
Length Waterline	27·33	27·17	26·8
Beam	9·21	8·75	8·6
Draught	6·25	6·25	6·15
Displacement	7·4	6·32 tons	6·03 tons
Sail Area	620 sq. ft.	539 sq. ft.	645 sq. ft.

The propeller factor Pf forming a multiple at the end of the formula will be noticed. cases of fully-feathered or two-bladed folding propellers the resistance is slight; but

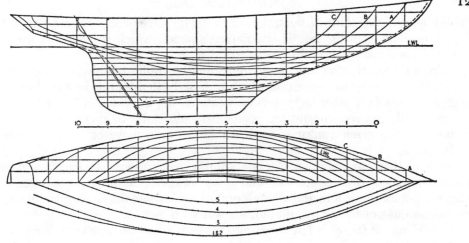

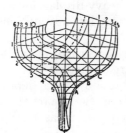

Fig. 51. *I.Y.R.U. 8-Metre cruiser-racer class yacht by James McGruer*

the importance of the allowance will be evident when it is realised that the resistance of a solid, locked, offset screw of 20 in. diameter and B.A.R. 0·35 will be about 120 lb. at 7¼ knots, and that at this speed the total resistance to motion of a 50-ft. waterline yacht, excluding propeller drag, may be about 560 lb.

Royal Ocean-Racing Club Rule. Structurally the formula is that of Rule (*a*) above, but with differences in the measuring of L and S, and with the displacement factor replaced by beam and internal depth measurements:

$$0·15 \frac{L + S^{\frac{1}{2}}}{(BD)^{\frac{1}{2}}} + 0·2 (L + S^{\frac{1}{2}}) = \text{Measured rating}$$

where B and D are the beam and internal depth measurements.

Certain of the most important features of this rule, which enable it to rate fairly a great array of widely different kinds of yacht, have no architectural significance (or should have none) and need not be considered here. Thus there are allowances for the engine weight, for iron instead of lead keels, for heavy scantlings, for light draught, even for a bowsprit. Their object is to level up, in terms of rating, the speed potentialities of yachts widely differing in the purpose of their design or their architectural merits.

Both the widespread use of this rule and the interesting and unintended influences it has had on yacht architecture have come from the fact that it is operated without the establishment of the plane of floatation or of the displacement. I should like in this connection to quote from the late H. R. Barrett's paper, which is lodged in the library of the Royal Institution of Naval Architects.

"From the purely practical angle, therefore, the author has always fought against the use of L.W.L. as a measurement on which to base L. Besides this he has always clung to the idea that the only other factor seriously influencing the value of L was beam.

"After all, however elegant the profile, it could easily be merely the end section of a plank, and this given a mast and sail would not even move off in the direction of its profile, but across it.

"When, therefore, Malden Heckstall-Smith tied up beam to length and made the basic measurement from which the final L was resolved the distance between two girth stations at points on the fore and aft ends of the vessel where the chain girth measurements were proportions of the beam, the author was with him . . ."

In the rule as it was a few years ago freeboard had an unintended effect on both length and depth, which produced a breed of very high freeboard, short-ended yachts of light displacement but with the rating advantages of heavy displacement. The rule then failed to reflect speed potentially accurately in its rating, but adventitiously showed the seagoing merits of an unusual type of yacht.

So far as the internal depth measurements were concerned, owing to lack of strict definition, it proved possible for these to contain large amounts of freeboard, thereby allowing a light displacement yacht with big freeboard to show equal depth measurements to a heavy displacement yacht with low freeboard. Thus the D part of the $(BD)^{\frac{1}{2}}$ factor became independent of the displacement it was intended to measure. But the resulting yachts proved the merits, which had hitherto been doubted, of light displacement combined with high freeboard for seagoing.

An important and active influence of this rule on modern yacht design lies in its draught stipulations. The maximum draught allowed, without a prohibitive penalty, is $(0.16 \times L.W.L.) + 2$ ft., and no bonus is received by yachts of less draught until this is below 80 per cent of the maximum. In view of the value both of aspect ratio of keel and a low C.G. of ballast the maximum draught allowed has inevitably tended to become the minimum chosen. The above expression allows a draught of 6 ft. to a boat of 25 ft. on the waterline, and 8 ft. to one of 38 ft. L.W.L. Such length/draught proportions are comparable with those reached during the period of the most extreme narrow and deep "plank-on-edge" cutters during the eighties, and only the more rational length-beam ratios of modern yachts disguise the fact that they are, in fact, very deep-draught vessels— inconveniently so for general purposes. A sliding scale of bonuses coming into operation immediately below the maximum draught allowance might encourage the adoption of more practical amounts of draught.

THE MEASUREMENT OF LENGTH   The problem of length measurements is complicated by the fact that it is effective sailing length that has to be assessed, and in the process the geometrical system involved should not encourage distortion of the ends of the hull. The difficulty of measuring length is further aggravated in Rule (c) by the requirement that the rule should be operable without the necessity of obtaining a yacht's exact plane of floatation.

The methods adopted in Rules (a) and (b), which are identical in principle and almost the same in detail, have long been used in former rules, and are able to encourage yachts with well-shaped ends having adequate reserve of buoyancy capable of also providing the increase in sailing length on heeling that offsets the increase in resistance due to the asymmetrical heeled hull.

The plane of measurement is taken at a certain proportion of the rating above the load waterline: in the case of Rule (*a*) this is 0·015 (rating), in Rule (*b*), 0·02 (rating). This length, therefore, includes a proportion of the overhangs, the exact amount depending, for any given boat, on the specified height of the measurement plane. The higher this is, the greater is the proportion of overhanging length included in the measured length, which has the effect of encouraging shorter overhangs and higher angles of incidence in the profile. It is logical that Rule (*a*), for small inshore racers, should be more lenient in its treatment of long overhangs than Rule (*b*), for yachts suitable for offshore cruising.

This part of the system of length measurement adequately controls the profile of the ends of the hull; though Rule (*a*) does contain another (probably unnecessary) safeguard in specifying that the angle of the after-profile with the waterline is not to be less than 1 in 5½ (10½ degrees). Associated measurements are needed to control the fullness of the sections in the overhangs. The method used in both these rules has a long history, and has proved successful. It is identical in either case, and the effect is to produce an addition to the measured length that increases in amount with the fullness of the girth of the sections in the fore and aft overhangs lying at the ends of the plane of measurement. The amount of the tax on section girth is arranged to be less aft than forward, greater fullness being reasonable at the stern; and the height to which the girth forward is measured is limited so that no direct penalty falls on adequate flare in the upper part of the topsides forward.

This system of measuring length has proved successful in the past. Once the rule-makers have established the height of the measurement plane and the weight of the end girth taxes a certain stereotyping of shape seems to follow, but in the past this had the beneficial effect, through the influence of the old International Rule on ocean-racing design, of allowing it to be proved that well-shaped overhangs were a desirable feature in seagoing yachts—a fact that had formerly been doubted. One slight eccentricity of shape, which is not without architectural advantages, may be produced by the measurement system. This is the abrupt snubbing of the load waterline and level lines immediately above it in the forward overhang. It allows the reserve buoyancy and the augmentation of length with heel to be little changed, whilst producing a substantial drop in the length at the measurement plane.

Without being able to use the load waterline as a datum, Rule (*c*) has been forced to assess sailing length by means of girth measurements derived from other features. The geometry of the present system is complex, lacking the sureness and elegance of the former systems, based on the direct and logical approach to the problem. This is the penalty that has to be paid for the administrative advantage of disregarding the plane of floatation.

Length is initially measured between fore and aft sections whose girth from covering board to covering board equals respectively, 0·5 (beam) forward and 0·75 (beam) aft. Corrections have to be made to the length so obtained to allow for the freeboard, which otherwise influences the measured length, greater freeboard shifting the girth stations towards the end of the hull. The effect of the corrections is to make the length virtually independent of the freeboard, but sensitive to floatation.*

THE SPEED-REDUCING FACTOR   In Rules (*a*) and (*b*) the stopping factor is taken, in the orthodox way, as displacement. In (*a*) the heavily weighted displacement factor in the denominator of the formula causes the rating to drop with increase of displacement within the limits allowed. In (*b*) displacement does not figure in the formula, but for each class there is a normal or base displacement expressed as 0·2 L.W.L. + *x* cu. ft., where *x* is a factor varying from 0·623 in the 7-Metre class to 0·5 in the 12-Metres. A deficit or an excess of displacement receives an allowance or a penalty according to a stipulated scale, and this appears as ±P in the formula. In Rule (*c*) we have seen that displacement is assessed on the basis of internal hull measurements.

It may be argued that displacement is the wrong speed-reducing factor to use, and that the result of doing so is to encourage the heaviest boat allowed within the limits of a rule. An increase in displacement allows an almost exactly equal addition to the ballast keel to be made. In Rules (*a*) and (*b*), in which the scantling requirements are not affected by the displacement, the added displacement may exactly equal the added ballast. The greater displacement, apart from receiving the bonus of additional length or sail area under the rule, immediately gets the advantage of a greater moment of stability, and hence of sail-carrying power, with its advantages of (*a*) lower augmentation of resistance to heel; (*b*) lower augmentation of resistance due to leeway angle, which is to some extent affected by heel; (*c*) greater effective sail area, which varies as the sine of the angle of heel; (*d*) greater lift coefficient per sq. ft. of sail area owing to the reduction of what, in effect, is the dihedral angle of the sail plan. Apart from these adventitious advantages accruing to greater displacement, if the bonus for the greater displacement is taken in the form of length, the result is a lower specific resistance. Nor, under the conditions of sailing, need additional displacement cause any significant increase in the resistance straight ahead (as opposed to yawed and heeled). The additional displacement may be concentrated low amidships, especially round the turn of the garboards, and produce a reduction in wetted surface thereby, and this is peculiarly valuable at the low average speeds of sailing craft. If the greater displacement is gained by additional draught it results in an increase in the lever arm of the ballast; and even if it is gained by more beam, the greater metacentric height allows more effective use to be made of the driving power.

Indeed, under sail, where the driving power that may be effectively used, and the various sources of yawed and heeled resistance are both closely linked to the stability, displacement tends to be self-rewarding; then, when it receives an additional bonus as well, the advantage to be derived from increasing it seems to be assured.

Accidentally, by its internal depth measurements which were meant, but for a time failed, to be a criterion of displacement, the Royal Ocean Racing Club's rule was freed from the effect of these reactions of displacement. The only attempt to discover a more sensitive speed-reducing factor is that evolved by the late H. R. Barrett, and fully described in his paper on yacht measurement already referred to. In its principle that "... what stops a yacht is the area and, to a certain extent, the shape of its effective cross-section ..." it may seem to be a reversion to certain of those discarded early nineteenth-century theories of ship resistance. But from the point of view of yacht measurement it

* See Appendix Eight, page 275.

28. *Rocquette* by Camper and Nicholson, forerunner of a new type of heavy-displacement R.O.R.C. rule yacht. Note the rail cut away in way of genoa sheeting.

29. *Fanfare* by C. R. Holman, 35 ft. waterline and with flush deck.

may be closer to the realities of performance than the use of displacement. Since this system is not used in the rating rules governing modern yachts it is not discussed any further.

In Rule (*c*) the (BD)$^{\frac{1}{2}}$ factor replaces the direct measurement of displacement, but is intended to serve the same purpose. The measurement of beam is straightforward. That of depth is made in two places, one at a quarter of the measured length from forward, the other at one-half the length, and respectively at one-tenth and one-quarter of the beam from the centreline. The values are corrected for freeboard, so that only the immersed portions of the internal depths are included in the measurements. There is a further correction to the forward depth measurement to allow for irrelevant variations in its position which the length of the forward overhang produces. In the final assessment of D length and beam components are included, which are necessary in view of the fact that both these features are able, irrelevantly in the architectural sense, to affect the positions and hence the amounts of the depth measurements. In avoiding the measurement of displacement the R.O.R.C. rule has been driven to adopt most complex geometry in its measurements; but the effect of the rule as it now stands does seem to be a freedom in the choice of hull form that no other rule offers.

PRINCIPLES OF SAIL AREA MEASUREMENT The measurement of sail area is basically a horse-power rating, but modified by three further considerations:

(*a*) Sails, in combination with the rudder, are an agency of control as well as a power plant. Safeguards have to be provided to ensure that the former role is not adversely affected by the latter. The fastest rig may be an unseamanlike one.
(*b*) Sails are expensive, and reasonable economy must be ensured by legislation.
(*c*) It is administratively and practically desirable to avoid having to measure actual sails. In the case of parachute spinnakers it is virtually impossible to assess their area. Spar measurements rather than sail measurements are needed.

MAINSAIL AREA Mainsail areas are found readily (we shall concern ourselves here only with the modern, triangular or Bermudan mainsail). The area is b × p/2, where b and p are distances along the boom and mast respectively representing the limits of the sail. Black bands on the spars indicate the points beyond which the sail may not be stretched without remeasurement.

The triangular mainsail has a curved leach, mainly for aesthetic reasons. The area within the curve is uncounted, but to prevent undue advantage being taken of this otherwise small amount, restrictions on the length and number of battens that may be fitted are made.

HEADSAIL AREA The measurement of headsail introduces more subtle problems, and it is necessary to review what has been done in the past to judge what is being done today and whether it is necessary.

An early system, which continued in use until the Second World War in the International rating classes, of which Rules (*a*) and (*b*) are the successors, and until last year in the Royal Ocean Racing Club Rule (*c*) assessed the area of all headsails as equal to 85 per cent of the area of the triangle ahead of the mast within which sails might be set.

I

The triangle is formed by the foreside of the mast at deck level, the point where the aft side of the foremost forestay on which a sail may be set cuts the deck or bowsprit, and the point where the aft side of the same forestay cuts the mast. That is, headsail area = 0·85 (I × J)/2, where I and J are respectively the height and base measurements of the fore-triangle.

The justification for the constant 0·85 lay in the fact that at the time of the system's formulation, when headsails were cut high in the foot and did not overlap the mast or each other to any great extent, the actual area of the sails set ahead of the mast approximated to 85 per cent of the foretriangle. By means of measurements that did not depend on the dimensions of the sails themselves an accurate assessment of sail area was thus achieved.

In 1927 the Genoa jib appeared, a triangular sail cut low in the foot and with its clew well abaft the mast. The sail became established, and was unrestricted by rule except for generous limits on the maximum amount by which the foot of the sail might overlap the fore side of mast. In the larger International rating classes this amount was limited to 0·4 of the rating, and under the Royal Ocean Racing Club to 0·5 (base of foretriangle (J)).

Three important effects followed this rule:

(a) The actual area of canvas carried ahead of the mast much exceeded its value measured on the basis of 0·85 (I × J)/2. The excess in normal cases ranged between 60–70 per cent. That is, only 30–40 per cent of the area of the largest Genoa was assessed in the measured sail area. In terms of the whole sail plan, approximately 20 per cent of the sail area carried was not counted in the measured area. This was the case in the International rating classes up to the outbreak of the war, and in the ocean-racers until this year.

(b) This entailed the provisions in the sail equipment of a number of Genoas and smaller jibs of graded area to suit any given weather conditions, and resulted in more expense than hitherto. Large Genoas are also prone to damage, and they need large crews to handle them.

(c) The apparent mathematical irrationality of the measurement was redeemed by the excellent effect that it had on the design of sail plans. Warner and Ober were the first people to show that the lift coefficient of a headsail is higher than that of a mainsail, owing to the effect of mast interference on the airflow over the leeward (low pressure) side of the mainsail. In spite of this, in designing a sail plan purely for speed, it is advantageous to concentrate a high proportion of the total sail area in the mainsail and have a relatively small area in the headsails. The advantage of a headsail's freedom from mast interference is lost, firstly, because a sail set on a wire inevitably develops a distinct curvature in its luff; secondly, because the luff itself is at an appreciable angle from the vertical, which becomes further exaggerated on heeling, so that the aerodynamic sweepback becomes excessive. In practice it appears that the highest lift coefficient is achieved when a given area of canvas is disposed approximately in the ratio 2:1 between mainsail and head-sail. This produces masts undesirably far forward in the ship, mainsails of unduly large area, and dangerously long main booms. The position of the mast has an adverse effect on the balance and tractability of the ship; the mainsail/headsail proportion makes a rig that is difficult to handle and essentially less seaworthy than one with a small mainsail.

A designer intent on speed has, therefore, to be encouraged to put area into the head canvas, and the free headsail area provided to him by the combination of the 85 per cent foretriangle measurement and large Genoas proved a sufficient incentive for him to do so. The 85 per cent rule produced the modern seaworthy rig of yacht.

It should further be noted that the Genoa and related overlapping headsails have a most beneficial effect upon the seaworthiness of rigs by allowing the necessary area of sail for light weather to be set without either undue height of mast, or the use of that now almost obsolete spar, the bowsprit. Overlapping headsails provide flexibility in the amount of sail that may be set, within the confines of a rig whose base is within the length of the hull, and the height of which does not preclude adequate, simple staying. Overlapping headsails, however, lower the lift coefficient of the rig as a whole. The potential Venturi effect of the slot between the overlapping portions of headsail and mainsail cannot operate with soft canvas sails sheeted within the hull, and experiments together with experience have indicated that most of the beneficial effect of a headsail on the airflow over the lee-ward surface of the mainsail is achieved with headsails having little or no overlap. Genoas also lower the aerodynamic aspect ratio of the rig as a whole, the latter being considered as $H^2/A \times C$, where H is the height of the rig, A the area, and C a coefficient allowing for the beneficial effect of the deck and sea's surface in modifying interference between the low and high pressure sides of the sail plan.

Overlapping headsails have a further particular value in modern yachts, in which modern developments in keel design have produced hull-keel combinations with a very much higher lift-drag ratio than hitherto. Owing to the effect of wave-making resistance at the higher speeds the direct proportionality of boat speed and wind speed, which exists in the lower speed range, is destroyed. This results in a more rapid increase in the lateral component of the wind force than in that of the counteracting water force, and to keep the leeway angle within bounds the area of the keel has to be sufficient to produce the necessary lateral thrust under strong wind conditions. A result is an excess of keel area at low speeds, so that such sails as Genoas may be carried with advantage in spite of their action in lowering the lift-drag ratio of the rig and increasing disproportionately to the thrust developed, the lateral component of the wind force.

We may summarise this aspect of rig measurement by saying that adequate headsail area, such as will produce a good mast position and a well-balanced rig, and the use of overlapping headsails which concentrate the sail area effectively will, as a result of their inherent aerodynamic inefficiency, only be produced when the system of measurement compensates for this by making headsail area cheap in terms of measurement.

PRINCIPAL RIG RESTRICTIONS Apart from the assessment of area measurement formulations embody definite restrictions on features of rig that might otherwise lead to expensive developments or the loss of reasonable seaworthiness.

The maximum height of the rig is usually limited. Our existing aerodynamic data as applicable to sails indicate that though the advantage of increase in aspect ratio is subject to diminishing returns, increases up to about $H^2/A \times C = 6$ would be profitable. But undesirably high sail plane would result. A limit on the height of a rig is, therefore, usual.

It has also been considered in the past that a limit on the height of the foretriangle is necessary and in the International rating classes before the war this was fixed at 75 per cent of the height of the rig. The principle of this restriction was the supposedly undesirably high stressing of the masting and rigging that was caused by headsails set from the mast-head.

SAIL-AREA MEASUREMENT IN CONTEMPORARY RULES

International 5·5 Metre Class Rule. Here the maximum height of the rig is limited to 36·4 ft. and that of the foretriangle to 29·11 ft. The area of the mainsail is found in the usual way, and there are batten restrictions. There are also other restrictions on the mainsail the reason for which has never been explained: "The breadth of the mainsail at half of lengths of luff and leech must never exceed 60 per cent of length of boom, and three-quarters of those lengths is not to exceed 35 per cent." Neither the syntax nor the rationale of this is clear, and it appears to be an example of the fussy legislation that appears from time to time in contemporary rating rules. (We may note here that in the formulation of international measurement rules by a gathering of technical representatives from many countries, an element of diplomacy is inevitable, and in the resultant compromise features of measurement may appear that have their origin in tact rather than technical requirements.)

In the measurement of the foretriangle the 5·5 Metre rule adopted the principle that gathered strong support shortly after the war under the slogan "measure the lot." It represents the full swing of reaction against large foretriangles, especially Genoas, and a high proportion of unmeasured area in the headsails. Here the actual area of the largest headsail is measured and marked on the sail. There are two further restrictions that have little apparent justification: (*a*) "The base of the foretriangle is not to exceed 50 per cent of the square root of the sail plan." (*b*) "No headsail shall be less than 80 per cent of the area of the foretriangle. Since there is no minimum area of foretriangle specified, (*b*) cannot have the one justification that might suggest itself, of legislating against unduly small headsails."

Under the influence of this system of measurement the masts of the boats have moved far forward, and the undesirable effects on the proportions and balance of rigs caused by expensive headsail area are becoming manifest. But the fact that the boats are small, open dayboats makes this development less vicious than it would be in seagoing yachts. However, the yachtsmen of most countries subsequently asked to be allowed to have the larger Genoas which it was the object of the rule to suppress! It will be evident that local rules allowing big Genoas cannot be safely introduced, for the greater sail area thus allowed would alter the balance of the other factors in the rating formula, and influence hull size and proportions.

International Cruiser-Racer Classes. Here the maximum height of sail plans is limited to ($1·65 \times$ class rating) $+ 1·6$ metres.

The foretriangle is measured as its actual area, $I \times J/2 =$ area. We find again a restriction on the base of the foretriangle, which in this case may not exceed $0·55/S$. Genoa overlap is permitted, but restricted to the usual $1·5 \times J$.

It will be evident that this measurement is a compromise between the older 85 per cent foretriangle rule and the actual measurement of sail area in the 5·5 Metre rule.

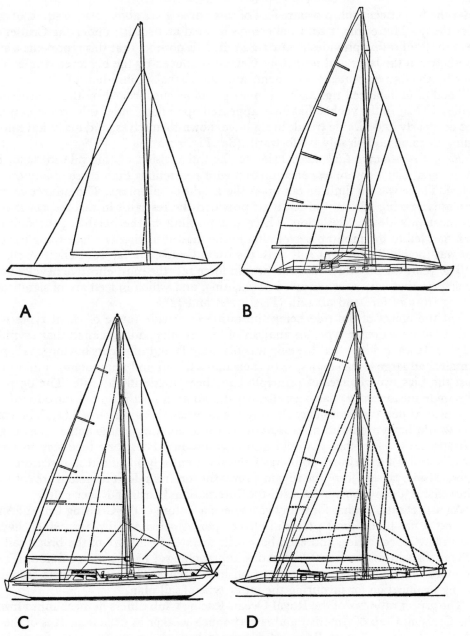

FIG. 52. *Various rated sail-plans*
A. *I.Y.R.U. 5·5-Metre*
B. *I.Y.R.U. 8-Metre cruiser-racer*
C & D. *R.O.R.C. rule*

Under the 85 per cent rule a square foot of rated area gives about 1·25–2 sq. ft. of canvas; under the 5·5 Metre rule, 1 sq. ft. of canvas is rated at 1 sq. ft.; under the Cruiser-Racer rule, 1 sq. ft. of rating provides about 1·2 sq. ft. It is possible that this represents a sensible mean between the large and numerous Genoas produced by the big foretriangles fostered under by the 85 per cent measurement, and the virtual prohibition of Genoas, and the likelihood of unbalanced rigs and bad mast positions encouraged by the measurement of actual sail area. In the yachts that have appeared up to date under this system of measurement no clearly undesirable trends in rig have shown themselves, and masts have not been tending to come undesirably far forward. (See Fig. 52(*b*).)

Royal Ocean-Racing Club Rule. Prior to the full revision of this rule in 1956, its sail measurement clauses were less encumbered with restrictions than those of any other rule in force. There was no limit or tax upon the height of sail plans. The subject of the rule being ocean-racing yachts, the sea itself provided the restraint in this respect that other rules must provide by legislation. There was no limit to the height of the foretriangle which had led to the profitable evolution of the masthead rig. The foretriangle measurement was the old 85 per cent rule with the usual Genoa overlap restriction of 1·5 × J.

The years during which this rule was in force saw the most effective developments in seagoing rig that have ever occurred in yachting, and which indeed are of significance in the long story of fore and aft sail. (Figs. 52(*c*) and (*d*).)

But the object of the rule being the rating of a wide range of yacht types without favour to any particular type, an analysis of race results had suggested that revision was necessary. It was evident that the rule was biased in favour of yachts having small, narrow mainsails and large foretriangles, with their masts far aft and approaching amidships. To adjust the bias two changes of principle have been made in the rule. The 85 per cent foretriangle measurement has been discarded, and an aspect ratio tax introduced.

It was at one time considered rating the foretriangle as 1·2 (I × J/2). The constant of 1·2 would have produced a measurement approximating to the actual canvas area of the headsails; the fact that it would also have produced a strong tendency towards big mainsails and a far forward position of the mast entirely justifies the discarding of the proposal. In its present form the rule measures the foretriangle at its actual area of I × J/2. It thus shares a common system with the International Cruiser-Racer rules.

An aspect ratio tax has for many years been a feature of the Cruising Club of America rule, and it has had a most powerful effect upon American sail plans, which have persisted in low aspect ratios, and even bowsprits to extend the base of the broad sail plans. Whilst in Britain mainsail luff-foot ratios approaching 3 have been common, a ratio of little more than 2 is usual in American offshore yachts. There seems little technical or seagoing justification for favouring the latter type of sail plan.

The aspect ratio tax of the Royal Ocean-Racing Club differs in mechanism from that of the Cruising Club of America and is very much weaker in its action. It is of the form: 20(J + b)/I + p = Aspect Ratio Allowance, where the symbols are as formerly. The tax is applied to the measured sail area (i.e. mainsail area + foretriangle area + any allowance and corrections), through the expression:

$$\left(\frac{\text{Measured Sail Area } (90 - \text{ARA})}{100} \right) \times \text{rated sail area} = \text{S.}$$

The object of the tax is to provide the benefit to the lower sail plans which experience has shown to be needed, without penalising the more advanced, more efficient rigs.

International 12-Metre Class Measurement Rule. The formula:

$$\frac{L + 2d + \sqrt{S} - F}{2\cdot37} = 39\cdot36 \text{ ft.}$$

where L is length, measured as described below, and is a most important factor: d is a girth difference (Fig. 53) and a matter of slight importance; S is the sail area, and a very important factor; F is a mean freeboard, and a trifle in the rule. So the formula basically reduces itself to this: length (ft.) measured in a particular way is added to the square root of the sail area (sq. ft.) also measured in a particular way; and to produce a 12-Metre the sum of these two combined with the two other relatively unimportant factors must be equal to 39·36 ft. Fundamentally, the rating is governed by the addition of length and the square root of the sail area.

Length is measured at a level approximately $7\frac{1}{8}$ in. above the L.W.L. The effect is to discourage either very long or snubbed overhangs, both resulting in a loss of effective sailing length. Furthermore, by means of girth taxes a designer is discouraged from drawing excessively full sections in the overhangs. Girths are measured at the sections at either end of the measurement plane. A full section produces a big girth tax, and the sum of the girth taxes is added to the measured length to produce the L of the formula. For a given L value, very full overhangs with big girth taxes will entail a sacrifice of waterline length. Thus, by means of a measurement plane above the waterline and taxes on fullness of section, overhangs of excessive length and bulk are discouraged. The girth tax is lighter at the stern than the bow since it is normal for the stern of a yacht to be fuller than the bow. The length measurement is illustrated in Fig. 53.

Sail area is rated as the area of the mainsail plus 85 per cent of the area of the fore-triangle, but there are a number of restrictions on rig which will be discussed below. It is the square root of the measured sail area that is entered in the formula, making rating less sensitive to changes in sail area than it would otherwise be.

We may pass briefly over the comparatively unimportant d and F factors. The d is a girth difference factor and illustrated in Fig. 53. Its object is to tax the amount of hollow in the sections amidships and so to encourage a fairly full-bodied hull and discourage skimming dish or champagne glass sections, which would have a high d factor. Originally introduced into a forerunner of the present rule in 1901, it is still retained presumably for the sake of "Auld Lang Syne"; for the fullness of the hull form is effectively controlled now by the displacement limitations we shall be noting in a moment. An effect of d is to discourage very hollow garboards.

The F factor is the mean of three freeboards measured near amidships and at the for and aft ends of the measurement plane. Being a minus quantity in the formula it encourages adequate freeboard. There is a stipulated maximum amount—about 4 ft.—which F may not exceed in the formula, which virtually standardises the freeboard of 12-Metres. Similar freeboard restrictions are used in the 5·5-Metre class, but here it does not appear in the formula, which is a neater arrangement.

Today the restrictions have a greater influence in fixing the type of the 12-Metre than the formula itself. Restrictions concern (i) hull, and (ii) rig.

Draught may not exceed 16 per cent of the waterline length plus 1·64 ft. In practice,

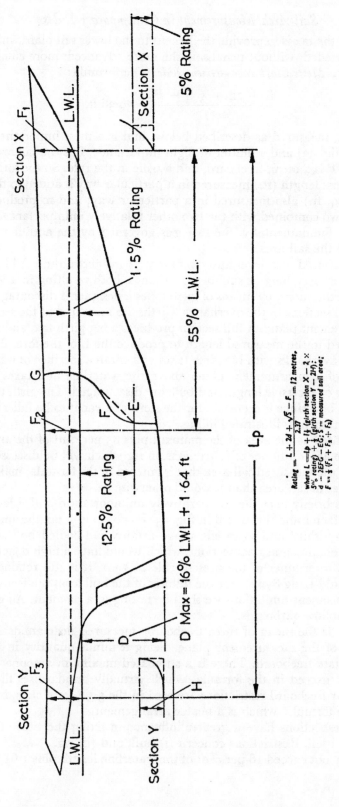

$$Rating = \frac{L + 2d + \sqrt{S} - F}{2.37} = 12 \text{ metres.}$$

where $L = L_P + 1\frac{1}{4}$ (girth section $X - 2$)^2 $\times$
5% rating $+ \frac{1}{2}$ (girth section $Y - 2H$);
$d = 2EFG - EG$; S = measured sail area;
$F = \frac{1}{3}(F_1 + F_2 + F_3)$

FIG. 53. *Basic features of I.Y.R.U. 12-Metre rule*

considering the acceptable waterline lengths for modern 12-Metres (see Table 13), this means that draughts will be a fraction of an inch more or less than 9 ft.; the total range of variation will not be more than about 2 in., or less than 2 per cent of the mean.

The beam may not be less than 11·8 ft. In 12-Metres ballast-displacement ratios are in excess of 60 per cent and may rise to 65 per cent. A designer is unlikely to be tempted to take much more than the minimum beam, which gives nearly four beams in the water-line length (they are narrow boats) owing to the tremendous inherent stability due to weight. We see from Table 14 that *Sceptre*, *Colombia* and *Weatherly* all have close to the minimum beam. *Gretel* has about 2½ in. more, and *Sovereign* about 5½ in. more, which in association with her big length and displacement makes her a most powerful 12-Metre.

In many rating rules displacement enters into the basic formula, when it may be balanced against the other factors, a designer being able to have more length or sail area if he accepts more displacement. In the 12-Metre there are simply stipulated minimum displacements for waterline lengths, and these preclude an excessively light hull. The following are approximate values:

TABLE 13

L.W.L.	Minimum Displacement
45·0 ft.	24·00 tons
45·5 ft.	24·75 tons
46·0 ft.	25·50 tons
46·5 ft.	26·25 tons

Since a designer cannot gain more length or sail area, as he may under the 5·5-Metre rule, for example, by having more than the minimum displacement, he has not much inducement to produce a heavier boat than the minimum. It will, however, enable him to have a bigger ballast ratio; for we may accept the fact that the structures of most 12-Metres will weigh much the same, being to a standard set of Lloyd's scantlings that does not vary with length or displacement; hence most of the displacement above the minimum may find its way into the weight of the lead keel. The Table indicates that most 12-Metres hover around the minimum displacement, a notable exception appearing to be *Gretel*.

I should add that Table 14 overleaf has been compiled from several sources, and checked where reported dimensions were in disagreement; but I would not dare vouch for its perfect accuracy. The two sets of figures for *Weatherly* indicate changes made in her trim between her first season, and her defence of the Cup against *Gretel*.

The rig restrictions are straightforward. The sail plan may not exceed a certain maximum height, and the foretriangle may not exceed three-quarters of this height. A low foretriangle rig is thus enforced. The largest headsail may not overlap the mast by more than 15 ft. 9 in.: a generous overlap considering that the base of 12-Metres' fore-triangles is commonly 21–22 ft.

There are a variety of other restrictions and requirements in the rule ranging from the length and number of the sail battens to the facilities of the W.C. These need not concern us in a general survey of the rule; but it may be noted that a large cockpit of the *Sceptre*-type has now been outlawed. Masts must be of a certain minimum diameter and weight, and permanently or mechanically bent booms are not allowed, although an insertion to the rule made in November 1963 states: "A boom which bends either vertically or horizontally is legal unless the bend is accentuated or induced by a force applied for the purpose of bending it."

TABLE 14

LEADING DIMENSIONS OF SOME MODERN 12-METRES

	Sceptre	*Sovereign*	*Colombia*	*Weatherly*	*Gretel*
L.O.A.	68·92	69·0	69·5	69·0	69·58
L.W.L.	46·54	46·5	45·5	45·0 (46·0)	45·0
Beam	11·82	12·25	11·83	11·88	12·0
Draft	9·08	9·0	8·92	8·96	9·0
Displacement	27·3	27·0	25·4	26·2 (26·4)	27·9
Sail Area	1,840	1,870	1,846	1,850	1,900

Dimensions in feet, square feet and tons.

It will be apparent from the above that a designer producing a 12-Metre is working within a pretty constricting framework. Many years' experience of the rule has established that the right waterline length for a 12-Metre is somewhere between 45 and 46½ ft. This means that the amount of sail area can be varied only within a small range. In rig a designer may adjust as he wishes the proportion of mainsail to foretriangle, the principal freedom he has in regard to the sail plan.

The maximum draught is virtually fixed. The architect is left to ring changes on beam and displacement; but no evidence suggests that any wide departure from the stipulated minimums of both is likely to be successful. Between the beamiest and narrowest boats in Table 14 there is a difference of 5⅛ in.; not much in boats the size of these. In displacement the range of difference is 2 tons. Small adjustments in proportions of this nature, combined with the effect that these may have on the hull lines, may lead to big differences in performance.

CHAPTER TEN

Mast, Sail and Rigging Plans

"... the capacity of the yacht engineer is nowhere more clearly indicated than in proportioning the various elements of the rig. .... Nothing will take the place of a thorough knowledge of the strength of materials and of the methods of determining stresses."

—*Norman L. Skene.*

"The best way to learn about spars is to study successful ones and forget about mathematics; for the spar, old as it may be, has developed mostly by trial and failure, and if there is any place in the whole design of a yacht where common sense is more useful than mathematics it is in the design of spars."

—*Francis Herreshoff.*

EACH of the above contradictory pieces of advice is true in its place; but if a choice had to be made between the loss of all data relating to spar and rigging sizes, and a sudden inability to do mathematics, the latter would be the lesser handicap when laying out spars and making a rigging list.

By making a sufficient number of assumptions, the loads carried by the spars and rigging of a yacht heeled by a known weight of wind may be approximately calculated. But the calculations are so long and the assumptions so broad that the answer bears little relation to reality.

The exact distribution of pressure over a given sail plan cannot be certainly known, and hence the resultant forces acting at different points on the mast can only be judged. The complex relationships of the stresses in the shrouds and stays, additionally complicated by the sails set on many of the stays and the loads carried by the sheets, make a system of forces which is beyond exact mathematical treatment. Also, such calculations do not take into account the sudden stresses which occur in a seaway, the magnified forces which come into play when a yacht is heeled suddenly by a squall which lets up for an instant, and then renews itself and strikes the yacht as she is swinging back to the upright.

Again, the strength of wood varies considerably. Allowance has to be made also, in seagoing yachts, for failure of part of the rigging. Yachts may lose their masts in a few moments whilst a runner jams on its winch, or when a rigging screw fails aloft. Masts must be able to stand against minor rigging failures. Lloyd's have not produced any rigging scantlings, regarding the matter as too involved for codification.

SAIL AND RIGGING PLANS The sail plan will usually be shown in a scale profile view of the yacht at rest on her designed waterline. As sail-making is a specialised art generally left to a firm with considerable experience, it is unnecessary to go into great detail concerning the method of cutting the sails themselves. What is required is the dimensions of all sails (working, storm and light canvas) the position of reef points and battens. If the builder is to deliver the boat with sails on board as part of the contract, the specifications will have to include certain other information such as type of material (synthetic or cotton), required draught (light-weather, heavy, etc.) and weight of canvas to be used in each sail. It is worth noting also that a designer may commonly design a larger sail inventory for a new yacht than her owner may wish to purchase initially. Many yachts are launched with working canvas only, the light canvas being added according to the designer's specifications at a later date.

As regards rigging, all spars should be sufficiently delineated so that the builder may make them according to the designer's specifications. Apart from the mast, all other spars, such as booms, bowsprits, bumpkins, spreaders, staysail or jib clubs, gaffs and spinnaker poles must be laid out, the amount of detail being dictated by the complexity of construction involved.

The sail plan will also serve the designer as a layout sheet for a stress analysis of the rig if he makes one. From the analysis or from collected data he will be able to specify diameters and materials for all standing rigging, construction of wire, the size of turnbuckles, shape and design of tangs, masthead fittings, and so on. All running rigging should be similarly specified including the size and location of all blocks, fairleads, winches and cleats, and the leads of purchases. As most of these items are of standard manufacture, they may often be specified by their catalogue number. All such details, which are usually too numerous to appear on the sail and rigging plan, are given in a rigging schedule. It should be pointed out, however, that each yacht presents a rigging problem unique in itself and that there is great merit in so designing the rig that no weight is wasted aloft. This may often require the design of special fittings which will be well worth the trouble in added performance and safety.

THE MAST   Today all seriously designed masts are hollow, it being impossible to gain the necessary strength in a tall, solid mast without exorbitant weight. Generally, too, they are of considerably greater scantling fore and aft than athwartships. This is the best disposition of material for strength, owing to the lightness of the fore and aft staying compared with that athwartships.

The direct wind resistance on a mast is unimportant compared with its effect on the airflow around it on to the mainsail. Between the oval and the pear-shaped mast there seems little to choose aerodynamically. The area presented to the wind, when close-hauled, by a pear spar is less than that of an oval one. The pear allows a smoother flow of wind on to the windward side of the sail, but it causes more disturbance to leeward. Since the driving power of the leeward side is about twice that to windward, disturbance on this side is more harmful, and though it may be less in degree, it is probably more damaging. This is suggested by the fact that model tests on mast interference show that with a thin, round mast, its disturbing effect is least injurious when it lies to windward of the sail.

Exact numerical answers to the problem are lacking, though investigations being made at present may provide them. Meanwhile, practical considerations hold the balance. The oval spar is the most easily built in wood, whilst alloy spars, and particularly those made from extruded sections, are equally easily produced in either shape.

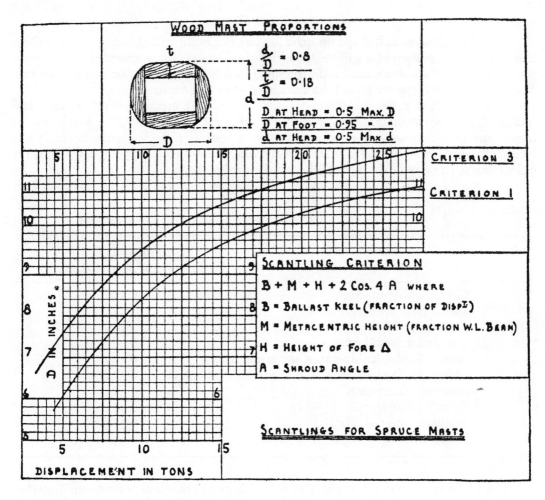

FIG. 54. *Mast scantling curves*

The principal factors governing mast scantlings are:

(i) Displacement.
(ii) Ballast ratio.
(iii) Stiffness due to hull shape.
(iv) Height of foretriangle.
(v) Angle of spread of shrouds.
(vi) Fore and aft staying.
(vii) Unsupported length of mast panel.

Stability is a function of displacement and the latter is the outstanding criterion of the stresses which a mast has to carry. Fig. 54 shows curves, based on displacement, indicating suitable scantlings for hollow, spruce masts. Two curves are shown, and the point between them indicating the most suitable scantling for any displacement is fixed by reference to the other features of the hull and rig.

The chief effect of hull shape on mast loading lies in the initial resistance to heeling, and in the quick motion of a stiff yacht, which produces greater momentum in the mast during a roll, and the more sudden destruction of this momentum at the end of each roll. Yachts under tow or power have been dismasted from this cause.

The criterion of stiffness is the metacentric height, the metacentre being easily and quickly found by calculation. Below is given, for a range of yachts, the height of the metacentre above the waterline, expressed as a proportion of the waterline beam. It will be seen to vary between 0·54 in a scow of the old Thames Rater type and 0·156 in the older *Genesta*, an extreme example of the plank-on-edge shape.

TABLE 14 (a)

Yacht	*(Metacentre above L.W.L. as proportion of Beam at L.W.L.)*
Genesta (plank-on-edge)	0·156
Dorade (narrow ocean-racer)	0·244
Conewago (8-Metre)	0·246
Z 4-tonner (small cruiser)	0·281
Stormy Weather (ocean-racer, moderate beam ..	0·303
Mystery (Robert Clark 11-ton cruiser)	0·312
Fidelis (8-ton cruiser)	0·329
Satanita (162-rater)	0·347
Windermere 17-ft. class	0·408
Thames Rater	0·542

The above ratios are indications of initial stiffness and quickness of motion. Together with the ballast ratio, which will range between 0·2 in small, heavily built cruisers, and 0·6 in the 6-Metres, and with the displacement a complete picture of the mast stresses caused by the hull design may be obtained.

The height of the foretriangle will be between the masthead and about 65 per cent of the mast length above the deck in a modest sloop. The higher the foretriangle, the greater must be the mast scantlings to carry the increased compressive loading of the forestay. This will be the result, firstly, of the steeper angle of the stay; and, secondly, of the greater tension needed in the stay to keep it straight, its length and the area of sail which it carries being greater.

Similarly, a small angle of spread to the shrouds increases the compressive loading in the mast, and also the tension in the shrouds. The angle is measured between the centre-line of the mast and the shroud, and the object of spreaders is simply to produce as big an angle as possible. The rate at which the mast and shroud loading varies with the angle of spread is shown in Fig. 55. The common range of shroud angles is between 15 and 20 degrees, and it may be seen that the larger angle reduces the loading by about 33 per cent.

The width of the spreaders will be governed by the cut and trim of the headsails, a subject which has been carefully examined by John Illingworth in his *Offshore*. Modern

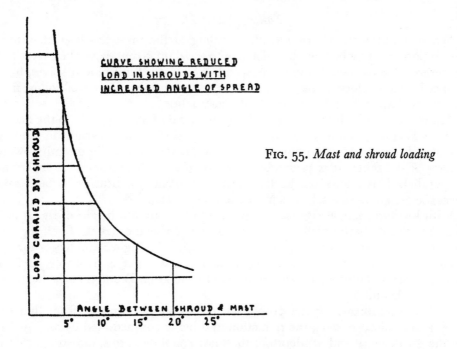

FIG. 55. *Mast and shroud loading*

headsails need narrow spreaders for their correct sheeting, and this means dividing the mast into shorter panels if the stresses in mast and shrouds are not to be excessive. The shorter panels help the mast in another way, the stiffness of a column being increased when its unsupported length is reduced.

A further feature governing the mast scantlings is the drift of the runners. The farther forward they are, the easier it is to handle the ship, but the compressive loading in the mast is increased for a given forestay tension.

The complex relationships of these variables prohibit rigid rules being made for the determination of mast scantlings. The empirical formula B + M + H + 2Cos4A may be used when determining the point between the two curves which indicates the scantlings for a given displacement. In this formula, the four most important factors apart from displacement are combined to produce a scantling criterion, which will range between 1 and 3, the values respectively of the lower and upper curves. The formula and key to the symbols is also given in Fig. 54.

The difficulty in establishing a formula of this kind lies in the weighting of the various factors so that they bear the right relationship to one another. Twice the cosine of four times the shroud angle is used in the formula. It should be noted that when determining this factor the shroud angle must be multiplied by four *before* the cosine is looked up in a book of tables. The cosine found is then multiplied by 2. Thus, if the shroud angle is 15 degrees, four times the angle is 60 degrees, and the cosine of this is 0·5. The value of the factor is twice this, i.e. one.

The foretriangle height is measured as the proportion which this height, above the mast's mid-point, bears to half the mast's length. Thus, the value for a masthead rig becomes one, and for a rig with the forestay 80 per cent of the mast height above the deck, it is 0·6.

When the maximum fore and aft scantling of the mast has been determined, the other proportions may be fixed by reference to the data given above the curves in Fig. 54. The method of construction shown, in which the mast is built of four staves, from which the taper is taken before gluing-up, is now very popular for all sizes of hollow masts. The scantlings will apply to other methods of construction.

Masts are usually slightly tapered from the point of maximum D to the heel, and the size at the heel may suitably be 0·95 D. But since the saving of weight in the lower part of the mast is comparatively unimportant, and anyhow is small in quantity owing to the slightness of the taper, it is preferable in craft of 20 tons and more to make the lower mast parallel. This allows the heel to have the maximum bearing surface, and hence reduces the compressive load per square inch on the step.

With low foretriangle rigs (say 80 per cent of maximum height of rig) it used to be customary to taper Bermudian masts to a diameter at head or truck of half the maximum diameter, which is still a common practice. But with the higher and larger foretriangles, and above all with the now usual masthead rig, less taper is desirable, and the head dimensions fore and aft and athwartships may be such that D and d at the head are about 0·6–0·7 max. D and d.

With the masthead rig the proportion d/D may be adjusted from that shown in Fig. 54, and reduced to 0·65, the reduction in d being compensated by an equal increase in D, the greater fore and aft depth of the mast enabling it to stand straight despite the considerable length of the unsupported panels fore and aft.

A rule for wall thickness, based on the analysis of many successful Sitka spruce masts, gives the maximum wall thickness at 18 per cent of the maximum fore and aft axis. Sometimes the aft stave of the mast is made thicker than the other three, this compensating for the weakening caused by the numerous track screws, and also giving them a better grip. The ratio of wall thickness to maximum D should be about 0·18, but may drop a little below this value for the forward and aft staves of the mast if the after-one is increased. An average value of 0·18 should be maintained.

In American practice, thickness ratios tend to be a little higher. One rule, originating in the office of Sparkman and Stephens, specifies that the thickness of the end and side walls should be 20 per cent of the fore and aft and athwartships axes respectively. If we take masts of average proportions this rule produces similar results to the former. Wall thickness may be varied along the length, tapering like the mast itself towards the head. But most masts have little internal taper.

Opinions are divided on the use of solid webs in hollow spruce masts. Some masts are made solid up to the gooseneck; and many have solid webs at the deck, gooseneck and the tangs and spreaders. These not only compensate for the weakening effect of bolts and screws at the fittings but seem to have a considerable stabilising effect on the mast; while those without webs prove hard to keep straight. Since their weight is slight the use of webs would seem commendable. They are fitted in the mast (Fig. 56) designed by Laurent Giles for a yacht of 4 tons displacement and 75 per cent foretriangle. A mast is more likely to cause greater loss of efficiency through lack of stiffness than the loss resulting from the meagre weight of the solid webs.

DRAFTING THE MAST The method of drafting a hollow mast is given in Fig. 57. The aft side of the mast will be straight, represented by the line KE, the taper

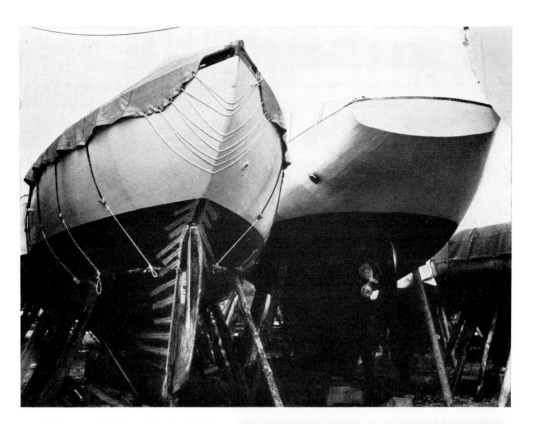

30. Extremes in stern design. Wide, flat counter of great breadth and a short, narrow canoe stern.

31. A finely-drawn after-body, finished with a veed transom without tumblehome.

32 & 33. A hollow spruce mast under construction. A scarf is being made in the left-hand illustration.

34. The moulds set up on the keel, before the laying of the ribbands.

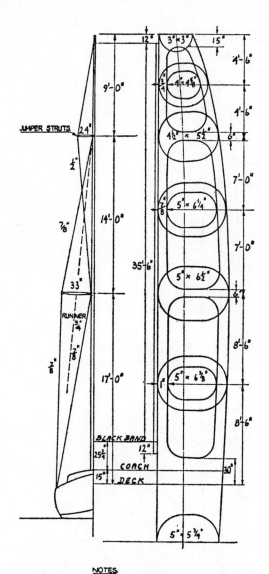

FIG. 56. Cohoe's *mast plan*

being taken from the fore side. At the position of the greatest fore and aft scantling, the amount should be set off square to KE (line AB), using a transverse scale, which may be anything between ten and twenty-four times that of the longitudinal one. The fore and aft diameters at the head and heel may also be drawn to this scale (lines EF and KL).

The taper of the fore side is found by drawing a semicircle equal in radius to the maximum fore and aft scantling—that is, equal to AB. This is represented by A_1B_1 in Fig. 57. The mast length above and below AB is now divided into a number of equal parts, the parts above AB not necessarily equalling those below. In one segment of the semicircle K_1L_1 is drawn, parallel to AB and equal to KL. In the other E_1F_1 is similarly drawn, equal to EF. The distances between these lines and A_1B_1 are divided into the same

FORE & AFT
TAPER

ATHWARTSHIP
TAPER

K   L

I   J

G   H

A   B   MAX. DIAS

C   D

E   F

W   X

U   V

S   T

M   N

O   P

Q   R

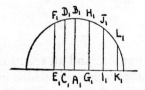

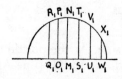

Fig. 57. *Drafting a mast*

number of equal parts as the corresponding distances on the mast elevation, and the lengths of the intermediate lines in the semicircle give the points through which the taper of the mast is drawn.

The thwartship taper, which is taken from both sides of the mast, is obtained similarly, the only difference being that the semicircle's radius will now be the maximum thwartship scantling of the mast. Sections of the mast may now be drawn, and are frequently superimposed on the fore and aft elevation. They are usually drawn at the points where the spreaders or other fittings are attached. But before the mast thicknesses can be indicated on the sections, the taper of the inner wall of the mast should be drawn. The thicknesses at head, heel and at the positions of maximum thickness, should be indicated on both mast elevations, and curves drawn through the points will indicate the inner wall. For strict accuracy, these curves should be laid off as were the curves for external taper.

LIGHT ALLOY MASTS Light alloy masts, from their tentative beginnings before the war, usually fitted in the larger yachts, have now become extremely common in all sizes of yacht from dinghies upwards.

The earlier light alloy masts were built up from a number of separate plates screwed and riveted together, and it may be of interest to consider the methods used.

Fig. 58 shows the hiduminium mast designed and built by Camper and Nicholson for the Royal Artillery Yacht Club's *St. Barbara*. The mast is 69 ft. 3 in. in length and of an oval section, having major and minor diameters of $10\frac{1}{2}$ in. and $7\frac{3}{4}$ in. It was designed to carry a masthead rig, and there were three spreaders. The plating of the mast is 0·16 in. up to the middle spreader, and 0·125 in. above, and the taper starts from this spreader which is 35 ft. 3 in. above the step. Below the spreader the mast is parallel-sided.

The shape of the mast at any section is formed by two plates each rolled to the half section of an oval and butted at the sides of the mast, internal hiduminium butt straps $1\frac{3}{4}$ in. by 0·125 in. covering these two longitudinal butts internally, and running from head to heel of the mast. There are altogether fourteen plates in the length of the mast, seven forming the fore side and seven the aft side, and the transverse butts of these plates are staggered along the length, those in the fore side plating falling between the aft-plate butts. The butts are covered with internal straps 4 in. by 0·125 in., which extend rather more than half round the mast, thus overlapping the butts slightly.

There are many other interesting points of building technique revealed by the plan. It will be seen that the longitudinal butt straps, running up each side of the mast, are fastened to the plating by cadmium-plated steel screws on one side of each butt, and by rivets on the other. The method of fastening alternates from side to side. Thus, in the two lowest plates of the mast, the plate forming the fore side of the mast, and extending 12 ft. 3 in. above the heel, has the screws to starboard and the rivets to port; in the fore-side plate above this one the fastenings are reversed. On the corresponding plates forming the after side, the lowest, which extends 7 ft. 6 in. above the heel, has the screws to port and the rivets to starboard, and the plate above has the reverse.

The use of screws on one side of the butt strap and rivets on the other is due to the difficulty of blind riveting. It will be apparent that the head of a rivet has to be held firmly whilst the point is hammered flat. The length of the plates forming the mast varies between 12 ft. 3 in. and 7 ft. 6 in., and it would not be practicable to hold the head of a rivet which is even 7 ft. 6 in. from the end of the tube. The butt strap is therefore riveted to one edge of the plate forming a side of the mast before the plate forming the other is in place. The second plate, with the butt strap riveted to its other side, is then placed to close the oval, and the screws inserted in the butt straps on either side. Thus, in building the mast, the half oval forming the lowest forward half of the mast would have the butt strap riveted to its starboard side. The corresponding aft-plate would have the butt strap riveted to its port side. The two halves would then be placed together, and the

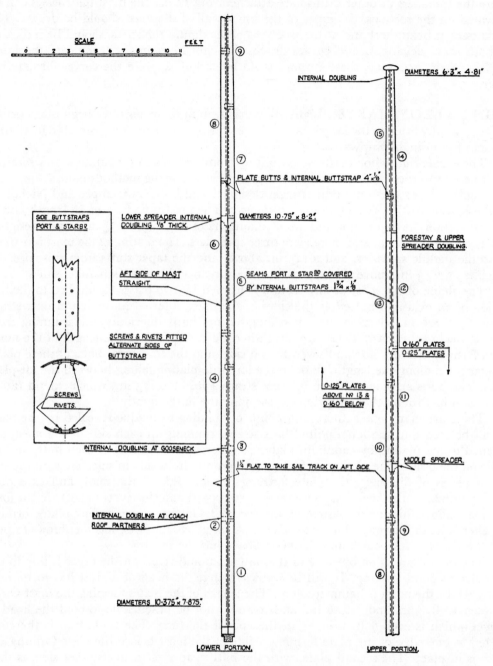

FIG. 58. St. Barbara's *alloy mast*

screws inserted to port and starboard respectively. Plates would then be added forward and aft alternately until the mast is completed.

At the tapering part of the mast, the flat plates, which are rolled to form the half ovals, are cut tapered prior to the rolling.

At points along the mast there are doublings to take the stresses of the various fittings. At the heel there is an external doubling 6 in. deep by 0·125 in. thick, riveted to the mast, and internally at the top of this doubling there is a steel angle bar riveted through both mast shell and doubling. This takes the pressure on the spruce plug which forms the mast heel. There are internal doublings at the levels of the coachroof, gooseneck, and at the spreaders and forestay attachments. These doublings are inserted as the mast is assembled, and the plates are arranged so that a butt in either the forward or aft mast plating falls under the doubling, which then serves also as a butt strap. And, as in the longitudinal doubling on either side of the mast, one side of each doubling is riveted, and the other (upper) side is always screwed.

The above were the main features of large alloy mast construction, and it may be seen that skilful design and workmanship were needed. The work would have been greatly simplified had the welding of alloys been advanced enough to replace the riveting and screwing. The latter work makes an alloy spar more expensive than one built up of spruce. Owing to electrolytic action all steel work in contact with the alloy was cadmium-plated. It will be seen that steel screws are used, this being because of the softness of alloy.

With the development of the technique for welding light alloy the complexity and expense of the riveting was eliminated; but now masts, even for the larger craft, are usually made from extruded sections.

Nowadays, the suppliers of light alloy masts have a considerable range of sections available from the stock size tubes on the market, and suppliers are able in their own workshops to modify the ratio of fore and aft to athwartship dimensions of tubes to suit the architect. The vital function of the latter is to ensure that the dimensions and sections of the tube chosen make the metal mast superior to one in spruce.

The variables involved are (i) Weight per foot; (ii) Stiffness; (iii) Breaking strength; (iv) Windage. A light alloy mast may be stronger than one in wood of the same weight, or lighter for the same strength, or have reduced windage owing to smaller dimensions and simpler staying, or some permutation of these qualities. Calculations based on Euler's column formula give the following comparisons for two pairs of spruce and light alloy masts, each pair being of equal strength—that is, of equal $E \times I$ value in the formula

$$W = \left(\frac{\pi}{L}\right) E \times I$$

where W is the breaking strength, E the modulus of elasticity, I the moment of inertia of the mast section, and L the length.

TABLE 15

	Spruce	Alloy	Spruce	Alloy
Major Diameter	8·5	7·5	13·6	13·6
Minor Diameter	5·5	4·5	9·13	8·3
Weight (lb./ft.)	4·55	4·55	12·1	8·9

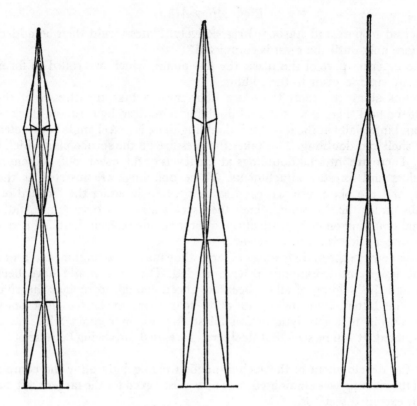

FIG. 59. *6-Metres' masts*—Circe, Juno, Firecracker

The first pair of masts was designed for a yacht displacing 8½ tons and the advantage gained here is the smaller dimensions of the alloy mast and hence the reduced windage and the smaller weight of the fittings. The second pair of masts have similar major diameters but the light alloy spar has a smaller minor diameter and 28 per cent less weight. The greater saving in weight for the larger masts is due to the impracticability of reducing wall thickness in the smaller masts to the minimum theoretically ideal owing to the need to retain sufficient thickness for the securing of tangs and spreaders and to avoid local buckling, which with thin plate will occur long before the critical load is reached.

It will be apparent that the weight of a light alloy mast may not always suitably be less than one of spruce, but it is the function of the architect to ensure that the chosen alloy section is superior to the spruce section in the balance of the counts given above. When masts of equal weights are or have to be accepted, it is not only the smaller size of the alloy mast that may give it superiority but also the simpler staying required. This is shown vividly in Fig. 59 comparing the masts for three 6-Metre class yachts. *Sceptre*'s shroud system may have been a little light, but it was a tribute to her aluminium mast that, unique amongst all 12-Metre masts, it was held up with a single pair of spreaders, in the manner of *Juno*'s, though she was a vessel of some seven times the displacement.

In Fig. 60 appear a number of metal mast sections for yachts of 80 ft. waterline to 18 ft. based on the big range of extrusions offered by Ian Proctor Metal Masts, Ltd.

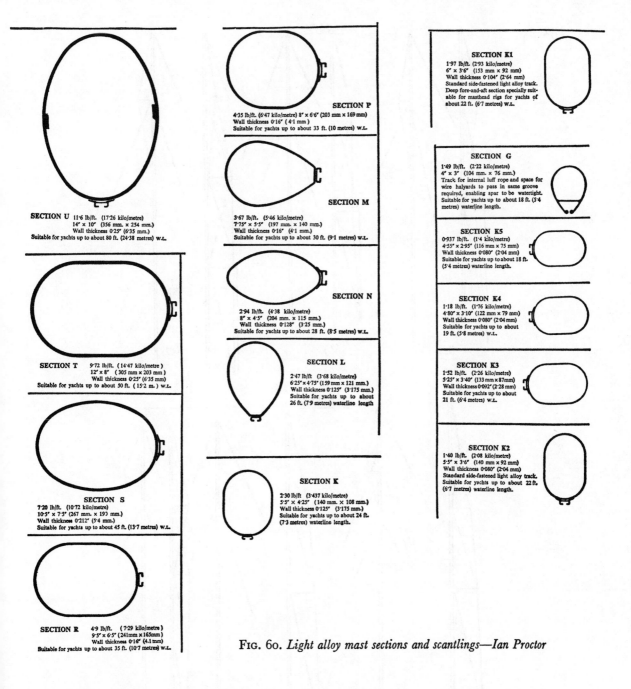

SECTION U 11·6 lb/ft. (17·26 kilo/metre)
14″ × 10″ (356 mm. × 254 mm.)
Wall thickness 0·25″ (6·35 mm.)
Suitable for yachts up to about 80 ft. (24·38 metres) w.l.

SECTION T 9·72 lb/ft. (14·47 kilo/metre)
12″ × 8″ (305 mm × 193 mm)
Wall thickness 0·25″ (6·35 mm)
Suitable for yachts up to about 50 ft. (15·2 m.) w.l.

SECTION S
7·20 lb/ft. (10·72 kilo/metre)
10·5″ × 7·5″ (267 mm. × 193 mm.)
Wall thickness 0·212″ (5·4 mm.)
Suitable for yachts up to about 45 ft. (13·7 metres) w.l.

SECTION R 4·9 lb/ft. (7·29 kilo/metre)
9·5″ × 6·5″ (241mm × 165mm)
Wall thickness 0·16″ (4·1mm)
Suitable for yachts up to about 35 ft. (10·7 metres) w.l.

SECTION P
4·35 lb/ft. (6·47 kilo/metre) 8″ × 6·6″ (203 mm × 169 mm)
Wall thickness 0·16″ (4·1 mm)
Suitable for yachts up to about 33 ft. (10 metres) w.l.

SECTION M
3·67 lb/ft. (5·46 kilo/metre)
7·75″ × 5·5″ (197 mm. × 140 mm.)
Wall thickness 0·16″ (4·1 mm.)
Suitable for yachts up to about 30 ft. (9·1 metres) w.l.

SECTION N
2·94 lb/ft. (4·38 kilo/metre)
8″ × 4·5″ (204 mm. × 115 mm.)
Wall thickness 0·128″ (3·25 mm.)
Suitable for yachts up to about 28 ft. (8·5 metres) w.l.

SECTION L
2·47 lb/ft (3·68 kilo/metre)
6·25″ × 4·75″ (159 mm × 121 mm.)
Wall thickness 0·125″ (3·175 mm.)
Suitable for yachts up to about
26 ft. (7·9 metres) waterline length

SECTION K
2·30 lb/ft. (3·437 kilo/metre)
5·5″ × 4·25″ (140 mm. × 108 mm.)
Wall thickness 0·125″ (3·175 mm.)
Suitable for yachts up to about 24 ft.
(7·3 metres) waterline length.

SECTION K1
1·97 lb/ft. (2·93 kilo/metre)
6″ × 3·6″ (153 mm × 92 mm)
Wall thickness 0·104″ (2·64 mm)
Standard side-fastened light alloy track.
Deep fore-and-aft section specially suitable for masthead rigs for yachts of about 22 ft. (6·7 metres) w.l.

SECTION G
1·49 lb/ft. (2·22 kilo/metre)
4″ × 3″ (104 mm. × 76 mm.)
Track for internal luff rope and space for wire halyards to pass in same groove required, enabling spar to be watertight. Suitable for yachts up to about 18 ft. (5·4 metres) waterline length.

SECTION K5
0·937 lb/ft. (1·4 kilo/metre)
4·55″ × 2·95″ (116 mm × 75 mm)
Wall thickness 0·080″ (2·04 mm)
Suitable for yachts up to about 18 ft. (5·4 metres) waterline length.

SECTION K4
1·18 lb/ft. (1·76 kilo/metre)
4·80″ × 3·10″ (122 mm × 79 mm)
Wall thickness 0·080″ (2·04 mm)
Suitable for yachts up to about 19 ft. (5·8 metres) w.l.

SECTION K3
1·52 lb/ft. (2·26 kilo/metre)
5·25″ × 3·40″ (133 mm × 87mm)
Wall thickness 0·092″ (2·28 mm)
Suitable for yachts up to about 21 ft. (6·4 metres) w.l.

SECTION K2
1·40 lb/ft. (2·08 kilo/metre)
5·5″ × 3·6″ (140 mm × 92 mm)
Wall thickness 0·080″ (2·04 mm)
Standard side-fastened light alloy track. Suitable for yachts up to about 22 ft. (6·7 metres) waterline length.

FIG. 60. *Light alloy mast sections and scantlings—Ian Proctor*

The waterline figures should, of course, be regarded as a guide only and related to the displacement when choosing a section.

BASIC STAYING ARRANGEMENTS The standing rigging arrangements illustrated in Fig. 61 are those found most generally suitable for the different sizes of sloops

SLOOPS.

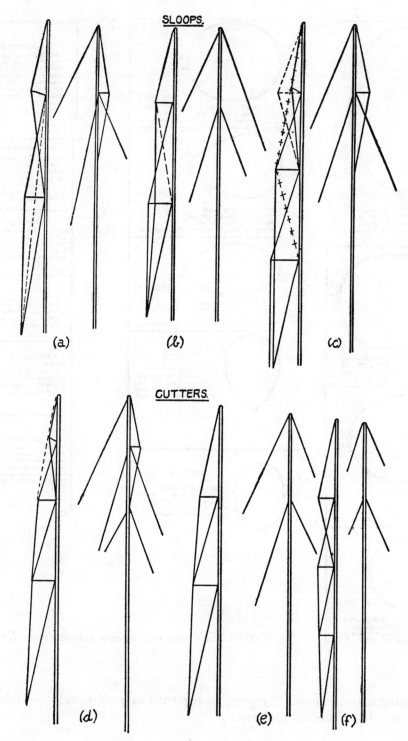

(a)   (b)   (c)

CUTTERS.

(d)   (e)   (f)

FIG. 61. *Basic staying arrangements*

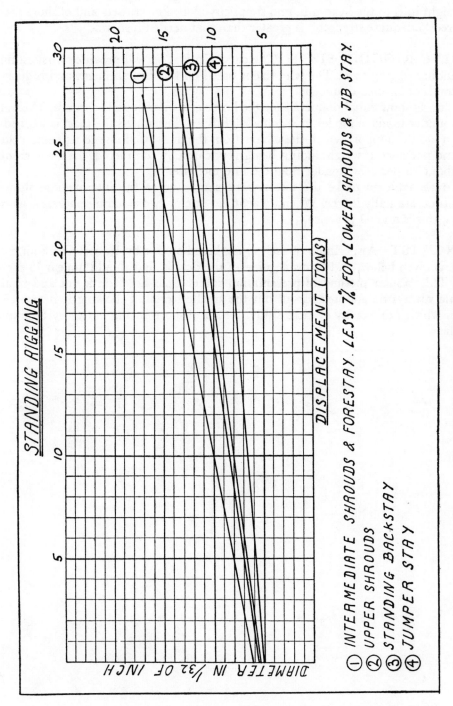

FIG. 62. *Guide to standing rigging sizes*

and cutters. The essence of the rigging problem is to get adequate strength, a straight track, straight luffs to the headsails, and simplicity aloft. For cruisers and offshore racers, the required "adequate strength" is greater than that needed inshore.

STANDING RIGGING SIZES The curves in Fig. 62 will provide a first estimate of the standing rigging sizes. The wire size is based on the displacement, and is given in thirty-seconds of an inch diameter.

The curves show equal diameters for the lower and intermediate shrouds. Theoretically it is sounder to make the lower shrouds slightly smaller, unless the mast is stepped on deck, owing to the support which these have from the mast itself due to its being held at the step and partners. If weight aloft is being very carefully considered, the lower shrouds may be about 10 per cent smaller than the intermediate.

It is reasonable to make the forestay the same size as the intermediate shrouds, though it is occasionally larger. When a yacht has one or two standing backstays as well as runners, this is a good practice.

RIGGING LIST A specimen of such a list, based on one by Robert Clark for a 15-ton ketch, is given below, and forms a guide to the details that should appear in such a schedule. This tabular method of presentation rather than notes on a sail and rigging plan should always be adopted for all but the smallest craft. Following it is a sail list, with notes which are worthy of close study, for an offshore racing cutter by Sparkman and Stephens.

TABLE 16

RIGGING SCHEDULE

15-TON AUXILIARY KETCH

Standing Rigging Main Mast

Description	No. off	Rope	Constr.	Circ. in.	Notes
Masthead Shroud	2	Stainless Steel	1×19	$1\frac{1}{8}$	Masthead strap to $\frac{9}{16}$-in. *rigging screw* at middle shroud plate.
Intermediate Shroud	2	Stainless Steel	1×19	$1\frac{1}{4}$	Upper crosstree strap to $\frac{5}{8}$-in. *rigging screw* at after shroud plate.
Lower Shroud	2	Stainless Steel	1×19	$1\frac{3}{8}$	Lower crosstree strap to $\frac{3}{4}$-in. *rigging screw* at forward shroud plate.
Permanent Backstay	1	Stainless Steel	1×19	$1\frac{1}{8}$	Masthead strap to $\frac{9}{16}$-in. *rigging screw* at deck.
Forestay	1	Stainless Steel	1×19	$1\frac{1}{8}$	Masthead strap to $\frac{9}{16}$-in. *rigging screw* at deck.
Inner Forestay	1	Stainless Steel	1×19	$1\frac{1}{4}$	Forestay strap to $\frac{5}{8}$-in. *rigging screw* at deck.
Runner	2	Stainless Steel	7×7	$1\frac{1}{4}$	Upper crosstree strap, lower end spliced to lower span.
Runner Lower Span	2	Galvd. Flex. Steel Wire	6×19	$1\frac{3}{8}$	Under runner sheave to runner lever.

Standing Rigging Mizzen Mast

Description	No. off	Rope	Constr.	Circ. in.	Notes
Masthead Shroud	2	Stainless Steel	1×19	$\frac{7}{8}$	Masthead strap to $\frac{7}{16}$-in. *rigging screw* at middle shroud plate.
Lower Shroud	2	Stainless Steel	1×19	$\frac{7}{8}$	Crosstree strap to $\frac{7}{16}$-in. *rigging screw* at after shroud plate.
Jumper Stay	1	Stainless Steel	1×19	$\frac{3}{4}$	Masthead strap to $\frac{3}{8}$-in. *rigging screw*.

Description	No. off	Rope	Constr.	Circ. in.	Notes
Forestay	2	Stainless Steel	1 × 19	¾	Forestay strap to ⅜-in. *rigging screw* at forward shroud plate.
Backstay	2	Stainless Steel	1 × 19	¾	Masthead strap to ½-in. screw slip hook. Davey 1384 to deckplate.

N.B.—Specify here the manufacturers of the wire rope, thimbles and rigging screws, adding any comments on the two latter or references to detail drawings.

Running Rigging Main

Description	No. off	Rope	Constr.	Circ. in.	Notes
Topping Lift	1	Galvd. Flex. Steel Wire	6 × 19	⅝	Shackle to boom end, over sheave in masthead to double block spliced in lower end for purchase, has shackle which slides on lower shroud.
Topping Lift Purchase	1	Terylene		1	Double block and wire part and single shackled to chain plate.
Main Halyard	1	Galvd. Flex. Steel Wire	6 × 19	⅝	Shackle for head of sail over masthead sheave, in length to turn up round winch when double reefed spliced to fall.
Fall	1	Terylene		1	Bitter end to swivel on small eye bolt.
Main Tack Purchase	1	Terylene		1	Single block with becket shackled to gooseneck slider, double block shackled to "K" eyeplate on mast above deck.
Main Sheet	1	Terylene		1½	Four part double ended.
Main Clew Outhaul	1	Galvd. Flex. Steel Wire	6 × 19	⅝	Eye splice to pin of outhaul slide over sheave in boom, block spliced to inner end for purchase.

Description	No. off	Rope	Constr.	Circ. in.	Notes
Purchase	1	Terylene		1	Single block with becket and sheave in cleat on boom.
Reef Pennant	2	Galvd. Flex. Steel Wire	6 × 19	$\frac{5}{8}$	Snap shackle to reef cringle, over sheave in boom, thimble in inner end for hook of double block and bow shackle for lashing 1st reef.
Purchase	1	Terylene		1	Double block on track and sheave in cleat under boom.
Lashing	1	Terylene		$\frac{3}{4}$	Spliced to lashing eye on boom to secure 1st reef.
Main Boom Fore-Guy	1	Galvd. Flex. Steel Wire	6 × 19	$\frac{1}{2}$	Outer end shackled to boom strap, large thimble in inner end for hook of purchase. Hambro' line tail for securing to boom.
Purchase	1	Terylene		1	Single and double blocks with hooks and foreguy spring.
Genoa Jib Halyard	1	Galvd. Flex. Steel Wire	6 × 19	$\frac{5}{8}$	Snap shackle for head of sail, through plate block on mast, spliced to fall.
Fall	1	Terylene		1	Long splice to wire. Bitter end in swivel.
Genoa Jib Tack Pennant	1	Galvd. Flex. Steel Wire	6 × 19	$\frac{5}{8}$	Spliced to tack. Snap shackle at lower end.
Genoa Jib Sheet	1 pr	Galvd. Flex. Steel Wire	6 × 19	$\frac{5}{8}$	Spliced to clew of sail, in length to turn up on winch.
Tail	1	Terylene		1	Long splice to wire.

Description	No. off	Rope	Constr.	Circ. in.	Notes
Staysail Halyards	2	Galvd. Flex. Steel Wire	6 × 19	$\frac{5}{8}$	Snap shackle for head of sail, through plate block on mast, in length to suit working staysail when turned up on winch.
Fall	2	Terylene		$1\frac{1}{4}$	Long splice to wire, bitter ends to swivels.
Halyard Span	1	Galvd. Flex. Steel Wire	6 × 19	$\frac{5}{8}$	Spliced to head of spitfire jib.
Staysail Tacks	2	Galvd. Flex. Steel Wire	6 × 19	$\frac{5}{8}$	Spliced to boom gooseneck and tack of spitfire jib, lower end to snap shackle, in length to suit sail plan.
Staysail Clew Outhaul	1	Galvd. Flex. Steel Wire	6 × 19	$\frac{5}{8}$	Shackle to clew of sail, over end of boom, block spliced to inner end for purchase.
Purchase	1	Terylene		1	Single block with becket and sheave on boom, forming three part purchase.
Working Staysail Sheet	1	Terylene		1	Spliced to bracket of block on traveller.
Spitfire Jib Sheet	1 pr	Galvd. Flex. Steel Wire	6 × 19	$\frac{5}{8}$	Spliced to clew of sail, in length to turn up on winch.
Tail	1	Terylene		1	Long splice to wire.
Burgee Halyard	1	Light Nylon			Through cheek block at mast head spliced double ended just short of dead length.

Running Rigging Mizzen

Description	No. off	Rope	Constr.	Circ. in.	Notes
Topping Lift	1	Galvd. Flex. Steel Wire	6 × 19	½	Shackle to boom end, through block at mast head. Thimble in lower end for fall.
Fall	1	Terylene		1	To belay on cleat.
Halyard	1	Galvd. Flex. Steel Wire	6 × 19	½	Shackle for head of sail, thimble in lower end for fall. Length for belaying on rope.
Fall	1	L.T. Italian		1	To belay on cleat.
Outhaul	1	Galvd. Flex. Steel Wire	6 × 19	½	Thimble for outhaul slide, over sheave, thimble for tail.
Tail	1	L.T. Italian		1	To belay on cleat.
Reef Pennant	1	Galvd. Flex. Steel Wire	6 × 19	½	Shackle to reef cringle, over sheave in boom, block spliced to inner end for purchase.
Purchase	1	Terylene		1	Single block on track and sheave under cleat on boom.
Mizzen Sheet	1	Terylene		1¼	Standing part at boom end, through double block on counter and single on boom strap.
Staysail Halyard	1	Galvd. Flex. Steel Wire	6 × 19	½	Snap shackle for head of sail, through swivel steel block on mast head, single block on lower end.
Fall	1	Terylene		1	Thimble for eye bolt on deck and through block on halyard to cleat.

Description	No. off	Rope	Constr.	Circ. in.	Notes
Staysail Tack Pennant	1	Galvd. Flex. Steel Wire	6 × 19	$\frac{1}{2}$	Spliced into tack of sail, snap shackle for deck plate.
Staysail Sheet	1	Terylene		$1\frac{1}{4}$	Whipped ends to hitch to sail.
Lazy Line	1	Hambro' Line			Rove through block at boom end to pull sheet through.
Burgee Halyard	1	Light Nylon			Through cheek block at mast head, spliced double ended just short of dead length.

N.B.—This schedule should be interpreted in accordance with best rigging practice and in particular the running rigging should be seamanlike and convenient for handling in normal yaching conditions. Shackles to be of "Tested" quality and to be of types and strengths suited to their respective purposes. Also such sundry items as may be required when installing and operating the ship's rigging fittings.

All halyards leading down mast to have bullseye fairleads at every mast band and wherever else necessary so placed as to ensure a fair lead at all times.

35. Carvel planking laid on bent timbers (D. Cheverton).

36. Cold moulded construction by Souter of Cowes.

37. *Feather III*, a cold-moulded Class III offshore racer by Illingworth and Primrose.

38. A 40 ft. waterline offshore racer of composite construction in frame. Each set of frame, floor and beam forms a complete unit, which is erected on the wooden keel, where it is held by the floor bolts and the overhead spur shores until the planking is laid.

TABLE 17

SAIL LIST AND NOTES FOR A 33-FT. L.W.L. 48-FT. L.O.A. OFFSHORE RACING CUTTER BY SPARKMAN AND STEPHENS INC.

	Material	Weight	Wind m.p.h.	Foot	Luff	Area	Remarks
Mainsail	Dacron	12	—				1″ 406A Mast Track 1″†406A Boom Track
Storm Trysail	Dacron	12	—	14′ 2″	18′ 0″	129	
Storm Staysail	Dacron	12	—	9′ 0″	23′ 0″	87	
Fore Staysail	Dacron	12	25·45	12′ 0″	33′ 2″	169	
No. 3 Jib Topsail	Dacron	12	33·40	13′ 2″	35′ 0″	168	
No. 2 Jib Topsail	Dacron	10	25·33	19′ 10″	46′ 0″	456	
26-ft. Genoa	Dacron	9	18·25	26′ 0″	46′ 0″	558	
RORC Heavy Genoa	Dacron	7	12·18	28′ 3″	52′ 0″	688	
RORC Light Genoa	Dacron	5	3·12	28′ 3″	53′ 0″	700	
Ballooner	Dacron	3·5	—	28′ 9″	53′ 0″	644	Sets Flying
Drifter	Dacron	2	0·3	28′ 4″	53′ 0″	682	Sets Flying
Spin Staysail	Nylon	1·5	—	24′ 0″	28′ 0″	370	
Heavy Spinnaker	Nylon	1·5	—	RO	RC	MAX	
Light Spinnaker	Nylon	1·0	—	RO	RC	MAX	
Storm Spinnaker	Nylon	2·0	—	RO	RC	—	Less Area in Head

* 408 Slides.   † 405 Slides.

GENERAL NOTES

1. Weight of material is ounces per yard U.S. standard width.
2. Dacron leech line on all Dacron Sails.   3. All headsail hanks to be side-pull type.
4. Extra heavy seizing on all slides and hanks.   5. Seizings on all luff slides to be hide-covered.
6. All batten pockets to be offset type with light ties.   7. Battens to be ash, tapered and varnished.
8. All sails to be marked at head with sail name, boat name and year.
9. All sail bags to be synthetic and marked in three places like sails.
10. Allowance to be made in leech dimensions of Genoas so clew height will be as indicated when sail is properly trimmed.
11. All sails to be Dacron unless otherwise noted.   12. Shape of leech to be responsibility of sailmaker.

L

CHAPTER ELEVEN

Construction

IT IS impossible to deal with the intricacies of construction in a small space. The difference between good and bad construction is so much a matter of detailed design and good workmanship that even a full treatise on building methods is only valuable when associated with a practical knowledge of the subject. Some designers give extremely full specifications, going even into such details as precisely how the annular rings should run in the laid planking. Such refinements in specification are not necessary with a good builder and probably will not be much regarded by the indifferent; but the value of full specifications lies in the cover they give to the architect and the evidence that they provide should arguments arise.

Yachts now represent a bigger proportion of their owners' capital than hitherto, and as their investment value grows so does the need for guarding against capital depreciation. For this purpose classification by Lloyd's is valuable. A classed boat is in a strong position on the market.

In the years before the Second World War Lloyd's Rules for scantlings and construction were obsolescent owing to developments that had taken place in constructional techniques. They demanded very heavy scantlings unsuitable for the modern relatively light displacement yacht, and methods of construction that had come into use were unacceptable to the Society. It was arranged at a meeting of the Technical Sub-Committee of the then Y.R.A. in April 1948 that Lloyd's should prepare revised scantling tables based on the principle of a general reduction in the Society's requirements. Early in 1949 the proposed new code was circulated for comment, and in 1950 the new rules, applicable to yachts not exceeding about 60 ft. in waterline length were published. Figs. 63(a), (b) and (c) show the order of the reductions in scantling sizes made at that time for side and deck planking, stringers and shelves and for the spacing of bent frames. (See below for the calculation of the transverse and longitudinal numerals.) Further amendments have been made in the 1954 and 1957 editions of the rules. For example, the use of all bent timber framing is now permitted up to a transverse numeral of 18, which means that whereas under the pre-war, or "A", rules all bent timbers were allowed only in boats of up to about 25 ft. waterline they are now permitted up to a size of about 40 ft. waterline.

The amended Lloyd's rules as they stand today are the best available general guide in existence to scantlings and constructional methods, based on fuller data and more scientific analysis than any single architect can accumulate or digest, and methods of construction not covered in the tabulated rules of the Society will always receive individual attention if submitted. However, experience is being gained so rapidly in the techniques of small yacht construction that already the latest Lloyd's rules could do with revision and a broadening of basic concepts.

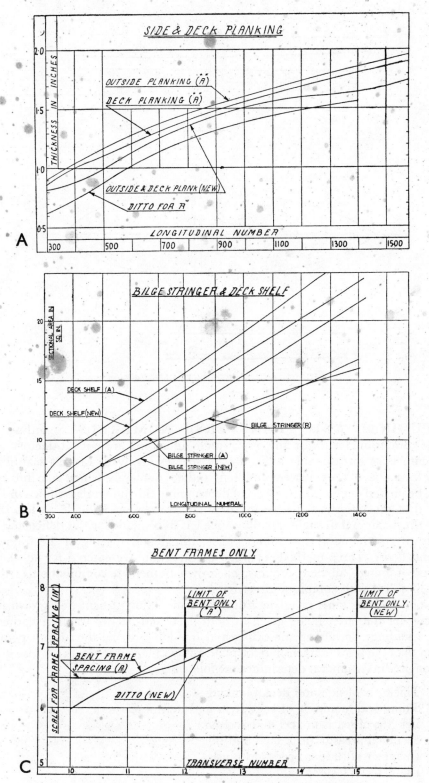

FIG. 63. *Comparison of Lloyd's old and new scantlings*

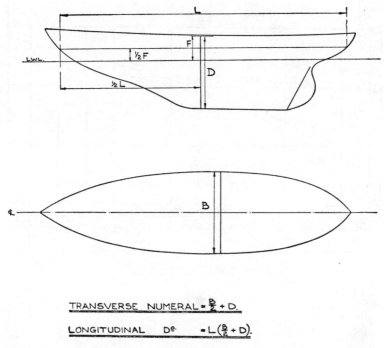

FIG. 64. *Derivation of Lloyd's numerals*

LONGITUDINAL AND TRANSVERSE NUMERALS Scantling tables based on the waterline length or any other single dimension are not satisfactory, no one measurement being a reasonable indication of stresses involved. Lloyd's scantlings are decided by the values of the transverse and longitudinal numerals, which take into account the length, beam and depth. The method of determining the numerals is shown in Fig. 64. When the draught amidships, where the depth measurement is made, is less than 90 per cent of the maximum draught, an allowance has to be made for this deficiency.

The transverse numeral determines the scantlings and spacing of the frames, side stringers and floors. Three methods of wood construction are catered for in the table which covers framing—all bent timbers, all grown timbers, a combination of the two separate tables deal with composite construction.

The wood-framing table gives the siding and moulding of bent and grown frames, the scantlings for the latter being given at both head and heel of frame. Another table gives floor scantlings, specifying the siding and moulding at the throat and point, and also the length of the arms. Dimensions for plate and wrought-iron floors are also given.

The longitudinal numeral determines the following:

  (i) Thickness of side and deck planking.
 (ii) Siding and moulding of keel, stem and sternpost.
(iii) Lengths of scarfs in keel and keelson.
 (iv) Sectional areas of deck shelf and bilge stringer.
  (v) Diameter of rudder head and pintles.
 (vi) Diameter of fastenings.

Important features not covered by the numerals are the deck beam sizes and the plank fastenings. The former are based on the maximum length of beam, the siding and moulding being given at the centre and ends. Beams have to be of the scantling indicated for three-fifths of the rule length, but at the ends the moulding and siding in the middle of the beams may be reduced to equality with that at their ends. The fastenings in the side planking are governed by the width and thickness of planking.

Except in the smallest sizes, Lloyd's require a bilge stringer. In the present rules the highest longitudinal numeral allowed to omit this member is 500. It seems doubtful whether bilge stringers, in spite of a traditional prejudice in their favour, are worth their weight except in shoal-draught yachts designed to take the ground regularly. The stringer tends to follow the line of the yacht's neutral axis, with the result that its effect on longitudinal strength is slight. The weight is better disposed in the planking, keel and deck shelf, which are the highly stressed parts of the girder. On the other hand, a short stringer running over the bow frames, and sloping downwards from the shelf in the region of the mast towards the waterline at the stem, is a valuable strength member, giving support to the forward frames and planking, which take so much punishment when a yacht is driven hard to windward.

A yacht having scantlings up to Lloyd's requirements may retain her class, subject to periodic surveys, for a certain number of years depending on the materials used in her construction. If the surveys are satisfactory, the original term of years may be extended at the end of the first period.

The main influence on the initial length of period is the timber used in the hull, and the term of years depends on the lowest grade of timber used. Teak has the longest life, and when the main parts of the structure, designated in the rules, are of this timber, a term of sixteen years is allowed. Pitch or Oregon pine planking reduces the life to ten years. Mahogany is allowed twelve years. If American rock elm is used for the keel the term is reduced to fourteen years, whilst oak in this position is allowed twelve years only.

Yachts built under a roof may have one year added to the prescribed period, and copper or naval brass fastenings allow extensions of up to three years. A teak yacht, wholly copper-fastened, and built under a roof, may therefore gain a period of eighteen years.

Teak is a sometimes brittle and virtually rot-proof timber ideal for most parts of a yacht's structure so long as weight and expense are unimportant. Unfortunately pitch-pine, which is an excellent substitute for teak planking, and ideal for the longitudinal strength members such as deck shelves, clamps, stringers, is not available.

The substitutes for pitch-pine are Oregon or Columbian pine (Douglas fir), and larch. Good larch is probably better than Oregon, but bad larch is definitely inferior. Oregon is an unstable timber and prone to rot in enclosed spaces, but if an initially sound wood is used, and it is well cared for, it can give good service. It can also make satisfactory planking. It may be used in the absence of spruce for masts. The respective weights are 37 lb. and 27 lb. per cu. ft. In the absence of pitch-pine, Oregon is much used today even on first-class work, and before the war many excellently built Scandinavian yachts were planked in this wood.

English elm has the advantage of cheapness, and may be used in place of oak for the keel. It must not be placed where it is subject to alternate wetness and dryness; but where large pieces are needed in the deadwood or false keel it has the advantage over oak in not developing the large cracks to which oak of large scantling is prone. Canadian rock elm is the best of the elms, but it is expensive.

Mahogany has always been a popular planking material for yachts. Honduras, and the mahogany from Central America, is the best. African mahogany is good though rather less durable, and Spanish mahogany is suitable for yacht work. Mahogany is slightly lighter than pitch-pine, but generally heavier than Oregon.

The timbers available in the Scandinavias, the U.S.A., Australia and New Zealand are numerous, and the above brief survey applies to England only.

The kiln-drying of timber, in place of natural seasoning, is common today, occupying as it does about three weeks compared with as many years when the wood is stacked for drying. If well done, kiln-drying appears to be as effective as air seasoning. The use of Cuprinol, or a similar preservative, is also general today, and seems effective in preventing rot if painted on the wood during construction.

Opposite is an example of the calculation of the Transverse and Longitudinal numerals and the Grading Numbers.

TIMBER AND GLUE Timber is, in Europe, still the usual material for building seagoing yachts of between 20–50 ft. on the waterline. Moreover, many of the woods used and the methods of handling them are still much as they were in 1930 or earlier. Within the framework of a continuing tradition two principal changes have occurred: firstly, the sizes of scantlings of the parts that form a yacht's structure are now, as we have seen, appreciably smaller than they used to be, which is due less to technical advance than to experience revealing that scantlings were once unnecessarily heavy. Now perhaps we err in the other direction. Secondly, the invention of waterproof glues has led to the wide use of laminations and, for the panel members in the structure, to that specialised type of lamination which is plywood.

In an age of technological revolution the continued use of wood for building the majority of yachts may appear reactionary until it is appreciated that it remains one of the most wonderful structural materials known to man. English oak, for example, may have a higher strength-weight ratio than mild steel or light alloy, and a reinforced plastic must have three times the strength of African mahogany to attain the latter's strength-weight ratio.

Timber suffers from faults. Nature designed it mainly to withstand the wind-loading on trees in leaf, and supplied it with great strength in the necessary direction but very little at right angles to it. This disadvantage may now be offset by the use of laminations and plywood. Secondly, it suffers from rot, sapwood, loose knots, resin pockets, shakes and other faults. The use of laminations or preservatives against rot and improved techniques of ventilation have done much to modify these faults. Certain good timbers have become unobtainable after so many generations of man ransacking the forests of his world, but here again plywoods and laminations have come to the rescue.

In fact, we come back to waterproof glue as the most vital development that has occurred during the last century in the technique of boatbuilding in wood. We have passed through the long era of fish glues, through the briefer reign of casein, when it was sometimes claimed to have qualities which it emphatically does not, to the day of the synthetic resins in the phenol group, together with which should be mentioned the urea and resorcinol groups, the former simple to use, the latter with exceptional qualities,

L.O.A.	40·90 ft.
L.B.P.	37 ft.
L.W.L.	32 ft.
Beam	11 ft.
Draught	6·25 ft.
Sail/Area	700 sq. ft.
Displacement	11·02 tons
Outside Ballast Keel	4·5 tons
T.M.	17·00 tons

Dimensions for Scantlings

Length	36·8 ft.
Freeboard (amids)	3·2 ft.
Breadth (beam)	11·0 ft.
Depth (D)	$3·2 + 5·1 = 8·3$ ft.
Transverse Numeral	$= \dfrac{11}{2} + \dfrac{8\cdot3}{10} = 13·80$
Longitudinal Numeral	$= 36·8 \times 13·8 = 508·64$

Grading of Materials

Stringers	Larch	12
Shelf	Larch	12
Beams	Larch	12
Floors	Oak	
	and laminated C.R.E.	24
Timbers	Oak	24
Deadwoods	Oak and Elm	24
Stem	Teak	48
Sternpost	Teak	48
Mainkeel	English Oak or Elm	36
Deck	Teak	64
Planking (Upper)	Teak	64
(Lower)	Teak	64

Total	=	432
Divisor	(=30) =	14·12/30
Add, for Copper fastenings		3·00
Add (built under roof)		1·00
Final Grading Number		18·12/30

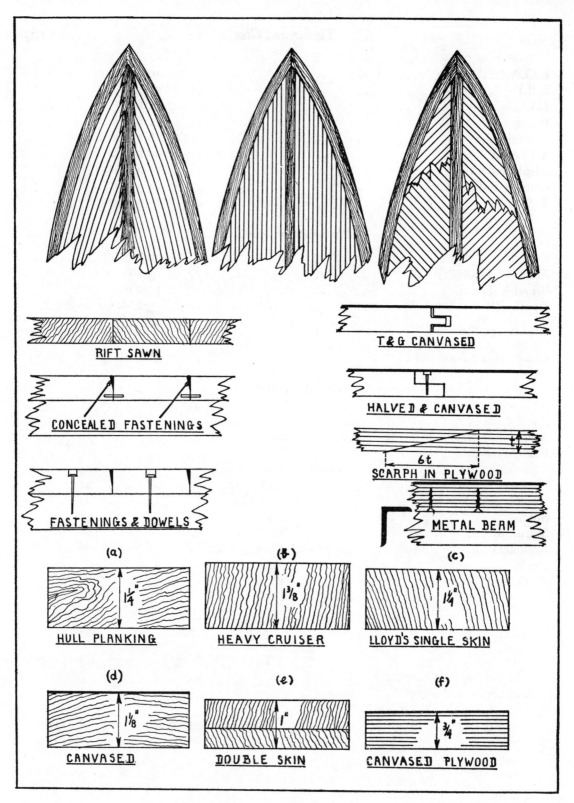

RIFT SAWN

T&G CANVASED

CONCEALED FASTENINGS

HALVED & CANVASED

FASTENINGS & DOWELS

SCARPH IN PLYWOOD

METAL BEAM

(a)

(b)

(c)

HULL PLANKING

HEAVY CRUISER

LLOYD'S SINGLE SKIN

(d)

(e)

(f)

CANVASED

DOUBLE SKIN

CANVASED PLYWOOD

FIG. 65. *Some layings of decks*

but needing a high temperature—about 60 to 80 degrees while setting—and very expensive. It is not too much to say that the day of fastenings by means of bolts, nails and screws is passing. Already there are boats held together by nothing but glue, notably a highly stressed 50-knot planing vessel, by Vosper, which has voyaged extensively in European waters.

So it seems appropriate to consider plywoods and laminations first. We are not going to concern ourselves here with chine hulls, and since plywood is a single sheet and cannot be applied to surfaces with more than a slight amount of compound curvature its use becomes mainly for those two important constructional features, decks and bulkheads. Boatbuilders have always been looking for something in the nature of plywood, which is unlike natural timber in being nearly isotropic and hence suitable for panel members, and before there was any suitable glue available for its manufacture S. E. Saunders, of Cowes, made plywood at the end of the last century by stitching layers of wood together with wire or twine. This was used in high-speed craft and flying-boats. Modern plywood is made from veneers peeled off the log by a large knife—rather like opening one of the Dead Sea scrolls. The "peelings" then go through various processes in which faults are removed and the water content reduced and made constant for all of them. Plywood is made of an odd number of veneers—that is, even numbers on either side of a core—and adjacent veneers have their grains running at right angles. They are then glued together in hydraulic presses at suitable temperature and pressure.

The resulting boards have a strength approximately equal to the average between the strength of the natural timber of which it is made measured along and across the grain. It is stronger than a double-skin bulkhead of the same timber and thickness and fastened by many nails but not glued, this presumably being because in the latter case there is an appreciable amount of slip between the layers however many the fastenings. Also, the strength of timber increases as the moisture content is reduced, and the careful control of the moisture in the best plywoods assures good strength.

Plywood, like the dog given a bad name, has still not wholly recovered from its wartime failures, when imperfectly prepared veneers and perhaps hurried gluing led to it failing, especially when placed in the bilges. The well-known B.S.S. 1088 plywood—a number now as well known to the boatbuilder as 1066—appears up to date to have withstood every test, including that of being boiled, which it must be capable of withstanding for a period of six hours. Though boats are more likely to be frozen than boiled, this stringent test is a comfort. On the other hand, plywood has been known to fracture under a sudden load when a double diagonal bulkhead would have survived.

SIDE PLANKING The side planking is the greatest single weight in a yacht's structure, amounting to about 15 per cent of the total weight of a bare and unballasted wood hull, and about $6\frac{1}{2}$ per cent of that of the completed yacht. Today, acceptable plank thicknesses are appreciably less than were usual some ten years before the war; for example, $1\frac{3}{16}$-in. planking may now be used where $1\frac{5}{16}$-in. timber was then usual, 1-in. wood replaces $1\frac{3}{16}$-in., and $1\frac{1}{2}$-in. that of $1\frac{11}{16}$-in. Such figures are approximate, but serve to indicate the saving in weight now achieved. Planking thickness will vary with the closeness of the timbering, and some designers favour thicker planking with greater frame spacing.

When weight is an urgent consideration the advantages of teak-bottom planking may be associated with mahogany topsides, which will give a saving of about 14 per cent in the weight of the side planking; but this will amount to only about 1 per cent of the total weight of the yacht, which seems hardly worth the sacrifice of teak topsides.

Double-skin planking is a more profitable means of saving weight, the inner skin in sailing craft being laid diagonally and the outer fore and aft. The same method may be used in the faster types of motor craft and in fully planing chine hulls, though the planking in the latter will be double diagonal. With double-skin construction Lloyd's allow a 10 per cent reduction in plank thickness. The skins too may be of differing timbers, say teak outer and mahogany inner, or teak and Canadian rock elm inner.

Double-skin construction is a step towards the cold-moulded hull whose planking consists of layers of plywood laid diagonally with gap-filling glue between them upon a wooden mould of the hull. This form of construction was adopted in the Illingworth and Primrose *Blue Charm*, built by Souters of Cowes, and these designers and builders have since developed the system. In *Blue Charm* the planking consisted of four skins of 3-millimetre plywood laid diagonally and bonded with resorcinol glue, making a total thickness of about $\frac{1}{2}$ in.

The advantages of lightness and watertightness gained by this method are considerable, and the former may be suggested by some figures published by Commander Peter Du Cane derived from experiments made by Messrs. Vosper some years ago. A test panel 2 ft. 6 in. square of double-skin mahogany, total thickness of 1 in., was tested under load against a similar panel of two skins of three-ply gaboon, total thickness $\frac{3}{4}$ in. The latter panel saved 26 per cent in weight compared with the mahogany, its deflection under load was only 55 per cent, and it broke under a load of 2,000 lb. compared with 2,100 lb. for the double-skin mahogany. We may expect the cold-moulding process to be widely used in the future.

Also the hot moulding, as used by Fairey Marine, in which hulls are made of veneers, resin-bonded, and baked under pressure in an autoclave. This is a method of construction peculiarly suited to the high-speed runabouts now becoming so popular, which at high speeds are encountering great stresses. Such hulls are completely watertight and have considerable resistance to rot and marine borers. The 28-ft. Huntsman type of fast launch by Fairey has bottom planking of seven laminations giving a total thickness of $\frac{3}{4}$ in., and topside of six laminations totalling $\frac{3}{8}$ in. At present this method of construction appears to be more expensive than either cold-moulding or orthodox carvel construction, but we may expect it to be applied to bigger boats in the future.

Still, however, it is the classical planking that is most usually employed in seagoing yachts, both power and sail. This may now be close-seamed, a variant of the more common practice of splining, the plank edges not being angled for caulking but laid in close contact with their edges glued. This can produce an unusually high finish, and when well done the planking virtually becomes a leak-proof solid mass. Indeed its very solidity may cause trouble, for the alternate swelling and shrinkage of the planking produce high stresses which the glued joint, unlike caulking, is unable to relieve, and cracks may result. This does not appear to occur in our kind of climate, but one European yard which specialises in close-seamed work does not now use it in yachts that are to be exported to hot climates. Also, the method is liable to be unsatisfactory with teak planking, owing to the difficulty of making good glued joints with teak; and with any timber the work is expensive, for it takes longer to plank with close-seams owing to the need for each plank joint to set before adding the next strake.

DECKS The beauty of the shipwright's craft is nowhere so fully revealed as in a deck built of narrow planks, laid to the curve of the rail, and then caulked and paid. Apart from their beauty such decks have a certain structural logic in modern yachts with big cockpits, long and wide coachroofs, large forehatches, and with the coach coamings sprung to the curve of the yacht's side. Laid planking may then be conveniently run over the narrow side decks and the small areas of decking forward and aft (Fig. 65).

The disadvantages of the laid deck in small craft are its expense, its weight, and formerly its thinness, and the need it has of regular attention if it is to remain watertight. In the past, unless a deck of this type was at least $1\frac{3}{4}$ in. in thickness, leaks were almost inevitable owing to springy seams and lack of depth for the caulking; which means, assuming normal scantlings, that they were suspect in boats of less than about 15 tons T.M. Today this disadvantage has been obviated by laying the teak planks on plywood and screw fastening from below. There is, as hitherto, the danger of water penetrating between the teak and plywood; but adequate screwing and the use of gap-filling glue between the layers obviates this.

There are a variety of ways in which decks may be laid. In the prettiest system the planks are narrow and sprung to the curve of the covering board. The planks may be tapered slightly fore and aft, and their ends are notched into the king plank (Fig. 65). As a variant on this system the planks may be more heavily tapered, the outer ones following the curve of the covering board and the planks progressively slackening in their amount of curvature as they approach the king plank, where they are straight. A method which is a combination of the two above, is sometimes seen, the inner planks being notched into the king plank, whilst the outer ones have a progressively slackening curve and run out into the covering board.

Decks of these types have to be laid in narrow planks, say $2\frac{1}{4}$ in. $\times$ $1\frac{1}{4}$ in., but the cheaper form of laid deck is run with straight and relatively wide planks, sawn parallel, and notched or simply butted into the covering board. In power craft with heavy curvature in the deckline at bow and stern, this is the usual system of laying the deck, and it is often adopted in sailing craft also. However the planks are laid, rift-sawn timber should be used for decking, having the grain in the planks running nearly vertically or at the worst at no more than 45 degrees from the vertical, this ensuring even wearing of the deck and obviating splinters.

The fastening of laid decks may be fully concealed, the planks being fastened by nails set at an angle through their edges, and with metal dowels connecting adjacent planks between the frames. Alternatively, planks may have vertical fastenings countersunk into the wood, with wooden dowels covering the heads. This is a less exquisite, though cheaper and probably stronger, method of fastening.

It used to be considered good practice in seagoing yachts for decks of unprotected wood to be about 10 per cent heavier than the side planking, this allowing for normal wear and periodic scraping. The earlier editions of Lloyd's rules were criticised for allowing decks to be thinner than the side planking. In their current rules decks are specified to be equal in thickness to the hull planking, and this we will accept as our norm in comparison with which the thickness of other types of decks may be considered.

Various constructions of deck are shown in Fig. 65(*a*) to (*f*) and their relative thickness compared, assuming, in each case, similar hull constructions and beam spacing. Any such comparisons are general, and amenable to modification in particular cases. Decks may be teak, isoko, Oregon or Columbian pine, larch, spruce or cedar, and many other woods. Lloyd's Rules take into consideration the kinds of materials employed in the construction, and the scantlings given in the Tables are based on the standard weights of materials as described in the text for the various members of the construction. Therefore, approved material of less or greater weight will be accepted subject to the scantlings being increased or decreased as the case may be. Any decrease is, however, limited to a maximum of 6 per cent of the Table siding or thickness, except for teak decks weighing more than 45 lb. per cu. ft., where a reduction of 12 per cent is permissible.

An alternative to a laid and paid deck is one of tongued-and-grooved planking covered with canvas or plastic compound. The planks are laid straight, and it is important that the tongues should not be driven hard into the grooves, a small allowance being made for swelling. The method of laying the canvas on the wood may follow one of two principles. The usual system is to lay it on wet paint, which preserves wood and canvas and gives a certain adhesion between the two without forming a too rigid bond. A less common method is to lay the canvas dry upon already painted wood, or sometimes upon unpainted wood. It is claimed that this, allowing as it does free movement between the wood and canvas, gives a longer life to the latter, preventing the development of cracks and the loss of watertightness. A system which should never be adopted is to make a rigid bond between the wood and canvas by means of glue or cement. Cracks will then certainly develop, whilst renewal of the deck canvas will probably entail a new deck also. When it is considered that visible wrinkles sometimes appear in the deck canvas of the more lightly built racing yachts when straining in a seaway, the nature of the stresses to which a rigid deck canvas may be subjected can be visualised.

A canvassed or plastics covered deck may be thinner than one of uncovered wood. Lloyd's allow a uniform reduction of $\frac{1}{8}$ in. below their normal specified thickness. If we consider a boat having outside planking of $1\frac{1}{4}$ in., Lloyd's require a normal, single-skin deck to be also of $1\frac{1}{4}$ in. thickness. For a really hard-working cruiser we might have a thickness of $1\frac{3}{8}$ in., while a canvassed or plastics covered deck may be $1\frac{1}{8}$ in. It is a common practice, however, to make greater reductions in the thickness of covered decks than that allowed by Lloyd's. Covered decks of $\frac{3}{4}$ in. are associated with 1 in. thick outside planking, or 1 in. decks with $1\frac{1}{4}$ in. planking. At the other end of the range there are yachts with covered decks equal in thickness to the side planking. The choice of scantlings is still partly an art, a matter of the proportioning of the structure with due regard to the precise nature of the wood used and to the purpose of the boat.

Double-skin decks, like hull planking of this nature, have certain advantages. They are lighter and of more certain watertightness than those of a single thickness. They may be laid on the double diagonal system (Fig. 65) or the upper skin may be laid fore and aft. If the upper planks are sprung to the curve of the yacht's side and lightly caulked the beauty of a laid deck is effectively imitated. But the possibility of leaks in the outer planks is seriously increased by this method, and it is a danger which has to be guarded against by good workmanship in all double-skin decks. A leak of this nature may pass undetected for a considerable time and cause severe rotting between the skins.

Various combinations of woods may be used in double-skin decks. When Claud Worth built *Tern III* in 1914 he used $1\frac{5}{8}$ in. pitch-pine for the lower layer with $\frac{1}{4}$ in. spruce laid in a mixture of white lead and varnish on top. The usual practice, however, is for the

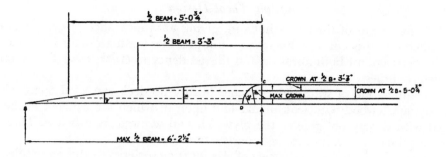

FIG. 66. *Laying off a deck camber curve*

top skin to be of about 60 per cent of the deck's total thickness to allow for wear. Teak and cedar may be used to produce a deck combining beauty and lightness and Western red cedar, which has a tensile strength equal to mahogany whilst weighing only 22 lb., may have isoko laid over it. The skins may be glued together, or more usually have calico laid in varnish or white lead between them.

The thickness of double-skin decks may be reduced below the normal. Laid decks lack homogeneity, being held together simply by the deck beams and fastenings. Double-skin decks have inherent homogeneity and may reasonably be 15 per cent thinner than a single skin, uncanvassed deck. A greater reduction is sometimes made. A saving in weight, an increase in strength, and a better guarantee against leaks are thus offered by decks of this nature.

Plywood decks are now very common, and may be laid almost like those of model yachts, in one piece even in large craft, the scarf in the plywood sheet being made by the manufacturers of the wood. When making scarfs in plywood, their lengths should be about six times the thickness of the wood, and the joints secured by gluing under pressure and screwing (Fig. 65).

The obvious advantage of a plywood deck is its comparative freedom from leaks, though this is impaired when holes for prismatic decklights are cut through it. Indeed, the difficulty of keeping decklights tight, which is chiefly due to the different expansions of the wood and the metal frames, makes a strong argument against this convenient and efficient form of natural lighting.

Phenolic resin-bonded plywood of the correct specification for external marine use has, too, shown itself apparently to be free from dangers of delamination and dry-rot. Owing to the considerable weight of the glue plywood is heavier than the same thickness of natural timber, but apart from any reduction in deck thickness which the use of plywood may allow, there is a further saving in the under-deck construction. The properties of plywood as a rigid panel giving strength athwartships equal to that fore and aft, allow a reduction in the weight and number of lodging knees; some designers are prepared to eliminate them altogether.

For decks the wood used will usually be of seven- or nine-ply. In principle, the covering of plywood decks is a redundancy, and they need simply to be painted; in practice, canvas or plastic compound is generally used. From the point of view of wear a thick surface veneer is an advantage; but it tends to crack or split, particularly if a deck is exposed for any length of time to a hot sun, giving an appearance of delamination. A thinner surface veneer is not so liable to split, but provides less margin for wear. Covering protects the deck against both abrasion and this tendency to crack, though it is unnecessary for watertightness.

For a combination of watertightness and beauty no deck can rival one of double-skin embodying plywood with teak planks laid upon it, which are caulked in the usual way, glued with waterproof glue to the plywood, and screwed from below. These have now become quite common in first-class construction.

There is still a reluctance on the part of classification societies to allow any substantial reduction in plywood decks as compared with those of natural timber, which results in yachts built to rules sailing with decks perhaps 20 per cent heavier than they need be.

Plywood also enables much simplified underdeck framing to be used. The following comparison is revealing. A yacht of 26 tons T.M. built shortly after the war has $1\frac{1}{2}$ in. laid decking. A more recent yacht of 32 tons had a deck of $\frac{3}{4}$ in. plywood, plastics covered. The weight of the former was 1,240 lb., of the latter 1,000 lb. The underdeck framing of the laid deck included tie-rods, brace straps and twenty-five lodging knees, necessary to restrain the laid deck from working. These were eliminated with the plywood deck giving a saving of 420 lb. Between the two yachts, the saving of weight in deck and framing was thus rather more than one-quarter of a ton, and had both craft been of the same dimensions it would have been about half-a-ton.

FRAMES   There are more diverse opinions on how a yacht should be framed than about any other aspect of construction. Except for the larger yachts, composite construction is not much considered today, though before the war several types of boat, even as light as 30 sq. metres, had their planking laid on bronze frames, and the combination of stainless steel main frames with intermediate bent timbers may be used today in yachts of 30 tons T.M. or so—but not often. Soon after the war it seemed that light alloy was going to provide the ideal material for composite construction in the new way, but one only, I think, experiment in the yachting fleet of Britain was enough to crush that idea owing to the quaint behaviour of the alloy. Now, in wooden craft, framing methods may be (i) All bent; (ii) All grown; (iii) A combination of (i) and (ii); (iv) All laminated; (v) A combination of bent and laminated; (vi) Composite. If we add to this the various proportions of moulding to siding that may be chosen for frames, and the frame spacing in relation to the plank thickness, we have a wide range for choice and disagreement.

Opinions may range between that of Alfred Mylne, who said: "We should not go above (say) 20 ft. waterline with bent timber construction . . ." to a Canadian architect of experience who wrote: "There should be no restriction on the use of bent timber construction. Herreshoff built 110 ft. steam yachts in this way, without a single grown frame, which lasted over thirty years. The combination of grown and bent frames is about as bad as anything I know of. The stiff grown members are stress concentrators which usually break up within a few years."

In these two statements we have epitomised the English and the Transatlantic points of view. On the west coast of the U.S.A., for example, and in Australia, grown frames are now little used in fishing-boats, nor laminated owing to the expense, and vessels of up to 125 ft. have all bent timbers. Olof Traung, Editor of *Fishing Boats of the World*, Vols. 1 and 2, and Chief of the U.N.O. Fishing Boat Division, has said that he personally had

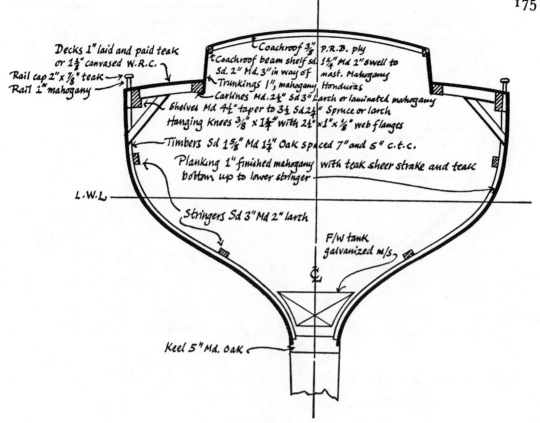

Decks 1" laid and paid teak
or 1¼" canvased W.R.C.
Rail cap 2" x ⅞" teak
Rail 1" mahogany

Coachroof ⅜" P.R.B. ply
Coachroof beam shelf sd. 1½" Md 2" swell to
Sd. 2" Md. 3" in way of mast. Mahogany
Trunkings 1", mahogany Honduras
Carlines Md. 2¼" Sd 3" Larch or laminated mahogany
Shelves Md 4¼" taper to 3¼ Sd 2¼" Spruce or larch
Hanging Knees ⅜" x 1¾" with 2¼" x 1" x ⅛" web flanges
Timbers Sd 1⅝" Md 1¼" Oak spaced 7" and 5" c.t.c.
Planking 1" finished mahogany with teak sheer strake and teak
bottom up to lower stringer

L.W.L.

Stringers Sd 3" Md 2" larch

F/W tank
galvanized m/s

Keel 5" Md. Oak

FIG. 67. *Scantling section for a steel hull by Alan Buchanan*

only in the last ten years come to the conclusion that all bent timber construction was stronger and longer-lived than planking laid on grown frames. Yet in the Scottish motor fishing vessels, which are acknowledged as the best designed and constructed in the world, loyalty to grown frames remains, and this is reflected in our prejudices in yacht construction. Lloyd's have marched with steady steps towards a recognition of all bent timbers as an admirable method of construction, and while in 1939 they would not allow yachts with a longitudinal numeral of more than 12 to be constructed, in the present rules the numeral stands at 18. The numeral values correspond to yachts of say 22 ft. waterline, 28 ft. overall, and 40 ft. waterline, 60 ft. overall.

In this matter both points of view have to be treated with respect. A frame is both a tie holding carvel planking together (which steamed timbers are admirably fitted to do) and a girder retaining the shape of the planking (for which grown or laminated frames are excellent). On the other hand, a grown frame of badly fastened futtocks with faultily grained timber in it is no less good as a girder than a cracked steamed timber is as a tie. And an uncracked timber of suitably proportioned moulding and siding will be a better

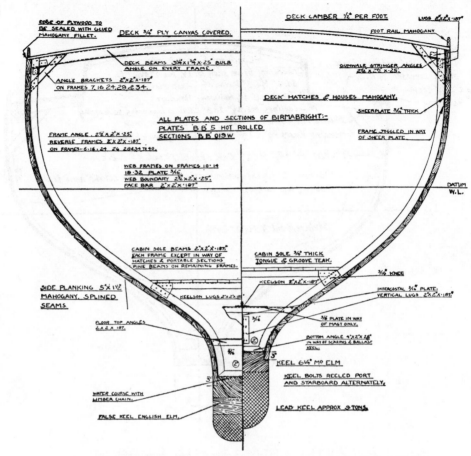

Fig. 68. *Scantling sections of alloy composite ocean racer by Robert Clark*

girder than a bad grown frame. It all comes back to a matter of proportion, of ultimate strength and of the relative importance attached in a frame of timber to the function of tie or girder. Of one thing at least we may be certain, but nobody has yet devised the way of calculating it: if either is going to fail under stress, then both framing and planking should fail simultaneously; the parts are wrongly designed if one gives way before the other.

STEEL CONSTRUCTION The Dutch began to build small craft in steel during the last quarter of the nineteenth century and soon developed a unique proficiency in the work. After several generations of building small steel barges and fishing vessels, steel motor yachts began to appear, soon after 1918. But it was not until the development of welding that small steel sailing yachts became practicable. Welding, by eliminating the laps and rivet heads, and allowing frames to be toe-welded to the plating and thereby develop higher strength and enable a reduction in scantlings to be made, gave enough

39 & 40. Pouring and subsequently transporting a lead keel. Slots for the trimming chocks will be noted in the lower illustration.

41. I.Y.R.U. 5·5-Metre *Yeoman XII*. Note that the wave formation extends to the extreme of the long counter.

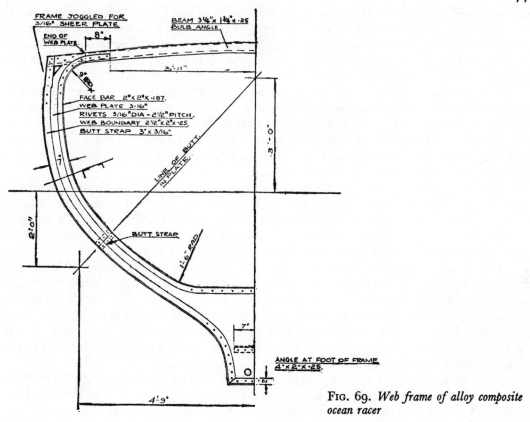

FIG. 69. *Web frame of alloy composite ocean racer*

saving in weight to make possible the construction of small sailing yachts with an adequate ballast ratio.

The limiting size for a steel yacht is governed by the fact that plating of less than 3 mm. thickness cannot be used. This means that unless an overall length of about 40 ft. is exceeded, the steel hull will be heavier than one planked in wood. Not that this precludes building steel sailing yachts of down to 30 ft. overall, but the design must then be governed by the method of construction. The weight of long overhangs must be avoided and the hull should have enough beam to regain the stability that she loses from the reduced ballast ratio.

Actually, data available from designers in steel tends to conflict. The well-known Dutch architect Van de Stadt recently produced a sloop of 24 ft. waterline and 32 ft. overall displacing 6 tons and with a ballast ratio of 33 per cent. This was adequate for the beamy type of hull involved; and it has to be remembered that the actual ballast ratio is higher, for to the keel weight should be added the weight of the steel floors and keel plating.

The same designer has given an example of two yawls of 36 ft. overall built to a common design in wood and steel respectively. Plated with 3 mm. plating above the

M

waterline and 4 mm. below the steel version displaced $7\frac{1}{2}$ tons compared with the 7 tons of the wood boat. The ballast ratio then dropped from 43 per cent to 40 per cent, and a British designer of wide experience with steel auxiliaries says that using Dutch scantlings he is able to reach a 38–40 per cent ballast ratio in a 30-ft. hull (this including the floors and bottom plating in the ballast weight).

We may say, therefore, that sailing yachts of down to 30 ft. overall may be built in steel and have an adequate ballast ratio provided the boat is of generous displacement, has modest overhangs, and that constructional weights above the waterline are reduced so far as possible. This indicates a wood deck and cabin top (which are desirable for other reasons too) but it is worth noting that a deck and cabin top in $2\frac{1}{2}$ mm. plating need not be much heavier than the wooden construction.

Here we come up against the question of scantlings. The Dutch use appreciably lighter scantlings than Lloyd's will accept. For example, where Lloyd's will demand 0·137 in. thick topside plating in a welded hull, the Dutch builders will use plating of 0·116 in. Where Lloyd's require frames 2 in. × $1\frac{1}{2}$ in. × 0·18 in., the Dutch will use, with the same frame spacing of 15 in. frames of $1\frac{1}{2}$ in. × $1\frac{1}{2}$ in. × 0·125 in.

This is not necessarily a criticism of Lloyd's. Though today means of inhibiting corrosion, by shot- or sand-blasting, zinc spraying and specially developed paints are much better than hitherto the Society is presumably concerned with allowance for wastage, and this they may feel is not achieved with the commonly used 3 mm. plating. Here experience alone can tell, and Lloyd's can hardly march ahead of experience. But it does mean that it is not practical today to build the smaller sailing yachts to Lloyd's requirements. F. Bandey, A.M.R.I.N.A., writes in this connection:

"The Dutch builders are quite happy to build under Lloyd's Survey, though they are critical of Lloyd's scantlings, which are considered to be far heavier than they need be. This is partly due to their 'canal mindedness,' but the scantlings of a steel cruiser built to Lloyd's requirements is greatly in excess of what would be used were the vessel not built under survey."

The relative woodlessness of Holland and its proximity to German steel have made the Dutch the greatest steel shipbuilders in small scantlings that the world has known. It is the result of special techniques. As Bandey says:

"Before the war their riveted steel yachts were perfect examples of fine workmanship, and after the war, when they concentrated on welded construction, they again made every effort to produce a finished craft which would be capable of continuing the good name already gained. The secret the Dutch have for producing their hulls with such a fair, even finish lies in the sequence of production and erection and upon completion of the hull, on the final stretching which is done with a blow-lamp, bags of wet straw, and the minimum amount of hammering."

Here we should mention another problem set by Lloyd's. The ultimate fairness of the hull depends not only on the welding sequence but also upon using the minimum amount of welding of the frames to the shell, for otherwise with 3 mm. plating the distortion becomes excessive and ineradicable. Also, for welded construction Lloyd's require a 10 per cent increase in shell plate thickness, which often entails either specially rolled plate or the use of over-thick stock sizes.

Below is a comparison of the basic scantling of a 10-ton sloop by Alan Buchanan as built in Holland and as required by Lloyd's.

	Scantlings to Lloyd's		*Scantlings as Built*
Shell			No. thickening of sheer strake
Sheer strake	0·16 in.		0·116 in.
Topsides	0·125 in.	} + 10 per cent.	0·128 in.
Garboard	0·15 in.		
Frames	2 in. × 1½ in. × 0·18 in. at 15 in. spacing		1·5 in. × 1·5 in. × 0·125 in. at 15 in. spacing.
Beams ordinary	2·5 in. × 2 in. × 0·24 in.		2 in. × 2 in. × 0·125 in.
Deck Plating	0·125 in.		0·116 in. (11 gauge).

THE SPECIFICATION. Specifications may be conveniently arranged under six sections:

> Section 1. General.
> Section 2. Hull Construction.
> Section 3. Accommodation and Fittings.
> Section 4. Rig.
> Section 5. Auxiliary Installation and Electrics.
> Section 6. Equipment.

Section 1 is prefaced by the dimensions and a general description of the vessel. This is followed by a detailed description of the plans that are to be supplied by the designer, and it is important that this should be comprehensive, so that designer, owner, and builder know the limits of responsibility. In the case of larger yards many detailed drawings may be prepared by their own drawing office. The demarcation line between the designers' and the builders' responsibility for drawing must be clearly defined; also the rights that the designer claims in the approval of drawings not done in his own office.

The routine of construction is also laid down here—whether or not the yacht is to be built under cover; the laying-off of the lines; the standards of workmanship; the rights of the designer to inspect; the date of delivery; costs and the methods of assessing them in the case of sub-contracts; any mutual agreement clauses in regard to alternative materials; any statutory requirements that the yacht is to satisfy such as Lloyd's, the certified testing of equipment, the rating under any system of measurement, or trial results in connection with running under power or the operation of the gear.

In Section 2 the special points in connection with their scarfing, shaping, and fitting, specification of the materials (but not the scantlings) of all hull members are given in detail, the methods of fastening them, the metals and treatment of fastenings. The weight of the finished, cleaned and faired keel should be given, and particulars of inside ballast. In this section all that it is thought the builder should know about the construction of the hull except for the sizes that appear on the construction drawings, or are lifted from the laid-off lines, should be explained so that there is no fear of subsequent misunderstanding.

Under more general headings, specifications of plywoods, glues, metals, seasoning

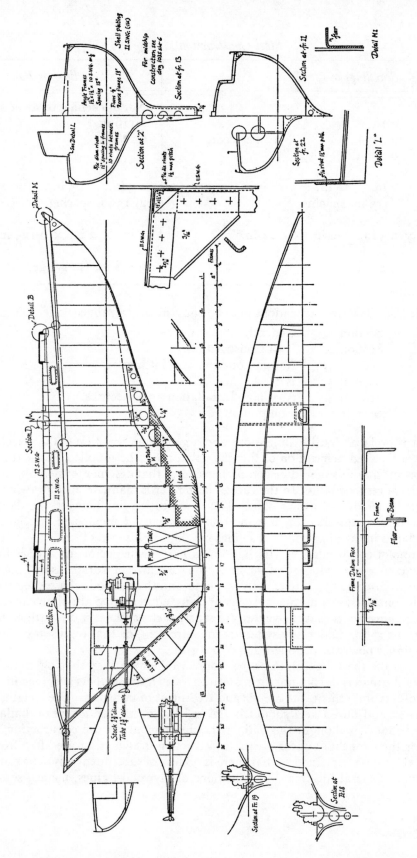

FIG. 70. *Steel construction by Alan Buchanan*

of timber, measures for the prevention of electrolysis and galvanic action, the system of ventilation and its fittings and all details that do not clearly fall under the heading of any separate part of the structure, should be given.

Section 3 goes into similar detail for the accommodational structure, such as bulkheads and their linings, the cabin sole, the berth, settee, and furniture joinerwork. An important part of this section is the list of the various proprietary fittings, ranging from drawer catches to galley stoves, from the shower to the hooks in the oilskin locker. Carpeting, mattresses, and upholstery are also specified in detail. The costing of these articles has already been detailed in Section 1.

In Section 4 details are given of the spars, sails and rigging. This includes the material of the spars, the construction of wire ropes used, and statements as to their splicing or swaging. In this section a variety of rig fittings, probably manufactured by a number of different firms, have to be specified in detail. In this respect British designers are at a disadvantage compared with American, who have available, in the catalogue of Messrs. Merriman, lists set out on engineering lines and with relevant data given, all the numerous fittings on deck and above that may be required. Fittings may be specified briefly according to their catalogue code number. In Britain, the blocks may come from one firm, the spinnaker boom fittings from another, the mast track from a third, the tang assemblies from a fourth, whilst the spreader fittings may be made at the yard. This all entails a full, explicit specification.

Section 5 covers details not shown in the drawings about the engine and its stern gear, and should include such details as tank vents, filters and cocks, the run of the exhaust, and so on. Nowadays there is justification for making "electrics" a separate section of the specification; and here we meet a point that every architect has to decide for himself. Some designers give most detailed description of how the shipwrights' work should be carried out, which it may be claimed tells a good builder nothing and will not help a bad builder. But the best builders may need the guidance from a good architect about electrics though they may need none about how to build a good boat beyond a proper specification.

The section on equipment is devoted to the items and their details that are to be supplied by the builder according to the contract. A clear line should be drawn here between what the builder is expected to provide and all else that is to be the owner's responsibility.

A specimen of a specification for an 11-ton cruiser-racer by Alan Buchanan appears in Appendix Seven. In detail it differs in layout from the above, but in no way of importance.

CONSTRUCTION IN GLASS REINFORCED PLASTICS (G.R.P.)

"Reinforced plastics" as a term is no less generic than "timber", and such plastics may vary widely in strength, weight, cost and many other qualities. They have in common the feature of being a combination of a low-strength resin reinforced by a high-strength filler. Various resins have been used in boatbuilding, but the present choice has generally settled upon those of the polyester group, which may be moulded without pressure and cured without heat. The curing entails an irreversible process in which the soft and sticky resin becomes hard, durable to an extent that we still have to learn, and as indissolubly wedded to the reinforcement as possible. G.R.P. becomes brittle with age, and the ultimate durability of the material has yet to be discovered. It should be noted initially

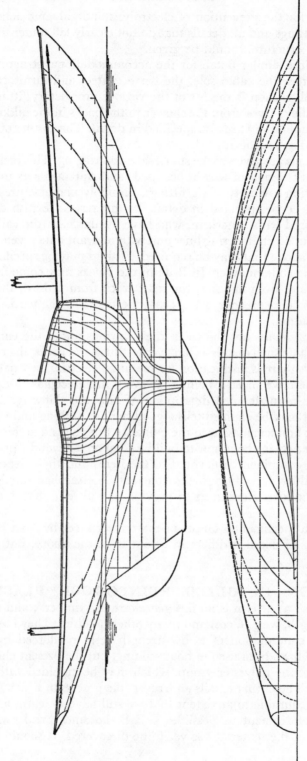

Fig. 71. *Heavy displacement centreboard yawl by Abeking and Rasmussen*

that the material is not anti-fouling by nature, though the claim that it is became widely believed for some years under pressure of publicity. It may be initially impregnated with colour, but at present this deteriorates fairly rapidly in sunlight, and normal painting then becomes necessary. G.R.P. boats have embarrassed navies that have adopted them owing to their liability to become quickly shabby in appearance with normal usage, and they have poor resistance to chafe. The saving in maintenence with glass fibre hulls is mainly due to their immunity from rot, corrosion and marine borers, and their lack of fastenings and small constructional members where leaks may occur. Only by a gross misuse of language, however, may a glass fibre hull be described by the now usual term of "monolithic". The junction between the deck and hull, apart from many other connections between individual parts, clearly deny monolithic integrity; and the hull-deck junction is of critical importance and a frequent source of weakness.

Plastics construction is inevitably associated with class boats or some form of line construction, and as the purely individual boat in any material is becoming less common and the architect increasingly hopes that a new design will become the prototype of a class, the use of plastics construction becomes more generally logical. Where price is concerned, so many variables enter the problem that definite answers are impossible. Reinforced plastics hulls are liable to be expensive firstly because the materials involved are highly priced. A glass reinforced polyester mat may cost per pound from five to ten times as much as a birch plywood of marine quality. To offset this disability, it will be obvious that there must be considerable saving in labour costs, and others aspects of construction (the cost of fastenings, painting and so on). Secondly, the cost of the strong and highly finished mould on which the plastics hull has to be laid up is a big initial outlay.

The finish of a plastics hull depends to a great extent on the finish of the mould. The most usual system is to use a female mould, laying up the resin-impregnated mat in the mould, which, when highly finished internally, ensures a good external finish on the outside of the moulded hull. With male moulds, the external finish depends on expensive hand operations during the last stages of laying up the moulding; also, the hull, then being built upside down, has to be turned over, a process best avoided with bigger mouldings.

A system occasionally used in Britain and more often in the U.S.A. is to make a wooden mould, which then becomes a core or plug for a plastics moulding laid up externally, and this subsequently becomes the female mould for further mouldings laid up internally. The initial wooden core may then be completed as a wooden hull. It will be evident that the moulds required for reinforced plastics hulls are elaborate and expensive productions, and if there is also to be a G.R.P. deck, this will require its own separate mould accurately made to camber and sheer.

Hence the importance economically of the number of boats that are to be built on any one mould. An analysis of one example shows that the cost of the mould was 17 per cent of the cost of the first boat excluding mould. Some figures given by two American authorities, J. B. Alfers and W. R. Grander, eight years ago were not favourable to plastics. They quoted the cost each of 45 G.R.P. motor boats 26 ft. in length as 9,500 dollars compared with 6,500 dollars for wooden hulls. Two hundred plastics wherries cost 720 dollars each compared with the wood price of 520 dollars. However, for 117 9 ft. dinghies, the cost was the same in either wood or plastics. These figures may now be unfavourable, and for medium-sized craft with little accommodation, equality between wood and steel prices may be achieved with the mould cost spread over about 20 craft. Mould cost becomes more easily absorbed as sizes become larger and boats more elaborate, when the hull is a proportionately smaller part of the total cost. It has even been claimed by a director of the well known British plastics hull builder Halmatic Ltd. of Portsmouth that between 30ft.–50 ft. a plastics hull may compete with wood provided two hulls are required from the same mould, while above 50 ft. a plastics hull can compete with a wooden hull even if only one hull is required from a mould. Such various opinions on costs are not surprising if it is considered that when several reputable builders estimate for even a wooden boat on the basis of a full specification, the difference between the highest and the lowest offer may be 50 or more per cent of the latter. In the U.S.A. the popularity of plastics hulls may be attributed to three main causes: (i) The extremely high price of shipwrights' work; (ii) The prevalence of worm in so many sailing waters; (iii) The enormous demand stimulated by high pressure publicity. What happens in the U.S.A. has a liability to happen in Europe tomorrow, and where plastics are concerned there is evidence that this is happening. At the Dutch Boat Show in 1965 fifty per cent of the boats exhibited were in G.R.P., and an increasing number of boatbuilding concerns are devoting part of their activity to such work.

Glass fibre hulls in the larger sizes may give a material saving in weight compared with wood construction, which is much in its favour for light-displacement sailing yachts. In a paper read before the 71st Annual Meeting of the Society of Naval Architects and Marine Engineers, New York, the authors, Robert G. Henry and Richards T. Miller, gave the following figures for hull weights applicable to the 30ft. waterline U.S. Naval Academy Yawls:

	Weight of hull per linear foot
Wood construction as designed	182 lb.
Wood construction to Herreshoff's rules	159 lb.
Wood construction to Lloyd's rule	170 lb.
G.R.P.	144 lb.
Aluminium construction welded	132 lb.

The very light scantlings involved under Herreshoff's rules demand standards of shipwrights' work of the most expensive order, but the weight figure above might be bettered today with hot or cold moulded wooden hulls. It will be evident that except for these methods of wood construction, the plastics hull offers a decided advantage in weight compared with conventional timber work.

Glass, as used for reinforcement, is drawn into very fine continuous filaments of less than 0·0004 in., which may have a tensile strength some sixty times greater than the resin. The filaments may be woven or laid up in a variety of ways giving different strength characteristics to the resin-filler compound; but initially the strength of G.R.P. depends on the proportion of filler to resin, which requires to be as high as possible to attain the greatest strength, and this adds to the expense of a laminate. It is also of great importance that excellent bonding should be achieved between the filler and the reinforcement during the laying up of the moulding. This is critical for the development of the full strength, and the filaments have to be treated after being drawn to assure the best adhesion. Apart from the proportion of filler to resin and the quality of the bonding between them, the effectiveness of G.R.P. when worked into a boat's structure is governed by the weave of the filler. Some arrangements of the filaments used in boatbuilding are woven cloth, which may be bidirectionally oriented to give equal strength in all directions; or cloth with the glass fibres oriented to give mainly unidirectional strength, like timber along the grain; or they may be laid as continuous parallel yarns, giving exceptional strength in one direction; or simply applied as a random mat, the filler being chopped into short lengths having no fixed orientation. A few specimen ultimate tensile strengths for various lays-up are:

Random glass mat	20,000 lb./sq. in.
Woven rovings	45,000 lb./sq. in.
Unidirectional rovings	110,000 lb./sq. in.

A particular use for the lay-up shown last would be for a sheer strake. In other positions, bidirectional lays-up may be particularly valuable.

Glass reinforced plastics have a low modulus of elasticity, which gives good resistance to shock loads but in other respects is structurally inconvenient in boatbuilding, and in-moulded stiffening is necessary. This stiffening may take the form of an angular glass fibre section, or a top hat section in light alloy, or plastics tube. These are laid up between the layers of the moulding, and may take the form of stringers, the outer shell of the hull not requiring closely spaced transverse frames of a carvel planked hull. The transverse framing may consist of the bulkheads and various in-built units of furniture and the tankage.

Different materials demand different approaches to design, and while fundamental hull shapes are not profoundly influenced by the use of plastics, other important features of design are. These may be grouped under the general observation that corners are to be avoided. Quite contrary to wooden construction, in which angles at the fastened junctions of members are natural, while big radius mouldings and all pronounced curvatures are extravagant in both labour and material, the essence of plastics design is large components, full curvature where junctions occur, and the absence of flat surfaces, a degree of curvature being an important contribution to the rigidity which the material naturally lacks. Glass fibre decks are thus suspect and require careful stiffening; and it will be evident that the vee-bottom hull, so eminently suitable for plywood construction, is the least desirable for plastics. Note page 78. On the other hand, for hulls that must endure extremely high shock loadings, such as offshore planing powerboats, the G.R.P. chine hull has impressively proved itself. The chine sailing yacht, however, would hardly justify the kind of stiffening used in such craft. A combination of plywood and plastics is logical, using the former for deck and bulkheads. This leads to the not perfectly rational but wholly comprehensible use of an appreciable amount of wood trim externally to bring warmth and grace to the chilliness of the plastics. Wood does have a practical justification, resisting abrasion better than G.R.P. which once roughened at the surface collects dirt and looks ugly, for being used for cockpit soles and bench tops.

CHAPTER TWELVE

Accommodation and Hull Shape

THE standard of accommodation expected today is much higher than was demanded in the past. Since Victorian times, when the quarters in some of the largest sailing craft were deplorable, accommodation has been improving steadily, better use being made of the available space. If there was a bath in a Victorian yacht it was generally a cold-water one under the saloon floor; cooking was done on a stove in the fo'c'sle, where the hands lived, ate and slept; there was little light below deck, and the joiner's work and furnishing, of mahogany, further darkened the scene; ventilation and artificial lighting were both bad. Yachts were characterised by smells and the whole sport by discomfort, mitigated sometimes by the attentions of well-trained stewards.

The improvement in accommodation has accompanied, strangely enough, the general decrease in the size of yachts which has been continuing since 1919. This has been made possible by a number of developments. The greater proportionate freeboard now common has added to the room inside a hull of given length, and bigger beam has had the same effect. Thirty-five years ago, yachts of only 26 ft. on the waterline had flush decks and a few skylights. The development of the coachroof, and its gradual extension until it found its way forward of the mast, opened up the space below deck wonderfully. And out of the coachroof came the doghouse, the last and belated offspring of the first deckhouse, seen in the Watson-designed *Rainbow* of 1898, and then criticised as unseamanlike and liable to be swept overboard by the main boom. At present, the wheel of change ever revolving, coachroofs and doghouses are tending to disappear as freeboards and deck cambers increase yet further, and we have small, flush-decked cruisers of a kind never dreamed of by our forefathers. Today we are nearer than our fathers were to that ideal yacht, defined by Froude, which combines in equal measure speed, beauty, habitability and seaworthiness.

The ocean-racer, by the attention it has focused on seagoing efficiency below deck, has exerted a mainly beneficial influence on accommodation. It has taught that the afterpart of the accommodation is the most important section for working space, amidships for sleeping. It has encouraged the provision of proper navigation space in the smallest craft, whereas formerly even 40-tonners were often without a chart table. It has shown how berths suitable for use at sea should be designed, and equally galleys. It must be remembered, however, that the ocean-racer carries a large crew of experienced hands who are intent on racing. This has led to the undivided layout, the saloon that is primarily somewhere to eat and sleep, the elimination of privacy, and of all inessential comforts. An important element in the philosophy of design is the correct assessment of the main purpose to which a yacht will be put and the provision, below deck as well as elsewhere, of the arrangements best suited to it. In craft of 10 tons and more this may lead to layouts unlike the thoroughbred ocean-racers. The saloon becomes primarily a day cabin, which will be less often used for sleeping in at sea. It is not necessary to pack in the maximum number of berths, to the exclusion of other comforts. The virtues of space, which is as much a matter of arrangement as cubic capacity, should be cultivated, and doors and bulkheads become features to be well arranged not ruthlessly eliminated.

ACCOMMODATION AND SIZE In yachts of about 30 tons T.M. and above, the shape of the hull need not be influenced by the accommodation unless unreasonable demands are made. The hull may be designed purely with an eye to performance, which is as it should be. It is in the smaller sizes that the accommodation influences shape. Since the demand for a big ship on a small length is never likely to die, we must discover how best to gain space below deck without spoiling the design of the hull.

There is not much elbow room for choice in the layout of yachts under 25 ft. on the waterline. The chief variable is the position of the galley, which is generally aft in these crewless days, and preferably under the doghouse if this is the only way of obtaining standing headroom. With the galley situation decided, the rest of the accommodation tends to fall into position, though perhaps needing a little forcing. Ingenuity in tucking the ends of settees under sideboards, and in ensuring that all space, even the most unpromising, may be put to some useful purpose, will produce a reasonable impression of comfort in the smallest cruisers. There is a temptation, when dealing with small craft, to swell the lines aft in order to accommodate the auxiliary and to make room for the quarter berth and more spacious lockers. Owing to the sensitiveness of sailing performance to the lines aft, great care must be taken not to sacrifice the more important quality to a few inches of berth width. It is always possible to accommodate the auxiliary lower in the ship or farther aft by deepening the sections of the quarters, but the effect which this has of coarsening the curve of the inner buttocks is a discouragement to the procedure.

Another result of crewlessness is the relegation of the fo'c'sle to the role of a large locker for sails, warps, lamps, chain and a W.C. In yachts of about 26 ft. L.W.L. and above, the lost fo'c'sle cot may be worked in between the saloon and the fo'c'sle with the foot possibly extending into the fo'c'sle. Since the fo'c'sle is generally most uncomfortable at sea for sleeping purposes, this is the best place for the forward berth. A length of about 30 ft. on the waterline is usually necessary if there is to be a separate forecabin as well as a reasonable size of forepeak, for storage only, ahead of the saloon.

When planning the accommodation, it has to be remembered that the outline of the deck gives a misleading impression of the amount of space available inside a hull. Unless care is taken when roughing out the layout, much of the furnishing may be placed so that it is not inside the skin of the ship. Particularly may this happen towards the ends, where the fine run of the lines constricts the floor space considerably. It is easy to sketch impossibilities, such as wash-basins or shelves which would be protruding a foot through the planking if placed where shown.

Fig. 72 shows the deck outline of a yacht, the pecked lines inside it indicating the cabin sole throughout the length of the yacht. To gain floor space forward and aft, the cabin soles are, of course, raised higher, and headroom is lost. The space between the pecked and the full lines indicates the yacht's sloping side. Fittings which are at the sole level have to be inside the pecked lines. Bunks, sideboards and the like may have their outer edges somewhere between the pecked and full lines, depending on their heights; only at the level of the deck beams is the full width of the yacht gained, and this is less

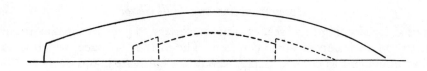

FIG. 72. *The line of the cabin sole*

than the maximum beam by the thickness of the planking, timbers and cabin ceiling—
a loss of about 10 in. in a craft of 15–20 tons T.M. If allowance is not made for these inches
in the preliminary sketching of the accommodation, difficulties can arise later. Lack of an
inch can prevent a door from closing, or make impossible the fitting of a proposed type of
sink and draining-board. An architect of international repute used not long ago to
circulate to prospective clients accommodation drawings of his propositions in which vital
items shown were not inches but feet outside any reasonable shape of hull.

MIDSHIP SECTION AND ACCOMMODATION In the small cruiser, full
headroom is not practicable. In the effort to obtain as much as possible, and to combine
it with reasonable floor space, the temptation is to swell the midship section to an extent
which spoils the sailing qualities. A full midship section with a low bilge, producing a
heavy displacement hull with little depth of keel, will make a yacht with surprising
roominess for her length, but she will not sail fast or be close-winded.

It is in smaller craft that the doghouse has its most material value in allowing standing
headroom to be provided at least in its own length, which covers the after part of the
accommodation. By this means the galley, the navigation space, and a few feet at the aft
end of the saloon, may have full headroom, even if unattainable elsewhere. Where headroom is limited, it is usually advantageous to drop the cabin sole and lose width, rather
than to retain width at the expense of height. This process shows to peculiar advantage
the full garboard (see page 55) which allows the cabin sole to be low without becoming
absurdly narrow. It is sometimes found that yachts, even of moderate size, lack comfortable headroom under the beams, though it is clear that the coachroof might have been
raised the vital inch, or the sole lowered, without producing any eccentricity in design.
Since the error which produces the discomfort is so small it may be accountable to
draughtsmanship, or a small discrepancy between plans and construction. It is obviously
to be avoided.

The slack garboard form is one that may be put to good use in light displacement
hulls, and the form has been carried to a logical limit in certain American craft, in which
the fin itself is thickened to contain the cabin sole, which is about 18 in. below the garboards. This necessitates a very thick keel section, but tank tests at the Stevens Institute
have indicated a low hull resistance. The arrangement has permitted 6 ft. of headroom
in a hull 19 ft. 6 in. on the waterline, but the berth tops are only just above the waterline,
whilst the cabin sole is on top of the keel. An absolutely dry ship is thus essential.

Once full headroom is possible, horizontal space becomes more valuable than any
excess in the vertical. The latter may be said to occur when it is practicable to provide

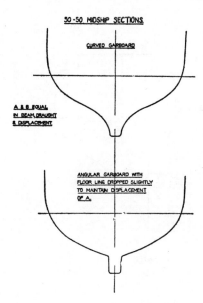

50-50 MIDSHIP SECTIONS

CURVED GARBOARD

A & B EQUAL
IN BEAM, DRAUGHT
& DISPLACEMENT

ANGULAR GARBOARD WITH
FLOOR LINE DROPPED SLIGHTLY
TO MAINTAIN DISPLACEMENT
OF A.

FIG. 73. *Curved and angular garboards*

more than 6 ft. to 6 ft. 2 in. under the beams. More than this probably has less value than an addition to width, which brings with it a sense of space as well as providing easier movement in the way of the saloon table.

Fig. 74 shows the midship sections of two yachts, both 30 ft. on the waterline, and having the same draught and displacement. Section B has less beam and a fuller body; A has a higher bilge, though it avoids any harshness in its curve. The headroom in each case is the same.

The two sections illustrate the benefit to accommodation of beam. Whilst giving the same headroom as B, A has more floor width and also some 10 per cent more volume of space above the cabin sole—and this on the same displacement. The amount of beam which a design can carry has to be decided from many considerations, of which accommodation is only one, but the effectiveness of beam for increasing internal space must be realised if this factor is to carry the weight it deserves.

One of the greatest advantages conferred by the extra floor width is that it allows a berth to be placed behind the settees (a pilot berth) on one or both sides. In terms of useful width of ship occupied by a berth, this is the most economical position for it. Being placed higher than the settee level, it makes use of the yacht's full beam. The economy is illustrated in Fig. 75. On the starboard side (B) the settee is at the ship's side, with only a shelf, or possibly cupboards, behind it. There is 3 ft. 4½ in. of floor width in the half-section. On the port side a berth of width 2 ft. 2 in. is shown behind the settee. The loss in floor space caused by the berth is 1 ft. 2½ in. If, as in Fig. 75, Section A, a berth was placed behind both the settees, the floor space would still be only 29 in. less than that of Section B.

Berths behind the settees may be curtained off from the saloon, or alternatively they may have hinged lids which, when lowered, convert them into sideboards. The latter gives

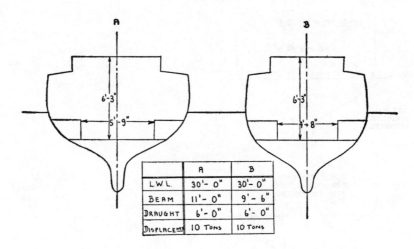

	A	B
L.W.L.	30'- 0"	30'- 0"
BEAM	11'- 0"	9'- 6"
DRAUGHT	6'- 0"	6'- 0"
DISPLACEM^T	10 Tons	10 Tons

Fig. 74. *The space inside hulls*

a great impression of space; the former makes a cabin look smaller than it actually is. If the yacht is large enough to have a berth on either side, one may be curtained and the other built with the sideboard lid. The space under the berth makes excellent lockers, reached through removable panels in the settee back, behind the cushions. This method of placing berths has now gained the popularity in England which it has long had in the States. In the past the comparative narrowness of English yachts precluded the arrangement.

Another feature affecting the beam available for accommodation is the overall coachroof, or built-up topsides, which have become increasingly popular in recent years. It is a form of hull which shows to the best advantage in very small cruisers, and in large cruisers with shoal draught.

In craft whose midship section does not allow sitting headroom (3 ft.) between the settees and the side decks, the built-up topsides are a help. But even here their advantage is not unquestionable, as Fig. 76 will show. Lockers are an essential part of the accommodation, and the best place for them is behind the settees. Those shown in Fig. 76 are used for bedding, but the blankets may equally well be stowed under the cushions, when the lockers become available for other purposes. By building up the topsides, the settees may be placed at the ship's side, but the valuable lockers are lost, and the additional floor space is hardly compensation enough.

We may say that the built-up topsides pay when the beam is too small to allow the settees to be moved inboard to the line of the coachroof and still retain reasonable floor space—say 2 ft. Thus, in yachts of under 24 ft. L.W.L. they may be of advantage. Above this size, the arrangement may be used to give an impression of greater spaciousness in the cabin, but there is little practical justification for it unless the draught is shoal or the displacement very light.

In larger shoal-draught yachts, and in those having a berth behind the settee, the raised deck form is useful in allowing headroom above the berth, which at a minimum

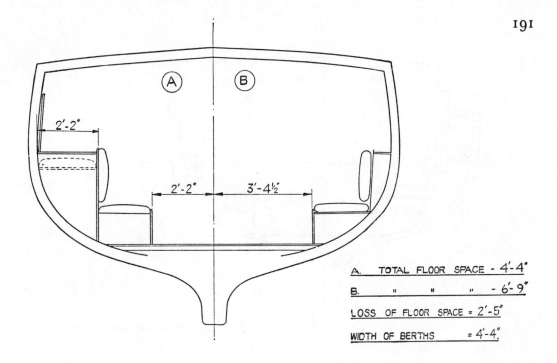

FIG. 75. *Arrangement of berths*

should be 2 ft. 3 in., and ideally should allow the occupant to sit upright. In the Thornycroft shoal-draught ketch (Fig. 77) the central turret is put to this use, whilst it also gives good headroom over the main part of the accommodation, combining this with considerable width of floor.

Apart from its influence on accommodation, there are certain other advantages and disadvantages of the central turret. The hull weights are slightly raised, particularly the deck and all that it carries, and getting forward in rough weather is more difficult. The raised midship portion forms a breakwater forward, where its level drops to that of the foredeck, and ports in this forward bulkhead are excellent for harbour ventilation, though a probable source of leaks at sea. The thwartship strength of the hull is increased by the full width deck beams, and the absence of the long break in the deck caused by a coachroof. There is another source of strength. The deck will be farther from the hull's neutral axis approximately by the ratio.

$$\frac{\text{Hull depth with raised topsides}}{\text{Hull depth without raised topsides}}$$

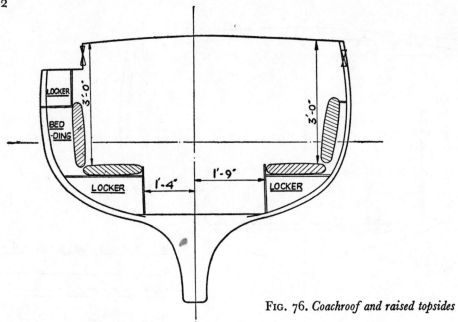

FIG. 76. *Coachroof and raised topsides*

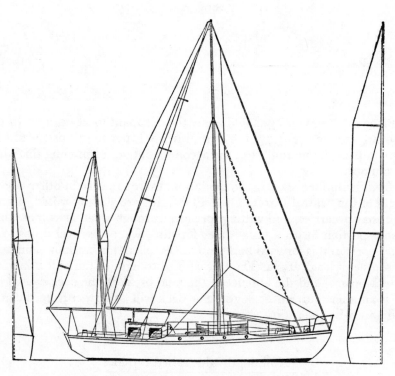

FIG. 77. *Thornycroft 38/47 shoal draught ketch*

42. Cockpit gear and instrumentation.

43. *Donella*, by Laurent Giles and Partners, a close union of sail and power in one yacht, and a style of design that has had a considerable influence on the modern highly powered auxiliary (Beken and Son).

This alone would have the effect of increasing the stress in the deck, but simultaneously the moment of inertia is increased in the approximate ratio

$$\frac{(\text{Hull depth with raised topsides})^3}{\text{Hull depth without raised topsides}^3}$$

The net effect on stress is therefore a reduction, in the ratio of

$$\frac{(\text{Hull depth with raised topsides})^3}{\text{Hull depth without raised topsides}^2}$$

It will be evident that this advantage accrues to all modes of increasing the hull depth by freeboard, whatever the profile adopted.

FREEBOARD, SHEER AND ACCOMMODATION The increase of internal depth, for a given length of boat, that has been achieved by means of higher freeboard, is one of the few fundamental changes in yacht hull design in the present century. It is the result of (i) A higher minimum freeboard than in the past beneath a conventional, concave sheerline; (ii) A straight line sheer; (iii) A broken sheerline, of which the central turret considered above is one example; (iv) A reverse curve, hogged or whaleback sheerline. Varieties of these are shown in Fig. 81(a) to (e). The relative merits of the styles is not clear-cut, and demand analysis for each individual case. From the aesthetic point of view (a) has advantages which even skilful design cannot confer on (b) and (c), whilst the two latter provide more space below and greater structural strength than a continuous concave sheerline and a long coachroof. The form (d) has been tried but discarded.

The comparison in Fig. 82 affords a digested survey of forty years of design in its attitude to freeboard. It shows superimposed the above-water profiles of *Tern III* (1912) and *Gulvain* (1949), seagoing yachts of similar lengths and proved ability. The much greater freeboard of *Gulvain* is evident. *Tern III* has a bulwark, and her deck level is indicated by the lower pecked line. Her freeboard amidships is about 60 per cent of *Gulvain*'s and her deck and its weights are lower by this amount. *Gulvain*'s displacement is one half of *Tern*'s, and the higher centre of gravity of the construction weights in the newer yacht, combined with the more lofty rig—which has the same actual area as *Tern*'s—shows the need for deep draught and a high ballast ratio if adequate stability is to be assured. *Tern* carried 40 per cent of her displacement in ballast, but 60 per cent of this was internal. With one-half the displacement and a hull of shallow body, *Gulvain* has rather more internal cubic capacity than *Tern III*. The success of the conception depends on the necessarily deep draught and ballast ratio to carry the higher weights without tenderness.

It is convenient to consider minimum freeboard as a proportion of the waterline length. Whilst with a normal sheerline one-twelfth was once considered the reasonable average, one-tenth is now most moderate, and in boats of up to 35 ft. on the waterline a ratio of 0·11 is commonly adopted. The idea that a boldly swinging sheer is seaworthy would seem to be without foundation, and several designs from which a number of yachts

N

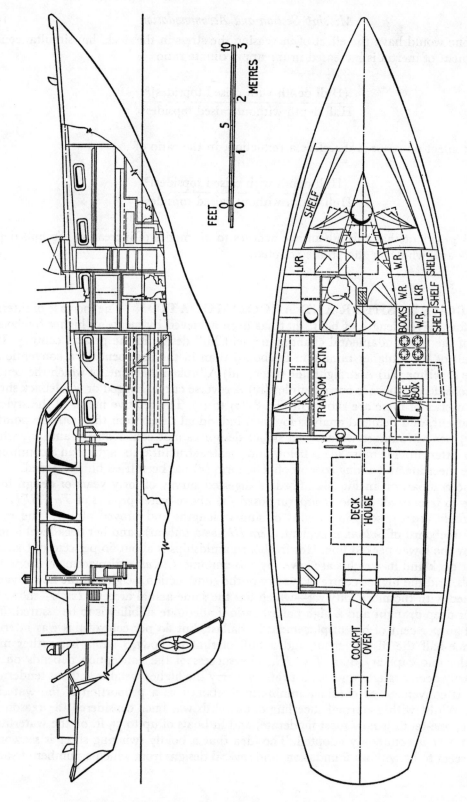

FEET

METRES

FIG. 78. *Lady Helene type by John G. Alden, having emphasis on the deckhouse and convenience of movement in the accommodation*

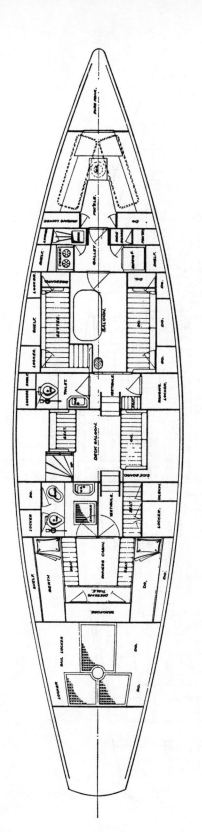

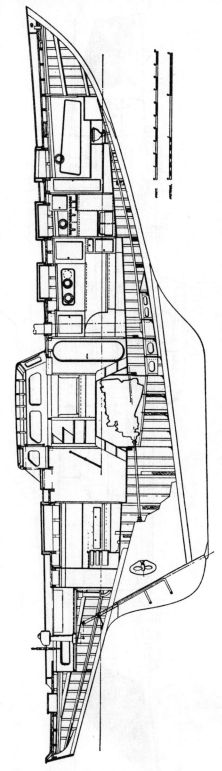

Fig. 79. *General arrangement by Laurent Giles and Partners for a fast cruising yacht*

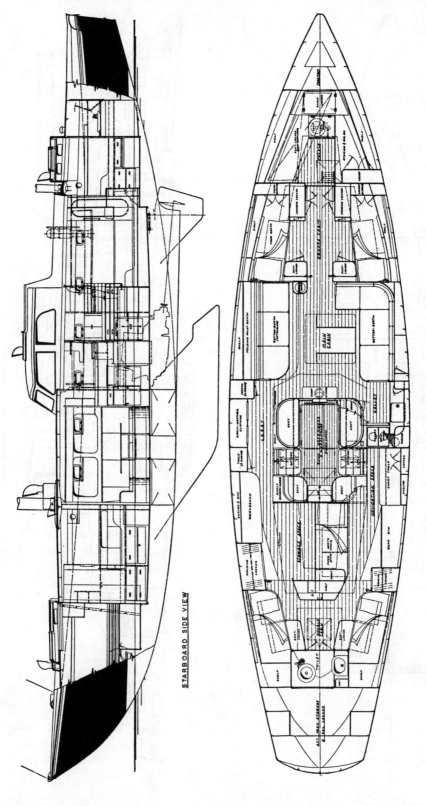

STARBOARD SIDE VIEW

Fig. 80. *General arrangement of Bluebird of Thorne. See Fig. 28*

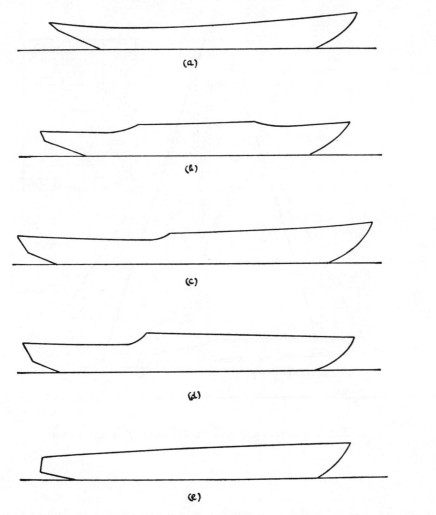

(a)

(b)

(c)

(d)

(e)

FIG. 81. *Sheerlines*

have been built—the *Vertues* and the R.N.S.A. 24 ft. class—were improved by later modifications involving a flattening of the sheerline and an increase in the minimum freeboard.
The maximum freeboard at the stem usually varies in modern practice between one-
sixth and one-eighth of the load waterline.

An interesting feature may be seen in the Thornycroft shoal-draught ketch (Fig. 77).
Aft there are dwarf bulwarks 4 in. high, but forward, in order to get full headroom in the
state-room, the deck is lifted and there are no bulwarks. The yacht, in fact, is a compromise between the central turret type of Fig. 81 (*b*), and the raised foredeck of (*c*), though
in appearance the characteristic of the central turret is retained by means of the artificial
sheerline.

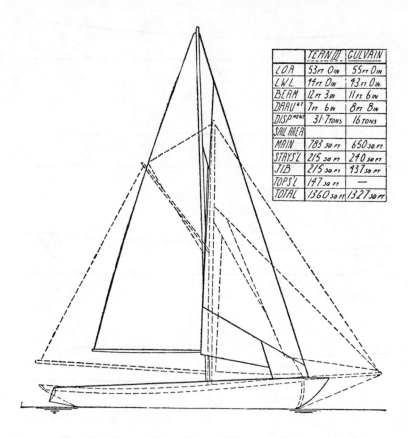

	TERN III	GULVAIN
LOA	53 FT 0 IN	55 FT 0 IN.
L.W.L.	44 FT. 0 IN	43 FT. 0 IN.
BEAM	12 FT 3 IN	11 FT. 6 IN
DRAU GT	7 FT 6 IN	8 FT 8 IN
DISP MENT	31·7 TONS	16 TONS
SAIL AREA		
MAIN	783 SQ FT	650 SQ FT
STAYS'L	215 SQ FT	240 SQ FT
JIB	215 SQ FT	437 SQ FT
TOPS'L	147 SQ FT	—
TOTAL	1360 SQ FT	1327 SQ FT

FIG. 82. *Sheer profiles of* Tern III *and* Gulvain *compared*

A similar device has been adopted in a number of yachts designed and built by Camper and Nicholsons. Externally the yachts have unbroken sheerlines, but there is a low bulwark aft, whilst forward the deck is flush with the bulwark top, the bulwark capping being continued to form a toe-rail.

The true reverse-curve sheer is the boldest answer to the freeboard problem in light displacement yachts. It is certainly the most artistic. Unbroken curves are more pleasing than broken ones; this seems to be an instinctive, aesthetic judgement. But whether the curve should sweep upwards or downwards would seem to be unimportant. Reverse-curve sheer craft may have a freeboard amidships of about one-eighth L.W.L., which allows a wonderful improvement in the under-deck space, and this is achieved without any great windage in the topsides. And the curve of the sheer is graceful and flowing, expressive of speed and lightness. In this connection, it should be appreciated that from the aesthetic point of view a sheerline that is straight on paper appears curved in three dimensions, and in some opinions is optically the most satisfactory form of "reverse curve" sheerline that may be adopted. Since the curving of the line usually entails dropping it slightly as it runs out to the stern head, this practice fractionally lowers the headroom forward.

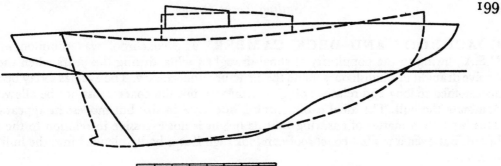

FIG. 83. *Comparison of concave and hogged sheerlines*

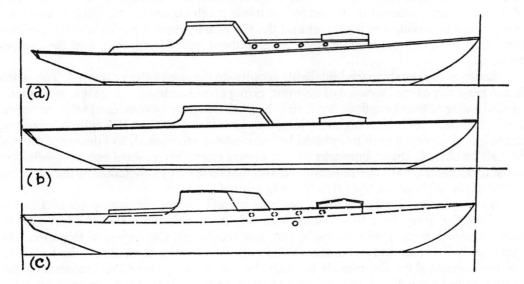

FIG. 84. *Straight and boldly concave sheerlines in light and heavy displacement cruisers*

The advantages of high freeboard have been stressed, but it must be emphasised again that if a conventional type of sheer curve be combined with high freeboard, performance will suffer unless the draught is also fairly high. As a rough guide it may be said that when the minimum freeboard is between one-ninth and one-tenth of the waterline length, the draught should be at least one-fifth of the waterline length, and preferably more. The length of the ends should also be considered. The amount of windage embodied in long overhangs is considerable. Though a hull with long ends is better able to stand, in appearance, relatively higher freeboard than one with short ends, the effect of freeboard on windage is greater in the latter case.*

* See windage ratios page 47.

COACHROOF AND DECK CAMBER The coachroof was common in the U.S.A., owing to the popularity of shoal-draught yachts, during the years when the excessive draught of English ones made the structure unnecessary. The eye has today become accustomed to long and relatively high coachroofs, but the coach must not be allowed to dominate the hull. The ideal cabin trunk is adequate in size but modest in appearance. This is partly a matter of ensuring that its height is not excessive in relation to the freeboard, but even a modest coachroof can look high if it is badly blended into the hull and sheerline.

The amount of freeboard affects the height of the cabin trunk. An extra inch of freeboard reduces the trunk by an equal amount, and the single inch will produce a marked difference in the relative heights of coach and freeboard. In yachts below 20 tons T.M., and of light to moderate displacement, the coachroof may be slightly more than a half of the minimum freeboard in height. When this is much exceeded, the trunk is made less conspicuous by having low coamings and the top heavily cambered. In heavier displacement craft the coachroof may be much lower without loss of headroom, and the camber reduced.

Large or too closely spaced sidelights accentuate the size of the coachroof. The coach is now generally carried forward of the mast, giving extra headroom where it is particularly needed owing to the rising floor level, and the forehatch may be combined with the trunk. But if the coachroof is both high and long the result is unpleasing. If length is necessary, the height of the coach must be reduced by increasing the freeboard, and the top of the roof be well cambered. Dwarf bulwarks do not always effectively conceal excessive height of cabin trunk; and it has to be remembered also that cove stripes, by reducing the apparent height of the freeboard, add to that of the coachroof.

The top edge of the coachroof coaming should be approximately parallel to the waterline, the rising sheer then reducing its height towards the bows. The line may be sloped upwards slightly, but except in very low coachroofs, the degree of slope must be appreciably less than that of the sheer. The line of the roof at the centre—the top of the camber—should slope downwards towards the bow except where the camber is slight, when it may be parallel to the top edge of the coaming. Purely from the aesthetic point of view, coachroofs repay careful study. Their importance increases as yachts become smaller and of lighter displacement, and it is one of the artistic problems of design to combine adequacy with beauty of line. Many pretty hulls are spoilt by having what looks like the top of an old-fashioned railway carriage placed on top of them.

The same applies to the doghouse, where considerable artistic judgement is needed to blend it happily with the hull. The slightest study of contemporary design will show the improvement in accommodation which the doghouse has produced, and the added grace which a well-designed one can give to a hull. In small, light displacement craft the doghouse may be the making of the accommodation. This is well illustrated in the little cruiser-racer *Sabrina* by Laurent Giles and Partners. Here the doghouse is carried the full extent of the small saloon, which is 5 ft. only in length, ends of the berths being tucked under the bridge deck; and from the berth-seats there is a perfect view of the outside world through the single large window in each side of the house. Yet the doghouse is modest in appearance and sits contentedly on the slim hull.

The use of extreme deck camber to obviate the coachroof has been tried successfully in certain types. It is particularly expedient in semi-dayboats and small craft with accommodation for an occasional night. Uffa Fox adopted the heavily cambered deck in his 30 sq. metre designs, of which *Avocet* is an example. Mr. Ian C. Bridge, B.SC., A.M.R.I.N.A., used the idea in a proposed design for a British one-design class. The boat was 20 ft. on the waterline, displaced 2·17 tons, and had two berths and simple cooking facilities beneath a cambered deck without coachroof. A delightfully sightly hull was the result. The camber of the foredeck in this case was about 2 in. per foot.

These early examples of the feature have been followed in many recent yachts, though their influence for many years was slight. The advantages of the system are a saving in weight and cost, an increase in strength, and greater amount of space below deck assuming that the deck camber be equal to the height of the coachroof which it replaces. The big arching of the beams, and the fact that they are unbroken from end to end of the accommodation, allows them to be of lighter scantling than usual, and the weight of coachroof coamings, carline and other constructional details is saved.

CHAPTER THIRTEEN

The Combination of Sail and Power

THE AUXILIARY We are concerned for the moment with engines which are purely auxiliary to the sails, and intended for getting in and out of crowded moorings, for pushing the boat home against foul tides, or when the wind fails. As with most other elements of design, the auxiliary problem becomes more acute the smaller the boat, for the speed needed under power is an absolute quantity, and does not become less with the size of yacht. A speed under power of 4 knots is not sufficient for practical purposes: it will hardly hold its own against the tides encountered in many crowded yachting centres, and we may say that 5-$5\frac{1}{2}$ knots is the minimum desirable. But whereas $5\frac{1}{2}$ knots gives a $V \sqrt{L}$ value of a little over 1 for a boat of 27 ft. L.W.L., the ratio is nearly 1·2 for one of 22 ft. L.W.L., and this is fairly high in the speed range. Combined with this fact is the less easily driven hull form of the small cruiser with its greater beam/length and displacement/length ratios. Thus the small yacht needs proportionately more power than the larger.

Horse-power is most simply related to the displacement since this, more than any other single factor, governs the resistance under power, variations in wetted surface between yachts being insufficient at the speeds concerned to produce an important effect; and the simple rule of allowing one horse-power per ton is as reliable as any other more elaborate formula. Estimations of horse-power based on accurate calculations of resistance are unnecessary, and also probably no more reliable in the end than this approximation. In either case propeller efficiency is neglected, and it may affect the speed by as much as 20 per cent one way or the other. One horse-power per ton will produce a speed giving a $V/\sqrt{L}$ ratio of about unity. The following speeds for length are thus achieved:

TABLE 18

L.W.L.	28	30	35	40	45	50
Speed	5·3	5·5	5·9	6·35	6·7	7·1

In the smaller sizes, powers in the region of 1·6 to 2 horse-power per ton are necessary. The exact power will probably be governed by the engine most suitable for installation.

The choice between side and central installation has next to be made. The resistance of a screw, its bossing and shaft bracket, increases with the depth of immersion, but the depth must be sufficient to keep the propeller in the water in a seaway, and, if offset, at the smaller angles of heel also. Screws placed at 30 to 40 per cent of the draught beneath the surface are very suitable.

For highest sailing efficiency, an offset installation with a small, fast-turning and feathering or folding screw is the best, and if the shaft bracket is a single, streamlined strut, the increase in total resistance may be as low as 0·8 per cent. The more common A-bracket offers greater resistance, and internal shaft chocks or bossings are better than those placed outside the planking. Possibly the best installation is that in which the engine is placed centrally, but at an angle, and with the screw coming out of the hull low down and near the deadwood. But practical rather than theoretical considerations govern the exact position of the engine, and in the design stage this means experimenting with a paper pattern of the engine on the drawings of the hull. A point to be kept in mind at this juncture is the lubrication of the engine, and the maker's instructions as to maximum angle at which the engine may be tilted—usually about 10 degrees—must be observed.

The disadvantages of the offset installation are: (i) Loss of power due to shaft angle; (ii) Bad steering and manoeuvrability, particularly astern. The former may be mitigated, of course, by placing the screw on the side which tends to counteract the steering effect of its rotation, but the latter is uncurable; (iii) The engine has usually to be placed farther forward than with a central installation; (iv) The screw is unprotected. When the shaft is run out very close to the centre line, just enough offset, to clear the rudderpost, these disadvantages are correspondingly slight.

Unless a folding or feathering propeller is used there is no advantage in the side installation, and the present tendency is to favour the centreline position. Its drawback lies in the aperture, which is bad both for speed and steering. Three qualities are essential in an aperture which is not to upset the sailing qualities of a yacht: (i) It must be small; (ii) It must not cut away much of the rudder. Some apertures are cut wholly from the deadwood, and it is not desirable to have more than half the aperture area cut out of the rudder. Sometimes the whole of it is taken from the rudder, and erratic steering is then inevitable, and is most pronounced in the smaller yachts; (iii) The deadwood must be well faired into the aperture.

Apertures and their propellers add to the resistance, but a propeller on the centre-line has only one-half to one-fifth of the resistance of an offset screw which does not fold or feather. But it is most important that the aperture should be carefully faired, and since it is cut from deadwood, which may have considerable thickness, this fairing is not always easy to achieve. The aperture causes great turbulence in the water, even when well faired, which not only adds to the resistance, but causes rudder inefficiency, the rudder having to operate in disturbed water.

The great advantage of the central installation is the better manoeuvrability under power which it allows, both at slow speed, and when going astern. The engine may also be placed lower in the boat, where it helps stability, and the shaft is well supported by the deadwood. But care must be taken in placing the keel bolts, which may interfere with the shaft boring.

A variation on the usual method of engine installation has been developed and used in some power yachts. This is the V-drive transmission. The propeller shaft is in two parts, connected in the V-drive box, which may also contain the reduction gear. Thornycroft adopted this system in the 38–47-ft. shoal-draught ketch (Fig. 77). The advantage of the V-drive is that it allows the auxiliary to be placed farther aft, and in a position which would be prohibited by the steep shaft angle were an orthodox transmission used. When an auxiliary is small and capable of being accommodated well forward and low in the ship, there is no advantage in the V-drive. But with more powerful engines, which would encroach on the accommodation if placed far enough forward to avoid an excessive angle of tilt, the V-drive is advantageous.

In the Thornycroft example the auxiliary is a large diesel, and if placed suitably for a normal power transmission it would occupy the middle of the deckhouse-saloon. By using the V-drive it was possible to place the engine below the floor of the self-draining cockpit.

PROPELLERS IN AUXILIARY SAILING YACHTS One method of reducing the resistance of the idle propeller, often adopted in practice and sometimes advocated in principle for a two-bladed propeller, is to arrange that it may be aligned vertically behind the rudder post when sailing. If the rudder post is thick enough to mask the propeller, the screw lying behind it thereby avoids adding to the already considerable eddy-making resistance due to the unfaired sternpost. If, however, the deadwood is properly faired the flow of water on to the screw will be little affected by the alignment. Under these conditions other methods of reducing drag must be found.

As in the motor-sailer, the sailing clutch and freely rotating propeller is one solution. Others are the feathering or the folding propeller, the first two solutions being applicable to two- or three-bladed screws, the last to two-bladed only. In the auxiliary the position of the screw may also be governed by considerations of low resistance.

The following summarises certain important facts about propellers and their resistance under sail:

(*a*) The resistance of a propeller increases with the depth below the waterline at which it is installed.

(*b*) A centreline propeller gives lower resistance than one offset, unless there is the resistance of a propeller aperture to add to that of the screw.

(*c*) Feathering and folding propellers give less resistance than solid ones of the same size and type.

(*d*) Folding propellers give lower resistance than feathering propellers.

(*e*) A reduction gear installation may give more resistance than one with direct drive unless special care is taken in the propeller design.

Of the above (*c*) is obvious, and (*a*) will be evident from general principles. (*b*) is the result of the stronger frictional wake on the quarter than on the centreline. The various rating rules have analysed the idle propeller-resistance in terms of propeller type and location, with a view to assessing the allowances that a yacht should receive on account of her installation. The most analytical rule in this respect is that of the Cruising Club of America, and the essentials of its allowances were adopted in the International Yacht Racing Union's Cruiser-Racer and Royal Ocean-Racing Club rules. The order of efficiency (or of low resistance) derived from these rules is as shown opposite.

In brackets are shown certain resistance figures derived from model tests in the Stevens Tank, Hoboken. It will be seen that they are generally in agreement with the rule. It will be seen also that for the lowest locked resistance the desirable features in a propeller, apart from small size, are shallow immersion, the centre-line position, and the two-bladed folding design. And each of these characteristics militates against efficiency in absorbing and delivering the power of the engine.

The fact that locked resistance, under any given conditions, is proportional to the blade area of the propeller, indicates the advantage of reducing the size of the screw. But here, too, there is a conflict of interest between sailing and power, for the coupling of fast-turning engines direct to propellers, without reduction gearing, is a cause of inefficiency. In one 35 ft. waterline sloop the original installation drove the propeller direct at 1,500 r.p.m. and gave a speed of 6 knots. When later a 2:1 reduction gear was fitted, and an appropriate bigger diameter screw, the speed was raised to 6¾ knots. Sometimes reduction gears are fitted whilst a small screw is retained; the resultant efficiency may then be no higher than with direct drive.

TABLE 19

Propeller Type and Installation

(a) Folding on centre not in aperture (0·8).
(b) Folding off centre.
(c) Feathering 2-blade on centre not in aperture.
(d) Feathering 2-blade on centre in aperture.
(e) Feathering 2-blade off centre.
(f) Feathering 3-blade on centre not in aperture (2·2).
(g) Feathering 3-blade on centre in aperture.
(h) Feathering 3-blade off centre (8·5).
(i) Solid 2-blade on centre not in aperture.
(j) Solid 2-blade on centre in aperture.
(k) Solid 2-blade off centre.
(l) Solid 3-blade on centre not in aperture (18·7).
(m) Solid 3-blade on centre in aperture (24).
(n) Solid 3-blade off centre (34).

This matter may be examined more fully. Let us consider an auxiliary of 20 b.h.p. which gives a speed of 7 knots driving through a 2:1 reduction gear and a solid, three-bladed screw. This is the first example given in Table 20. The optimum propeller will have a diameter of 20 in., a pitch of 15 in., and, as there is no danger of cavitation, the blades may be narrow in the interests of reduced resistance under sail. The efficiency of this screw will be 0·59, which is satisfactory. Its resistance if locked when sailing (we shall consider the question of a freely rotating screw) will be about 120 lb. In a 40-ft. waterline yacht sailing to windward in a speed-length ratio of unity the drag of the locked screw will increase the total resistance by about 35 per cent. The visual evidence of this drag will sometimes be seen in a small wave crest under the quarter on the side of the offset screw.

If, in the interests of sailing efficiency, we eliminate the reduction gear and so obtain a smaller optimum diameter of screw, one of 13 in. diameter and 8½ in. pitch is the best; but its efficiency will be only 0·47. It is important to note that this efficiency will be attained only if cavitation in this small, fast-turning screw is avoided; and to ensure this, wide blades are necessary, giving a blade area ratio of 0·6 instead of 0·35 as formerly. (See Table 20.)

The locked resistance of a propeller depends primarily on the area of the blades and not on the diameter. This means that the advantage of the smaller diameter propeller is partly offset by the proportionately larger blade area. The locked resistance in this case will be about 90 lb., a reduction of 25 per cent compared with the larger propeller and

TABLE 20

Gearing and Propeller	Diameter	Pitch	B.A.R.	Efficiency	Resistance Locked
Reduction 2:1	20 in.	15 in.	0·35*	0·590	120
Direct	13 in.	8½ in.	0·60†	0·470	90
Reduction 2:1 and Reduced Diameter	15¼ in.	20½ in.	0·55†	0·455	115
Two-bladed Folding 2:1 Reduction	20 in.	15 in.	0·30*	0·590	—

* Narrow blade.   † Wide blade.

reduction gear. If the blade area of this screw is further reduced to lower the locked resistance a heavy price will be paid in performance under power, for the blade area chosen is the minimum necessary to avoid undue cavitation.

It is often the case that a reduction gear is fitted, but either because there is not enough clearance between the shaft and hull or deadwood, or in order to reduce the sailing drag a propeller is fitted which is appreciably less than the optimum in diameter. In the third example of Table 20 a propeller of 15 in. diameter is used in conjunction with the 2:1 reduction gearing. The significant facts to note are that the efficiency is lower than that of the direct drive propeller, and its locked resistance is higher. The installation represents a loss under both sail and power, and to achieve these disadvantages the boat is burdened with the weight of a reduction gear.

The above examples are calculated for an individual case, but a general picture may be sketched from them. Elimination of a reduction gear will lower the resistance under sail, but unless care is taken to provide the small, fast-turning screw with enough area to avoid cavitation the price paid in speed under power will be heavy. If cavitation is prevented the price will be kept within bounds, but there will still be an appreciable loss under power. But if, when there is a reduction gear, a propeller of appreciably less than the ideal diameter is fitted the case should be carefully analysed to ensure that the propulsion is not going to be less efficient than without gearing, and the worst of both worlds be achieved.

There are now various types of feathering and folding propellers available for auxiliaries. Three-bladed screws capable of feathering and reversing have blades which are controlled by an operating rod in the bore of the hollow shaft. Two-bladed folding screws may simply have the blades arranged to hinge aft. When driving, the thrust developed ensures that they remain open. When stopped, the water pressure closes them. Opening of the blades is achieved initially, as soon as the shaft turns, by centrifugal force, and continued by the thrust which the blades immediately develop, and which opens them fully. As a result of stiffness in the hinge centrifugal force is sometimes insufficient to achieve the initial degree of opening, and when this fault occurs it may be desirable to arrange that the propeller blades are not allowed to shut completely, but remain at a slight angle, which will add little to the resistance.

When feathering, three-bladed propellers are fitted in the above examples, the resistance under sail of the various arrangements will probably not differ enough to merit the elimination of the reduction gearing, unless singularly little importance is attached to performance under power. The argument applies more strongly when the propeller concerned is of the two-bladed folding type. Details of the two-bladed installation are given in the fourth example. This propeller might be expected to be a little more efficient than the three-bladed screw of the first example; but the theoretical advantage would probably be lost in the unfavourable shape of the folding blades, and by a degree of cavitation.

THE MOTOR SAILER   The motor sailer, of whatever type, embodies two separate means of propulsion of approximately equal value. The power yacht, with a little steadying canvas, does not qualify for the description, for the steadying sails are unable to give effective propulsion, and will allow no more than a limited degree of control to be maintained over the boat when the wind is abaft the beam. Nor, at the other extreme, does the auxiliary yacht which happens to have the engine and a large deckhouse amidships. This combining of two forms of propulsion is an ancient practice of naval architecture, and was common about 500 B.C. when galleys had their oar propulsion supplemented by sails. Perhaps the worst power-sailers which the world has ever seen were those of the navies in that uncertain period when warships had adopted steam engines but did not trust them sufficiently to discard their rigs. Then there was a generation of battleships and cruisers which were of uncertain reliability under power, and sometimes actively dangerous under sail. Successful compromise is never easy.

Four fundamental compromises have to be made when combining sail and power, each arising at a point where sail and power requirements come into conflict.

(i)   Efficient performance under sail demands a ballast-displacement ratio of 35–45 per cent. Weight of ballast represents loss of speed under power without any compensating gain.

(ii)   Windward ability depends on draught or an effective lateral area of keel. The former entails heavier displacement and greater wetted surface, which reduces speed under power. Clearly in the motor-sailer the argument for the centreboard is very strong.

(iii)   The form of hull required for economical performance under power at the higher speeds ($V/\sqrt{L} = 1\cdot34$ and above) is unsuitable for sailing. The form of hull demanded by sailing cannot be pressed to the higher speeds under power.

(iv)   The heavier engines and greater fuel capacity required for effective power propulsion detract from sailing performance by reducing the practicable ballast ratio, and so likewise does the drag of larger propeller needed to absorb the power efficiently.

The governing feature in planning a motor sailer must be the speed under power which it is desired to attain. This inevitably dominates the conception of the boat, and decides the balance that is to be struck between sail and power.

Fig. 85 illustrates in a general way the speed problem as it applies to motor sailers. On a base of yacht's length, the ratio of b.h.p. per ton of displacement required for speeds of between 6 and 9 knots is plotted, the curves being drawn as partially full and partially dotted lines. For clear reasons the power required per ton increases rapidly for any given speed with decrease in length, and more rapidly so with the higher than the lower speeds. Thus, whilst a little more than 1 b.h.p. per ton will give a 50-ft. boat a speed of 7 knots, 4 b.h.p. per ton will be needed for the same speed in a 30-ft. boat.

The speeds, for various lengths, at which wave-making becomes a feature that must govern the form of the hull is indicated in Fig. 85 by the heavy line labelled XY and crossing the various speed curves. From this it will be seen that the speeds are 7 knots for a 28-ft. boat; 8 knots for a 35-ft. boat; 9 knots for a 45-ft. boat, lengths being measured on the waterline. It will also be found that for these speeds between 4–5½ b.h.p. per ton of displacement are needed. At speeds lying, for any length, below this line XY a boat may be given the hull form of a sailing yacht. Her ballast ratio may be high without entailing exceptionally uneconomical propulsion under power, and the boat need not be dominated by engine and tanks to the detriment of the ballast ratio. British motor sailers are sometimes below this line—a long way below it.

If the sailing type of hull is adopted and the speed under power is coaxed up to the level of, or a little over, line X (that is, the speeds for lengths given above) the powering will have to be extravagant in relation to the size of the boat, which is often accepted in American motor sailers; rarely in British ones.

This leads to a consideration of the dotted portions of the speed lines. It will be seen that at and below a length of 30 ft. the 8-knot speed line is dotted; at 40 ft. the 9-knot line is dotted and the 8-knot line solid; at lengths exceeding 45 ft. all the speed lines are solid. The dotted lengths of the curves indicate the power speed range, for each length of boat, which lies outside the capacity of motor sailers designed to have a high sailing performance. Hydrodynamically, once boats reach such speeds they are riding on a single wavelength, the after-wave crest lying abaft the stern of the boat. The hull becomes, technically, overdriven, with a tendency to squat by the stern, and unless she possesses pronounced power yacht characteristics, with light draught and displacement, and easy buttock lines in combination with a fairly wide transom stern, increases in power will have little effect on the speed, and simply create abnormal disturbance in the water. In this range of speeds it is not practicable to satisfy the five fundamental compromises between power and sail, and motor sailers having speeds under power which, for their length, bring them on to the dotted portions of the curve, must be basically power yachts with enough canvas simply to give them reasonable control in reaching and running winds. But sailing ability must be sacrificed. A certain number of American motor sailers with a pronounced emphasis on sailing qualities in hull and rig are powered with between 6–7 b.h.p. per ton, which may bring them appreciably above line XY, and on to the dotted portion of the curves; but it does seem unlikely that they are making economical use of the high power installed, the main value of which must in practice be to allow lower speeds to be maintained in broken water, when perhaps 50 per cent more power will be needed for the speed than in smooth water.

44. American motor-sailer *Virginia Reel* by Philip Rhodes, 65 ft. length overall, 59 ft. length waterline, steel built by G. de Vries Lentsch, Amsterdam.

45. *Blue Leopard* by Laurent Giles and Partners. She has a very light displacement, and her sail area provides a higher sail area displacement ratio than that of a J-Class racing cutter of similar length, while the twin engines give greater b.h.p. per ton than many fully powered motor yachts.

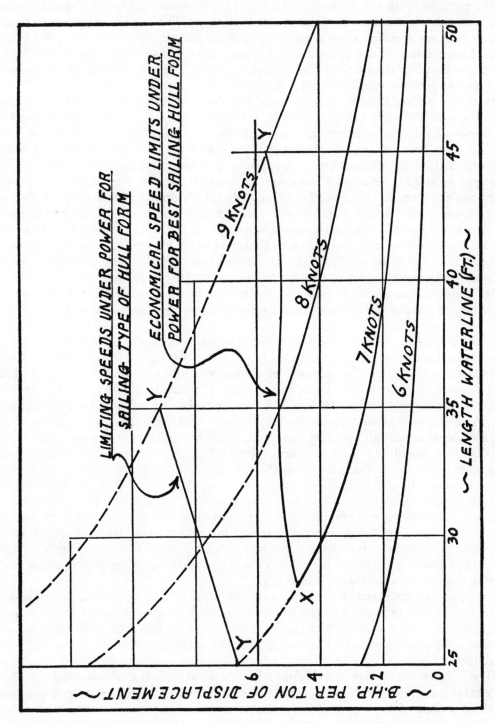

FIG. 85. *Power per ton displacement and corresponding speeds for sailing hull forms of moderate displacement*

The portions of the curves lying above line YY are beyond the limits of speeds under power which may be attained in motor sailers of any type. The line YY indicates the point in the speed range at which a motor sailer turns into a power yacht with a little steadying canvas. Motor sailers of the pronounced "seventy-thirty" class may have speeds lying close to this line, but their hulls have to be designed with close regard to power performance, and with heavy sacrifice to the sailing qualities.

It will be evident from the above study that the firmest marriage between sail and power (the true "fifty-fifty" in fact) is to be achieved in yachts of light displacement for their length—light displacement, that is, in terms of a sailing yacht of the same size. Since it is the relation of their displacements that makes the basic discord between hulls suitable for sail, or for efficient power propulsion, a drawing together of the sailing and power type of hull in this respect is a long step towards effective compromise. It allows a speed under power to be attained economically which compares favourably with the wholly power yacht, whilst light displacement, unlike other aspects of compromise between sail and power, does not operate against sailing efficiency. In England, Laurent Giles, we have seen, has taken advantage of this fact in his most highly developed motor sailers, producing what are in effect light displacement sailing hulls, perhaps of less draught than usual, and powering them so that speeds are obtained which lie well above line XY of Fig. 85. Thus the best qualities of sail and power may be combined without loss of windward ability or the installation of extravagant horse-power for the size of boat.

THE SAIL PLAN Motor sailers have three methods of propulsion at their disposal— sail, power, sail in combination with power. In the "thirty-seventy" type of predominantly power-driven motor sailer, the sails will be considered purely as steadying canvas until the wind draws abaft the beam. Then, in a moderate to fresh wind, they may be capable of assisting the engines, or even of giving a speed equal to the economical speed under power. A 50-ft. motor sailer may have a total resistance of about 800 lb. at a speed of $7\frac{1}{4}$ knots, and would require 40 b.h.p. for this speed. With the wind on the quarter about 1,600 sq. ft. of canvas would be needed to attain this speed under sail alone. Using power and sail together—that is, in effect, doubling the drive applied to the boat—perhaps a knot more speed would be obtained. The average "thirty-seventy" type of motor sailer would not, in fact, carry this amount of sail, or be capable of setting it effectively in quartering winds, and the advantage of combining sail and power would usually be little in speed, though possibly considerable in terms of easier motion, which would itself reflect upon the speed obtained. We may say that in the motor sailer which is predominantly of the type, the sail power is chiefly of use when dawdling, quietly cruising in free winds, and for easing the motion in awkward seaways.

The important characteristics which have to be taken into account when planning the rig are a hull lacking draught, and of a shape which will handle badly when heeled to any extent, and also having only light ballasting. The yacht thus lacks the ability to produce the lateral force which is necessary for sailing with the wind forward of the beam, and also the stability and hull form needed to carry effective areas of canvas on this point of sailing.

Thus a rig having its highest efficiency when the wind is abaft the beam, and one able to develop this efficiency with as small a heeling moment as possible, is needed; and this is provided by one of low aspect ratio, probably set on two masts. For our purposes we define low aspect ratio as a luff-foot ratio of less than 2:1. It is the aerodynamic characteristic of low sails to develop higher thrust per unit area when the wind is abaft the beam. It is further to be noted that the superiority of the low aspect ratio sail plan is at its greatest in strong winds, which are those in which the motor sailer of this type, with her small sail area and powerful engines, will find best use for her sails. Luff-foot ratios of as low as 1·5:1 will be profitable if the required sail area can be arranged in a rig of this proportion, and apart from the greater thrust per unit area delivered by such low rigs there is the further advantage, which may be demonstrated mathematically, that if the rig is considered in terms of heeling moment instead of canvas area, a greater thrust per unit of heeling moment may be derived from low aspect ratio sails. This may benefit this class of motor sailer when running under power and sail, and hence drawing the apparent wind a little forward of the beam.

In the true "fifty-fifty", and to a greater extent in the "seventy-thirty", the sails become of value on all points of sailing and it has been proved to be of advantage, in a moderate wind of perhaps 16 m.p.h. blowing from about 50 degrees off the bow, to sail rather than motor when it is possible to point within 10 degrees of the course. We find that the logic of design drives us to different proportions in rig for motor sailers of the "seventy-thirty" type, or in those in which sail and power are equal partners. Such boats must have a good performance with the wind forward of the beam, but they suffer from two disadvantages compared with the pure auxiliary—less sail area, and a hull lacking the auxiliary's ability to develop lateral resistance. These two features clearly suggest that the rig must be capable of developing, per unit area, high thrust when sailing with the wind forward of the beam, and to achieve this at the minimum of side thrust, which the hull is ill-equipped to counteract. In terms of sailing aerodynamics the rig should develop a high ratio of thrust to side force; and this is the peculiar ability of the high aspect ratio rig, which we will define as one having a luff-foot ratio of about three.

When sailing with the wind forward of the beam a rig of this proportion has a thrust coefficient of about 25 per cent more than the low aspect ratio rig, and simultaneously a much reduced side force, the ratio of thrust to side force of a rig having a 3:1 aspect ratio being about 10 per cent higher than that of a 2:1 rig. The high aspect ratio rig thus has two qualities which make it especially suitable for motor sailers of the class that take their sailing seriously: it is highly efficient for its area; it suits the type of hull which is lacking in the pure sailer's ability to resist leeway.

The high aspect ratio rig is less common in America than in England, and with a few exceptions is uncommon in both countries in the motor sailer type of yacht; even in those having an emphasis on sailing qualities, apparently as a result of some vague feeling that a rig which looks highly efficient should not be set above a hull which obviously is not devoted wholly to sail propulsion. Yet this would seem to be a mistake. Whilst we may justify the low, broad rig above motor sailers which are primarily motor yachts, those which are designed to use sail propulsion effectively benefit from the highly efficient high aspect ratio plan.

In "fifty-fifties" it is possible to practice what we may call "power-sailing" when the wind is forward of the beam. In terms purely of speed, the improvement obtained by using both power and sail concurrently is not so great as may be thought—and this applies in free winds also as we have noticed. The setting of sail will produce an angle of heel probably exceeding 5 degrees, and this will increase the resistance by about 20 per cent—an amount which the sails will have initially to overcome before they begin to show profit. If, when achieving under either sail or power alone a speed of, say 6 knots in a 30-footer, 7 knots in a 40-footer, or 7¾ knots in a 50-footer, a further knot of speed will require about double the power to be applied, whether by wind or engine, to the hull. Thus, when already moving fast under one source of power, the help of the other will not be valuable in terms of speed; it may, however, be economical.

Power-sailing, however, is perhaps the most comfortable method yet devised of working a small vessel to a point lying up to windward. The violent motion of the pure power yacht is eased, the steadiness of the sailing craft is achieved, and this without the uncomfortable angle of heel produced by a big sail plan; whilst the speed lost due to the limited area of canvas is compensated by the motor. But power-sailing by its nature requires sail plans able to develop high thrust with the wind forward of the beam; hence the high-aspect ratio sail plan is needed.

PROPELLERS IN MOTOR SAILERS In sailing craft with auxiliary power the drag of the idle screw, if locked when sailing, may amount to 20 per cent of the total resistance; and in the motor sailer with large propeller, or twin screws, it will be correspondingly more. If performance under sail is not to be severely impaired, the reduction of this sailing drag is an important problem to be solved.

The drag of an idle screw, or of two in certain motor sailers, represents a greater addition to the total resistance at sailing speeds than may at first be appreciated. If we consider a 45-ft. motor sailer of 30 tons displacement powered with one 75 b.h.p. engine giving a speed of 8 knots, an efficient propeller, turning at 1,000 r.p.m., would be of 2·16 ft. diameter and 1·4 ft. pitch. Under sail at 6 knots, when heeling about 10 degrees, the resistance of the yacht, excluding the propeller, is about 600 lb. That of the locked propeller is 350 lb. It therefore increases the total resistance by some 58 per cent. In a free wind, when the yacht is sailing without heel, the drag of the propeller would represent about 70 per cent of the total resistance.

In terms of speed the picture is, of course, less depressing. The increase in resistance from 600 lb. to 950 lb. would entail a loss in sailing speed under the above conditions of about 1 knot, from 6 to 5 knots. Even this, however, is clearly to be avoided.

One method of reducing screw drag is offered by the sailing clutch, by means of which the screw and tail shaft are disconnected from the engines and allowed to rotate freely under the action of the waterflow when sailing. This method, which may provide, under the right conditions, an effective solution to the problem, may under others produce surprises; as apparently it once did for Clinton Crane,* who tells this story in his memoirs.

"I arranged a method of disconnecting the engine and allowing the propeller to rotate in the auxiliary barque *Apache*, which belonged to Edwin Randolph ... we steamed out of harbour in a stiff breeze and decided to try the effect of allowing the propeller to rotate. We had been logging on the patent log a little better than 10 knots under sail when we were dragging the propeller, and I expected an improvement in the speed when the propeller was disconnected and allowed to rotate. Much to my surprise and the owner's disappointment, as soon as the propeller began to rotate the speed decreased from 10 knots to 9½ knots. Freewheeling was obviously not the answer for an auxiliary."

Clinton Crane was justified in his opinion with the evidence before him; but now, many years later, we may put our finger on the element in the problem which misled

* *Clinton Crane's Yachting Memoirs*, Van Nostrand Company Inc.

him. It may be briefly stated thus: if owing to friction in the shaft and similar causes the speed of the freewheeling propeller is reduced below a certain amount, its resistance may actually be higher than when locked. If a speed in excess of this critical one be achieved the resistance of the spinning propeller will be lower than when locked; though it will not become zero unless the number of revolutions required for no drag are reached.

Table 21 shows the drag, in lb., of a screw of 28 in. diameter, 29 in. pitch, at various r.p.m. between zero and 270, when moving ahead at a speed of 7½ knots. It is based on tank data collected by Dr. Conn and presented in a paper before the Institution of Engineers and Shipbuilders in Scotland. The significant characteristic of the figures is the initial rise above a drag of 480 lb. until the screw is turning at almost 150 r.p.m. This is the range of r.p.m. values at which the screw's drag is higher than when locked. 150 r.p.m. represents the speed at which the screw must freewheel to give lower resistance than when locked.

TABLE 21

R.P.M.	0	50	100	150	200	250	270
Resistance in lb.	480	525	600	480	290	50	0

If, however, we consider the relative amounts of the resistances at various r.p.m. it will be seen that though the resistance is more at the lower r.p.m. than when locked, the excess, under the worst conditions, at r.p.m. of a little below 100, is about 20 per cent, whilst provided the propeller can be coaxed into rotating a little faster—at between 150 r.p.m. to 260 r.p.m.—the drag is decreased rapidly and finally eliminated. Thus, the gain from allowing a propeller to rotate freely may be great; the loss, at the worst, very much less severe. Clearly the object in design must be to reduce the friction in the free-shafting to a minimum.

One type of sailing clutch, made by Parsons, has thrust bearings incorporated with the clutch, which is operated by a small lever integral with the body of the clutch. It has, therefore, to be arranged that this should be accessible, through a hatch in the cockpit floor, or in the open in the engine room when this is amidships.

An alternative to the sailing clutch in motor-sailers is offered by the controllable pitch screw of the type capable of being locked in the neutral or fully-feathered position. Twin screws of this kind, by Slack and Parr, are fitted in the British Aluminium Company's motor sailer *Morag Mhor*. Compared with a solid screw and sailing clutch the controllable pitch screw suffers from its lower efficiency under power and a drag when sailing that is higher than that of a freely rotating solid propeller. This is caused by the drag of the large boss, and also the impossibility of feathering the blades so that all drag but friction is eliminated. Under either power or sail alone the C.P. screw is likely to be less efficient than the solid screw with efficient declutching mechanism; but it shows to advantage when sail and power are being used in combination, when the pitch may be adjusted to suit the altered speed of advance and thrust.

CHAPTER FOURTEEN

The Calculations

THE mathematics involved in practical sailing yacht design need not be advanced. They are chiefly a matter of adapting simple calculations to a specialised purpose. It is important, in the process, to adopt a rational standard of precision. The number of figures after a decimal point, for example, are often the result merely of the arithmetical process, and three figures may indicate no higher degree of absolute accuracy than one, or than none; for this is dependent on the original data put into the sum, which may themselves have been accurate to no more than one place of decimals. Calculations should therefore be worked sensibly, not blindly, and their results checked arithmetically and by common sense. The latter will often reveal the mistake that slips through the mathematical check.

The most important calculations are those concerned with areas and volumes, and with the locating of their centres of gravity. Displacement, the fundamental calculation, is found by measuring the immersed cross-section areas of the hull, and then applying one of two mathematical rules which will convert the areas into a volume. There are rules other than the two above, but their practical value in yacht design is slight. The proofs of mathematical rules are not given here; they will be found in any standard textbook on naval architecture.

The two rules are known respectively as Simpson's and the trapezoidal. The cross-sections used when calculating displacement are those employed for the designing and fairing of the hull lines, and the number of sections which were drawn for this purpose will govern which of the two rules will be suitable.

The immersed cross-section areas are measured with a planimeter. Alternatively, each section may be divided into triangles, as shown in Fig. 86, and the areas of the triangles found by the mathematical method. This way of measuring section areas was used by the old shipwright-designers, and though tedious can be quite accurate, but it will certainly not appeal to the professional today.

When measuring section areas by planimeter it is best to run the pointer round each section twice; or, alternatively, having traced in the clockwise direction, to return anti-clockwise and ensure that the dial reading shows the initial value. Planimeters seem to have a certain amount of temperament and single readings should not be trusted. Some planimeters have correction factors for use with different textures of paper.

Before applying the areas to the displacement calculation, there is a further check to be made on their accuracy. The curve of areas should be plotted. Since the hull lines are fair, the curve should also be fair, though sometimes slightly humped amidships by the keel. If the plotted points show any unfairness, the areas of doubtful sections should be checked.

Table 22, columns 1, 2, 3 and 4, shows a calculation of displacement by Simpson's rule, using the usual eleven sections dividing the waterline length into ten equal parts.

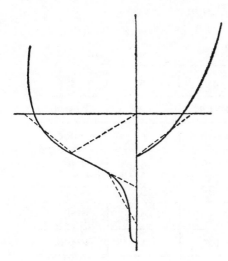

FIG. 86. *A method of measuring section areas*

Columns 5 and 6 may be disregarded for the moment. For Simpson's rule the waterline must always be divided into an *even* number of equal parts, the one exception being the modified calculation shown later. Ten is the usual number; in very small yachts and dinghies eight may be convenient. In all normal displacement calculations, the first and last ordinates, or sections, will be at the waterline endings, and hence will have no immersed area.

It will be seen from Table 22 that to obtain the displacement, the first and last ordinates are multiplied by $\frac{1}{2}$, and the intermediate by 2 and 1 alternately. Thus the penultimate ordinates' multiplier at either end will always be 2, and since the end ordinates in yacht calculations will be zero, the $\frac{1}{2}$ multipliers will have no effect. The functions of the ordinates are added together, and the sum multiplied by two-thirds of the spacing between them. The scale must be enlarged to full size, the section areas having been measured in square inches. To obtain the volume of the yacht's underwater body in cubic feet, the answer to the Simpson's rule calculation is multiplied by the square of the scale inverted. Thus, if the scale of the drawings is $\frac{1}{2}$ in. to 1 ft., the multiplier becomes 2 squared, or 4. Multiplying by the square of the inverted scale both converts the volume to full size and changes the units from cubic inches to cubic feet. Since 35 cu. ft. of salt water weigh a ton, the volume of the underwater body in cubic feet is divided by this figure to obtain the displacement in tons. A further point to be noticed is that half section areas only are measured and the answer must be multiplied by 2 for both sides of the ship.

In many descriptions of Simpson's rule, the multipliers are expressed as 1, 4, 2, 4, 2, 4 ... 1, and the sum of the functions is multiplied by one-third instead of two-thirds of the spacing. This is a less convenient form of the rule, producing more bulky figures.

Owing to the sharper curvature of the hull at the ends, half-ordinates between the normal, equally-spaced ones are sometimes introduced for accuracy at both ends of the waterline. The multiples for Simpson's rule are then changed to those shown in Table 23, the figures of which apply to the same yacht as Table 22. A half-ordinate has been placed between section 0 and 1, and between 9 and 10. The first three multipliers then

TABLE 22

1	2	3	4	5	6
Section	Area	Multiplier	Function	Arm.	Moment
0	0·000	$\frac{1}{2}$	0·000	5	0·000
1	0·310	2	0·620	4	2·480
2	0·990	1	0·990	3	2·970
3	1·770	2	3·540	2	7·080
4	2·400	1	2·400	1	2·400
5	2·730	2	5·460	0	14·930
6	2·550	1	2·550	1	2·550
7	2·070	2	4·140	2	8·280
8	1·320	1	1·320	3	3·960
9	0·585	2	1·170	4	4·680
10	0·000	$\frac{1}{2}$	0·000	5	0·000
			22·190		19·470

$$\text{Displacement} = 22 \cdot 190 \times 3 \times \tfrac{2}{3} \times 2 \times 4 \times \tfrac{1}{35}$$

$$= 10 \cdot 14 \text{ tons}$$

Longitudinal C.B. Excess Moment $= 19 \cdot 47 - 14 \cdot 93$
$$= 4 \cdot 54 \text{ aft.}$$

$$\text{C.B. aft. of Section } 5 = \frac{4 \cdot 54}{22 \cdot 190} \times 3 = 0 \cdot 614 \text{ ft. aft. No. 5}$$

N.B.—Section spacing is 3 ft. (i.e. A 30-ft. waterline divided into ten parts).

become $\frac{1}{4}$, 1, $\frac{3}{4}$, and the last three $\frac{3}{4}$, 1, $\frac{1}{4}$, the multiplier of the half-ordinate at either end being 1. Like the first Simpson's rule, this modification needs an odd number of ordinates— i.e. the waterline divided into an *equal* number of parts before the introduction of the half-ordinates. Half-ordinates at the ends are therefore easily introduced in the common eleven-ordinate drawing.

Sometimes it is convenient to use Simpson's rule when the waterline is divided into an *unequal* number of parts—say seven by eight ordinates, which is not sufficiently close spacing for the trapezoidal rule. Such spacings may occur in dinghy designs. It is not

TABLE 23

1	2	3	4
Section	*Area*	*Multiplier*	*Function*
0	0·000	¼	0·000
½	0·130	1	0·130
1	0·310	¾	0·233
2	0·990	2	1·980
3	1·770	1	1·770
4	2·400	2	4·800
5	2·730	1	2·730
6	2·550	2	5·100
7	2·070	1	2·070
8	1·320	2	2·640
9	0·585	¾	0·438
9½	0·280	1	0·280
10	0·000	¼	0·000

22·171

$$\text{Displacement} = 22·171 \times 3 \times \tfrac{2}{3} \times 2 \times 4 \times \tfrac{1}{35}$$
$$= 10·15 \text{ tons.}$$

always realised that Simpson's rule may be used with an even number of ordinates by the introduction of a half-ordinate at one end only. This calculation is shown in Table 24. The half-ordinate is placed at the bow, where the lines run in sharply to the stem; aft, in the way of the transom, where there is no abrupt change in the run of the lines, a half-ordinate is not needed anyway, and by this simple device of using one half-ordinate Simpson's rule is made practicable where otherwise the sections would have to be respaced, or the less accurate trapezoidal rule used. In Table 24 the figures refer to a dinghy. It was therefore convenient to express the displacement in pounds. To do this, the volume of the displacement is multiplied by 64 instead of being divided by 35, there being 64 lb. of salt water to the cubic foot.

A quick check may be made on the displacement by an adaptation of a rule much used in general naval architecture, and called Tchebycheff's. In the form here described it is an

TABLE 24

Section	Area	S.M.	Function
1	0·000	$\frac{1}{4}$	0·000
1$\frac{1}{2}$	0·855	1	0·855
2	1·440	$\frac{3}{4}$	1·080
3	2·550	2	5·100
4	3·000	1	3·000
5	2·670	2	5·340
6	1·635	1	1·635
7	0·690	2	1·380
8	0·000	$\frac{1}{2}$	0·000
			18·390

Displacement = $18.39 \times \frac{2}{3} \times 1.75 \times 64 = 1{,}389$ lb.

N.B.—Full section areas and not half-sections are used above. Scale of drawing was one inch to one foot. No correction is therefore needed for scale.

approximation of Tchebycheff's very accurate calculation. It is applicable only when the usual eleven-ordinate spacing is used for the waterline. Four sections are used: they are numbers 4 and 6 (i.e. those on either side of the section at mid-length) and sections 1 and 9, which are the ones immediately forward and aft of the waterline endings. The displacement is the product of one quarter of the waterline length and the sum of the above sections' areas:

$$\frac{\text{L.W.L.} \times \text{Sum of Measured Section's Areas}}{4} = \text{Volume of Displacement}$$

Using the figures in Table 22 the displacement is:

Section		Area
1	..	0·310
4	..	2·400
6	..	2·550
9	..	0·585
		5·845 = Sum of Areas

$$\text{Displacement} = \frac{5.845 \times 30}{4} \times \frac{2 \times 4}{35} = 10.02 \text{ tons}$$

The approximation in this adaptation of Tchebycheff's rule is in the section spacing. The four Tchebycheff ordinates do not correspond exactly with any of the normal eleven ordinates, and we have assumed them to do so. But the error involved is slight, and the rule produces a displacement which, with the usual yacht form, varies between 0·1 and 1·0 per cent *under* the actual, for which allowance may be made. The modified Tchebycheff rule is useful for finding the displacement in the early stages of design, and in many other cases where a quick estimation is needed. Using it, the displacement may be calculated, once the four section areas are known, in under a minute.

The trapezoidal rule is the obvious one to use for calculating displacement when the waterline is divided into about fifteen or more parts. Even with only eleven ordinates, the error involved in this rule is only about one-half of 1 per cent, which is sufficiently close for much yacht work. This means that with a yacht displacing 12 tons, the error involved in using the trapezoidal rule with eleven ordinates would be 134 lb., or about twice the weight of the windlass. It is to be noted that the trapezoidal rule produces an answer which will invariably be *under* the actual, though only by the above small amount.

For the rule, the waterline may be divided into either an even or odd number of parts. The multiplier of each section area except those at the ends is one; that of the end ordinates is one-half, and since these usually have no area, the half-multipliers may be disregarded. The rule therefore resolves itself into adding up the section areas, the sum of which is then multiplied by the spacing to obtain the volume of displacement. The usual corrections for scale, and the conversion of the volume into a weight, is made as in Simpson's rule.

The following standards of accuracy are to be expected, assuming that the section areas are correctly determined, with Simpson's and the trapezoidal rules and various spacings of sections:

TABLE 25

Number of Intervals	Percentage Error—Positive or Negative	
	Simpson's	Trapezoidal
8	+ 0·30	— 1·00
10	+ 0·12	— 0·68
12	+ 0·06	— 0·48
15	+ 0·03	— 0·32
20	+ 0·02	— 0·16

The error involved, even with the trapezoidal rule and only ten intervals, is probably less than that inherent in the yacht's weight estimate and other approximations. And the fact that the error is an underestimate is helpful.

We should not, however, become too conceited about the accuracy of our calculations. When assessing the merits of rated racing designs such as 12-Metres, 5·5-Metres, the International C.R. classes, and other high class work in the testing tanks, it has become evident that the errors inherent in the architects' basic calculations from their drawings are liable to be big enough to submerge the differences in performance that the tank seeks to measure.

For example: the analysis of tank results may show that within the chosen speed range 12-Metre Model A is superior to 12-Metre Model B. But the analysis is the outcome of many calculations, such as the displacements of the two yachts, and their centres of buoyancy and gravity, and the errors involved in making these calculations by conventional methods may be enough to reverse Model A and Model B in order of merit. We may be trying, in fact, to get out of model experiments results to a degree of accuracy greater than the data put into them.

One source of the trouble appears to lie in the continuous expansion and contraction of paper, which means that all planimeter readings are subject to an error beyond the possible considerable one involved in the instrument itself and its operation. In one drawing office the movements of paper were measured by micrometer during the course of several days and the results plotted as a curve. This showed considerable expansions and contractions during the period in our climate, and a source of crucial error when research as opposed to practical construction is concerned.

THE LONGITUDINAL CENTRE OF BUOYANCY This may be found by poising a paper pattern of the curve of areas on a knife edge. There is nothing unscientific in this practical method, though designers may be a little coy about using it. The pattern should be folded into a spill for stiffness, the creases being made parallel to the base of the curve. The point of balance of the resulting spill will be at the C.G. of the paper pattern, and hence the fore and aft C.B. of the yacht, since the curve of areas represents graphically the yacht's distribution of displacement.

The method of calculating the centre is shown in columns 5 and 6 of Table 22 (p. 216). Moments may be taken about any point; the fore end of the waterline (section 0), or amidships (section 5), are usually chosen; the latter is the most convenient, the figures being smaller. This is the section about which moments are taken in Table 22.

In order to reduce the amount of figuring, section spaces instead of distances are used for expressing the arms by which each area is multiplied when calculating its moment, and the section spacing is used as a multiple at the end of the calculation. The moments of the fore- and after-bodies are totalled independently, the greater total indicating on which side of section 5 the C.B. lies. In all normal yachts the after-body moments will be the greater, and the C.B. will lie aft of No. 5 section. The distance of the C.B. aft of this section is found by dividing the excess moment—that is, the difference between the totals of the fore- and after-body moments—by the sum of the functions of the areas (column 4) and multiplying the dividend by the section spacing.

If the moments had been taken about section 0, the total of all the sectional area moments would have been used instead of the excess moment, and the calculations completed as before. The answer would then be the distance of the C.B. aft of the forward waterline ending. The C.B. is found by a similar method when the trapezoidal rule is used for calculating displacement.

The vertical position of the centre of buoyancy is determined by the same integrating process, using successive waterlines instead of sections. Their areas are measured by planimeter, and a vertical displacement curve may be drawn to confirm their accuracy.

Moments are most suitably taken from the load waterline, the arms for the moments being the spacing of the waterlines. Unless the bottom of the keel is horizontal, and conveniently falls at the depth of an exact waterline interval, intelligent allowance must be made for the volume of the keel lying below the lowest waterline. In comparison with the total volume of displacement this will usually be small, and not worth elaborate mathematical correction.

POUNDS PER INCH IMMERSION It is sometimes necessary to know the changes in draught and freeboard which will result from weight alternations. In general naval architecture the tons per inch immersion is calculated for a number of different waterlines. The ton is too large a unit for yacht work, and pounds or hundredweights should be used. Knowing the area of the L.W.L. plane, measured by planimeter and corrected for scale, the number of pounds needed to lift or sink the yacht by one inch is

$$\frac{\text{Waterplane area} \times 16}{3}$$

Expressed in hundredweights it is:

$$\frac{\text{Waterplane area}}{16}$$

In correcting the waterplane area for scale, the square of the inverted scale is again used, as in the displacement calculation. It should be added that as the waterplane area varies at different draughts, it is not absolutely accurate to use the area of the designed L.W.L. plane for big increases or decreases in draught. In practice, when the changes in immersion will not be more than a few inches on either side of the L.W.L. the error may be neglected.

A serviceable approximation may be derived from the above expressions making use of the fact that the waterplane coefficient (ratio of the waterplane area to that of the circumscribing rectangle) is about 0·7 for average sailing yachts. In full-ended yachts it may reach 0·75, and some fine-ended boats have ratios as low as 0·65. The P.P.I. may be approximated:

$$\text{P.P.I.} = 3 \cdot 73 \ (\text{Length Waterline} \times \text{Beam Waterline}).$$

MOMENT TO CHANGE TRIM The moment to change trim one inch (M.C.T.1″) is the moment of weight in ft./lb. or ft./tons needed to produce a change of trim totalling one inch at the bow and stern when these are added together. In altering trim a boat pivots over her centre of floatation, which is at the centroid of the load waterline, and with normal shapes this is a little abaft amidships, resulting in a slightly greater change of trim forward than aft.

The moment of change trim is governed by the longitudinal metacentric height, which compared with the transverse height is considerable. The expression is:

$$\text{M.C.T.1″ (ft./lb.)} = \frac{\text{Displacement (lb.)} \times \text{G.M. (Longal.)}}{12 \times \text{Length Waterline}}$$

For beamy and heavy displacement craft such as sailing yachts the longitudinal

G.M. is approximately equal to the waterline length. The serviceable approximation then appears:

$$\text{M.C.T.1}'' \text{ (ft./lb.)} = \frac{\text{Displacement (lb.)}}{12}$$

The change of trim caused by movement of ballast, modification in the stowage of sails or ground tackle thus equals:

$$12 \left(\frac{\text{Weight} \times \text{Distance Moved}}{\text{Displacement}} \right)$$

ADJUSTMENTS TO BALLAST KEEL Adjustments in the position of the vertical centre of gravity may be made by modifications to the draught, at the design stage or sometimes on a completed yacht, having the effect of bodily raising or lowering the ballast keel (Fig. 103). The change in the yacht's V.C.G. by such alterations in the height of the ballast keel's C.G. may be found thus:

If ballast keel is bodily raised or lowered by a decrease or increase of draught:

$$G\,G_1 = gg_1 \times \frac{w}{W}$$

where w = weight of keel; W = displacement; g = original position of the keel's C.G.; g_1 = adjusted position of keel's C.G. ; G = original C.G. of yacht; G = adjusted C.G. of yacht.

That is, if the C.G. of the keel is lowered, the C.G. of the yacht as a whole will be lowered by the product of the distance the keel's centre has been lowered and the fraction which the keel weight bears to the total displacement.

Thus if the keel is 40 per cent of the total displacement and its C.G. is lowered by lift, the C.G. of the yacht will be lowered by 0·4 ft.

If the ballast keel is increased in weight, resulting in a corresponding increase in displacement:

$$G\,G_1 = \frac{Gg \times \text{increase in weight of keel}}{\text{increase in displacement}}$$

If the ballast ratio is increased (i.e. weight of ballast keel) added to without corresponding increase in displacement:

$$G\,G_1 = \frac{Gg \times \text{increase in weight of keel}}{\text{original weight of keel}}$$

VOLUMETRIC HULL BALANCE As a check on the harmony of the fore- and after-bodies, it must be ensured that there is no considerable change of trim as the hull heels. This is done by plotting a curve of heeled areas of the hull assuming no change of trim. If the heeled C.B. does not fall in the same fore and aft position as when upright, a false assumption has been made, showing that actually the hull will alter trim so as to bring the heeled and upright C.B.s into coincidence. The common statement that "the C.B. moves aft on heeling" is a convenient but not accurate statement.

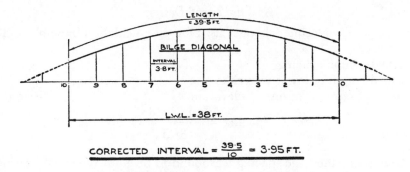

CORRECTED INTERVAL = $\frac{39.5}{10}$ = 3·95 FT.

FIG. 87. *Finding the mean value of section spacing*

Heeled waterlines are struck across the body plan, and the immersed heeled area of each section measured by planimeter. The areas are plotted to the same scale as the upright, and exceed them by an amount representing the excess of the in-wedge over the out-wedge at each section. The C.B. of the heeled curve is then found by poising.

Great accuracy is not needed in this test, and the position of the heeled C.B. need not be calculated. If the coincidence of the two centres is within about 4 per cent of the waterline length, the hull may be considered satisfactory. It must be noted, however, that there is absolute coincidence in many well-balanced yachts, this indicating that no change of trim occurs on heeling.

WETTED SURFACE AND AREA OF PLANKING Wetted surface area will be needed if sail area/wetted surface comparisons are to be made with other yachts; and a similar calculation, but including the topsides, will give the area of the planking. This is used when estimating hull weights.

The method is to measure the girth of each half section and to put the result through Simpson's or the trapezoidal rule. The multiplier at each section will be the same as that used in the displacement calculation, but girths instead of areas are now the multiplicands. The half-girths are measured either by bending a flexible spline round each section in turn or by using a straight slip of paper and rotating it round successive points of contact on each curve. For wetted surface, girths are measured to the waterline only.

The section spacing will not be the same as that used in the displacement calculation. The spacing, as measured along the yacht's planking, will vary from place to place depending on the run of the lines; amidships, in the topsides, it will be almost the same as the normal spacing, whilst forward and aft it will be appreciably more.

A mean value of the section spacing is found by measuring the length of the bilge diagonal between the waterline endings, and dividing this length by the number of section spaces in the waterline length. This is shown in Fig. 87. Another method is to measure the girth, or actual length, of a waterline at about half of the hull depth (excluding keel) below the L.W.L. and to compare this expanded length with that of the same waterline in the elevation, where it is represented as a straight line. The proportion of the one to the other will give the proportion which the corrected section spacing must bear to the normal. For the 38-ft. waterline schooner used for the calculation in Table 26 the figures are:

Normal section spacing   ..   ..   3·8 ft.

Girthed length of lower waterline   33   ft.

Length of same waterline in elevation   ..   ..   ..   31·5 ft.

$$\text{Corrected spacing} = \frac{33 \times 3\cdot8}{31\cdot5} = 3\cdot98 \text{ ft.}$$

Using the diagonal method the spacing was found to be 3·95 When calculating the area of the planking, it is probably more accurate to use the bilge diagonal method.

TABLE 26

No. of Section	½-Girth of Section	Simpson's Multiplier	Function
0	0·00	½	0·00
1	5·75	2	11·50
2	7·95	1	7·95
3	9·50	2	19·00
4	9·75	1	9·75
5	9·85	2	19·60
6	9·80	1	9·80
7	9·25	2	18·50
8	8·50	1	8·50
9	7·50	2	15·00
10	5·75	1	5·75
11	3·15	2	6·30
12	1·70	½	0·85
			132·50

$$\text{Corrected interval} = \frac{39\cdot5}{10} = 3\cdot95$$

$$\text{Area of side planking} = 132\cdot5 \times \tfrac{2}{3} \times 3\cdot9$$
$$= 344\cdot5 \text{ sq. ft.}$$

46. *Chesapeake '32*, an American class of plastics sloop.

47. *Rhodes Meridian*, another class of American plastics sloop. Compare with Plate 46.

It is convenient in wetted surface calculations not to use any conversions for scale, but to measure the girths to scale in the first place.

The very involved Mean Secant method of measuring wetted surface, though described in some textbooks, should never be used for yacht work, and is indeed rarely used in general naval architecture.

WEIGHT CALCULATIONS These are not often made for small craft, except when built to rated classes, or of an uncommon breed on which there is little data. With larger craft weight approximations are sometimes necessary, and particularly so when no inside ballast, except a little for trimming purposes, is to be used. Indeed, if weight calculations were not so time-consuming, it is doubtful if the praises of inside ballast would ever have been sung so cheerfully. With wood construction, however, weights are always approximate owing to the uncertain density of timber, which varies by 20 per cent or more between the green and seasoned states. Weight calculations are to a large extent common sense and dreary arithmetic, palliated by the intelligent use of approximations.

One of them is the cubic number. By its means the structural weight of a yacht may be approximated from that of a similar yacht, of the same type of scantlings, but of any size. The cubic number may be accepted as:

$$\frac{\text{L.O.A.} \times \text{Max. beam} \times \text{Depth of hull}}{100}$$

the latter quantity excluding the fin keel, and being measured to the point of greatest body depth. The structural weights vary in different yachts in the same proportion as their cubic numbers. A yacht of 40 ft. L.O.A., 10 ft. beam and 3 ft. depth of body will have a cubic number of 12; that of a yacht 50 ft. L.O.A., 12 ft. beam and 4 ft. depth will be 24. Assuming the yachts to be of reasonably similar type and proportionate scantlings, the constructional weight of the larger will be double that of former. Below is given the weight analysis of a 26-ton T.M. yacht of 47 ft. L.O.A., the scantlings of which are to Lloyd's. This example will serve as a guide to weight estimations of smaller or larger craft, basing the comparisons on the cubic numbers.

When making more detailed weight calculations, a yacht is divided into units, the weight of each being found by multiplying the volume of timber in the unit by its weight per cubic foot. The following methods of calculation will be found serviceable:

Planking. The area is multiplied by the thickness to determine the volume, care being taken here, and everywhere else, not to make the error of mixing units. The area of planking will be in square feet; the thickness must therefore be expressed as a fraction of a foot, and not in inches.

Frames and Timbers. The area of the frames will be a certain proportion of that of the planking, the proportion depending on the siding and spacing of the frames. Thus, frames with a siding of 1 in. and spaced 12 in. will have a surface area of one-twelfth of the planking. The volume of the frames is the product of this area and the moulding of the frames.

When the construction embodies both grown and bent timbers, the two varieties should be treated separately. Grown timbers are not of constant moulding, being thickest at the keel, and tapering towards the head. An average must be struck between the head

P

and heel mouldings, this mean moulding being the thickness by which area is multiplied to obtain the volume.

Keel, Stem, Sternpost, Deadwood and Floors. Approximations are best made when dealing with these members, since their irregular shapes make the calculations of volume difficult.

Stringers, Gunwales, Shelves and Clamps. The lengths of these may be measured from the drawing. Length is multiplied by the cross-section area, allowance being made for the taper in the members.

Deck. The area is most simply measured by planimeter, deductions being made for hatches, coachroof and cockpit. No allowance need be made for the deck camber, the effect of which on area is insignificant.

Deck Beams. The siding and spacing of the beams will show what proportion they bear to the deck area. A mean value for the moulding has to be judged. The moulding is generally the same at the ends of all beams, except those heavier ones in the way of the mast and deck breaks, but it varies at the middle. To determine the volume, the mean moulding is multiplied by the area. Allowance must be made for heavy beams, and for hanging and lodging knees.

Joiner Work and Furnishing. This may be worked out by proportions from similar craft. The only other method is to consider each item in turn. Hardware catalogues usually give the weight of the larger fittings described.

Auxiliary. The weight of this will be known. The additional weight involved in the installation must be allowed for. The fuel tanks may also be included under this heading.

Fastenings and Paint. This is best calculated by proportion. Five per cent of the hull construction and joiner work weights is a reasonable allowance to make for fastenings. Two and a half per cent of the same weight will cover the painting and finishing.

The following is a full weight analysis for one yacht designed to Lloyd's Rules:

Weight Analysis of Yacht

L.O.A.	..	47 ft.	Beam	..	12 ft.
L.W.L.	..	38 ft.	Draught	..	5 ft.
		Displacement	17·13 tons		

Item	Weight	Item	Weight
Hull Structure		Engine bearers	190
Side Planking	2,980	Fo'c'sle bulkhead	170
Keel	600	Stateroom bulkhead	353
Stem and Apron	480	Saloon bulkhead	390
Sternpost and deadwood ..	320	Galley bulkhead	350
Bent timbers	682	Rudder	150
Grown timbers and floors	940	Rudder stock and tube	80
Bilge ceiling	380	Forward deck beams	80
Main gunwale	370	Amidships deck beams	180
Upper gunwale	147	Aft deck beams	40
Gunwale packing pieces	58	Forward deck planking	410
Centreboard and ironwork	250	Amidships deck planking	810
Centreboard case	40	Aft deck planking	90
Centreboard tackle	15	Hanging and lodging knees ..	305

Item	Weight		Item	Weight
Rail capping	70		Folding table..	7
Rubber	70		Two Calor gas containers	112
Keel and stem bolts	140		Cutlery and Crockery	25
Doghouse sides	22			
Doghouse roof	137		**W.C.**	
Doghouse front	20		Fore and aft bulkhead	68
Doghouse beams	20		Cupboard	10
Doghouse carlins	8		Washbasin (S/L No. 286)	40
Cockpit coaming	34		W.C. (Blake Victory)	80
Cockpit side seats	70		"Lacotile" lining	21
Cockpit aft seats	26			
Cockpit lockers	30		**Saloon**	
Skylight sides and carlins ⎫			Settees	160
Skylight front and back ⎬	60		Settee cushions	64
Skylight top and fittings ⎭			Sideboard and bunk	90
Forehatch sides and carlins⎫			Cupboard (aft port)	60
Forehatch front and back ⎬	54		Cupboard (aft starb'd)	60
Forehatch top ⎭			Table	100
Cockpit floor and bearers	37		Chair	20
Doghouse sole and bearers	135		Desk	50
Galley and W.C. sole and bearers	100		Bar Cupboard	80
Saloon sole and bearers	220		Sideboard (starb'd aft)	75
Stateroom sole and bearers	122		Sideboard (starb'd for'd)	75
Fo'c'sle sole and bearers	50		Bookshelf	10
Paint, varnish, stopping	450		Calor stove	20
Fastenings	737		Extension speaker	12
Cockpit bulkhead	338		Cabin ceiling..	90
	———			
	12,820		**Stateroom**	
			Wardrobe (port)	60
			Wardrobe (starb'd)	60
			Dressing table and drawers	30
			Cupboard (starb'd)	13
			Cupboard (port)	13
Accommodation Furnishing and			Ceiling	24
Fittings			Berth, bedding, drawers	120
Doghouse			Berth, bedding, drawers (port)	120
Berth and cushions (starb'd)	78			
Berth and cushions (port)	78		**Fo'c'sle**	
Companion steps	30		Bench (port)	30
Lockers behind berths	90		Wardrobe	60
Table top	30		Pipe cot	20
Cupboard (starb'd)	60		Sail bin	12
Cupboard (port)	60		Shelf and chain locker	50
Wireless	25		Folding wash basin	15
			W.C. (Blake Victory)	80
Galley				———
Sink and cupboard	53			2,650
Dresser	60			———
Table and Refrigerator	50			
Stove and bench	50			

Item	Weight
Hull and Deck Fittings	
Windlass (S/L No. 497)	168
16 Sidelights (S/L No. 1070 No. 3)	265
Stanchions and wire..	112
Bilge pump and piping	40
Steering wheel and gearing.. ..	15
Sundry deck fittings	200
Fuel tanks	280
Water tanks in saloon	259
Batteries, boxes, wiring	325
	1,664

Item	Weight
Fire extinguishers	12
Nav. lights, boards, brackets ..	50
Compass and mounting	20
Ensign staff and socket	6
Two lifebuoys	5
Six fend-offs	12
Dinghy	150
Boom crutches	50
Lifebuoys and jackets	15
Flags	20
Dinghy davit	30
	1,034

Item	Weight
Auxiliary and Installation	
R.T.R.4. Engine and Rev. Gear ..	1,120
Reduction gear	56
Sailing clutch	50
Exhaust	40
Seacock and strainer	10
Pipes	15
Engine tray	40
Circulating water and oil	25
Propeller	30
Propeller bracket	50
Propeller shaft	40
Stern tube	20
Spares and sundries	50
	1,546

Item	Weight
Rig	
Mainmast (inc. ironwork)	850
Foremast (inc. ironwork)	263
Mainboom (inc. ironwork) ..	100
Foreboom	63
Staysail boom	23
Sails	182
Standing rigging	145
Running rigging and blocks ..	140
Foresheet horse	11
Staysail sheet horse	11
Mainsheet horse	15
Rigging screws	60
Two Highfield levers	12
	1,875

Item	Weight
Outfit	
1st bower anchor	45
2nd bower anchor	45
Kedge anchor	30
45 fthm. $\frac{3}{8}$ in. cable	427
Hawser 45 fthm. 2½ in. hemp ..	65
Warp 45 fthm. 2 in. hemp	41
Two boathooks	11

Item	Weight
Load	
Fuel—120 gallons	1,010
Water—114 gallons	1,040
Stores	500
Crew (5)	800
	3,350

SUMMARY

Item											Weight
Hull structure	..	..	..	..	..	..	..	..	..	..	12,820
Accommodation Furnishings and Fittings..		..	..	..	..	..	..	..	2,650
Hull and deck fittings	..	..	..	..	..	..	..	..	..	1,664
Auxiliary and installation	..	..	..	..	..	..	..	..	..	1,546
Outfit	..	..	..	..	..	..	..	..	..	..	1,034
Rig ..	..	..	..	..	..	..	..	..	..	..	1,875
Ballast keel	..	..	..	..	..	..	..	..	..	14,560
Inside ballast ..	..	..	..	..	..	..	..	..	..	2,500
											———
Dry weight	..	..	..	..	..	..	..	..	..	..	38,649
Load ..	..	..	..	..	..	..	..	..	..	..	3,350
											———
Full load displacement	..	..	..	..	..	..	..	..	41,999

Displacement—18·75 tons.
Proportion of ballast keel to displacement 34·6 per cent.
Proportion of inside ballast to displacement 5·95 per cent.
Proportion of total ballast to displacement 40·55 per cent.
T.P.1 (salt water) 0·81 tons.

CENTRE OF GRAVITY AND BALLAST KEEL To float at the trim indicated in the drawings, the longitudinal C.G. of a yacht must fall in the same line as the longitudinal C.B. The varying density of timber causes trim as well as weight calculations to be fallible in wooden craft; when a new yacht slips down the launching ways and lies afloat, for the first time, with her designed marks kissing the water, luck as well as the designer's judgement should be praised.

Data from existing yachts will generally be relied on when judging the position of the C.G. of the hull and structural fittings, the latter including the bulkheads and normal furnishing. The point will usually be slightly aft of amidships, and nearly coincident with the C.B., with the result that such weights, which amount to a large proportion of the total, will have a small moment and little effect upon trim. If exceptional care is to be taken, the weight and moment of each member of the hull structure and furnishing may be calculated.

The heavy, concentrated weights which must be considered separately are: (i) The auxiliary and its installation; (ii) Fuel and water tanks; (iii) Chain; (iv) Mast; (v) Batteries; (vi) Doghouse if large. Moments are found by multiplying the weight of an item by the horizontal distance of its C.G. from any fixed point. The mid-point of the waterline length is usually chosen; or sometimes it is convenient to use the fore and aft position of the C.B., this saving one step in the calculations subsequently. Sometimes weights other than those listed below may have to be considered—a particularly heavy windlass placed far forward for example, or a charging set with petrol tank situated in the counter. (See Table 27).

The excess moment is aft of the C.B. The distance of the C.G. aft of the C.B. is equal to the excess moment divided by the sum of the weights. That is, $17,614 - 15,919 \div 19,891$, which equals 0.085 ft. aft.

The greatest, single concentrated weight in a sailing yacht is the ballast keel, and this has to be placed to redress the balance of the other weights. The moment of these in the above example is $19,891 \times 0.085$ aft of the C.B. The weight of the ballast keel must be so placed that the combined C.G. is in the same fore and aft position as the C.B. Taking moments, $12,000 \times x = 19,891 \times 0.085$ where x is the distance of the keel's C.G. forward of the C.B. and 12,000 lb. is the weight of the keel. From the equation, x equals 0.14 ft.

The line of the ballast keel is then struck in by eye, the slope and height of the line being adjusted and tested by successive calculations until the right weight and location of C.G. is achieved. For this work the keel drawing should be enlarged from the lines plan, and a number of closely spaced sections plotted in the way of the ballast—about one-third of the normal section spacing is suitable. Lead and iron are respectively twenty and twelve times heavier than salt water: working out the weight and C.G. of the keel is

TABLE 27

Item	Weight in lb.	Arm about C.B. in feet	Moment fwd.	Moment aft
Auxiliary and Installation	850	9·4 A	—	7,940
Chain	486	16·5 F	8,019	—
Fuel tanks	420	8·0 A	—	3,360
Water tanks	1,340	1·2 A	—	1,608
Batteries	325	0·5 A	—	162
Mast	650	5·0 F	3,250	—
Doghouse	320	14·2 A	—	4,544
Hull, Joinery, Fittings	15,500	0·3 F	4,650	—
Sum of weights	19,891	Sums of moments fwd. and aft	15,919	17,614

essentially another displacement calculation, with the necessity for added accuracy owing to the weights of the metals used. The sections should be arranged suitably for a Simpson's rule calculation.

A good practice sometimes adopted is to regard the keel line as tentative until the yacht has been laid off on a mould loft floor, and then to lift the full-size keel sections from the floor and check the areas. Slots in the keel casting, which may be filled with either lead or wood according to the trim, provide a further safeguard.

A small amount of internal ballast is used to correct unavoidable errors in the weight and ballast calculations; and the fact that some rated racing yachts carry it, including 6-Metres, indicates the difficulty of absolute accuracy. In small cruisers there is also the weight of the crew, concentrated aft for so much of the time, to be considered. With modern, light displacement yachts, which are both sensitive to trim when sailing, and also more subject to alterations in trim owing to the proportionately greater weight of crew, it is theoretically ideal that they should float down by the head when at moorings. This is aesthetically unsatisfying, which is a reason for avoiding the ideal.

CHAPTER FIFTEEN

Design

THE hull of a sailing yacht is a form that cannot be defined by any regular geometric pattern. It is the purpose of the lines drawing and table of offsets to delineate and record this complex shape in such a way that the builder may accurately reproduce the desired shape at full size. A second purpose of the lines drawing is to give the designer a form from which to work out such calculations as displacement, stability, required ballast, trim, and so on. Thirdly, the lines drawing will be used by the builder not only to reproduce the general shape of the hull, but in many instances to determine the bevels, rabbets and patterns of small parts of the vessel's structure which must be shaped to fit her hull. Lastly, the lines drawing gives the designer some indication of performance and the aesthetic appearance of the finished yacht.

The lines of a hull are ordinarily produced in a scale drawing by methods of descriptive geometry. This basically involves the construction of a suitable, three-dimensional grid and the superimposition of the hull and appendages on this grid in three views: sheer or elevation plan, half-breadth plan and transverse section or body plan. The grid forms a series of planes cutting through the surface of the hull at regular intervals and parallel to some normal line of reference (such as the centreline of the hull, the designed waterline and a line perpendicular to the designed waterline) so that the lines, as developed, may be scaled off and reproduced full-size on the mould loft floor.

Previous designs play a big part in a new production. When a range of yachts has been drawn, subsequent designs tend to be developments from those done earlier, to be improvements on them or modifications to suit slightly altered specifications. The most experienced designer would find it difficult, bereft of all his data, to produce a design conforming to closely fixed requirements. A designer works less from first principles than from his data, and particularly from the evidence afforded by any previous designs of yacht similar in size and type to the one contemplated. This is not copying, but the building upon of experience.

EQUIPMENT Drawings should not be on too small a scale, particularly the lines plan from which the hull is faired and the offsets lifted. But large drawings take space and need more elaborate equipment, whilst ones which are too large cannot be properly absorbed by the eye, and lack of harmony in the various curves may not be detected. One of a designer's most important acquirements is an unerring eye for curves, and the ability to detect in them the least deviation from fairness. This is most easily done when the drawing is small, and one designer has said that he finds himself best able to judge his work after he has seen it as a much reduced photostat print or published drawing.

The following scales for different lengths are suitable:

60 ft. to 50 ft.	..	$\frac{3}{4}$ in. or $\frac{1}{2}$ in.
50 ft. to 30 ft.	..	1 in. or $\frac{3}{4}$ in.
30 ft. to 20 ft.	..	$1\frac{1}{2}$ in. or 1 in.

In each case, if the larger of the alternative scales is used for the greater length of hull, a rather big drawing will result, though lines plans five feet long have been done by experienced draughtsmen. The lesser scales combined with the smaller lengths will produce drawings which are smaller than desirable, but suitable for early, amateur efforts. Thus a 1-in. scale plan of a fifty-footer will be over four feet long, which is on the big side, but a $\frac{3}{4}$-in. drawing of a thirty-footer will be under 2 ft. in length which is not big enough for close accuracy. Thirty inches is a reasonable average length for a set of hull lines.

Good cartridge paper is suitable for the hull lines drawing, and linen-backed cartridge is ideal. For construction, accommodation and sail plans, detail paper is adequate. Detail paper is only slightly transparent, but it is stronger than tracing paper, which is brittle and in the less good qualities tears along the pencil lines when the drawing is handled. One variety of tracing paper, which is yellow in colour, like parchment, and rather less brittle than most, should be avoided in spite of this quality. Pencil lines drawn on the paper make an impression on it like that of a stylo on a wax sheet, and though the colour of the line may be erased, the impression will still appear on any print taken from the drawing. The value of transparent tracing, or semi-transparent detail paper, is very great when drawing accommodation plans. It allows the profile, deckline and the required sections to be traced from the lines plan, saving time and increasing accuracy. Today there is an increasing use of plastics cloth in drawing offices, and general arrangement, construction and detail plans are done in a not too hard pencil, allowing prints to be taken directly from the drawing. Ink work is avoided as far as possible, and when it is necessary, the older fashion of leaf pen using Indian ink is discarded, and in up to date practice, replaced by the reservoir pens with exchangeable head pieces giving various line thicknesses.

Nowadays it is not very common to draw on stretched paper, though no better surface can be used. But it is an advantage to stretch a sheet of cartridge paper on to the drawing-board to serve as a background for the thinner, transparent papers. To do this, take a sheet of cartridge about half an inch smaller on all sides than the board, and out of each corner cut a square having one-inch sides. Turn up the edges of the paper to form a tray and lay it on the board. With a wet sponge soak the paper which forms the base of the tray. Then run a quick setting glue along the outside edges of the tray, and turn them down on to the board, pressing out the surplus glue. Sponge away any water which gathers into the wrinkles of the wet paper. When it has dried it will form a tight, flat surface, excellent as a background, and which will last many years.

It is not only the bad workman who blames his tools, but also the good one who is forced to work with the second-rate. Which means that the best, and consequently the most expensive, equipment is desirable; but there is a difference between the best and the merely lavishly expensive. Good splines, weights, curves and drawing instruments should be used, but the number need not be great. Good equipment, like an epicure's dinner, may be slight but excellently chosen.

The splines used for drawing curves are the most important part of the equipment.

FIG. 88. *A selection of yacht curves*

They may be made of close-grained pine or lancewood, the latter being the best, and for some purposes celluloid splines are of value. It is possible to buy boxes containing sets of splines, but the better and cheaper procedure is to get them separately, as experience shows the length and thickness which will best suit the work.

Since the purpose of splines is to ensure the fairness of all curves drawn, their degree of flexibility must suit the nature of the different curves; one which takes the curvature too easily is not able to test fairness properly, and an over stiff one can cause distortion. Sheerlines need a very stiff, parallel-sided spline; one of lancewood $\frac{3}{8}$ in. $\times$ $\frac{1}{8}$ in. $\times$ 48 in. is suitable, and when striking in the gentle sweep of a sheer, it should be laid with its broad edge on the paper.

Closest to the sheerline in the flatness of its curvature is the outline of the deck in plan. The deckline of narrow racing yachts, and many fast cruisers, may be drawn with the above spline placed with its narrow edge on the paper. A number of cruisers, and most power yachts, have a deckline which is comparatively flat along the middle part of its length, and falling into sharper curves at the ends. Particularly will this be so in beamy yachts with cruiser sterns. A tapered spline, thick in the middle and thinner at the ends, is needed for such lines. If of lancewood its dimensions may be $\frac{1}{4}$ in. $+$ $\frac{1}{8}$ in. tapering to $\frac{1}{4}$ in. $\times$ $\frac{1}{16}$ in.

A similar spline is needed for the buttocks, but it may be tapered at one end only and be thinner at the end, for buttocks tend to be flat in their curvature aft, whilst turning up sharply to the deckline forward. Unless a big collection of splines of varying length and taper is to be made, it is often necessary to draw a curve in two parts. This applies especially to the lower waterlines. When drawing a line in two lengths, the spline must be made to follow for a few inches the part of the line already drawn, this ensuring a fair junction. A parallel-sided celluloid spline is useful for sharp curves, such as the bow endings of the buttock lines, and the after end of waterlines, where there may be a reverse curve. Fairness at the point of contraflecture of the lower waterlines is not always easy to achieve. The celluloid spline will also be helpful in drawing the body plan sections.

A number of yacht curves is also needed. Dixon Kemp's famous Pear set is excellent, and a useful selection of other curves are chosen in Fig. 88. Actually, one can go on adding

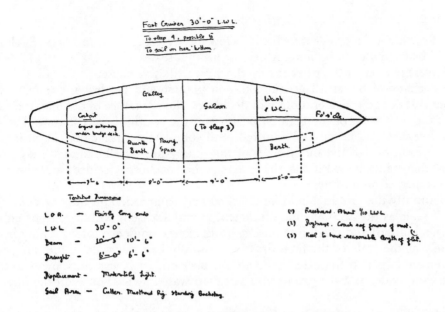

FIG. 89. *A preliminary sketch for a new design*

almost indefinitely to a set of curves, but it is surprising how much may be done with a very few well chosen ones. And though there are numerous standard shapes, it will be found that a set of curves made from the sections of any normal yacht, will serve for an infinite number of subsequent designs. Curves can be misused. Unlike splines, their purpose is not to form curves, but simply to fair up those that have already been sketched freehand. Thus, when a section of the body plan has been lightly sketched in soft pencil, a suitable curve and a harder pencil will serve to clean up the line. Large curves, having gentle curvature and known as sweeps, may be used when inking in the waterlines and other parts of the plan; they should not be used in lieu of splines when drawing the lines initially, though more than one designer does use them occasionally for this purpose. But an unerring eye is needed, and really it is a lazy practice.

Drawing weights, used to hold the splines in position, should be of lead, unless a designer likes having large lumps of cast iron littering his drawing-table. They should be so shaped that the bulk of the metal is concentrated in the nose. But they should have a base extending $\frac{1}{2}$ in. beyond the metal so that the body of the weight is clear of the spline. Otherwise the hand is cramped when ruling a line.

THE FIRST STAGES The specifications for a proposed yacht may be very full, or may be as brief as "Ketch, 45 ft. O.A., shoal-draught," from which a yacht recently grew. The initial conception of a proposed yacht is best illustrated in a dimensioned, freehand sketch of the layout, and in notes giving the leading dimensions and any particular features of the yacht. In Fig. 89 the *motif* of the design is shown to be a fast yet comfortable cruiser, uninfluenced by the rule.

The next step is to embody the information in the rough sketch into a small scale drawing of the layout, a profile above and below the water, and the sail plan. Such drawings should be from 9 to 12 in. long, which means that scales of $\frac{1}{4}$ in., $\frac{3}{8}$ in. or $\frac{1}{2}$ in. will suit yachts of average size. In the present case the $\frac{1}{4}$-in. scale was chosen.

The deckline of the small accommodation plan should be drawn carefully with a spline. General design considerations will determine the curvature of the line, the fullness of the ends, the location of the greatest beam, and the width of the transom. The curve should be swept in and faired and adjusted until completely satisfactory. Later it will be enlarged to form one of the initial lines of the lines plan. The bulkheads may now be ruled in at their tentative positions, the extent of the coachroof decided, and the accommodation indicated in outline.

Concurrently the profile should be sketched and balanced. This may be done on the same small scale as the accommodation sketch, in which case it will have to be enlarged later for the final sail and rigging plan. Or, if sufficient confidence is felt, it may be done immediately at the scale of the final drawing—usually half the scale of the lines, or less if the latter are large. In the case of the 30/42 racer-cruiser it was convenient to do the lines on a $\frac{3}{4}$-in. scale, and the profile and sail plan was drawn at once on the final $\frac{3}{8}$-in. scale.

In the profile drawing the freeboard amidships and at the ends, the curve of sheer, outlines of stem and stern, together with the lines of the coachroof, doghouse, and the many smaller features which have so great an effect on appearance, are drawn and harmonised. Any details which will help to bring the drawing to life, such as the ventilators, windlass, sidelight boxes, should be sketched in at this stage. In this drawing the general proportions and appearance of the yacht will be fixed. Her character will be formed, and the remarks which will pass between the people who will see her through the clubhouse window in the future will be largely decided.

It may be mentioned that it is the usual practice to show the bow to the right-hand side of the paper. The convention is unnatural. It is like drawing the profile of a face with the nose to the right, a thing which most people are unable to do. However, the first object when making drawings is absolute clarity, and it is best to adopt the convention which is best known to those who will have to read them.

Whilst harmonising the various features of the profile, it is a good practice to turn the paper over and to gain the entirely different impression of the work which its reversal will produce. The device is useful when balancing the features of larger craft, and particularly power yachts, with their different levels of deckhouses, their masts, which may be placed where best suited for appearance, their big windows, and probably broken sheerlines. It is rare for the profile to seem equally pleasing when viewed from the opposite side to that on which it was drawn. Which leads to the peculiar conclusion that however clear-cut an idea may be in the designer's mind, its expression will vary slightly depending on whether he draws the bow to the left or right of the sheet of paper.

The type and purpose of the yacht will determine the profile of the keel and the disposition of the sail area. The mast position must be judged by the relationship desired between the mainsail and foretriangle, and it will be affected too by the accommodation which has been drawn. The keel should be sketched in on the profile drawing, from which it may be subsequently enlarged to the scale of the lines. The keel will not be shown when the sail plan is traced. The keel and sail plan must now be balanced, using the C.E. and C.L.R. convention and a great deal of good judgement.

The freeboard, coachroof and doghouse heights shown on the profile drawing are tentative, since no midship section has been drawn from which the cabin sole level may be fixed with certainty. But the designer will already have in his mind the shape of mid-ship section which the leading dimensions demand, and the sole level may be judged with reasonable accuracy from experience.

We now have drawn the profile above and below water, the layout, and the sail plan. The leading dimensions of the hull are known, and a deckline has been drawn. The midship section must now be sketched at a size convenient for the eye to judge, and from which it may be enlarged to the scale of the lines drawing without difficulty. It may be preferred to draw it immediately at the latter scale. To help the eye in judging its shape it is useful to draw both sides of the section. A convenient, though not very workmanlike way of doing this is to fold the paper down the centreline when one side has been drawn, and to trace it on the other side of the paper. As the second side is only a visual aid, great accuracy is not needed.

The shaping of the midship section is the second major step in the development of the hull form, the deckline being the first. The form of the midship section will influence that of the whole hull, for the character of each section in the length will resemble that of the one amidships.* Thus a high, hard bilge will be reflected in the fullness of the overhangs, while a deeper and more rounded section amidships will allow softer ends. There are craft in which the character of the ends may seem markedly dissimilar from the midship section. The Itchen ferry boats are an example. Here a fairly shallow-bodied midship section, which might easily be drawn out to a full forward overhang, actually ends in a straight stem of narrow V-section. The sections forward of amidships have, in fact, undergone a subtle change in character, but the change is progressive from one to the other; the blend-ing is beautifully done, and it is an extreme example of what every designer has to do when drawing a yacht with fine ends. In fuller-ended craft it will be found that the sections throughout the length are almost parallel with one another, differing simply in breadth and depth.

When forming the midship section, the facts of resistance and stability must be kept in mind. The section must also have the necessary area under water to produce a hull with the chosen displacement. To determine the requisite area, comparison with a com-pleted design is necessary. The features which must be in common are length on the water-line and draught. The keel profile should also be similar, for it will be apparent that a considerable part of the displacement is in the keel.

Having found from an earlier design or from data the area of midship section which will produce a hull with the required displacement, a new midship may be sketched and adjusted until its area under the waterline is suitable. In the example the displacement chosen was 10 tons, and the necessary area of midship section was found to be 21 sq. ft. This is an approximation only; two designs may have identical dimensions and midships sections, yet differ in displacement owing to varying degrees of fullness in the ends. But the difference will not be considerable, and in this matter judgement must be used. In yachts not built to a rating rule, the exact displacement is not of vital importance.

In yachts of about 10 tons T.M. and under, the headroom and width of cabin sole must be considered when sketching the midship section. Fig. 90(*a*) shows superimposed two tentative midship sections for a certain 11-tonner. Section A has the lesser area, a

* See Chapter Four.

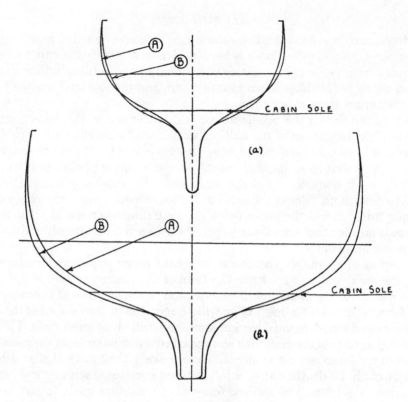

FIG. 90. *Trial midship sections*

high but soft bilge, and flat floors. This section lacked the desired width of cabin sole, and it was not possible to raise the sole without losing full headroom; also, though a light displacement hull was projected, the area of section A was rather on the small side. In section B the waterline beam was reduced and the bilge drawn with a slacker curve; the section was padded out lower down, the floors being more rounded. The area was slightly more than that of A, and the sole width was increased by six inches. The hull drawn round section B would have less wetted surface than A, and less stiffness owing to the reduced waterline beam. After balancing these factors, section B was chosen.

Fig. 90(*b*) shows two trial midship sections for a shoal-draught yacht. A set of lines, already drawn, and based on section B, was found to have more displacement than the detailed weight estimate showed to be needed. With scantlings up to Lloyd's standard there was still 40 per cent of her displacement available for ballast, and this was considered excessive in view of the beam and inherent stiffness of the hull. Also, it was subsequently decided to use iron for the keel, and it was not possible to place a sufficient quantity of the metal in the keel as drawn. The design was redrawn round the section A, having less waterline beam and fullness of body, and more width of keel. The proportionate reduction in the displacement was almost the same as that of the midship section area. The above examples will serve to show the nature of the problems encountered when forming the midship section.

When judging the internal space offered by a trial midship section, a line should be sketched lightly inside the section indicating the inside of the hull—that is, deducting the thickness of planking, timbers and ceiling, these being estimated. Owing to the oblique angle at which the floor line crosses the cabin sole, the width of sole lost will be considerable, and this is not apparent from such drawings as Fig. 89. It is also helpful to sketch in the settees and berths in section, as arranged in the accommodation plan. If an inadequacy of floor space is then revealed, it must be decided whether to raise the cabin sole and reduce headroom, or to fill out the section as in Fig. 90(a). It may prove desirable at this stage to increase the freeboard or the height of the coachroof. It is now, when a tentative accommodation plan, profile and midship section have been drawn, that the small adjustments and compromises must be made which will fix the character and appearance of the design.

Before starting the large-scale drawing of the hull lines, it is often helpful to draw a trial load waterline at the same scale as the small accommodation plan. Three points on the curve are known; the fore and aft endings, and the amount of maximum beam. The nature of the curve will be decided from general design considerations, and together with the deckline and midship section it will define the shape of the hull very closely.

THE LINES The lines drawing may now be started. The straight lines which form the basis must be ruled with great accuracy. The three projections of the hull have to be arranged on the paper so that they do not overlap, and it is best not to superimpose the body plan on the middle of the elevation, though it may subsequently be traced in this position. It is convenient, if the width of the paper allows, to place it in the middle of the sheet between the elevation and the waterlines, but usually, with deep draught yachts, it has to be moved to the right to prevent overlapping. A good deal of manipulation with small splines and curves is necessary when working on the body plan, and accessibility is important; there are advantages in drawing it on a separate, small board.

The horizontal lines representing the waterlines and buttocks must be spaced and struck in with a straight-edge, then checked at points along their length to ensure absolute parallelism. The spacing of the lines is a matter of judgement; the closer they are the more certain will be the fairness of the hull shape, and many designs would benefit from having them closer together. But the time taken to complete the drawing becomes much longer. Since the spacing of the lines will have to be used when the offsets are lifted, and subsequently when the yacht is laid off full size, they should be a conveniently measurable distance apart. Multiples of 3 in. are suitable. On a yacht of 40 ft. on the waterline, waterlines spaced at 9 in. or 1 ft., and buttocks at 15 or 18 in. would be satisfactory. A yacht of big beam and flat floors should have closer spaced buttocks than a narrow craft with a big rise of floor, since the buttocks are the best lines for fairing the bottom. The waterlines serve best above the turn of the bilge. Sometimes the waterlines above the L.W.L. are more widely spaced than those below, but this tends to spoil the impression of form derived from the waterline plan, for shape is best visualised when the defining lines are equally spaced, like the contours on a map.

When the horizontal lines have been drawn, the vertical ones representing the sections may be struck in. They are usually spaced so as to divide the waterline into an even number of equal parts—ten is a common number—and this facilitates the calculations. The effect of the section spacing on the mathematical work is considered elsewhere. There is also the shipwright to be considered. It is helpful if the section spacing is also suitable for that of the moulds or, in a bigger ship, if the section spacing is a multiple of that of the grown frames on which the hull will be ribanded out. In order to achieve this, some designers are ready to space the sections so that they do not equally divide the waterline length, but this makes the calculations awkward. Whatever the spacing chosen for the straight lines, they must be drawn absolutely accurately. The work may take a couple of hours or more. A T-square is not true enough for this work.

The hull lines may be started by drawing the following:

(i) Profile.
(ii) Midship section.
(iii) Deckline.
(iv) L.W.L.

Their shapes will already have been decided in the preliminary sketches, and it is a matter of scaling from these and fairing the curves. If the yacht has a pronounced fin-keel, as in the example, it is a good practice to treat the keel and the canoe body separately. In heavy displacement, full-bodied yachts the separation of the two is not practicable.

Firstly the profile, including keel, is enlarged from the smaller drawing, and also the midship section. Then the point of greatest body depth may be located on the midship section by projecting the line of the floor on to the centreline. This is really the natural line of the body, and we may regard the keel as an appendage blended into the body by the reverse-turn of the garboard. The point of greatest body depth (G.B.D.) must now be placed on the elevation drawing. If it is amidships, at section 5, the line of the canoe body will tend to be symmetrical about this point. If it is placed ahead of amidships, the curve will be more abrupt forward, but longer and flatter aft. In an extreme case, we have the racing dinghy with its greatest depth of body about one-third of the length from the bows. Considerations of balance will not allow this extreme shape in craft which have to be sailed heeled, and it is a delicate decision how long and flat the run may be made. The line of the G.B.D. will, of course, decide the form of the outer buttocks (the G.B.D. is really a buttock on the centreline) and yachts in which the point of greatest depth is well forward have flat buttocks aft and long, clean runs to the after-bodies. But if the point of G.B.D. is placed too far forward, heavy weather helm usually results. In the cruiser-racer the point was one-twentieth of the waterline length ahead of section 5.

The waterline plan is begun by drawing the deckline, taking the shape from the pre-liminary drawing and fairing the enlarged curve. The point of greatest beam was placed a little aft of section 5. A straight line drawn across the waterline plan connecting the points of G.B. and G.B.D. is a raking master section, and it is shown dotted in Fig. 91. Yachts of a few decades ago had much raked master sections—it was considerable in the cod's head and mackerel's tail type—and there is a model in the Science Museum showing the extreme amount of rake present in some old yachts. Considerable separation of the points of G.B. and G.B.D. is a dangerous feature, however, producing a hull whose heeled waterlines have a bad shape. The use of the raking master section is to ensure that, since the points of G.B. and G.B.D. are not in the same fore and aft line, the maximum depth of the hull fairs harmoniously into the greatest beam. Thus the greatest breadth of each waterline, above and below the L.W.L. should fall on the raking master section— that is, on the dotted line drawn across the waterline plan. The lower waterlines, in fact,

48. An example of beam and long ends, producing a large yacht for a given length of waterline.

49. *Tasman* class of British motor-sailer, with small sloop rig.

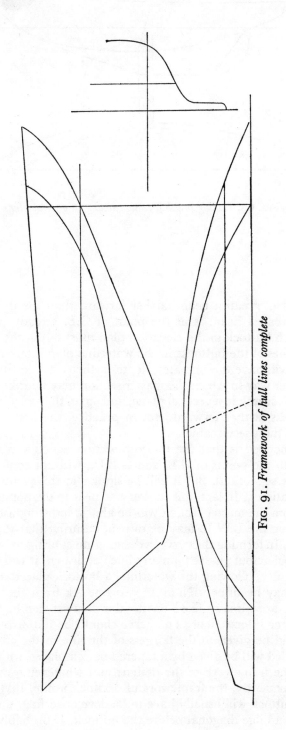

Fig. 91. *Framework of hull lines complete*

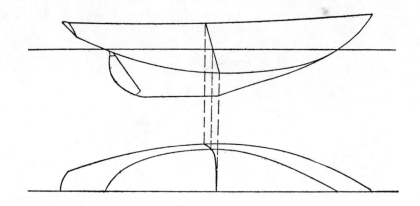

FIG. 92. *Raking midship section swung in vertical plane*

will have their point of greatest beam farther forward than the upper ones, and at the deckline itself the greatest beam is at the point of G.B. already plotted. Likewise the greatest depth of each buttock in the elevation plan must fall in the fore and aft position where the straight lines of the buttocks in the waterline plan intersect the master section. The inner buttocks will have their greatest depth farther forward than the outer ones.

There is a further way in which the master section may be raked. It is shown in Fig. 92. Here the section is swung in a vertical plane, and again the effect is to bring the greatest depths of the buttocks farther forward. But in practice, the first method of raking the section will be found most serviceable.

A point to be noticed is that the midship section which was initially drawn, and which combined both the points of G.B. and G.B.D., will not conform exactly in shape to any of the transverse sections. But it will be similar to the eventual shape of the true midship section at station 5. In fact, this station is so near to the points of G.B. and G.B.D. that its difference from the master section will be almost indistinguishable.

After the deckline the L.W.L. may be drawn, ensuring that the greatest beam falls on the raking section. In forming the curve, a designer must bring to bear all his knowledge of yachts and their behaviour; more than any line yet drawn, it will influence the underwater shape of the hull. Following the waterline, a buttock placed at about a quarter of the beam inboard may be drawn. Number two buttock from the centreline is usually suitable. Five points are already fixed on it—the greatest depth, two waterline intersections, and two sheer intersections. The curve should be flatter aft than forward, and particular care should be given to the fairness of the line in the after-body. A guide to the sort of curve needed will be given by a tapered batten placed with its thick end aft.

Fig. 91 shows the framework of the design; and whatever routine for drawing the lines is adopted subsequently, the framework of decline, profile, L.W.L., midship section and quarter beam buttock will usually have to be developed first, though some designers may favour drawing a bilge diagonal before the buttock. It probably needs a surer sense of form to develop a diagonal than a buttock, and if the curve of the diagonal is badly chosen it can cause great distortion in the lines later. Whereas the buttock shape is more clearly envisaged.

The straight lines forming the basis of the drawings may now be ruled in ink. The ink should be kept, for the sake of neatness, within the boundaries of the deckline and profile, and since only the midship section has yet been drawn on the body plan, we may defer inking in the lines on this plan until later. It is not a good idea to ink in the straight lines as soon as they have been drawn. They will then sprawl outside the lines of the hull, which is distracting to the eye.

With the framework set, the following procedure may be adopted for completing the hull lines:

(1) Trial sections at 3 and 7.
(2) Bilge diagonal.
(3) W.L. above L.W.L.
(4) W.L. below L.W.L.
(5) Remaining sections.
(6) Diagonal above bilge.
(7) Diagonal below bilge.
(8) Remaining waterlines.
(9) Remaining diagonals.
(10) Remaining buttocks.

As the work proceeds, each line must be faired with those which have gone before; the later lines drawn will have more spots through which they must pass than those done earlier. Thus, on the trial sections at 3 and 7, the spots fixed by the framework are the deck breadth and height, the lowest point on the centreline, the waterline breadth, and the depth at the buttock—a total of four points. The fairness of the sections drawn will be indicated by the bilge diagonal, drawn next, which will have to pass through the points made by the two sections, as well as those set by the framework. If a fair batten curve cannot be made to do so, the sections will have to be adjusted.

On turning to A.W.L. and 2 W.L., there are seven points fixed on each of them: the fore and aft endings (from the profile), the half-breadths at sections 3, 5 and 7, and two buttocks intersections, one forward and one aft. There are then seven points fixed on each of the sections: three waterline breadths, a buttock depth, the bilge diagonal intersections and the top and bottom points at the sheer and keel.

The order in which the various lines are drawn is an individual taste. The fact to remember is that the best fairing lines are those which cross the sections most nearly at right-angles. Thus the waterlines are of most value in the topsides; below the turn of the bilge, where they cross the sections obliquely, they are of less use, the points of intersection being difficult to determine. For the same reason, the outer buttocks, where they cross the topsides of the sections, are poor fairing lines. The curve of the garboard is most accurately faired by a diagonal struck through it as near to the middle point of the curve at each section as can be arranged. The inner buttock may also be of value in fairing the garboard. But if the garboard is of large radius, a buttock which is too close to the centre-line will drop suddenly amidships, where the hull turns down into the keel. It will show a bulge, which is inevitable and not an indication of unfairness.

There are two schools of thought over the arrangement of the diagonals; one favours that they all should be struck at 45 degrees, and the other that the angles should be adjusted to suit the convenience of fairing. The former method gives the prettiest effect on the finished drawing, for the diagonals are then parallel planes, like the waterlines or buttocks, and bear a constant relationship to one another. But the latter is the more serviceable. In the course of fairing the lines it may be found that a diagonal struck at a certain angle will pick up spots on the section which seem to be inadequately tested for fairness by the waterlines or buttocks. A diagonal at a steep angle may be needed to fair the floor line below the turn of the bilge, where the sections make oblique crossings with the other fairing lines. A designer is more likely to achieve fairness if he retains freedom to place the diagonals as he finds convenient. Wherever there is any doubt about the fairness of the hull, a diagonal, which need not be shown on the finished drawings, should be struck in and plotted, and to tie them to a constant angle is to destroy the useful elasticity of these lines. When diagonals are not at a constant angle, the lower ones should be at steeper angles than those higher, and when plotting it will sometimes be found that diagonals cross one another; if they radiate from a common point on the centreline they will frequently do so. This is immaterial.

Like seamanship, the art of drawing and fairing lines is learned only with practice. It has to be remembered that a spline, held in place with not too closely spaced weights, is a guide to fairness, but not an infallible one. The eye must be the ultimate judge. Sometimes it may be thought that there are flats or bumps in a curve where actually none exist. This occurs sometimes at the ends of the upper waterlines aft, where the curve may be drawn a little sharply in to the centreline, leaving an impression of a flat immediately forward of it, though the curve itself may in fact be fair.

The routine for drawing a set of lines will be adjusted according to circumstances and experience. If the type of yacht is well known, or if the new design is only a slight modification of a previous one, much of the preliminary, exploratory work on small sketches will be omitted. Thus, a new design may be basically similar to an earlier one, but having more or less beam, greater length but similar in section, or a fuller body and more displacement whilst remaining similar in profile and layout.

A method of design practised more abroad than in England is that of fairing the sections by means of closely spaced diagonals only. It is used by the Swedish designer Knud M. Reimers, the creator of the *Tumlare* type, and it has peculiar advantages for those working in limited space or without much equipment. But it perhaps needs a more certain sense of form than other methods.

The framework of the design is laid as before. Proceeding from the stage shown in Fig. 91, the lines are completed by sketching in all the sections. The embryo body plan should appear as in Fig. 93. The waterlines and buttocks are drawn, and the four spots fixed on each section by the framework are located. Once again it will be found best, if the type of hull is suitable, to draw the canoe body first, and subsequently to add the keel, fairing the keel into the canoe body with the garboards. The spots derived from the framework may conveniently be marked in ink, for they should not need any subsequent alteration, and it is annoying to find them being constantly lost through erasure as work on the sections proceeds.

To draw a fair set of sections by eye, guided only by the four points on each, needs practice and a clear vision of the shape of hull being developed, but with experience it becomes possible to detect where the curve of any section departs from the character of those on either side of it.

When the sections are drawn, they are faired with closely spaced diagonals—about double the usual number. Sometimes these diagonals may be contracted in their longitudinal scale when they are plotted. This means that their curves are sharpened, and a batten's test of their fairness then becomes more sure. Thus, on the 30–42-ft. yacht, if the

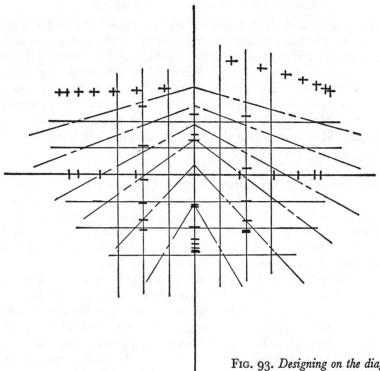

FIG. 93. *Designing on the diagonals*

body is drawn on a 1-in. scale, the longitudinal scale for the spacing of the sections, when plotting the diagonals, may be a $\frac{1}{2}$ in.

It should be mentioned that in modern yachts the lines are usually faired to the face of the stem; that is, the stem timber itself is shaped to the lines and carries on the run of the planking. The line of the rabbet, where the planking joins the stem, thus falls on the smooth curve flowing up to the face of the stem, which may be very narrow. Or sometimes the stem is rounded with a big radius at deck level, this allowing a full deckline forward, the radius decreasing towards the L.W.L. The line of the rabbet also blends into the garboards, when these are curved. It need not, therefore, be considered when drawing the lines. But it is not strictly correct to bring the waterlines, in plan, and the sections in the body to points on their respective centrelines, though this is often done. The thickness of the stem face should be allowed for and shown at each section. The fore endings of the diagonals are also affected by this. The method of determining the endings of the diagonals is a well-known problem in ship geometry which need not be repeated.

The lines of a yacht are reconstructed by the shipwright from a table of offsets, the measurements being lifted from the original pencil drawing of the lines. The whole shape of a yacht is thus embalmed in a table of figures. Dimensions are taken to the outside of the planking, deductions for planking thickness being made by the shipwright.

The form of such a table is well known. Half-breadths of the deckline, sheerline and the various waterlines, taken at each of the sections, are measured from the centreline.

Sheer, deck, and buttock, heights and depths, are usually measured above and below the waterline. All the essential information must be given in the offset table, such as the spacing of sections, waterlines and buttocks, placing of diagonals, and the overall dimensions of the hull, so that it may be reconstructed without other references. A profile of the stem and stern, with dimensions measured horizontally from the forward and aft perpendiculars, must be shown to allow their being redrawn correctly, and there must also be ordinates showing the run of the rabbet line. All measurements are given in feet, inches and eighths of an inch. The entry 4-7-5- therefore means four feet seven and five-eighths inches.

ACCOMMODATION DRAWINGS Having already considered the question of accommodation, it is necessary only to add a few words on the draughtsmanship involved. Drawing and tracing a detailed accommodation plan is a long process, and the style of the drawing will depend on the time available. When time is money, it may be justifiable to make the drawing no more than plain and serviceable. In small yachts the construction drawing may be combined with that of the accommodation.

But marine draughtsmanship has a noble tradition; the draughts shown in Chapman, and other early works, have never been bettered in later years. They are works of art. The amateur designer has the opportunity of making his accommodation drawings models of clarity and a delight to study. It has to be remembered that a plan which gives a picture is more readily comprehensible, and more tempting, than one which has to be read. A sideboard with a glass-fronted cupboard above it is more easily appreciated if drawn on the plan to look like what it is, than if two rectangles are labelled with what they represent. Shaded upholstery work, tiles on bathroom floors, turned down counterpanes on the bunks, and many other less obvious touches like books in bookshelves, and even charts on chart tables, bring a drawing wonderfully to life if drawn carefully.

The elevation and plan of the accommodation drawing may be traced from the lines. In elevation, the line of the deck at centre should be traced, and also the rail if there is one. The thickness of the deck should be indicated, and possibly the top and bottom of the deck shelf may be drawn, the dimensions being taken from the scantlings. The distance between the bottom of the deck and the top of the shelf then represents the depth of the beam camber. The amount of hull constructional work indicated on the accommodation drawing is a matter of taste. Sometimes the stem, keel and deadwood members may be shown, but if a detailed construction drawing is to be done they may well be omitted. A study of completed drawings will be the best guide here.

In plan, the deckline should be traced from the lines drawing. If the yacht has considerable tumblehome, a mean line may be drawn between the deck and the maximum tumblehome beam, but this is not really necessary, and the deckline is the best guide. A line inside the deckline by an amount equal to the combined thickness of the outside planking, the frame moulding, and an allowance for cabin lining, should be drawn. The bulkheads and floor levels may then be shown on the plan and elevation, the latter being placed with the help of sections, which will show the best compromise possible between floor space and headroom.

The number of sections found necessary will depend on the familiarity of the hull shape and layout. It may be necessary to draw one at each of the ten sections used in the lines drawing. It may happen too that a certain feature in the layout or engine installation

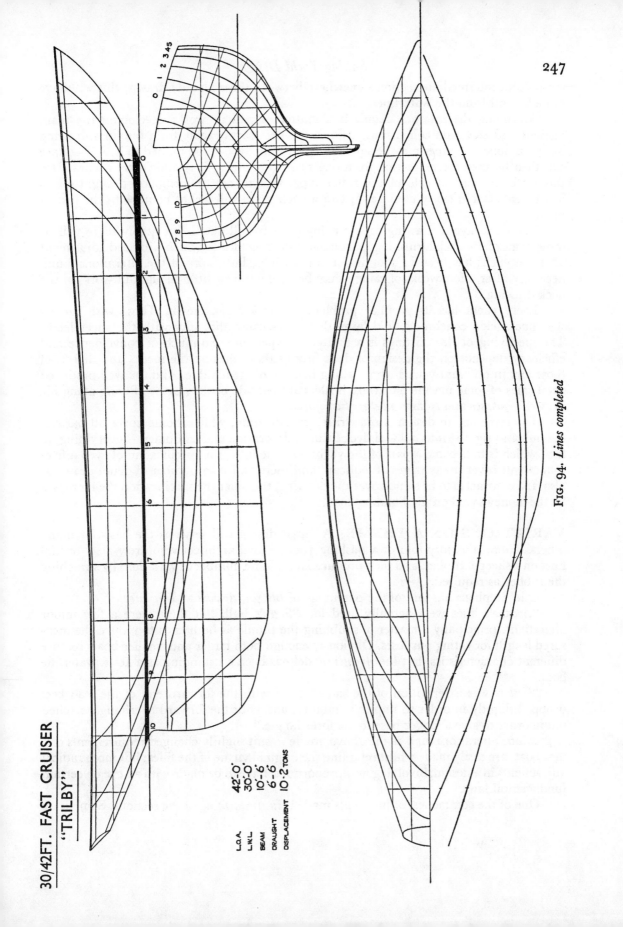

30/42FT. FAST CRUISER
"TRILBY"

L.O.A.	42'-0"
L.W.L.	30'-0"
BEAM	10'-6"
DRAUGHT	6'-6"
DISPLACEMENT	10·2 TONS

FIG. 94. *Lines completed*

requires an intermediate section somewhere between those already drawn; this will have to be laid off from the waterlines.

Arranging the internal details is a matter of patient work, developing the plan, sections and elevation concurrently. Once the necessary tracing from the lines drawing has been done the paper may be squared up with the board and pinned to it. A T-square can then be used for projecting from one plan to another; it is sufficiently accurate for this work. A parallel rule of the roller type, though not an orthodox draughtsman's instrument, is frequently useful also, and a yachtsman will feel at home with the instrument.

The deck layout drawing repays being done in full detail. Inevitably there will be some items of the deck furnishing, particularly the sheet leads, which will need adjustment after the yacht has been in commission for a while; but many of the alterations found necessary after a few weeks of sailing may be avoided by a little thoughtful work on the deck drawing.

Every yacht has its peculiar problems in deck arrangement. Those with broken sheerlines, wide coachroofs, and large doghouses cause difficulty with the sheet leads. The specifying of deck fittings is a matter of experience. So much of convenience and efficiency depends on the design of deck fittings that notes on the merits and defects of those met in different yachts when sailing become of great value. And the well produced catalogues of some marine hardware dealers are bedside books worthy of lying alongside Boswell's *Johnson* and Adams's *Letters from Japan*.

The last stage in design is the written specification, which should cover all parts of the hull and rig, the internal and deck fittings, decoration and equipment—everything, in fact, which is to become a part of the yacht. If done fully, the specification of even a five-tonner will cover many pages of foolscap, and there will be a number of detail drawings also. If a contract is to be signed over the drawing, the fuller the specification the more will be the money saved on the building costs.

VARIATIONS ON A THEME　A tested design will serve as the basis for many others. There is a story told of a pushing young naval architect who drew a set of hull lines on a sheet of rubber, and then produced an infinite number of variations by stretching the rubber as required.

Olin Stephens has said of the parentage of *Blitzen*, *Avantie* and *Gesture*:

"*Avantie*'s lines were actually used for *Blitzen*'s hull, but there were a few minor alterations, principally a matter of snubbing the profile at both ends to reduce the measured length for rating purposes. Obviously enough both larger and smaller boats require different characteristics, but the *Avantie* model has been outstanding as a 40-ft. waterline boat.

"*Gesture* was a repetition of the same design with the forward end of the lead keel dropped slightly in order to improve stability, and with the forward overhang stretched out in order to give a longer base to the foretriangle."

Minor alterations such as the above, made to suit slightly changed requirements of a new boat, are easily made whilst retaining the original virtue of the lines; but more radical adjustments in a design, involving new proportions, have to be made with an eye on certain fundamental laws.

One of the commonest adjustments made is in the spacing of the sections. Sometimes a design will stand the sections being spaced closer together or farther apart. Whether it will do so depends on the length-beam and displacement-length ratios. Thus a design for a small cruiser with considerable beam may suitably have the section spacing extended to make a design for a longer ship. More draught may also be needed, but this may be gained by deepening the keel, which will not affect the basic hull lines. Likewise, a design with comparatively small beam may have the section spacing contracted to produce a smaller boat.

Displacement has also to be considered when judging whether a set of hull lines may suitably be adjusted in length. Displacement varies directly as the length. Thus, the displacement of the new design will be:

$$\frac{\text{New section spacing}}{\text{Original section spacing}} \times \text{Original displacement}$$

When a design is lengthened by respacing the sections, there follows a considerable reduction in the displacement-length ratio. If in the original design this is already small, the yacht may be unsuitable for enlargement in this way. In the case of Fig. 94 the length beam ratio of 2·86 shows that an increase in length is practicable. If the sections were spaced out to produce a design 32 ft. on the waterline, the ratio would become a little more than 3, which would be suitable for the length. Her displacement, on the new length, would be

$$\frac{3·2}{3·0} \times 10·1 \text{ which equals } 10·8 \text{ tons.}$$

Her original displacement-length ratio was 372, which is moderate. On a 32-ft. waterline, with a displacement of 10·8 tons, it would be 330 and this is a little low if the yacht is to be regarded as a reasonably comfortable cruiser. Of course, the lengthening might be accompanied by a slight deepening of the keel. which would add to the displacement. When considering the suitability of any design for adjustments of this nature, the requirements of the new design must be clearly in mind, together with the effect of the adjustments on stability, resistance and general performance.

Sometimes it may be wished to make an alteration in the beam or draught of a design whose lines have been drawn. Three inches more beam, for example, may be needed. An adjustment of this sort causes a more fundamental change of character in the hull form, for the shape of the sections as well as the hull proportions will be altered.

SPECIAL INSTALLATIONS On larger yachts the owner may require the installation of special equipment which must be laid out in some detail by the designer. The electronics age has broken upon the yachting world, and such instruments as depth recorders, automatic pilots, radio-direction finders, electrical refrigeration, and so on, all of which may now be found on board a yacht of only 27 ft. 6 in. on the waterline, must have their installation worked out.

Obviously, the design of an electrical system capable of handling a load of this capacity is not a matter of mere wiring to be left to the builder to puzzle out alone. Such systems, also including fire-prevention, bilge-exhaust, hot water, cabin heat and even air-conditioning may well come within the province of the designer, requiring much detail work and a good deal of ingenuity to "get it all in" within the required hull dimensions and still leave room for the crew. The above constitutes a very brief outline of the plans that must be drawn, the specifications to be assembled.

While no two designs are ever precisely alike, it is a rare experiment (not to be entered upon by the beginner) where every feature of hull and rig represents a total innovation. Therefore, the designer, after determining the owner's needs and desires as to general dimensions, type of rig, shape of hull and individual limiting factors (draught is often the commonest) may often consult his files seeking a prototype or prototypes to guide him in laying out the new design. For this purpose all young designers should keep a clip file of designs culled from the yachting journals and covering the range of yachts of the type his interest is in. It should be pointed out that the information given on these designs is very fragmentary, yet, partial as it is, it is an invaluable aid to the inexperienced.

Appendices

APPENDIX ONE

THIRTY-SECOND OF AN INCH EXPRESSED AS DECIMALS

$\frac{1}{32}$	0·03	$\frac{9}{32}$	0·28	$\frac{11}{32}$	0·53	$\frac{25}{32}$	0·78
$\frac{1}{16}$	0·06	$\frac{5}{16}$	0·31	$\frac{9}{16}$	0·56	$\frac{13}{16}$	0·81
$\frac{3}{32}$	0·09	$\frac{11}{32}$	0·34	$\frac{19}{32}$	0·59	$\frac{27}{32}$	0·84
$\frac{1}{8}$	0·13	$\frac{3}{8}$	0·37	$\frac{5}{8}$	0·63	$\frac{7}{8}$	0·88
$\frac{5}{32}$	0·16	$\frac{13}{32}$	0·41	$\frac{21}{32}$	0·66	$\frac{29}{32}$	0·91
$\frac{3}{16}$	0·19	$\frac{7}{16}$	0·44	$\frac{11}{16}$	0·69	$\frac{15}{16}$	0·94
$\frac{7}{32}$	0·22	$\frac{15}{32}$	0·47	$\frac{23}{32}$	0·72	$\frac{31}{32}$	0·97
$\frac{1}{4}$	0·25	$\frac{1}{2}$	0·50	$\frac{3}{4}$	0·75	1	1·00

INCHES AND EIGHTHS EXPRESSED AS DECIMALS OF A FOOT

		1 in.	2 in.	3 in.	4 in.	5 in.	6 in.	7 in.	8 in.	9 in.	10 in.	11 in.
0		·083	·167	·250	·333	·417	·500	·583	·667	·750	·833	·917
$\frac{1}{8}$	·010	·094	·177	·260	·344	·427	·510	·593	·677	·760	·844	·927
$\frac{1}{4}$	·021	·104	·188	·271	·354	·437	·521	·604	·687	·771	·854	·938
$\frac{3}{8}$	·031	·115	·198	·281	·365	·448	·531	·614	·698	·781	·865	·948
$\frac{1}{2}$	·042	·125	·208	·292	·375	·458	·541	·625	·708	·791	·875	·958
$\frac{5}{8}$	·052	·135	·219	·302	·385	·469	·552	·635	·719	·802	·885	·969
$\frac{3}{4}$	·063	·146	·229	·312	·396	·479	·562	·646	·729	·812	·896	·979
$\frac{7}{8}$	·073	·156	·240	·323	·406	·490	·573	·656	·740	·823	·906	·990

APPENDIX TWO

VALUES OF $\left(\dfrac{\text{L.W.L.}}{100}\right)^3$ FOR USE IN CALCULATION OF

DISPLACEMENT/LENGTH RATIO $\left(\dfrac{\text{DISPLACEMENT}}{\left(\dfrac{\text{L}}{100}\right)^3}\right)$

L.W.L.	$\left(\dfrac{\text{L.W.L.}}{100}\right)^3$	L.W.L.	$\left(\dfrac{\text{L.W.L.}}{100}\right)^3$	L.W.L.	$\left(\dfrac{\text{L.W.L.}}{100}\right)^3$
20	0·008	35	0·043	50	0·125
21	0·009	36	0·047	51	0·133
22	0·010	37	0·051	52	0·141
23	0·012	38	0·055	53	0·149
24	0·014	39	0·059	54	0·157
25	0·016	40	0·064	55	0·166
26	0·018	41	0·069	56	0·176
27	0·020	42	0·074	57	0·185
28	0·022	43	0·079	58	0·195
29	0·024	44	0·085	59	0·205
30	0·027	45	0·091	60	0·216
31	0·030	46	0·097	61	0·227
32	0·033	47	0·104	62	0·238
33	0·036	48	0·111	63	0·250
34	0·039	49	0·118	64	0·262

APPENDIX THREE

Values of (Displacement)$^{\frac{1}{3}}$ for Use in Calculation of Sail Area/Displacement Ratio $\left(\dfrac{\text{Sail Area}}{(\text{Displacement})^{\frac{1}{3}}}\right)$

Disp't (tons)	D.$^{\frac{1}{3}}$	Disp't (tons)	D.$^{\frac{1}{3}}$	Disp't (tons)	D.$^{\frac{1}{3}}$	Disp't (tons)	D.$^{\frac{1}{3}}$
2	1·58	18	6·87	34	10·49	50	13·58
3	2·08	19	7·12	35	10·70	51	13·75
4	2·52	20	7·37	36	10·90	52	13·93
5	2·92	21	7·61	37	11·10	53	14·11
6	3·30	22	7·85	38	11·30	54	14·30
7	3·66	23	8·09	39	11·50	55	14·46
8	4·00	24	8·32	40	11·70	56	14·65
9	4·33	25	8·55	41	11·90	57	14·80
10	4·64	26	8·78	42	12·10	58	14·98
11	4·95	27	9·00	43	12·27	59	15·15
12	5·24	28	9·22	44	12·48	60	15·33
13	5·53	29	9·44	45	12·65	61	15·50
14	5·81	30	9·65	46	12·85	62	15·68
15	6·08	31	9·87	47	13·03	63	15·83
16	6·35	32	10·08	48	13·20	64	16·00
17	6·61	33	10·28	49	13·40	65	16·17

APPENDIX FOUR

IMPORTANT LIQUID WEIGHTS AND MEASURES

SALT WATER weighs 64 lb. per cu. ft. and occupies 35 cu. ft. per ton.
FRESH WATER weighs 62·4 lb. per cu. ft. and occupies 36 cu. ft. per ton.
FRESH WATER: 1 gallon weighs 10 lb. There are 224 gallons per ton.

There are 0·1605 cu. ft. per gallon and 6·235 gallons per cu. ft.

PETROL: 7·4 lb. per gal. and 1 cu. ft. weighs 46 lb.
DIESEL OIL: 8·83 lb. per gal. and 1 cu. ft. weighs 55 lb.
PARAFFIN: 8·15 lb. per gal. and 1 cu. ft. weighs 50·9 lb.

Note.—In American measure there are 7·48 gallons per cu. ft.

APPENDIX FIVE

Weights and Strengths of Timbers

	Lb. per cubic foot	Tensile Strength	Crushing Strength	Bending Strength	Modulus of Elasticity
Ash (English)	46	1·7	3·1	5·2	640
Ash (American)	30	2·4	2·4	3·8	390
Cedar	32	1·3	2·0		
Elm (English)	38	2·4	2·5	2·4	280
Elm (American)	47	4·1	4·0	5·5	700
Fir (Douglas)	33				
Greenheart	62	3·9	6·8	8·0	490
Larch	36	1·9	2·7	3·8	730
Mahogany (Honduras)	38	1·3	2·7	5·2	550
Oak (English)	51	3·4	3·4	4·3	450
Oak (White)	58	3·1	3·1	4·9	590
Pine (Oregon)	37				
Pine (Pitch)	41	2·1	2·9	5·3	850
Pine (Yellow)	31	0·9	3·3	3·3	600
Spruce	28				580
Teak	51	1·5	2·8	5·3	600

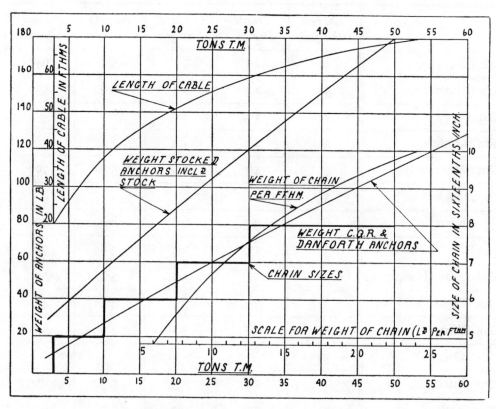

FIG. 95. *Data for ground tackle for cruisers*

Sample Specification

Designed by: Alan H. Buchanan, Ltd., Naval Architects, 45 High Street, Burnham-on-Crouch, Essex, England.

L.O.A.	.. ..	37 ft. 3 in.	Draught ..	6 ft. 2½ in.
L.W.L.	.. ..	26 ft. 5½ in.	Lead keel ..	2·8 tons approx.
Beam	.. ..	9 ft. 7 in.	Displacement ..	7 tons

Part I—General

Generally, the layout and appearance of the yacht to be in accordance with the drawings supplied by the Architect. To be insured by the builder against fire and usual building risks. To be measured for tonnage and fees for registration to be paid by the owner. The hull to be carefully and strongly constructed in accordance with the detailed construction drawings and specification. Special attention to be paid to the drainage of the bilges and care to be taken to provide adequate water-courses under the floors throughout the yacht. Limber holes are to be provided through solid floors and bilges are to be levelled off wherever drainage cannot be arranged. Fillings of bitumen solution and granulated cork.

All timber to be carefully selected, well-seasoned and reasonably free from knots and other defects. All ironwork to be hot-dipped galvanised after drilling and before fitting. All ironwork to be given two coats of yellow chromate. All fastenings to be of copper or yellow metal unless otherwise stated.

The vessel to be built in a suitable shed, protected from the weather during construction. To be laid off and faired up to the approved lines and sheer draught. The lines are to be laid down in first-class style to the entire satisfaction of the Architect. Every precaution is to be taken to preserve the design shape of the ship during building. Templates are to be prepared as desired by the Architect to check the shape if necessary.

The yacht to be built strictly in accordance to Lloyd's 100 A.1 class.

The yacht to be built with mahogany planking with three planks each side in the bottom of Aframosia. All bent timbers are to be of Canadian Rock Elm, carefully selected, straight-grained. Decks to be ribbon laid teak, fitted round the shape of the ship and into king plank with teak rails and covering boards. All main deck beams are to be of Oak. All interior joinery work to be of the highest possible standard, to be constructed of Cedar and plywood with teak trim. Workmanship and finish throughout to be of the highest class. All joints to be of good fit. All faying surfaces are to be given a liberal coating of white lead before fastening. Outside planking to be carefully laid off. No planking to be wider than $4\frac{1}{2}$ in. in the topsides. No butts of the outside planking to be nearer than 5 ft. to the next unless there be a strake wrought between, then a distance of 4 ft. will be allowed. No butt to be in the same transverse plane unless there be three strakes wrought between. No butts will be permitted in the garboard strake.

The caulking of the outside to be with cotton and to be well executed to the satisfaction of the Architect.

Part II—Hull Construction

The construction is to be generally in accordance with the construction plan and fully detailed drawings. All sizes are to be final sizes.

Centre Line Structure. Keel to be Oak and to be in one piece $4\frac{1}{4}$-in. moulded, sided to suit lines and lofting.

Stem. English Oak may be scarphed as shown on drawing. Lower stem to be approximately 7-in. sided. Stem head to be built up and rounded off as shown on lines plan.

Stern Post. To be English Oak fitted as shown on plan.

Horn Timber. To be English Oak in one length moulded and sided as shown on plan.

Deadwood. English Elm.

Transom. To be built up on heavy Oak frame. To be curved in accordance with lines plan. Outside face to be at least $\frac{7}{8}$-in. mahogany. Alternatively, the transom to be cut from solid timber.

Stern Knee. To be 12 s.w.g. galvanised steel as shown on plan, or grown Oak.

Stop Waters. To be fitted in back rebate where considered necessary.

Ballast Keel. To be of cast lead. Pattern to be inspected and checked before casting. Great care to be exercised in the fairing of the lead into the hull lines. Keel bolts to be of Crotorite bronze supplied by Manganese Bronze and Brass Co. of Ipswich in accordance with the detailed construction drawing.

Bent Wood Frames. To be of Canadian Rock Elm. Ordinary frames over 3/5L. to be $1\frac{7}{8}$ in. sided by $1\frac{7}{16}$ in. In ends beyond 3/5L. frames to be $1\frac{3}{4}$ in. $\times$ $1\frac{7}{16}$ in. Heavy frames at end of deck opening in way of mast to be $1\frac{7}{16}$ in. $\times$ $3\frac{1}{8}$ in. Spacing to be as shown on plan approximately 7-in. centres. Timbers to be carefully steam bent without bending or lifting grain and to be accurately positioned in accordance with the construction drawing.

Floors. Galvanised wrought iron floors to be fitted as shown on the drawing on every timber of the centre 3/5ths and alternate timbers in the ends. The size of the floors to be as indicated on construction drawing. All floors to be carefully fitted and fastened to the bent wood frames with galvanised bolts. Throat fastenings and fastenings through wood keel to be $\frac{5}{8}$-in. diam. maximum. All fastenings and ironwork to be given 2 coats yellow chromate at time of fitting. Web steel floors 0·16 in. to be fitted as required by Lloyd's and shown on detailed construction plan.

Planking. To be of selected mahogany with 3 planks each side in the bottom of Aframosia. To be $\frac{7}{8}$-in. finished thickness (see note on planking and butts, Part I). Finished thickness to be carefully maintained throughout the ship. Butts in the sheer strake and covering boards to be kept well clear of one another and of parts of the hull taking rigging strains. Butt blocks to be same thickness as planking and to be thoroughly fastened.

Bilge Stringers. To be of Spruce in one length. To be fastened at every frame. Sizes to be $3\frac{1}{4}$ in. and $1\frac{1}{2}$ in. to be reduced at ends beyond 3/5L. to $2\frac{1}{2}$ in. $\times$ $1\frac{1}{2}$ in. to be equally pitched between keel and shelfing. Stringers to be accurately pitched in accordance with construction drawing.

Beam Shelf. 5 in. $\times$ $1\frac{1}{4}$ in. Spruce in one length to be tapered beyond 3/5L. to $3\frac{3}{4}$ in. $\times$ $1\frac{3}{4}$ in. to be properly fastened at every frame with at least $\frac{5}{16}$-in. Copper clenches. Beam Clamp to be 5 in. $\times$ $1\frac{3}{4}$ in. Oak thoroughly fastened to shelfing and beam ends.

Breast Hooks. To be of galvanised wrought iron to be fitted to stringers and shelfing. To be the size stated on drawing adequately fastened with 4 fastenings in each arm. Throat bolts to be $\frac{3}{8}$-in. diameter. Quarter knees to be fitted at after-end.

Deck Beams. All deck beams to be of Oak properly dovetailed and fastened, all in accordance with detailed construction plan.

Carlins. Carlins of Oak 2 in. $\times$ 2 in. to be shaped to fit coamings. Deck beams to be properly dovetailed in and adequately fastened as shown on detailed construction plan. $\frac{3}{8}$-in. yellow metal tie rods to be fitted each side as shown on construction plan.

Main Deck. To be of ribbon-laid Burma teak $1\frac{3}{4}$ in. $\times$ $\frac{7}{8}$ in. fitted with teak covering board and king plank. Planking to be parallel with covering board. Deck planking to be secret fastened and to be screw fastened and dowelled at every third plank on each beam with No. 12 wood screws.

Doghouse and Coamings. To be properly framed up from $\frac{7}{8}$-in. teak. Ports and doghouse windows to be $\frac{5}{16}$-in. armoured plate glass fitted from outside with cast bronze frames or yellow metal. All to be fitted with secret nosings of teak as shown on construction plan. Cabin top decking to be $\frac{3}{8}$-in. waterproofed ply B.S.S. 1088 covered with fibreglass. Doghouse top to also be $\frac{3}{8}$-in. B.S.S. 1088 ply covered with fibreglass. Cabin top and doghouse beams to be of Oak in accordance with detailed construction plan. All to be properly dovetailed and fitted. All other beams to be as shown on detailed plans. 2–6-in. deadlights to be fitted in cabin top.

Foot Rails. To be of teak properly fastened with teak capping and continuing forward into stemhead fitting and to run aft to connect with transom. Space between deck and top of transom to be fitted up with solid radiused teak chock. Hatches to be constructed of teak in accordance with the detailed drawings.

Other items of deck work to be arranged as shown on deck plan or in details.

Sills in hatches and cockpit, etc., to be fitted with metal chafing strips. 6-in. deadlight to be fitted in forehatch. Forehatch to be fitted with wings so that this can be partly opened at sea.

Cockpit. To have $\frac{3}{8}$-in. plywood sides properly fitted into teak sills and have toe-pieces at side of cockpit. Sides of cockpit are to be set back from cockpit seats. Lockers at after-end to be provided with adequate water-courses and to be fitted with flush bronze lifting rings. Removable teak gratings to cockpit floor. Cockpit to be fitted with copper tray. Cockpit drains to be fitted at forward end. Seat gutters to be deep type constructed of teak with a fall of at least 15 degrees. Copper drain-pipes to be fitted in corners of cockpit seats draining into cockpit. Cockpit to be fitted with proper teak gratings and sheet beam and heavy brass lifting rings in all hatches.

Rudder. To be of mahogany carefully faired into the ship. Rudder stock and tiller as shown on detailed drawings. The bottom pintle to be of cast bronze. Stock to be of bronze. Tiller head to be hinged.

Mast Reinforcing. Mast to be stepped in keel. Oak mast step properly fitted with through clenches and drainhole, to be carefully cased in. Cast bronze mast coat ring to be fitted on deck where mast passes through coachroof with rubber coating and stainless steel clips. Two steel reinforcing angles are to be carefully fitted round coachroof top and down into sides of hull as shown on detailed construction drawing.

Fresh Water Tank. To be made of 16g. galvanised steel carefully fitted. Tank must be easily removable through cabin sole without removing any of the fixed structure. To have deck filler and suction line to pantry pump at sink. Tank to be vented to sink. Tank to have large manhole for access for cleaning and to be fitted with at least one baffle. Tank to be cemented before use. Alternatively, tank to be fibreglass, to be quoted as extra. Tank to be as large as possible.

Chainplates. To be as shown on drawing. To be galvanised iron bolted to frame with angle under shelfing.

Fastenings. All fastenings to be copper or bronze throughout. All bolts to be hove-up on washers of adequate size. All clenches to be hove-up on cooper rooves. Hull planking to be fastened with at least 10g. copper clenches. In throats of floors, keel, stem and stern post, counter, frames, deadwood and breast hooks $\frac{3}{8}$-in. diameter bolts to be used. This is the minimum size. In scarphs to keel and sternpost $\frac{5}{16}$-in. copper clenches is minimum size. In arms of floors $\frac{5}{16}$-in. galvanised bolts 4 in each arm. In heel of timbers and in garboards heavy bronze or monel screws are to be used. All fastenings in covering boards, coamings and brightwork to be carefully dowelled off. Plank fastenings to frames in way of steel floors to be screwed from outside. The holes to be properly dowelled off. This will enable a floor fastening to fit down closely against timber. Copper clenches are to be carefully pitched to avoid fastenings of planking to frames and plank seams. All bolts for centreline to be Crotorite bronze. All nuts to be hexagonal.

Mast. To be hollow Spruce stepped in keel, size as shown on spare drawing. To be fitted with internal aerial. Mast track to be Gibbons Y.1 screwed to mast every 2 in. with stainless steel screws which must be properly countersunk to allow free passage of slides. Slides to be Gibbons Y.6 and thimbles Y.9. 5 ft. of Y2a track to be fitted on forward face of mast to take spinnaker slide fitting. All mast fittings to be in accordance with detailed drawings and to be of galvanised iron, as follows: Masthead fitting with light, Main shroud attachment and spreader. Mast to be fitted with 1 Merriman reel winch and 1 Simpson Lawrence top action winch. A half gate to be fitted clear of stowed mainsail.

Main Boom. To be hollow spruce, round, with Gibbs reefing gear modified type and patent outhaul fitting and winch.

Spinnaker Boom. To be hollow Silver Spruce fitted with proper end fittings of adequate size supplied by Simpson Lawrence.

Rigging. To be in accordance with rigging schedule. All standing rigging to be galvanised plough wire. Wire running rigging to be extra flexible galvanised. The lower ends of the shrouds to be covered with P.V.C. sleeving. All rope rigging to be of best quality hemp. All blocks to be Gibbs tufnol in accordance with rigging schedule. All sheets to be fitted with U.S.M.P. $\frac{1}{2}$-ton clips or Merriman snap shackles in accordance with rigging schedule. All sheets to be of hemp. All rigging screws to be Davey 1397 galvanised. All shackles to be galvanised, tested. Builder to supply all running and standing rigging, warps, sheets, kicking strap, sail tiers, sheet tacks and blocks, necessary for the ship.

Constructionally, no galvanised steel is to be used unless specifically mentioned. All eyebolts and fittings on the main deck are to be of yellow metal or stainless steel.

Part III—Accommodation and Finish

Cockpit. Two after-lockers to be provided with access each side of the tiller head. Port side of cockpit to have large locker extending right down to bilges, not to be fitted with floor. Cockpit to be finished off in bright varnish except cockpit seats which are to be left bare. The main after-bulkhead to be teak properly framed up, to have solid sill with brass strip at entrance to cabin, to have drop boards. All tanks to be installed to Lloyd's requirements, easily removable through locker tops.

Quarter Berth and Engine Casing. Quarter berth to be $\frac{3}{8}$-in. plywood with teak capping. Berth bottom to be of Spruce with ample access to stowage under berths. Stowage to be built in behind berths port and starboard. These to be of $\frac{1}{4}$-in. plywood and Cedar as shown on plan. Forward face of engine casing to be of $\frac{3}{8}$-in. plywood fitted on cedar. Frame to be easily removable for access to engine. Top of engine casing to be $\frac{5}{8}$-in. teak, to be hinged in middle. Teak companion ladder to be fitted on top of engine casing. Removable step to be fitted forward of the engine casing between the quarter berth and galley. Stowage for battery in lead-lined tray properly secured under engine bay. After-end of quarter berth to have partition at end of mattress to form stowage, for personal gear. Small shelf with at least 3-in. fiddle to be fitted at side.

Galley. Main galley bulkhead to be constructed of $\frac{5}{8}$-in. Western Red Cedar with $\frac{1}{4}$-in. Marine plywood, to B.S.S. 1088. All bulkheads and partitions to be side-fastened to existing frames. No extra cleating is to be fitted if possible. Galley to have lockers and plate racks as shown on detailed plan, all to be constructed of $\frac{1}{4}$-in. and $\frac{3}{8}$-in. ply with teak trim. Galley to be lined with Formica, all edges to be masked with teak capping. Locker doors to have brass hinges with yellow metal fastenings, chromium plated. Stainless steel sink with copper drain-pipe to be fitted as shown on plan. Sink waste to be fitted with pump. Galley stove to be Simpson Lawrence gas cooker with stowage under for contractors type gas cylinders. Stove to be in gimbals. Whale fresh-water pump to be fitted in galley.

Chart Table. To be constructed of Cedar and plywood with teak cappings as per galley. Chart table-top to be covered with Formica. Below chart table, hinged down flap to provide access to chart stowage. Below lockers with shelf for stowage. Above chart table stowage to be built-in for Woodsons radio and all equipment (if required). Shelves and stowages to be built-in for all navigational books and equipment. All in accordance with detailed plan.

Main Saloon. To be constructed as shown on drawing. Berth tops to be constructed of $\frac{1}{2}$-in. Cedar with traps and stowage under. Teak kicking-board to run the whole length of the saloon and galley. Lockers to be constructed as shown on plan. Doors are to stand proud. Sideboard tops and shelves to be constructed of teak or mahogany covered with formica and the whole to be finished off with teak trim and white paint. Cabin sole throughout ship to be $\frac{5}{8}$-in. teak with grating in forward hatch and grating in toilet. All screw fastenings to be put down in cups. One drawer to be fitted under each saloon berth with patent locking device and one small hinged door in each for access. Shelves behind berths to be wide enough to set books on with at least 4-in. fiddle.

Toilet Compartment and Hanging Lockers. Toilet bulkheads to be constructed of Cedar covered with plywood. Hanging locker to be properly framed up in two sections;

after-section to have door. Toilet door to be flush-type with grille, to open up to close off fo'c'sle. Hanging cupboards to be fitted with rails and hanging hooks. Toilet to be fitted with hanging hooks for oilskins. Curtain to be fitted between fo'c'sle and saloon when toilet door closed.

Forward Cabin. To have one built in berth finished off white with teak cappings. To have drawer and stowage below, shelf over foot. Small forward bulkhead with stowage beyond teak steps to be fitted on toilet bulkhead with access to forehatch. Berth bottom to be of Spruce. Chain stowage forward for cruising cabin. Main chain to be carried under cabin sole aft. Port side to have sail bin with teak capping and canvas root berth and Dunlopillo mattress, to stow back against skin when not in use.

Plumbing. Toilet to be Baby Blake in white with plastic tubing and sea-cocks. Flanges are to be turned down and let into hull, all finished off flush. Two main water tanks as large as possible, to be fitted under cabin sole, to have filler cap on deck and vented to galley sink. Tanks to be cement washed. Sink to be fitted with Whale pump. Sink waste to be pumped out with $1\frac{1}{4}$-in. Whale pump mounted in recess at angle in galley face. Toilet to be fitted with porcelain wash-basin unit draining into toilet with fresh water pump mounted on bulkhead, "Whale" type. Cockpit drains to be of copper piping, all fitted with sea-cocks. $2\frac{1}{2}$-in. Whale bilge pump to be mounted in bridge deck and fitted through ship's side and suction at lower end.

Upholstery. Two forward berths and quarter berth and two saloon berths to be fitted. with 4-in. Dunlopillo mattresses covered with light canvas ticks and Vynide coverings. Backrests in main saloon to be 2-in. Dunlopillo upholstered in Vynide with piping. (Colours to be selected by owner.) Canvas leaboards to be fitted to each berth with lashings to deckhead.

General Note—Interior Finish. The whole of the interior to be finished off in white paint with teak cappings. The cabin sole, coamings, side board tops, etc., to be left bright wood or wax-polished as required.

It is understood that the builder will supply and fit all necessary drawers, stowages, book-cases, cutlery drawer and interior fitments to the owner's requirements as part of the contract.

Deck Fittings. Pulpit to be of galvanised steel to detailed drawing with stainless steel double lifelines, top wire covered with P.V.C. 7-24-in. Reynolds stanchions to be fitted each side, with sockets. Special stemhead roller of galvanised steel electrically welded as per detailed drawing. Chain plates to be properly finished off where they come through the covering boards with collars and plates. A section of flat bronze track milled and drilled, fitted with standard bronze sliders, as detailed drawing supplied by the Architect to take Genoa and staysail sheet leads. Sliders each side to be fitted with Gibbs blocks. Bronze chain navel to be fitted forward. 5-in. mushroom ventilators to be fitted fore and aft. Flush-type fairleads to be fitted forward. Fairleads and mooring cleats to be fitted aft. Sheet winches to be fitted on cockpit coamings, to be Gibbs 8 C.R. on 10g. mounting with teak chafing block on forward face. Main sheet sliders and track to be fitted in cockpit as per detailed drawing. Grab rails to be fitted on cabin top and doghouse top, to be $2\frac{3}{4}$ in. $\times$ $1\frac{1}{4}$ in. teak. All cleats to be of adequate size 10–12 in. properly fastened. 2 Dorade type box vents to be fitted on cabin top, to be made of extra heavy gauge brass, made up specially from at least 16 gauge with 5-in. diameter bases. Waterproof sockets for 3-in. masthead light to be fitted as detailed plan. 5-in. mushroom ventilator flush-type to be fitted on foredeck. 1-6-in. deadlight to be fitted in fore hatch and one each side of mast, making 3-6 in.

Engine. To be Stuart Turner P55ME direct-drive fitted with self-starter, to be installed just off centre with the shaft running on the port side of the rudder stock. Engine to be properly fitted with drip-tray. Drip-tray to have sump. Fuel tank to be at least 6 gallons capacity, to be supplied and fitted by builder with filling-can and water-trap draining into engine sump. Tank vents to be run out to atmosphere. Tank to be fitted with filters and cocks, all in accordance with Lloyd's requirements. Stern gear to be of bronze with remote greaser. Propeller to be 2-bladed folding. Exhaust to be run under cockpit sole and out through centre of transom. Silencer to be fitted under after-deck. The whole of the exhaust system to be water-jacketed and water to be run in at the forward end of the exhaust. Engine to be 12v. starting with non-spill battery in proper stowage. Throttle control to lead up into cockpit and also gear control. Engine and all equipment to be supplied and installed by builder.

Electrical Installation. The ship to be wired out with lead-covered cable and watertight junction boxes. All switches are to be heavy yellow metal tumbler type. Lighting is to be from engine starter battery which is to be of sufficient capacity for lighting and engine starting.

Watertight socket on after-deck for stern light.

Watertight socket in cockpit for lighting compass.

Watertight socket under bridge deck for lead light.

Light over head of quarter berth.

Light over chart table.

Light over galley.

Centre light in doghouse.

Light at head of each saloon berth.

One central overhead light in saloon.

Overhead light in toilet.

Overhead light in forward cabin.

One overhead light at head of each berth.

Waterproof guarded light in fo'c'sle.

Waterproof socket on deck for masthead light.

Waterproof socket forward for pulpit navigation light.

Pulpit navigation light.

Stern light.

Masthead light.

Compass light to be fitted with Rheostat.

Equipment. Equipment to be in accordance with Lloyd's requirements for a vessel of this class.

2 bower anchors, 35 lb. C.Q.R.

2-15 fathom lengths galvanised $\frac{5}{16}$-in. diam. chain to Lloyd's full test.

1 hawser, 30 fathoms $2\frac{1}{4}$-in. circ. lightly tarred Italian hemp.

2-15 fathom warps $1\frac{3}{4}$-in. circ. hemp.

Sails. To be supplied by builder in first quality heat set Terylene:

Mainsail complete with number, battens, bag, tiers, slides, etc.

No. 1 staysail complete with hanks and bag.

No. 2 staysail complete with hanks and bag.

No. 1 Genoa complete with hanks and bag.

Spinnaker complete with swivel and bag, in Terylene or Nylon.

Mainsail cover.

Builder to supply all sheets, U.S.M.P. clips, tacks, etc.

Painting. The yacht to be cleaned of all sawdust and shavings.

The hull to be primed inside and out with at least 4 coats Metallic Pink Primer, where painted. Topsides after priming to receive 1 application stopping cement, 1 application Metallic Pink Primer, 2 undercoats and 1 coat of enamel.

All brightwork to receive at least 6 coats International varnish.

Bottom to receive after-priming, 1 coat stopping cement, 1 coat. Metallic Pink Primer, 2 coats underwater undercoat and 1 coat Kobe anti-fouling.

Internally, the vessel to receive after priming, 1 application stopping cement, 1 application Metallic Priming, 2 undercoats and 1 coat enamel throughout.

Bilges after priming with Metallic Pink Primer to receive at least 2 coats International Danboline.

All spars to receive 6 coats International varnish.

Boot top to be carefully cut in as indicated on lines drawing. Yacht's name and club to be applied on transom.

Gold line round topsides.

Sundry metal and wooden fittings not specified but covered either on the drawings or in the specification are to be supplied by the builder in order that the yacht may be completed in the spirit of the specification and drawings.

It is understood and agreed that there will be no extras unless they are specifically mentioned by the owner, agreed by the Architect and quoted for in writing by the builder.

Carvings for tonnage and registration to be carried out in the main beams by the builder and the builder is to supply rubbings for the Ministry of Transport and carve in official number.

Yard to assist R.O.R.C. measurer and to paint on black bands and fit stops to spars.

The vessel to be completed, transported and launched and to be under the care of the builder until completion of trials.

Builder to carry out any adjustments to gear and fittings which may be found necessary after trials and to be responsible for the vessel until the owner takes full delivery.

The vessel to be built to the satisfaction of the Designer or his representative, in accordance with the specification and detailed drawings supplied by Alan H. Buchanan, Ltd.

All materials to be approved by Alan H. Buchanan, Ltd.

Equipment to be Supplied by Builder

Saloon table.

2 Dorade ventilators, heavy gauge, 5-in. base diameter.

1 Whale bilge pump $2\frac{1}{2}$ in.

2–5-in. mushroom ventilators.

1–5-in. mushroom ventilator, flat type.

1 horseshoe lifebuoy with Yacht's name. *Onazote.*
Ensign staff and socket.
1 canvas bucket.
1 mop.
1 deck scrubber.
Sestrel Minor compass mounted on beam.
Toilet and fitments as specified.
2 yacht fenders.
1 galley pump "Whale".
1 toilet pump.
2–8 C.R. winches.
1 Merriman winch.
1 Simpson Lawrence top-action winch.
Baby Blake toilet with sea-cocks and plastic piping.
Porcelain folding wash-basin.
Simpson Lawrence calor gas stove in gimbals.
Contractor size cylinders and piping.
Boathook.
Sail cover.
Sail tiers.
5 Dunlopillo mattresses and 2 back-rests.
Root berth for fo'c'sle.
Anchors and chains as specification.
Electric lighting as specification.
8 h.p. Stuart Turner P55ME with all equipment.
2 fresh-water tanks, as large as possible.
Masthead light.
Stern light.
Bi-colour navigation lights.
Light alloy boom crutch.
Chain navel.
Deck stowage for spinnaker pole.
1 fire extinguisher 14-in. Pyrene.
Stainless steel sink and piping.
Fairleads, as required.
Cleats, as required.
Sundry deck fittings, as required.
Fo'c'sle curtain.
Pulpit, stanchions and lifelines, top wire covered P.V.C.
Gibb modified roller reefing gear and winch outhaul.
Sails as specified.

APPENDIX EIGHT

DISCUSSION ON RATING RULES (See Chapter 9)

Mr. James McGruer (*Associate Member*): Yacht rating rules are of a very complex nature and a close study of the 70 pages of print referred to in the author's opening remarks is essential before the values of even the main features can be assessed. I should like to congratulate Mr. Phillips-Birt on producing so concise a paper on the subject.

I personally regret, however, that he did not also include the rating rule of the Cruising Club of America, known as the C.C.A. Rule and the International Rating Rule for yachts under $14\frac{1}{2}$ metres, both of which have considerable influence on the rules discussed, and to which references are made throughout his paper.

It is too early yet in the life of (*a*) the 5·5 Metre class rule, and (*b*) the Cruiser-Racer Rule, to say that they are "type" rules. They have quite a long way to go before it can be said, as it has been said about the 6 Metres, that "they are more alike than the International One Design Dragons."

Rule (*c*), the R.O.R.C. Rule, came into being between the wars to serve the purpose of measuring a large variety of yachts which wished to go in for long-distance racing. They were of varying proportions, were built over a large number of years, and their vital statistics were not available.

The International 5·5 Metre rule cannot be compared with any other or any previous international rule in that it is the only international rule the purpose of which is to produce a purely day sailing yacht. It is the only alternative to one-design classes, which do not make any contribution to design development. Criticism of this rule can be made only on the rule features other than the main features, for instance, the sail plan.

The Cruiser-Racer rule has two basic features:

(i) The main part of the formula is based on the rule for $14\frac{1}{2}$ metres and under, which is commonly called the old International Rule, and includes the 6 Metres which sail in the British America Cup, etc., and the 12 Metres, which is to be used for the famous America's Cup, with a slight change in the divisor, as follows:

$$\text{Old International Rule} \quad \frac{L + 2d + \sqrt{S} - F}{2\cdot37} = R$$

$$\text{C/R Rule} \quad \frac{L + \sqrt{(S)} - F}{2} = R$$

That basic formula has been retained in the C-R rule, but they have dropped from it the item $2d$, which was an attempt to control the cross-section—an item the author has gone into very carefully when he discusses the speed-reducing factor.

(ii) Various other factors which give the designer freedom of choice in selecting beam, draught/displacement, and the shape of the profile, and make allowances for yachts with transom sterns, iron keels, and yachts fitted with engines, which, as the author says, gives the rule its similarity to the C.C.A. rule. The exception is that the normal values are those common to European yachts, and the main difference from the C.C.A. rule is in beam and draught "normals."

The C-R rule does not take into direct account the ballast/displacement ratio which surely has had considerable influence in giving the shallow draught beamy American yacht its rule advantage.

The author goes into the various measurements taken in the R.O.R.C. rule with great care and has explained their purpose. However, to my mind, the rule still has the defect inherent in the fact that no basic line of flotation is used—I am in favour of the inclusion of that line. The reason of it not being included to begin with was lack of information, but basic measurements should now be available from the designers or builders, and use should be made of them. In my opinion, this should have been incorporated in the latest changes.

In the C.C.A. rule, not only must the line of flotation be found and the displacement for that line given, but also the weight for the ballast keel must be provided.

The author states that in rules (*a*) and (*b*) increased displacement means a direct increase in ballast, which is so in any open class yacht such as a 5·5, but does not work out so in any craft that is to be a cruising yacht. A narrow, heavy displacement cruiser-racer would be very uncomfortable; to perform the function of a cruiser it must have beam, displacement, and ballast complementary to one another.

It is not strictly true to say that in rule (*b*) increased displacement does not require any increase in scantling as in this rule the control of construction is by Lloyd's, which is by far the best method. If you increase the beam you must have increased scantling.

The author has an interesting reference in the paper to the control of the displacement and has given a further explanation by his illustration on the blackboard. I cannot wholly subscribe to his inference in this section that increased displacement does not require increased sail area. Adding displacement in way of the garboards, while decreasing the resistance at slow speed, is otherwise a disadvantage. In most cases an increase in draught incurs a penalty or at least a loss of bonus which would probably cancel any bonus gained by the increase in displacement. From the author's remarks about the beam, while discussing the 5·5's in Section IV, it would seem that added beam does cause greater resistance in certain conditions, as, for instance, when going to windward. But I would agree that in the cruiser-racer rule the additional beam, along with the additional sail area gained because of it, could be carried to advantage, for the reason he has given. A good rule is one which draws the correct balance.

With regard to the author's remarks about measuring the cross-section, this was fairly common in some of the older rules and, in fact, usually developed into a control of the section, as illustrated by the small values of 2*d* in the old international rule. It is possible, although too early yet to tell, that the quarter beam depth measurement on the R.O.R.C. may develop similarly if it is found that the boats with this measurement as large as possible do well.

Sail area measurements, rightly occupy a good deal of the author's paper, and are interesting, and while he has confined his remarks to Bermudian sails it appears to me that we are still to some extent influenced by the change from gaff rig to Bermudian rig. For example, in the 6 Metres, when the change from gaff to Bermudian rig took place, the new sails were so much more effective that the "Sixes" became much larger yachts and still faster. Whereas, due to the efficiency of the sail plan, in this country we now tend, in cruiser-racers, to have the sail area too small for the size of the yacht and certainly for racing round the buoy it would be better if they carried more sail.

I was interested to note the author's remarks about the American sails becoming old-fashioned with their low aspect ratio—I would have thought these sails would become inefficient. The American rules, however, give more free area.

The author does not mention, in his section on sail area, the spinnaker which has become a very important item in the sail area of a yacht, and I cannot think that the modern spinnaker is what it ought to be. The R.O.R.C. spinnaker is too tall and narrow, especially when used with a masthead rig, and the C.C.A. spinnaker, which is the same as the R.O.R.C., seems to fly too high; so that all these yachts are fitted with an additional sail, namely, a spinnaker staysail to fill the space below.

In the 5·5's the restriction on the base of the foretriangle has a bearing on the size of the spinnaker, and my criticism of this class, from the sailing point of view, is that it is a three-man yacht with a four-man spinnaker.

The author has said that in the C-R rule the masthead rig is prohibited. That is not so: there is no absolute prohibition of the masthead rig, and it can be obtained by operating the bonus for reduced mast height and accepting the penalty for an increased height of I. This serves to give a good rig for ocean racing purposes by reducing the total height.

In the R.O.R.C. rule there was always a restriction on mast height. It was, however, of such a nature as to be non-restrictive.

Finally, I am of the opinion that both the R.O.R.C. and the C.C.A. should insert in their rules a compulsory requirement that all yachts to be measured should have flotation marks fitted at their datum waterline and a further set of marks at some convenient distance above, say, 6 in. Under any system of measurement these marks would be well worth while, even if only for checking freeboards; to do so from some mark near the waterline is much easier than trying to measure from the covering board.

May I again congratulate Mr. Phillips-Birt on his very worthwhile paper.

Mr. P. R. Crewe, m.a. (*Associate-Member*): Firstly, I must confess that I know very little about sailing; but I have had some experience of aerodynamic problems and there is one matter in that connection that I would like to raise.

Before doing so, however, I should like to congratulate Mr. Phillips-Birt very much indeed on this paper, and particularly on his exposition this evening, which I found very clear and extremely interesting. I had not realised just how much is involved in designing yachts, nor that there are quite so many pages of regulations to be satisfied.

Being associated with a tank, I am very fully in agreement with the remark that more tank tests of a systematic type would be of use. It seems to me, however, that the problem is mainly economic and not primarily a technical one. There should not be much difficulty in designing valuable tests and in developing model yacht test techniques beyond the point so far reached. On the other hand, it is unfortunately not generally practicable for the yacht designer to include in addition to his other charges, the appreciable cost of tank tests on a particular craft he is designing.

If a co-operative arrangement is tried the trouble is, of course, that the members do not gain individual advantage, for everybody receives the same results. May I suggest that the most important problem of yacht tank testing is to devise a co-operative scheme in which each member derives individual benefit, depending upon the ideas he contributes. Methods by which this might be done have been tentatively suggested to us, but further progress must depend upon the designers deciding that they really do want more information of the type that we can provide.

Turning to my aerodynamic point, this concerns aspect ratio. It is stated that high aspect ratio should be aimed for, but this belief may require very careful qualification.

Systematic tests on low aspect ratio aerofoils or laminae are not very readily available, and some of their implications may have escaped attention. Results I have recently some across are particularly interesting. Some examples follow in tables:

(a) Rectangular Planform

Aspect ratio	0·5	1·0	5·0
Maximum lift coefficient	1·1 approx.	1·36	0·82
Approximate corresponding attitude, deg.	36	36	15
Approximate L/D .:	1·2	1·3	3·5
Maximum L/D	3·3	3·7	8·3
Corresponding attitude, deg.	11	9	4
Approximate corresponding lift coefficient	0·3 approx.	0·33	0·32

General variation of L/D with incidence and aspect ratio:

Incidence ..	2	4	8	14	20	30	40
Aspect ratio:							
5	6·5	8·4	6·3	3·7	2·7	1·7	1·1
1·0	1·8	2·8	3·6	3·3	2·6	1·7	1·1
0·5	1·5	2·2	3·1	3·1	2·5	1·6	1·0

(b) Elliptic Planform

Aspect ratio	1·1	0·2	0·6	1·2	2·0	4·5
Maximum lift coefficient	0·8	1·10	1·62	1·29	0·80	0·72

It will be observed that the maximum lift coefficients occur at low aspect ratio combined with high attitude.

Peaking of maximum lift coefficient at low aspect ratio is considerably more pronounced for the elliptic planform than for the rectangle.

The lift coefficient at maximum L/D is not much affected by aspect ratio.

The L/D variation with attitude is not much affected by aspect ratio, at low aspect ratio.

The maximum L/D occurs at high aspect ratio combined with low attitude.

This supports the view that where total sail force is more important than L/D, low aspect ratio is best. It is therefore of interest to consider how far reduced aspect ratio might be permissible when sailing to windward.

The important geometrical relationships of the parallelogram of velocities may conveniently be written

$$\frac{2V_{mg}}{V_T} + 1 = \frac{1 - v^2}{1 + v^2 - 2v \cos \beta} = \frac{1}{\eta} = \text{say}$$

where v denotes V_S/V_a, while

$$\frac{V_S}{V_T} = \frac{v}{\sqrt{\eta (1 - v^2)}}$$

Thus

$$v = \frac{\cos \beta - \sqrt{(\eta^2 - \sin^2 \beta)}}{(1 + \eta)}$$

It follows that for given V_{mg} and V_T, the angle between course and relative wind β, must not exceed $\sin^{-1} \eta$.

Take *Gimcrack* results for example:

$$\text{At } V_T = 8 \cdot 7 \text{ knots, } \beta = 27 \text{ deg., } v = 0 \cdot 4,$$

Thus β must not exceed $32 \cdot 4$ deg., where $v = 0 \cdot 55$.

The variation of β, V_S and V_a, in this case for V_T and V_{mg} to remain constant is of interest:

β				0	10	20	30	32·4
$\frac{V_S}{V_T}$	..	..	..	0·435	0·449	0·504	0·674	0·9
$\frac{V_a}{V_T}$	..	..	..	1·44	1·44	1·46	1·52	1·63

Note the rapid rise in V_S as the limiting β is approached, and the comparatively small change in V_a.

Now if the sail L/D in a horizontal plane, relative to V_a, is denoted by $\cot^{-1} \epsilon$, and C_L is the horizontal sail lift, the water resistance R and horizontal side force Y of the hull satisfy

$$\frac{R}{Y} = \tan (\beta - \epsilon)$$

while

$$R = \tfrac{1}{2} \rho S V_a^2 C_L \sec \epsilon \sin (\beta - \epsilon)$$
$$Y = \tfrac{1}{2} \rho S V_a^2 C_L \sec \epsilon \cos (\beta - \epsilon)$$

Typical hull tests give Y/R lying between 0 and, say, 3·6, while R varies with V rather faster than V_S^2, other things being equal.

This gives $\tan (\beta - \epsilon) \geqslant 0 \cdot 28$, i.e $\beta - \epsilon \geqslant 16$ degrees, which limits permissible values of ϵ to less than 16·4 degrees. The corresponding sail L/D must therefore exceed 3·4.

Consider the limitingly low value of L/D of 3·4, in comparison with the *Gimcrack* value of about 7.

To a first approximation R is independent of Y and varies as V_S^2. Thus to obtain equilibrium in the low aspect ratio case it is necessary to increase C_L at least in the ratio of $v^2/\sec \epsilon \sin (\beta - \epsilon)$, i.e. as 2·3 to 1, while Y will then increase in the ratio of $V_a^2 C_L$, i.e. as 2·8 to 1. The rolling moment will not go up as rapidly as this due to the lower centre of action of the low aspect ratio sail.

	Limitingly low aspect ratio cone	Gimcrack *case*
β	32·4	27
ϵ	16·4	8
$\beta - \epsilon$	16	19
$\sec \epsilon \sin (\beta - \epsilon)$ ..	0·264	0·322
$\sec \epsilon \cos (\beta - \epsilon)$ ..	0·92	0·93
V_S	7·8	5·2
V_a	14·2	13
v	0·55	0·4
R/Y..	0·286	0·326

The low aspect ratio results previously quoted will just permit an L/D of 3·4, near maximum L/D conditions, but do not appear to offer the C_L increase required. However, the physical behaviour of low aspect aerofoils is as yet imperfectly understood, and an appreciable increase in C_L might be obtained by suitable choice of planform. It is known, for example, that a delta wing at high altitude produces very large tip vortices which sweep in air from beyond the wing tips. If the tips are clipped, reducing geometrical aspect ratio, the lift remains almost unaltered, and the effective aspect ratio is also larger than (geometric span)²/area would suggest.

Further investigations of this point would appear worthwhile, as might also an evaluation such as that given above, but for lighter airs.

The above reasoning supports the view that very low aspect ratio sails can be an advantage when not sailing close-hauled, but they are not satisfactory to windward. Some reduction in aspect ratio might, however, be made without loss in speed made good to windward, if special sailforms were employed.

Many of these low aspect ratio effects are published in a Russian textbook on fishing gear which has just reached this country. (1958)

MR. J. LAURENT GILES, B.A. (*Member*): Mr. Phillips-Birt's paper is a painstaking and lucid exposition of some of the mysteries of yacht measurement. I admire his skill in selecting essentials out of a complex and abstruse subject.

I would like to make a few remarks about one or two points.

Major Heckstall-Smith, in fact, invented the form of the 5·5 Metre Rule in 1912; it was used then for the British Racing Association's 18-ft. class and in the international model yacht racing A-class rule still in use; subsequently (1926) in the R.O.R.C. rule here dealt with at length; and for a short-lived class of 5-Metre yachts in 1933 by the Royal Corinthian Yacht Club. It therefore has a substantial background as well as being the product of the greatest analyst and critic of yacht design the world has known.

The author in discussing the measurement of length uses the expression "effective sailing length." That is a very controversial expression and I would like him to explain a little more fully what he understands by it, and to ask him and perhaps one or other of the tank experts to say what value they think may be placed to the credit of the immersion of the counter in the stern-wave.

The immersed length is of course increased to a greater or less extent even if assessed in the static condition as is normal for stability calculations: in practice we are concerned only with the yacht in motion so that she will be sunk in her own wave pattern relatively to the smooth water surface. Therefore the displacement/length ratio and the wave-making resistance must be reduced; on the other hand, the wetted surface is clearly increased and this must cost resistance.

Now the increase of length will be the greater with fuller, flatter sections in the ends. Such sections will contribute greatly to the "stability of form" as we call it. The author has stressed the great importance of stability as related to ballast in his discussion of displacement and I would like to ask his views on the possibility that "sailing length" is an illusion, and that the means adopted in the various rules to assess it are in reality measures of the stability of form of the ends—therefore of sail-carrying power and therefore of speed potential.

I am glad that the author finds that the 5·5-Metre yachts are under-canvassed. I think it was unfortunate that the permitted limits should have been so tightly drawn in a new class with this new and very restrictive sail area measurement. The limits have precluded the normal self-adjustment of the hull and sail area proportions. So tight are the limits that no clear trend has been able to emerge, but I think that, freed from restraint, we should see smaller hulls with larger sail plans. I think, however, that in the end the present sail area measurement will be found a failure and that flexibility will be given back by allowing Genoa jibs.

I would add one word of warning on developments engendered by rules and say that any rule can be regarded as innocent of evil propensities only in so far as evil types of hull and sail plan have been effectively tried under it and have been proved unsuccessful.

Mr. Arthur C. Robb: So far as the R.O.R.C. rule is concerned the policy has always been to make it practicable to measure any odd boat that might unexpectedly appear, and which could not be slipped, or the waterline measured due to the weather.

Almost no boats of this category race today, so the tail wags the dog, and we have a highly complicated rule to avoid waterline measurement, at a time when the plans of 99 per cent of the boats are, or could be, available. It would take little ingenuity to produce a device to measure the waterline, as is done with ships for an inclining experiment. As things are, the rule-makers insist that the waterline *cannot* be measured, and then set out to base several vital measurements *on* the waterline—some with heavy multiplier-effect factors.

The C.C.A. rule is mentioned for comparison. It provides gradually increasing debits and credits from reasonable average basic proportions, whereas the R.O.R.C.

rule arbitrarily fixes several measurements without making any gradual allowances beyond or below its fixed measurements—draught, for example.

With regard to the 5·5-Metre rule, I regard this as a good one, its only faults in measurement effect on design being its too severe bow measurements, and too low stern measurements. A very strong criticism I have of this rule is its quite ridiculous scantlings—½-in. planking for boats upwards of 35 ft. overall. and floors larger than in many 10-ton cruising boats, are examples.

I have one criticism of *all* rules—they are largely illiterate, being full of confusions for lack of grammatical editing, as you will have experienced.

Mr. W. A. Crago, b.sc. (*Associate-Member*): My first comment can best be illustrated by means of a very simple example. I understand that in ancient Egypt a tax was levied on land ownership. This tax was based on the productive capacity of the land, which was very reasonably thought to be a direct function of the area of the land in question. Unfortunately, the officials concerned believed that the area of a field having the shape of a parallelogram was given by the product of the length of two adjacent sides. Thus if the included angle of the two sides departed very much from 90 degrees the land-owner was taxed very much more than he ought to have been. This unfortunate situation was attributable entirely to the officials' lack of knowledge of a precise method of evaluation of the particular parameter which they wished to calculate.

I take it that the aim in formulating yacht rating rules is so to penalise or "tax" yachts so that all the yachts concerned in any particular race will pass over the winning line together. Such a procedure will be possible only when we know a great deal more about the precise calculations of yacht performance and I feel that at present we may very well be in the same position as the Egyptian tax collectors.

In an endeavour to find a satisfactory method for calculating yacht performance, many attempts have been made to analyse full-scale yacht racing results, but it is very difficult to determine how far success in a race can be attributed to ability on the part of the crew, to honest to goodness luck, and how far to the yacht design. I know that attempts have been made to eliminate some of these factors in the analysis, but there is still the weather to be reckoned with, and when one arranges for a particular yacht to be sailed over a specified course twice with different crews, one generally finds that the weather is also different during the two experiments.

In view of the difficulty of analysing full-scale data I would like to ask the author's opinion as to the possibility of carrying out relatively elementary tank tests on a series of models, in which the major parameters are systematically varied, with a view to finding out how one could calculate a reasonable overall performance "number" or "characteristic" for any given yacht. I feel that only in this way will it be possible to formulate a reasonable rating rule which leads to a reasonable penalty for any given yacht shape that comes along, and does not lead to weird designs being built in an attempt to take advantage of some loophole.

I do not think such tests would necessarily cost a great deal of money, since they would be concerned only with isolating the main parameters which affect a yacht's performance.

From the work that has been carried out at Saunders-Roe on quite a number of yachts on various occasions, I have already been able to isolate at least some of the more important parameters concerned in yacht performance. I have found, for example, that the hull resistance and the hull side force as defined in Fig. 96 A are related to each other in a very simple manner, as shown in Fig. 96 B. Each line corresponds to a particular water speed and the intercept on the vertical axis is, of course, the upright unyawed resistance. The slope of the lines can be calculated and is a function (as would be expected from simple aerodynamic theory) of the wetted hull area in elevation and also its aspect ratio.

Of course there is a certain amount of scatter of the test points, but the effect of heel is relatively small, and this fact tends to support the curve the author drew on the blackboard.

From this work one could fairly conclude that the wetted area of the hull in elevation, together with its aspect ratio, ought to appear in some way or the other in the ideal rating rule.

Various flattering references have been made to tanks in general, and as a Tank Superintendent I would like to say that I hope we can justify the confidence placed in us and be of service in some way if it is felt that model work could help to clarify some of the problems of yacht rating.

Mr. A. H. Paul: I am on my feet because there has been some sniping at the R.O.R.C. rule of measurement, and several suggestions have been made that we should adopt the load waterline as a basis of length measurement. This matter has been discussed for many years. The basis we have had to work on in producing this rule is that it must be possible to measure a yacht afloat in various states of trim, a yacht which has come from France, Holland, America, or elsewhere, and for which it is impossible to obtain data. Often it is difficult enough to get the yacht measured at all. They arrive at short notice, and some owners are very unknowledgeable about the details of their yachts.

With regard to the establishment of datum marks on the hull, I am afraid there are some designers who do not seem to be able to get the plane of flotation within about 6 in. of the lines on paper. Weights of keels vary enormously and often seem to be very widely different from what they are supposed to be.

Anyway, we did think we had found an improved method of assessment of length in the new rule that was brought in this year. If I may criticise a little, I think Mr. Phillips-Birt did not do justice to our length measurement when he stated that "The geometry of the present system is complex, lacking the sureness and elegance of the former systems, based on the direct and logical approach to the problem." We thought the basis of our length measurement was very simple and fairly logical.

If we measure various girths around the ends of the hull taking various arbitrary points, and drop a perpendicular from the freeboard equal in length to the half girth, we arrive at a curve something like this (Fig. 96 C).

It seems to me that if we establish the measured length between the point forward where the half girth equals the freeboard, i.e. where the curve of girths cuts the surface of the water, we have a fairly reasonable measure of the effective length of the overhang. For instance, for an overhang with considerable fullness, the perpendicular would be longer than one having a narrow V-shaped end, with the same freeboard. So that a full bow boat would have a curve like this (Fig. 96 D), and a narrow-ended boat would have a curve perhaps there (Fig. 96 E). So that the full-ended hull would have a greater length than the narrow-ended hull.

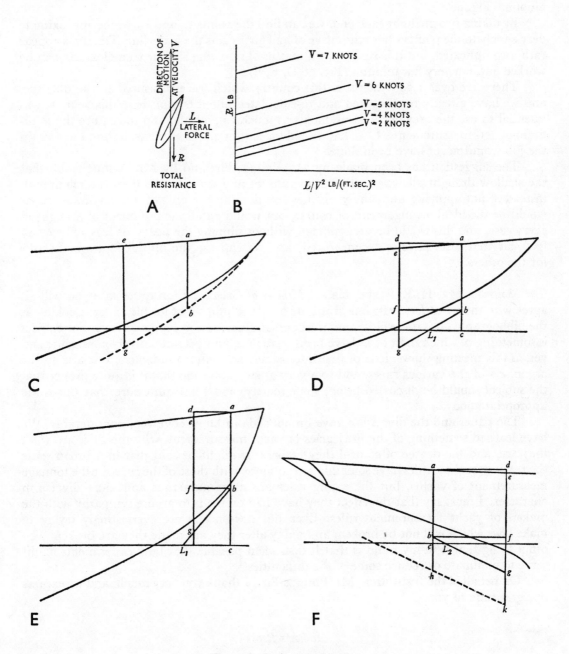

FIG. 96. *Rating measurements*

Treatment of the after overhang is similar, but as the curve of girths cuts the waterline a long way aft, B/8 is deducted from the half girths and the curve is lifted up by that amount (Fig. 96 F).

By taking two girths at each end, we can find the points L₁ and L₂, which approximate very closely to the points where the curve of half girths cuts the waterline. The sums appear rather complicated, but it is really just a matter of resolving similar triangles, and can be worked out in a very few minutes (Fig. 96 D, E, F).

There are over 1,200 yachts in this country which were measured to the old rule, and we have already re-measured and re-calculated about 600 of these this year. It was essential to use the previous measurements as much as possible, and to require the minimum of new measurements. If we had called for datum marks at the waterline I am afraid the job would never have been done.

The suggestion has been made by Mr. Phillips-Birt and by Mr. Arthur Robb that the shallow draught allowance should operate for any draught less than the maximum, instead of not applying until the yacht has less than 80 per cent of the maximum. That would be the ideal arrangement, of course, but would entail measurement of draught in every case, and this would be very difficult without slipping the boats. As it is, only a very few marginal cases have to be measured, and we can use the official figure in Lloyd's for the others.

The Chairman, MR. H. E. STEEL, C.B.E. (*Member of Council*): I am quite sure you will all agree with me when I express our gratitude to Mr. Phillips-Birt for his paper. Looking at the bibliography, it is quite clear that is a good addition to our TRANSACTIONS. The subject is something of which most of us have been conscious, and yet not actively conscious; and yet, as this meeting shows, it is of first importance not only to designers, but also to the organisers of the various races, and to a very great public. So that it is quite proper that the subject should be discussed before some society, and I am quite sure that this is the appropriate body.

The paper and the discussion have broadened our knowledge very considerably. We have learned something of the intricacies of yacht measurement, why the rules are what they are, and the degree of control they enforce. It might be said that in a broad sense the reasons for these rules have something in common with those of the rules for the tonnage measurement of yachts, but the rating rules are more numerous and more diverse in character. I must say that the effect they have had on me is to arouse sympathy with the makers of yacht measurement rules. Even our law-makers are everlastingly trying to make laws which will not be broken, and a day after they are made they are broken. The other thing that is in my mind is that it does seem possible that tank experiments might serve to eliminate or reduce some of the difficulties.

On behalf of the Institution, Mr. Phillips-Birt, I thank you very much, and we express our gratitude to you.

Author's Reply

I should like to thank the speakers and authors whose contributions have added so much to the value of the paper.

Mr. McGruer raises many points, each the product of great thought and practical experience in rule-making and design. The rule of the Cruising Club of America, the omission of which he regrets, was not discussed because it was felt that as there was a pressure on space a rule applying in American waters only was the one most reasonably excluded. But it has to be owned that this rule, through its influence on American design, and the recent strong influence of American design on our own, has had a distinct effect upon the shape of British yachts. I now regret myself that the International Rule for yachts under $14\frac{1}{2}$ metres was not given in detail in view of the renewed interest in it caused by the America's Cup challenge. (This is now included in Chapter 9.)

I agree that spinnakers are not what they ought to be—or, rather, that they are too much of what they ought not to be. Instead of the tiresome meddling with foretriangle and Genoa measurements that has characterised post-war rating rules, effective steps should have been taken to limit the size of these frail and expensive kites.

Mr. Crewe's figures for the lift-drag ratios and lift coefficients of low aspect-ratio aerofoils provide most valuable data where they are scarce. Some of the figures are not wholly surprising. I find, for example, in a standard work on naval architecture, values of the normal force coefficient for flat plates at various attitudes, which show that the peak value for a plate of aspect-ratio 0·5 is 1·4 and occurs at 40 degrees incidence. That for aspect ratio 2 is 0·9 and comes at 23 degrees incidence. It will be seen that the values for the 0·5 plate are in close agreement with Mr. Crewe's; but his fuller data are significant, and provide a partial answer for the success of American yachts with their low rigs when in competition with our own higher sail plans.

A point to be noticed in Mr. Crewe's figures is that at 14 degrees, which is an approximation to the angle of incidence when close hauled, the difference in lift-drag ratio between aspect-ratios of 1·0 and 5·0 is only about 12 per cent. On the basis of these figures the difference in lift-drag ratio between the modern high and low rig, whose aspect-ratios might be about 2·7 and 3·5, would hardly exceed 4 per cent. This indicates that any heavy aspect ratio tax, such as that of the American rule, is bound to lead to undesirably low rigs—as indeed it has. We are, however, in this connection faced with a problem that has not been solved: namely, how the aspect ratio as a complete sail plan should be calculated to make it comparable with the aspect ratio of rectangular and elliptic planforms tested in a wind tunnel. Might it be suggested that a paper reviewing the present state of knowledge about the aerodynamics of normal sail plans would be welcome? At present most of the studies of sail aerodynamics are confined to freak sail plans of no seagoing interest whatever.

Mr. Laurent Giles questions whether the supposed advantage of sailing length, as derived from overhangs, may not be an illusion. It would seem to have a bearing on this matter that after a small, initial angle of heel of about 5 degrees, tank test results from various sources have shown that the ratio

$$\frac{\text{heeled resistance}}{\text{upright resistance}}$$

tends to remain constant until an angle of heel is reached when the deck edge becomes immersed. This was so in the *Gimcrack* experiments, and later results have reinforced the conclusion. In his contribution to the discussion Mr. Crago also mentions that the effect of heel is small. I am unable to find any other explanation for the fact that, in spite of the growing asymmetry of the hull form with heel, there is little augmentation of the upright wave-making resistance, unless this is attributable to the greater wave resistance being offset by increased sailing length. But this does not preclude valuable stability effects coming from the immersion of the overhangs, and as Mr. Giles suggests, only the tanks can separate the two results of overhang immersion.

That all rating rules, and particularly those of the International Yacht Racing Union, contain illiteracies must be confessed. I particularly like Mr. Crago's comparison between yacht measurers' technique and the ancient Egyptian tax-gatherers' most inaccurate method of finding the area of a parallelogram. Perhaps in the past it might have been justified. The same contributor's suggestion for using as a parameter in yacht measurement the wetted area in elevation and its aspect ratio is of great interest. It is possibly a hang-over of the Egyptian tax gatherers' mentality that this characteristic, which has been known for some years to be one of the principal arbiters of performance, has never been directly assessed in a rating formula; though it has been indirectly approached through draught limitations or penalties, and to some extent by factors governing displacement. To make this parameter fully effective it would seem essential to make allowance for the fact that the wetted surface in elevation consists partly of keel, with a fairly high lift coefficient, and a canoe body having a low value. The proportions of the two parts vary widely in different types of yacht.

We are most grateful to Mr. Paul, Secretary of the Royal Ocean Racing Club, for presenting his most lucid demonstration of the rule's new system of length measurement.

Finally, and perhaps irrelevantly, may I express the hope not only that this Institution will continue its traditional policy of devoting a small part of its time to problems of yachts, but also that papers on the many and virtually unstudied problems of the application of scientific naval architecture to the design of the smaller power craft may be read. This is a field where rule of thumb is still in command.

APPENDIX NINE

International Offshore Rule
I.O.R. Mark III

MEASUREMENT RULE FOR OFFSHORE RACING
EFFECTIVE AS DETERMINED BY LOCAL AUTHORITY
AND WITH TIME SCALES AT THE DISCRETION OF THE ORGANIZING
AUTHORITY FOR THE RACE CONCERNED
RECOMMENDED LIMITS OF RATING 16·0 TO 70·0 FT.

Alphabetical Index of Symbols in the Rule

AW, BW, CW, DW	705	Inclining weights
AWD, BWD, etc.	703	Weight distances
APD, BPD, etc.	704	Pendulum deflections
ARM, BRM, etc.	707	Righting moments one degree

Symbol	Para.		Symbol	Para.	
AGO	327	After girth overhang	BD	841	Boom depth main
AGS	311	After girth station	BDF	873	Ditto foresail
AIGS	311	After inner girth station	BDY	857	Ditto mizzen
AOC	332	Aft overhang component	BF	321	Beam forward
AOCC	333	AOC corrected	BFI	321	Beam forward inner
AOCG	332	AOC girth	BHA	323	Buttock height aft
AOCP	332	AOC profile	BHAI	323	Buttock height aft inner
APB	609	Aperture width bottom	BLP	840	Batten leech penalty
APH	609	Aperture height	BLPS	873	Ditto foresail
APT	609	Aperture width top	BLPY	856	Ditto mizzen
B	319	Rated beam	BL 1-5	845	Mainsail battens
BA	321	Beam aft	BS 1-5	873	Foresail battens
BAD	838	Boom above deck	BSC	317	Beam sheer correction
BADS	877, 873	Ditto schooner foresail	BMAX	310	Beam maximum
BADX	879	Ditto	BY 1-5	861	Mizzen battens
BADY	854	Ditto mizzen	BWL	320	Beam waterline
BAI	321	Beam aft inner	CBDA, B	706	Centreboard CG drop
BAL	836	Sheet limit main boom	CBLD	507	Centreboard CG lateral
BALF	873	Ditto schooner foresail	CBP	510	Centreboard proportion
BALY	852	Ditto mizzen	CD	504	Centreboard extension
BBS	318	B below sheer line	CGF	711	Centre of gravity factor
			CMD	326	Centre mid depth

Symbol	Para.	
CMDI	335	Ditto immersed
D	337	Rated depth
DB	508	Base draft
DC	514	Draft correction
DD	513	Draft difference
DF	611	Propeller drag factor
DK	511	Depth of keel equivalent
DM	324	Draft measured
DMT	324	Draft measured total
DSPL	509	Displacement
E	836	Foot of mainsail
EB	865, 875	Distance between masts
EBC	881	Ditto corrected
EC	836	Foot of mainsail corrected
EF	873	Foot of foresail
EFC	873	Ditto corrected
EM	604	Engine moment
EMF	605	Engine moment factor
EPF	601	Engine and propeller factor
ESC	609	Exposed shaft clearance
ESL	609	Exposed shaft length
EW	602	Engine weight
EWD	603	Engine weight distance
EY	852	Foot of mizzen
EYC	852	Ditto corrected
FA	328	Freeboard aft
FAI	328	Freeboard aft inner
FB	402	Base freeboard
FBI	328	Freeboard base of I
FC	401	Freeboard correction
FD	326	Forward depth
FDI	335	Ditto immersed
FDM	324	Freeboard draft measured
FDS	313	Forward depth station
FF	328	Freeboard forward
FFD	328	Freeboard at FDS
FFI	328	Freeboard forward inner
FGO	327	Forward girth overhang
FGS	311	Forward girth station
FIGS	311	Forward inner girth station
FM	403	Freeboard measured
FMD	328	Freeboard at MDS

Symbol	Para.	
FOC	330	Forward overhang component
FPD	325	Freeboard propeller depth
FS	328	Freeboard at stem
FSP	814	Forestay perpendicular
G	843	Gaff length
GD	311	Girth difference
GF	873	Foresail gaff
GSDA	327	Girth station difference aft
GSDF	327	Ditto forward
GY	860	Mizzen gaff
H	842	Hoist of gaff mainsail
HB	839	Headboard of mainsail
HBF	873	Ditto foresail
HBS	819	Ditto spinnaker
HBY	855	Ditto mizzen
HC	847	Gaff hoist corrected
HF	873	Hoist of gaff foresail
HFC	873	Ditto corrected
HY	859	Hoist of gaff mizzen
HYC	863	Ditto corrected
I	809	Height of foretriangle
IC	829	Ditto corrected
IS	880	Height of schooner mainmast
IY	858	Height of mizzen mast
J	807	Base of foretriangle
JC	826	Ditto corrected
L	334	Rated length
LBG	327	Length between girths
LBGC	331	Ditto corrected
LL	828	Luff limit of spinnaker
LLA	314	Limit of length aft
LOA	301	Length overall
LP	827	Longest perpendicular
LPG	813	Ditto of jibs
LPIS	815	Ditto of inner jib
MACG	517	Movable appendage CG
MAF	518	Movable appendage factor
MAW	516	Movable appendage weight
MD	326	Midship depth
MDI	335	Midship depth immersed
MDIA	336	Ditto adjusted

Symbol	Para.	
MDS	313	Mid depth station
MSA	803	Measured sail area
MSAT	844	Ditto of topsail
MSATF	873	Ditto of foretopsail
OF	876	Schooner foresail overlap
OMD	326	Outer mid depth
OMDI	335	Ditto immersed
P	837	Mainsail hoist
PC	846	Mainsail hoist corrected
PBW	607	Propeller blade width
PD	325	Propeller depth
PL	702	Pendulum length
PRD	606	Propeller diameter
PS	608	Propeller size
PSF	875, 878	Foresail hoist schooners
PSFC	873	Ditto corrected
PY	853	Mizzen hoist
PYC	862	Ditto corrected
RD	512	Rated draft
RM	708	Righting moment
RMC	709	Ditto corrected
RSA	804	Rated sail area
RSAB	882	RSA between masts schooners
RSAC	887	RSA combined abaft masts
RSAF	830	RSA foretriangle
RSAG	874	RSA schooner foresail
RSAK	869	RSA mizzen staysail
RSAL	890	RSA low limit
RSAM	850	RSA mainsail

Symbol	Para.	
RSAT	889	Total rated sail area
RSAY	864	RSA mizzen
RSBS 1-6	304	Rated sheer below sheer
S 1-3	Appx. I	Sides of mules and topsails
SATC	888	Sail area total correction
SBMAX	327	Length bow to BMAX
SDM	327	Length bow to draft station
SF	822	Spinnaker foot length
SL	821	Ditto luff/leech length
SMG	823	Ditto mid girth length
SMW	820	Ditto maximum width
SPD	327	Length bow to PD station
SPH	810	Spinnaker pole height
SPIN	831	Spinnaker rated area
SPL	808	Spinnaker pole length
√S	189	Square root RSAT or SPIN
ST 1-3	609	Propeller struts
TR	710	Tenderness ratio
VHA	322	Vertical height aft
VHAI	322	Vertical height aft inner
WCBA, B	505	Centreboard weights
WCBC	506	Centreboard weight total
Y	327	Distance AGS to LLA
YSAC	870	Combined RSA mizzen sails
YSD	867	Mizzen staysail depth
YSF	866	Mizzen staysail foot
YSMG	868	Mizzen staysail mid girth

Part I—General

101. *Introduction.* It is the spirit and intent of the rule to promote the racing of seaworthy offshore racing yachts of various designs, types and construction on a fair and equitable basis. Consistent with that purpose, it is the policy of the Offshore Rating Council to seek constant improvement in the rule and to make such changes in it from time to time as may appear necessary to keep pace with advances in the design of yachts and in the use of new materials and new methods of construction. Changes in the rule are made only after careful consideration so that evolution of the rule can be accomplished gradually on the basis of proven experience and with a minimum of hardship to existing yachts. Similarly, changes usually will be made effective only after as much advance notice as, in the judgment of the Council, circumstances permit.

Notwithstanding the foregoing, the Council recognizes it is not possible for the rule to cover every eventuality nor to anticipate every innovation in design or construction. Accordingly, any yacht which in the judgment of the Council incorporates design or other features that exploit loopholes in the rule will be assigned such rating as the Council considers equitable. Additionally, whenever such loopholes are discovered, the Council may take such further and early action by way of interpretations of or amendments to the rule as would alleviate any undue advantages resulting from such loopholes. Designers and owners of yachts intending to undertake ‘questionable design, construction or other features, therefore, are forewarned to consult the Council for interpretive rulings. The Council in such instances shall interpret the rule so as not to discourage developments tending to increase the speed of yachts, but to minimize the incorporation of features tending by unusual methods to reduce the rating.

102. *Rating Certificates.* No yacht shall have more than one valid rating certificate at any one time. The rating certificate issued under this rule shall, except as mentioned below, be valid for four years from the date of measurement unless a change is made in any of the rule parameters or there is a change of ownership of the yacht in which case the change shall be notified to the measurer or rating authority and the existing rating certificate automatically.

The rating authorities may, where convenient, allow the validity to exceed four years to the end of the yachting season following the date of measurement providing this extension does not exceed one year. Remeasurement will give a full four years' extension of validity only when the remeasurement includes complete sail area remeasurement, free boards and an inclining test. A smaller remeasurement or recalculation shall not extend the formal date of expiration in any way.

The authority having custody of rating certificates shall supply a copy of any rating certificate to any person on payment of a copying charge. Rating certificates shall be in the form shown at Appendix One. To be valid the certificate must bear the name or stamp of the National Authority issuing the certificate.

103. *Measurements.* All measurements shall be taken in a manner consistent with these rules. Where hollows or projections or other local deviations from the fair surface of the hull occur in the way of a point of measurement the Measurer shall adjust the measurement by relating it to the fair surface of the hull. Special rules in this respect apply to:

.1 *B and BWL.* These measurements are controlled by radius of curvature requirements specified in 318, 319, 320.

.2 *Edge of Working Deck.* The edge of the working deck is defined as the most outboard point on the deck at the sheer line. Where, at any point abaft the FD station, the line of the edge of the working deck extends outboard as a projection bounded, in plan, at its fore and/or aft ends by angles or curves with double inflection such projection shall be bridged by a straight line not less than 7·0 ft. in length.

    Such straight line shall be taken as the edge of the working deck for all purposes under this rule and under paragraph 6.6. of the Special Regulations as regards life line stanchions. The straight line defined above shall not be used to reduce the measurement of BMAX which shall be taken to the maximum beam of the hull including the projection. Where the measurement of BMAX is so taken the location of the BMAX station (see 310) shall be where the beam at the edge of working deck defined above is the greatest.

.3 In Depth Stations where any bump generated by an inflection occurs at a measurement point the measurer shall measure a series of depths to the hollows in the section. By plotting these points he shall draw a curve to represent the section of the yacht drawn without inflection and to nullify any such bumps placed at the Depth Stations.

    The Depth Measurements to be used for rating shall be taken from the plotted section, none of which shall be greater than the one actually measured on the hull.

.4 Where local deviations from the fair surface of the hull are found which might effect the measurement of "L" the measurer shall take extra girths. There shall be at least three girths taken fore and aft of the deviation, so that the procedure of 330.2 and 332.3 can be carried out equitably.

    The extra girths shall be measured in accordance with Section 307 or 308 as individually applicable.

.5   A. Where, at any section abaft the FD station, there is inflected flare occurring, wholly or in part, above a level 1/6 of BMAX below the sheerline, the edge of the working deck shall be defined as the point at which the tangent to the hull at the point of inflection would if extended cut the deck. The edge of the working deck shall not however be required to be taken inboard of the point vertically above the point of maximum beam

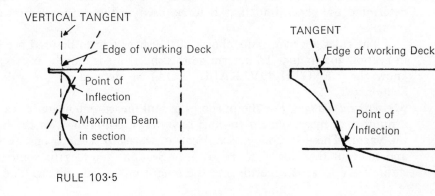

VERTICAL TANGENT

Edge of working Deck

Point of Inflection

Maximum Beam in section

TANGENT

Edge of working Deck

Point of Inflection

RULE 103·5

in the section occurring on the hull surface between the point of inflection and the centre line.

B. Stanchion bases shall not be situated outboard of the edge of the working deck. Where inflected flare has caused a deck area outside the edge of the working deck, it shall be considered as an outrigger as restricted in I.Y.R.U. Rule 54.2.

104. *Units of Measurement.* Dimensions of sails shall be taken in feet to one place of decimals. All other measurements including headboards and battens shall be in feet to two places of decimals. Measurements shall be taken from the yacht wherever practicable but where this is unduly difficult the Measurer shall have the option of using the plans or other such sources of information as he considers reliable. Weights shall be measured in pounds.

Where measurement is in the metric system dimensions shall be in metres to three places of decimals except that dimensions of sails shall be to two places of decimals. Weights shall be in kilograms and constants or dimensions given in the text or formulae shall be converted in accordance with the requirements of Part IX, Rule 901, METRIC EQUIVALENTS.

Intermediate stages of calculation shall use the full capacity of the computer to run out decimal places. The printout on the rating certificate shall be to a suitable number of decimal places, but the full value will be carried forward into subsequent calculations.

The RATING shall be calculated in the units (feet or metres) in which the yacht was measured. The final rating shall in addition be converted (before any rounding of decimal places) into the alternative units (RATING FT/3·281 = RATING METRES).

Final ratings shall be given on the rating certificate to the NEAREST single decimal place in FEET and the NEAREST two decimal places in METRES (0·050 and 0·0050 being rounded up). The rounded figures should be used in any calculations required for the TIME SCALES used for racing.

105. *The Principles of Measurement and Rating under the I.O.R. Rule*

.1 *Measurements with the Yacht Ashore.* The principal hull measurements are taken with the yacht ashore. A résumé of the principles of hull measurement is given below.

A. *Sheer Line.* Before detailed measurement can be started it is necessary to determine the sheer line that is to be used as the datum for measurement.

The rules governing the choice of the sheer line to be used are given in Section 302 to 305. To determine this sheer line it may be necessary to know the LENGTH OVERALL (LOA) as defined in the rule (see Section 301).

B. *Measurement Stations.* For the purposes of hull measurement under the rule a number of measurement stations have to be established on the hull of the yacht. These stations are vertical athwartship sections on the yacht and rules for their location are given in Sections 309 to 316. Some of the stations are located according to the length of the hull girths. The rules governing the measurement of girth lengths are given in Sections 306 to 308.

C. *Measurements at Measurement Stations.* The rule requires certain measurements to be taken in the measurement stations established.

These measurements are taken in the plane of the station and are either vertical measurements, known as depths, heights, or draft, or horizontal measurements, known as beams.

The measurements to be taken and recorded at the various stations are detailed in Sections 317 to 326.

D. *Length Measurements.* The rule requires certain length measurements to be taken. These are horizontal distances between measurement stations. The length measurements required are detailed in Section 327.

.2 *Measurements with the Yacht Afloat.* The rule requires certain measurements to be taken on a single occasion with the yacht afloat in measurement trim (as defined in 202.2). These measurements are:

A. *Freeboards.* The freeboards that the rule requires to be measured are defined and detailed in Sections 328 and 329.

B. *Waterline Beam* (BWL). The details of the waterline beam measurement are given in Section 320.

C. *Inclining Measurements.* The details of the inclining procedure, the measurements required, and the formulae to obtain the centre of gravity factor (CGF) are given in Sections 701 to 706.

.3 *Measurement Formulae.* The hull measurements, taken ashore and afloat, are combined in a number of formulae:

A. *Rated Length* (L) and *Rated Depth* (D), representing the sailing length and bulk of the yacht, are determined from the hull measurements by the formulae given in Sections 330 to 337.

B. The *Freeboard Correction* (FC) is determined from the formulae given in Sections 401 to 404.

C. The *Draft Correction* (DC) is determined from the rules and formulae given in Sections 501 to 514.

D. *Engine and Propeller Factor* (EPF) is derived from hull measurements, engine and propeller installation details and formulae detailed in Sections 601 to 611.

E. The *Movable Appendage Factor* (MAF) is determined from the rules and measurements detailed in Sections 516 to 518.

.4 *Sail Area Measurement.* The sail area measurements required for any rig, together with the formulae required to determine the figure for the square root of the rated sail area (S) are detailed in Part VIII.

This part also contains rules governing the proper setting and sheeting of sails while racing under the rule. It is particularly important that owners and crews should be conversant with these requirements.

.5 *Rating Formulae.* Hull and sail area measurements are finally combined to determine the rating by the following formulae:

A. *Measured Rating* (MR):

$$MR = \frac{0 \cdot 13L\sqrt{S}}{\sqrt{B \times D}} + 0 \cdot 25L + 0 \cdot 20\sqrt{S} + DC + FC$$

B. *Rating* (R):

$$R = MR \times EPF \times CGF \times MAF$$

Owner's Responsibilities

106. Before any Certificate under this Rule is valid it must be signed by the owner of the yacht. By this signature he signifies that he understands his responsibilities under the Rule.

The paragraphs below summarize these responsibilities with reference to the appropriate sections of the Rule.

The owner's responsibilities are clearly divided into three categories:

1. Owner's responsibilities prior to and during measurement.
2. Owner's general responsibilities after measurement.
3. Owner's special responsibilities during a race.

107. *Owner's Responsibilities: Measurement.* The owner is responsible for arranging measurement with the rating authority in his country of residence.

.1   A. He shall present the yacht for measurement ashore in an accessible location, clear of obstruction, and properly and firmly chocked level both fore and aft and athwartships. The measurer shall satisfy himself that the weight of any keel is supported from below.

B. If the yacht is of a class for which standard hull measurements are available the owner shall inform the measurer of any modifications that have been made to the hull, propeller or engine installations so that the measurer may determine whether, and to what extent, the hull standard applies to the yacht. The owner shall make the yacht available ashore for the checking of any measurements that the Measurer may require.

.2   A. He shall at another occasion make the yacht available at a suitable location agreed with the Measurer so that flotation measurements may be taken.

B. He is responsible for preparing the yacht in measurement trim as laid down in para. 202.2 of the Rule. If he is in doubt about the proper conditions of tankage for measurement he shall consult with the Measurer.

C. If the yacht has portable tanks he shall declare their size and intended location.

D. If the yacht is fitted with a drop keel and/or a movable appendage which is to be locked for measurement and racing under Rules 502.3 or 518, the owner shall be responsible for ensuring that a positive locking and locating device is fitted at the time of measurement. If the device is to be freed for cruising or at other times when the yacht is not racing the device must be of a form that will positively locate and retain the keel in one predetermined position.

.3 *Sail Areas*. The owner is responsible for declaring to the measurer all spars and sails that he proposes to carry on the yacht, and the locations in which he proposes to set them, so that they may be properly measured.

108. *Owner's Responsibilities after Measurement*

.1 It is the owner's responsibility to declare to the rating authority any changes made to the yacht or its rig which could change any of its measurement under the Rule.

Such changes could be:

A. Changes of ballast in amount or location. Note that unwarranted quantities of stores shall be considered as ballast under this Rule.
B. Change of tankage, fixed or portable, in size or location.
C. Any changes in the engine and/or propeller installation.
D. Addition, removal, or change of location of gear or equipment, or structural alteration to the hull, that affect the trim or flotation of the yacht.
E. Movement of any measurement bands used in sail area measurement, or any changes in spars.
F. The addition of sails to the yacht. Where these are not measured it shall be the owner's responsibility to ensure that they do not exceed the maximum dimensions permitted for them on the Rating Certificate and that they are of a type permitted by the Rule.
G. Changes to the shape of the yacht's hull by the addition or removal of filling pieces, micro-balloons, etc.

109. *Owner's Responsibilities while Racing*

.1 The owner is responsible that all members of his crew fully understand and comply with the limitations on sail setting and sheeting contained in the Rule. These are summarized below for reference.

A. Sails shall only be set in those areas declared for measurement, and no sail shall be carried on board that exceeds the limiting dimensions for such a sail as shown on the Rating Certificate, nor is of a shape or has features not permitted by the Rule: see 812 to 816 for jibs, 817 to 825 for spinnakers and 851 for mainsails.
B. *Setting and sheeting of Sails*. The rules for the setting and sheeting of sails are listed below for easy reference.

> Jibs (832).
> Squaresail (834).
> Mizzen staysails (871).
> Sails measured to spars (802).
> Spinnakers (833, 810).
> Heavy weather running sails (835).
> Schooner foresails (844, 885).
> Where spars are measured to measurement bands sails may not be set outside these limits.

.2 *Engine and Propeller.* The owner is responsible for ensuring that when the engine is run for any purpose the propeller shaft is secured to prevent rotation.

.3 *Drop Keels and Movable Appendages.* The owner is responsible for ensuring that any locating device for a locked drop keel or movable appendage, called for by the Rule, is at all times in place while racing.

If for any reason such a device is removed during a race the owner shall declare the fact to the race committee on completion of the race.

.4 *Shipping, Unshipping or Shifting of Ballast.* Attention is called to Section 22.2 of the I.Y.R.U. Racing Rules: "Shipping, Unshipping, or Shifting Ballast; water. No ballast, whether movable or fixed, shall be shipped, unshipped, or shifted, nor shall any water be taken in or discharged except for ordinary ship's use, from 9 p.m. of the day before the race until the yacht is no longer racing, except that bilge water may be removed at any time." (Except that water may be taken on up to the 10 minute gun for races of 100 miles or more.)

.5 *Tankage.* Tanks, fuel or water, which are always to be empty when racing may be declared as such and shall be empty at the time of measurement providing each declaration is entered on the rating certificate and the owner accepts responsibility that these limitations will be observed. One fuel tank normal for the installation shall, however, be operable if the yacht is to qualify for an EPF. The condition of this tank shall be governed by Rule 202.2 I at the time of measurement.

.6 *Movement from Stowage.* Portable equipment, gear, sails and stores may only be moved from stowage for use in their primary purpose. Stowage in this respect is the position for any item of equipment or stores, to be maintained for the duration of a race or series, when such item is not in use for its primary purpose.

Part II—Preparation for Hull and Rig Measurement

201. *General Measurement Procedure.* To secure an accurate and fair measurement, it is necessary to have close co-operation between owner and Measurer. It is desirable that the owner should be familiar with all parts of the measurement rule.

202. *Hull Measuring Procedure*
Hull measurement shall be in two stages:

.1 *Ashore.* The principal hull measurements shall be taken ashore with the yacht approximately level. As regards longitudinal trim, level may be taken to mean "in a trim which, by inspection, the yacht might reasonably be expected to assume when afloat in measurement trim".

.2 *Afloat.* Inclined stability, freeboards and waterline beam shall be measured with the yacht afloat in measurement trim. The owner or his representative must be present and available at this time and the yacht shall be presented for the Measurer in Measurement Trim as defined below.

A. The yacht shall be completely rigged and ready to sail. Sheets and guys shall be stowed abaft the mast with the sails on the cabin sole.

B. The mainsail, the schooner foresail and the mizzen of a yawl or ketch shall be in place and furled. Booms shall be secured at the low points of P, PY, PSF, H, or HY, as the case may be. Spinnaker pole(s) shall be in their normal stowage.

C. Sails, except those mentioned above, shall be stowed below decks on the cabin sole and not forward of the forwardmost mast. In the event it is necessary to pile the sails, they shall be distributed aft of the mast over the length of the main cabin or its equivalent, with the heavier sails on the cabin sole and lighter sails piled over them but no higher than necessary. Sails below decks at time of measurement shall not exceed:

> Four jibs including the largest and smallest.
> Two spinnakers.
> Two topsails per mast in gaff-rigged yachts.
> Storm trisail.
> The two largest between mast sails of schooners or staysail ketches.
> The two largest mizzen staysails in yawls.

D. All mattresses, cushions and pillows shall be stowed in their normal bunks, and all navigational and cooking appliances and all movable gear normally stowed aft of the foremost mast shall be in its normal position for racing and all movable gear normally stowed forward shall be placed aft of the foremost mast for measurement, unless otherwise specified in this rule. The batteries shall be in their proper stowage.

E. No clothing, food, or stores shall be on board.

F. The life raft (or rafts) may be on board, stowed in the position used for it when racing, and that position shall be entered on the Rating Certificate. In this case it shall always be so carried when racing.

   If no life raft is on board at the time of measurement one may be carried when racing and this shall not invalidate the Certificate.

   In either event the stowage of the life raft shall be in conformity with the Special Regulations issued by the Offshore Rating Council.

G. The yacht's head shall not be depressed through lying to a mooring.

H. Trimming ballast (which must be secured against involuntary movement and must not thereafter be changed in weight or location), anchor chain and anchors shall be stowed in the positions used for them when racing. The weights of these items and their distances from the stem will be recorded on the Rating Certificate. Anchor rope shall be stowed abaft the forward mast.

I. *Tanks: Water, Fuel and Sump Tanks.* If, in the opinion of the Measurer, any tanks are of such unusual capacity, or so unusually located, that they clearly affect the performance or rating of the yacht, the yacht shall be measured with tanks in such condition (all full, all empty, some full and others empty) as will result in maximizing the rating.

   As a general guide, all tanks the major part of which is located aft of a point 0·65LBG from FGS should be full. Tanks forward of this point should be empty.

Any tanks shall, at the time of measurement afloat, be either full and pressed up or completely empty.

J. Tanks of hydraulic systems shall be full for measurement and the system shall remain full when racing.

K. Bilges shall be pumped dry.

L. No one shall be on board while flotation measurements are being taken.

M. Centreboard(s) and drop keels shall be fully raised. If any drop keel or movable appendage is to be locked when racing (under Sections 518 or 502.3) it shall be so locked for measurement and the locking device shall be in place.

N. Painted measurement bands on masts and booms shall be in place.

O. If an outboard motor, where it is the yacht's engine, is to be carried when racing it SHALL BE provided with a proper locker and/or mounting bracket. It shall be in this stowage at the time of measurement and at all times when racing. The fuel tankage for such motor shall be governed by the terms of sub-paragraph I above.

If the above conditions are not fulfilled, MEASUREMENT WILL BE REFUSED.

203. *Sail Measuring Procedure*. All sails must be made available to the Measurer for measuring or for checking marked dimensions. Measurements of all sails required to be measured must be measured with such tension between measurement points as will remove all wrinkles across line of measurement and must include the fabric length between measurement points. Measuring point at corner of a sail shall be the intersection of the adjacent outside edges projected. All other measurement points shall be at the extreme outside of rope, wire or fabric of the sail's edge.

204. *Measurement Bands*. Measurements may be taken to locations defined by painted bands, of black or other contrasting colour, only when these bands are in place at the time of measurement. Where measurements are taken to such bands, movement of the bands or a failure to display them while racing shall invalidate the Rating Certificate.

205. *Ballast Material*. No yacht shall be measured, rated or raced under this rule that has in its keel or ballast any material with a density greater than that of lead.

Part III—Hull Measurements

301. *Length Overall* (LOA). The length overall of a yacht will be measured to include the whole hull, but not spars or projections fixed to the hull such as bowsprits, bumpkins, pulpits, etc. It will be measured from:

.1 A point forward being the forwardmost of the following points:

A. The stem of the yacht, whether carried above deck level or not.

B. The bulwarks of the yacht where these are extended above the stem.

.2 A point aft, being the extreme after end of the hull and bulwarks or taffrail of the yacht whether at, above, or below deck level. Rubbing strakes at the stern will be included. If rudder and/or push-pit extend abaft this point, neither one nor the other will be included.

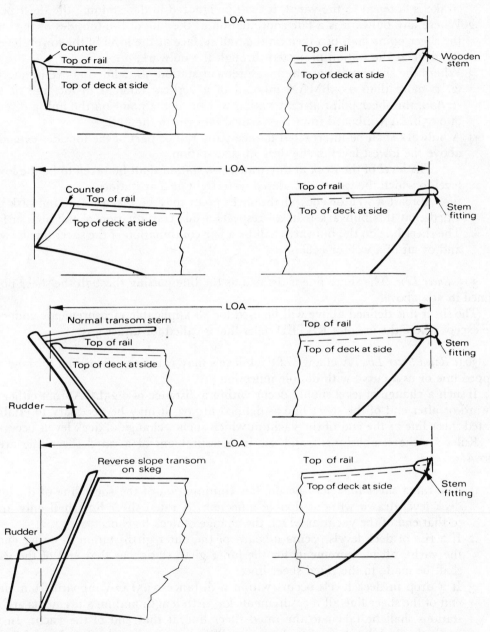

302. *Sheer Point.* The sheer point at any measurement station shall be defined by the following rules:

1. The sheer point shall normally be the lowest point on the topsides of the hull where a tangent at 45° can be rested on the hull. The sheer point shall not, how-

ever, be taken to any point that is above the lowest level of the deck, or its extension where it intersects the topsides at that station. Where any bulwark or rubbing strake is fastened to the yacht, it shall be ignored in determining the sheer point.

.2 Where any bulwark is a fair continuation of the line of the topsides of the yacht the sheer point shall be taken on the hull surface at the level of the lowest level of the deck at the station projected through the bulwark.

.3 Where the sheer point at any measurement station, as defined above in 302.1 or .2, is more than 0·05BMAX inboard of a vertical tangent to the hull at that station, the sheer point at that station will be at the point on the hull a distance of 0·05BMAX inboard from the vertical tangent to the hull.

.4 A bulwark shall be interpreted to mean any rail or part of the topsides extending above the lowest level of the deck at that station.

The level of the deck at any transverse station shall be taken to be the lowest level to which the yacht is rendered watertight at that station.

Abreast a well or cockpit the sheer point may be taken to the bulwark provided that this bulwark is in all respects a fair continuation of the hull surface. The sheer line on the bulwark shall be a fair continuation of the sheer line forward and/or aft of a well or cockpit.

303. *Sheer Line.* The sheer line is defined as the line passing through the sheer points defined in 302 above.

The sheer line defined above will be used for all applicable measurements under the rule except where the use of a RATED sheer line is called for under 304.

304. *Rated Sheer Line.* A change of deck levels may cause the sheer line to show as a stepped line or as a curve with double inflection.

If such a change of level should occur within a distance of 0·25LOA from either the forward or after end of the sheer line as defined in 303, it may be necessary to establish a rated sheer line at the end of the yacht at which such a change of deck levels occurs.

Rules for the establishment and use in measurement of a rated sheer line are as follows:

.1 The rated sheer line shall be the fair continuation of the sheer line of the lower deck level drawn without double inflection. A rated sheer line shall only apply to that end of the yacht at which the change of deck level occurs.

.2 If a rise of deck levels occurs inboard of the outer girth station at either end of the yacht, all measurements for the inner girth station at that end of the yacht shall be made to the rated sheer line.

.3 If a drop in deck levels occurs within a distance 0·25LOA inboard from either end of the sheer line all measurements for girth length and measurements at girth stations shall be taken to the rated sheer line at that end of the yacht. In this event the deck level, used to determine BSC under 317 and FS under 328.8 shall also be taken at the rated sheer line.

.4 Where the rated sheer line is used for measurement at any station, the vertical height of the rated sheer line below the sheer point (as defined in 302) at that station shall be recorded as RSBS (1 to 6).

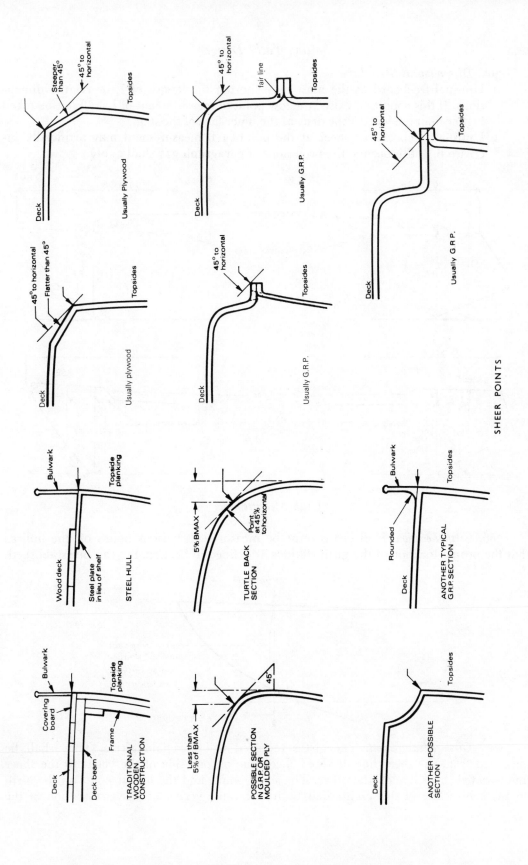

SHEER POINTS

305. *Discontinuous Sheer Lines*

.1 Unusual freeboard at the mast may shorten the length of I, or related dimensions. If this condition exists, the low point of measurement of I shall not be taken higher than the level of the deck at the inner face of the stem.

.2 Unusual freeboard or sheer at the point of B measurement may artificially increase B. If this occurs, the provisions of paragraph 317 shall apply.

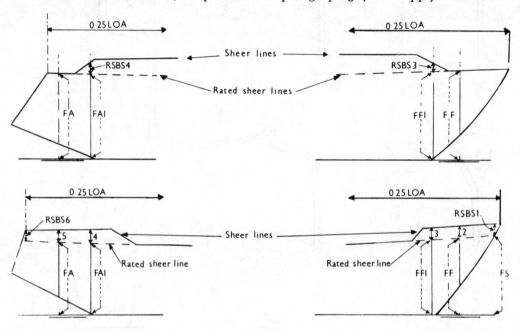

Girth Measurements

306. *Girth Location.* Hull girths must be measured at various points on the hull so that the proper location of the girth stations as defined in Section 311 can be established.

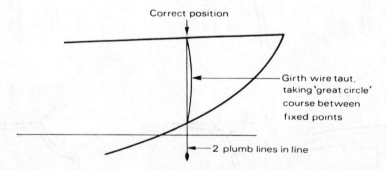

307. *Girth Measurement.* The girths required will be chain girths. They shall be measured from the sheer line or rated sheer line on one side of the yacht to the sheer line or rated sheer line on the other. The sheer points and the lowest point on the girth on the centre line of the yacht shall be in the same vertical transverse section of the

yacht. In between these points the girth line shall follow the shortest course and all hollows except as defined in 307.3 and 308 shall be bridged.

.1 Rubbing strakes or similar projections from the hull shall not be girthed and the girth line shall be projected through them.

.2 No girth shall be measured in any section that allows the natural girth, following a great circle course, to cross the edge of a transom. Such would call for use of a girth difference (GD).

.3 If a girth has to be measured in a section where the hull of the yacht is carried downwards through a reverse curve, however sharp, so as to form a skeg, deadwood, or other similar extension (which may include the rudder when this is faired into the section of the yacht), the girth shall not be measured around the low point of the extension but shall be measured as detailed in 308. For the conditions of this sub-section to apply it shall be a further requirement that the depth of the hull extension below the 0·04B buttock line in the section shall be greater than 0·02B.

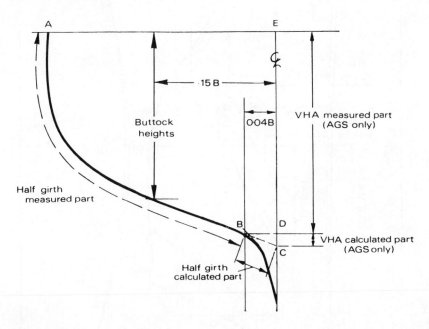

308. *Girth Measurement at a Section in way of a Skeg.* Girth length shall be determined in two parts on each side of the yacht. The girth length shall be the sum of the four parts.

.1 The measured part shall be measured on each side of the yacht from the sheer line or rated sheer line to a buttock line drawn at a distance 0·04B from the centre line of the yacht. The sheer points and the points on the buttock lines shall lie in the same vertical transverse section of the yacht. Between these points the girth wire shall follow the shortest path and all hollows shall be bridged.

.2 The calculated part (BC in the diagram) shall be calculated for each side of the yacht. It shall be the hypotenuse of a right-angled triangle (BDC in the diagram)

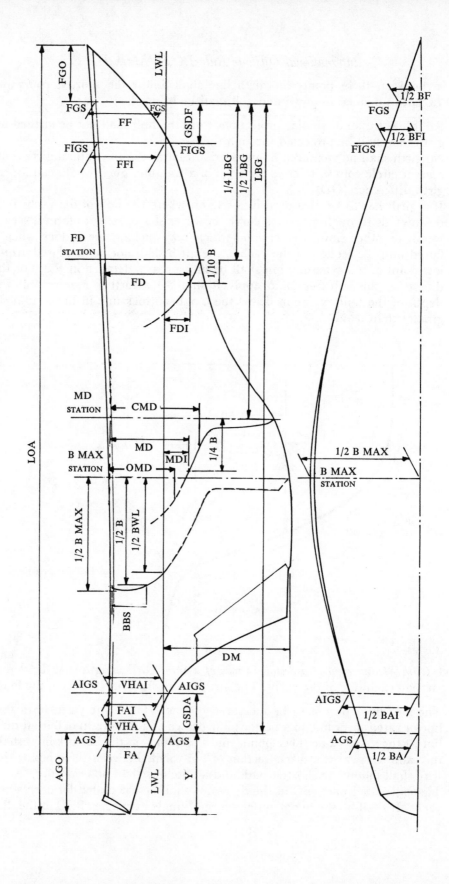

having a base of 0·04B and an angle known. The angle shall be the angle that the tangent to the measurement section at the 0·04B buttock makes with the horizontal, except that this angle shall never be taken for the purpose of calculation as greater than 45°.

Establishment of Measurement Stations

309. Measurement stations are defined as vertical transverse sections at right angles to the centre plane of the yacht.

Measurement stations shall be established on the yacht as defined below.

310. *BMAX Station.* The BMAX station shall be established where the beam of the yacht, excluding any rubbing strakes or other extraneous features, is the greatest. The maximum beam at this point shall be recorded as BMAX.

311. *Girth Stations.*

.1 Forward there shall be two girth stations.

A. *Forward Girth Station* (FGS). FGS shall be established where the girth length as defined in 307 is equal to 0·5B (for definition of B see 319).

B. *Forward Inner Girth Station* (FIGS). FIGS shall be established where the girth length is equal to 0·75B (but see 311.1 C below).

C. Where there is a hollow in the profile in which the normal position of FIGS would occur, that hollow shall be bridged but the upper end of the bridge shall not be taken forward of FGS. The forward inner girth station shall be located at the lower tangent of the profile and the straight edge used to bridge the hollow. The girth length at this station shall be measured. The difference between the measured girth length and 0·75B shall be recorded as girth difference forward inner (GDFI). Where FIGS is established as in 311.1 B GDFI shall be recorded as zero.

D. If any yacht has a "bulbous bow" it shall be measured in accordance with Rule 311.1 C except that, if the bulb extends forward of the normal 0·5B forward girth station the forward end of the bulb shall be taken as the location of FGS. In addition GSDF shall be taken as 0·0 thus making FOC zero also. In this latter case FF, FFI and FIS shall be measured to the forward end of the sheer line of the normal deck.

.2 Aft there shall be two girth stations (except on yachts with transom sterns (see 312 below)).

A. *After Girth Station* (AGS). AGS shall be established where the girth length is equal to 0·75B (or 0·75B + GD, see .3 below).

B. *After Inner Girth Station* (AIGS) shall be established where the girth length is equal to 0·875B plus the GD, if any, used at AGS.

.3 *Girth Difference* (GD). If an after girth of 0·75B in length cannot be placed on the yacht or is found to cut the transom, a girth will be taken as far aft as possible and its position recorded as AGS. The length of the girth will be measured and the difference between its length and 0·75B will be recorded as girth difference (GD). The after inner girth station, AIGS, will then be established with a girth length of 0·875B + GD.

(Note that the after inner girth shall always be 0·125B longer than the after girth length.)

On yachts where a GD is not required, it will be recorded as zero.

312. *Transom Sterns*

.1 A yacht shall be deemed as having a transom stern only when ALL the following conditions are fulfilled:

    A. The after side of the sternpost, on which the rudder must be hung, and the transom board at the centre line of the yacht must be in the same plane.

    B. The sternpost must be joined to the main keel of the yacht by dead-wood of not less depth than the sternpost (i.e. a separate skeg does not qualify).

    C. In a fixed keel yacht the bottom of the sternpost must have at least 85% of the maximum draft of the yacht.

    D. In a centreboard yacht the bottom of the sternpost must have at least 85% of the maximum draft of the yacht when the centreboard is raised and at least 35% of the maximum draft of the yacht when the centreboard is lowered.

.2 *Location of AGS in a Transom Sterned Yacht.* The low point of the transom shall be taken as the point where the overall width of the transom is 0·10B. The high point of the transom shall be taken as the highest point on the surface of the transom at deck level. If the transom slopes aft from its low point AGS shall be located aft of the low point a horizontal distance equal to 40% of the horizontal distance the high point is abaft the low point. If the transom slopes forward from its low point AGS shall be located at the low point.

When AGS is located as detailed above, BA, BHA, VHA and Y shall be recorded as zero. AOCC shall also be zero.

.3 In a transom sterned yacht there shall be no aft inner girth station. GSDA and all measures relating to AIGS shall be recorded as zero.

313. *Depth Stations.* There shall be two depth stations.

.1 *Forward Depth Station* (FDS) shall be established at one quarter of the horizontal distance between FGS and AGS abaft FGS.

.2 *Mid Depth Station* (MDS) shall be established at one half of the horizontal distance between FGS and AGS abaft FGS.

314. *Limit of Length Aft* (LLA). LLA is defined as a vertical transverse section located as defined below.

.1 Except as required by .2 and .3 below, LLA shall be located at the aftermost part of the hull, excluding the rudder, either above or below the water line.

.2 Where the transom of the yacht slopes aft from its low point, LLA shall be located abaft the low point of the transom at a horizontal distance equal to one half of the horizontal distance from the low point of the transom to the aftermost point of the yacht at deck level.

.3 On yachts with transom sterns (see 312), LLA shall be located at AGS.

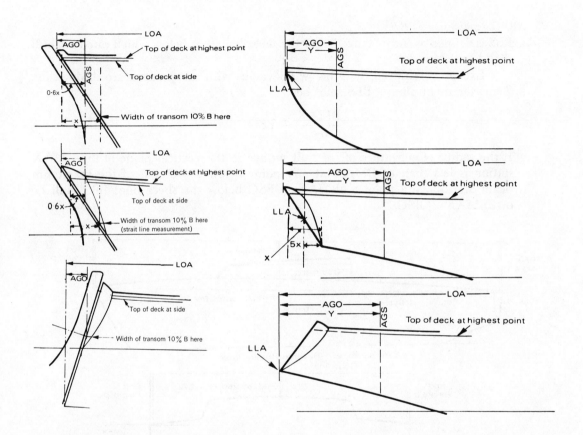

315. *Maximum Draft Station.* The maximum draft station shall be established at the deepest point of the keel. If the base of the keel is horizontal the maximum draft station shall be located at the foremost position of maximum draft as defined in 324, or at the mid depth station (MDS) where this is abaft the foremost point.

316. *Propeller Station.* The propeller station shall be established at the junction of the centre line of the propeller shaft with the axis of the propeller blades (when open if the propeller has folding blades).

Measurements in the BMAX Station

317. *Determination of Beam Sheer Correction* (BSC). BSC is defined as the vertical distance, at the BMAX station, that the sheer line is above a straight line joining points at

the level of the sheer line at its fore and aft extremities on the yacht. Where they apply rated sheer lines shall be used.

On a yacht with reverse sheer or a stepped sheer line BSC shall be measured but shall never be taken as less than zero.

On a yacht with a straight or a concave sheer line BSC shall be zero.

318. *Determination of BBS*

.1 BBS is defined as the distance below the sheer line at or below which rated beam B shall be measured.

Except as required by .2 below for yachts with sharp curvature through the B measurement planes, BBS shall be

$$\frac{\text{BMAX}}{6 \cdot 0} + \text{BSC}$$

.2 If the radius of curvature of the hull surface in the vertical plane of the BMAX station is less than $0 \cdot 1$BMAX at any point below the height of the maximum beam and above a point $0 \cdot 2$BMAX + BSC below the sheer line; BBS shall be $0 \cdot 18$BMAX + BSC.

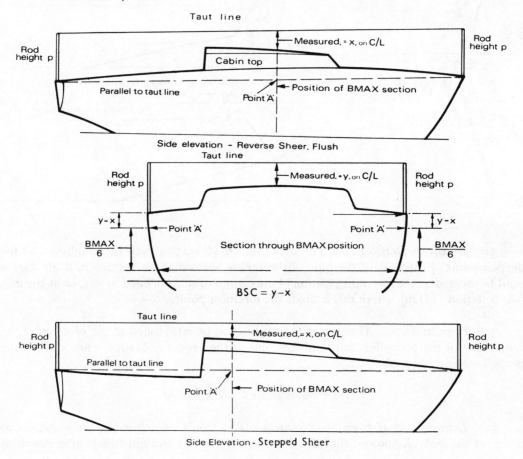

Side elevation – Reverse Sheer, Flush

Section through BMAX position

BSC = y−x

Side Elevation – Stepped Sheer

319. *Determination of B*

.1 The rated beam (B) is the maximum beam of the hull measured in the BMAX station at a height not above points located at a distance BBS below the sheer line.

.2 If, on the horizontal plane through the B measurement point defined in .1 above and within a distance 0·25BMAX forward and aft of it, the radius of curvature of the hull surface in the horizontal plane is at any point less than 1·0BMAX then rated beam B shall be determined as detailed below.

Beams shall be measured as in .1 above but at stations 0·25BMAX forward and aft of BMAX. Rated beam B shall be the mean of these two beams.

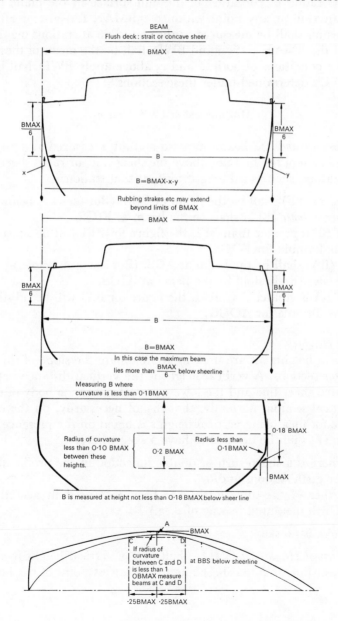

320. *Determination of BWL.* BWL is defined as the beam at the waterline, measured as detailed below, when the yacht is floating upright in the trim at which the freeboards and inclining measurements were taken.

.1 Except as required by .2 and .3 below, BWL shall be measured at the waterline in the BMAX station.

.2 Where the radius of curvature of the hull surface in the vertical plane of the BMAX station is less than 0·10B, within a vertical distance of 0·02B of the waterline, beams shall be measured at a distance 0·02B above and below the waterline. BWL shall be the mean of these two beams.

.3 Where the radius of curvature of the hull surface in the plane of the waterline is less than 1·0B at any point within 0·25BMAX forward or aft of the BMAX station, beams shall be measured at the waterline at stations 0·25BMAX forward and aft of the BMAX station and BWL shall be the mean of these two beams.

.4 Should the conditions of both .2 and .3 above apply BWL shall be the LESSER of the BWL's determined under these sections.

Measurement at Girth Stations

321. *Beam Forward and Aft.* Beams forward and aft, measured at a girth station, shall be the maximum beam of the hull not above the sheer line, or rated sheer line, excluding any extraneous features such as rubbing strakes, at that station.

.1 *Beam Forward* (BF) shall be the beam at FGS. (But see .2 A below.)

.2 *Beam Forward Inner* (BFI) shall be the beam at FIGS.
   A. If BF is greater than BFI, the figure for BFI will be substituted for BF in the formula for FOC.

.3 *Beam Aft* (BA) shall be the beam at AGS. (But see .4 A below.)

.4 *Beam Aft Inner* (BAI) shall be the beam at AIGS.
   A. If BA is greater than BAI, the figure for BAI will be substituted for BA in the formula for AOCG.

322. *Vertical Heights*

.1 The vertical heights aft are used to approximate the slope of the run of a yacht in the after sections. A vertical height is the vertical distance between the sheer line or rated sheer line and the lowest part of the canoe body of the yacht at the same vertical section, normally, though not necessarily, on the centre line. The procedure for measuring vertical heights is based on the presence or absence of a skeg. A yacht shall be deemed to have a skeg where:

   A. There is a sharp turn or double inflection in the profile abaft or between the girth stations and/or
   B. Either of the after girths has been measured in accordance with 308. (Girth measured in way of skeg.)

.2 Where there is no skeg:

   A. *Vertical Height Aft* (VHA) shall be the vertical height measured from the sheer line or rated sheer line to the lowest point of the hull at AGS.

B. *Vertical Height Aft Inner* (VHAI) shall be the vertical height measured from the sheer line or rated sheer line to the lowest point of the hull at AIGS.

.3 Where there is a skeg.

A. *Vertical Height Aft* (VHA) shall be measured as in 322.2 above except that if the after girth has been measured in way of a skeg as in 308, VHA shall be as determined below.

Vertical height aft shall be determined in two parts. The vertical height shall be measured from the sheer line to the 0·04B buttock line used in determining the girth. To this shall be added the calculated vertical side of the triangle used to determine the calculated portion of the girth.

B. *Vertical Height Aft Inner* (VHAI) shall be calculated from the buttock heights and the formula in 323.3 below.

323. *Buttock Heights* shall be used to approximate the rated slope of the profile of a yacht having a skeg. They shall be measured to buttock lines drawn 0·15B from the centre line of the yacht. Buttock heights will be measured on all yachts having a skeg as defined above.

.1 *Buttock Height Aft* (BHA) shall be the vertical distance measured from the sheer line or rated sheer line to the 0·15B buttock line at AGS.

.2 *Buttock Height Aft Inner* (BHAI) shall be the vertical distance measured from the sheer line or rated sheer line to the 0·15B buttock line at AIGS.

.3 *Vertical Height Aft Inner* (VHAI) shall be determined from the formula:

$$\text{VHAI} = \text{VHA} + (\text{BHAI} - \text{BHA})$$

Measurements at Maximum Draft Station

324. *Determination of DM.* DM is defined as the vertical distance from the waterline to:

.1 In the case of fixed keel yachts the lowest point on the keel, hull, skeg, or rudder whichever is the deeper.

.2 In the case of centreboard or drop keel yachts the lowest point on the hull, fixed keel, or drop keel or centreboard in its fully raised position, whichever is the deeper. In centreboard or drop keel yachts a rudder skeg shall be considered as fixed keel to the lowest point at which the chord of the skeg is equal to or greater than the chord of the rudder.

Measurements at Propeller Station

325. *Determination of PD.* PD shall be the vertical distance of the propeller shaft below the waterline. The distance of this point below the sheer line at this station shall be measured as propeller depth total (PDT). The freeboard at this station shall be measured as freeboard propeller depth (FPD). PD shall be the difference between these two measurements.

326. *Depths* shall be measured on each side of the yacht and the mean value determined.

  .1 At the *Forward Depth Station.*

      Determination of forward depth (FD). FD shall be measured vertically from the sheer line to points on the outside of the planking or skin of the yacht at the station, offset 0·10B from the centre line of the yacht.

  .2 At the *Mid Depth Station.*

      A. *Determination of OMD.* OMD shall be measured vertically from the sheer line to points on the outside of the planking or skin of the yacht at the station, offset three-eighths of B from the centre line.

      B. *Determination of MD.* MD shall be measured as is OMD but to points offset one-quarter of B from the centre line.

      C. *Determination of CMD.* CMD shall be measured as is OMD, but to points offset one-eighth of B from the centre line.

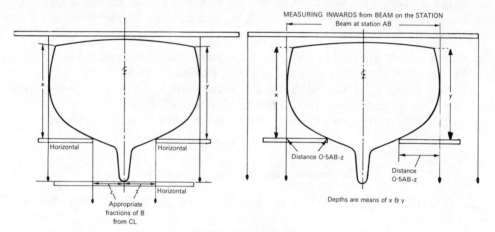

Length Measurements

327. *Length Measurements* are defined as horizontal distances between measurement stations.

Length measurements defined below shall be measured and recorded as:

  .1 *Length Overall* (LOA). LOA shall be the horizontal distance between the forward and after measurement points of the yacht as defined in 301.

  .2 *Forward Girth Overhang* (FGO). FGO shall be the horizontal distance between the forward end of LOA and the forward girth station (FGS).

  .3 *After Girth Overhang* (AGO). AGO shall be the horizontal distance between the after end of LOA and the after girth station (AGS).

  .4 *Length between Girth Stations* (LBG). LBG shall be the horizontal distance between FGS and AGS.

      Note that by definition LBG = LOA − (FGO + AGO).

.5 *Girth Station Difference Forward* (GSDF). GSDF shall be the horizontal distance between the forward girth stations FGS and FIGS.

.6 *Girth Station Difference Aft* (GSDA). GSDA shall be the horizontal distance between the after girth stations AGS and AIGS.

.7 *Length Limit Aft* (Y). Y shall be the horizontal distance between AGS and LLA.

.8 *SBMAX*. SBMAX shall be the horizontal distance between the forward end of LOA and the BMAX station.

.9 *SPD*. SPD shall be the horizontal distance between the forward end of LOA and the propeller station.

.10 *SDM*. SDM shall be the horizontal distance between the forward end of LOA and the maximum draft station.

Freeboards

328. *Freeboards*. Freeboards shall be measured at the stations listed in sub-paras .1 to .10 below. Freeboard is defined as the vertical distance between the sheerline, or rated sheerline where used, and the waterline when the yacht is afloat in measurement trim. They shall, however, be measured in the first instance to a horizontal datum at the time the hull is measured ashore. They shall subsequently be converted by the computer to flotation freeboards by the rules and formulae in 329, 1004 and 1005.

.1 *Freeboard Forward* (FF) shall be the freeboard at FGS.

.2 *Freeboard Forward Inner* (FFI) shall be the freeboard at FIGS.

.3 *Freeboard Aft* (FA) shall be the freeboard at AGS.

.4 *Freeboard Aft Inner* (FAI) shall be the freeboard at AIGS.

.5 *Freeboard at Forward Depth* (FFD) shall be the freeboard at the forward depth station.

.6 *Freeboard at Mid Depth* (FMD) shall be the freeboard at the mid depths station.

.7 *Freeboard at Base of I* (FBI) shall be the freeboard abreast the fore side of the mast (foremost mast if more than one mast). (For application see 806.2.)

.8 *Freeboard at the Stem* (FS) shall be the freeboard at the junction of the deck with the inner face of stem. (For application see 806.2.)

.9 *Freeboard at the Maximum Draft Station* (FDM) shall be the freeboard measured at the maximum draft station.

.10 *Freeboard at the Propeller Station* (FPD) shall be the freeboard at the propeller station.

329. *Freeboards measured afloat, and for measurement of Standard Hulls*
All the freeboards listed in 328 are required to be measured to a horizontal datum at the time of the original measurement of the yacht ashore.

When a yacht is measured afloat, or when a yacht with a standard hull is measured, only FF and FA, FBI and FS shall be measured.

The remaining freeboards shall be calculated from the original or standard sheer line as detailed in Part X (Standard Hull Dimensions) 1004.6 and .7 and 1005.

.1 *Freeboard Forward Measured* (FFM) shall be the freeboard at FGS measured afloat in measurement trim as defined in 202.2.

.2 *Freeboard Aft Measured* (FAM) shall be the freeboard at AGS measured afloat in measurement trim.

Length Formulae

330. *Formula for Forward Overhang Component* (FOC)

.1 FOC is intended to approximate the horizontal distance from FGS to the point where a line, drawn at a distance below the sheer line equal to the half the girths of the sections minus 15% of the beams at those sections plus 5% of B, intersects the water plane.

.2 FOC will normally be satisfactorily determined from the formula given in this paragraph. If for any reason this procedure appears to give an FOC greatly at variance from the above intentions, the Chief Measurer may at his discretion direct that a yacht be measured by extra girths located as deemed necessary to determine the proper forward end of "L".

.3 *Formula for FOC:*

$$FOC = \frac{GSDF\,(FF - 0\cdot3B + 0\cdot15BF)}{0\cdot125B + FF - FFI - 0\cdot15\,(BFI - BF) + 0\cdot5GDFI}$$

FOC shall not be taken as greater than $\dfrac{1\cdot5 \times GSDF \times 0\cdot25B}{0\cdot25B + GDFI}$

If both the numerator and denominator in the FOC formula are negative FOC shall be taken as negative and its absolute value shall not be taken as less than FGO.

331. *Formula for LBG Corrected* (LBGC):

$$LBGC = LBG + \frac{GD \times GSDA}{0\cdot125B}$$

332. *Formula for After Overhang Component* (AOC)

.1 AOCP is intended to approximate the horizontal distance from AGS to the point at which a line drawn at a distance of $0\cdot018$LBGC below the profile intersects the water plane.

.2 AOCG is intended to approximate the horizontal distance from AGS to the point where a line below the sheer line drawn at a distance equal to the half girths of the sections minus 20% of the beam at these sections intersects the water plane.

.3 AOCP and AOCG will normally be satisfactorily determined from the girth stations AGS and AIGS and by the formulae given in the paragraph. If for any reason this procedure appears to give an AOCP or AOCG greatly at variance from the above intentions, the Chief Measurer may at his discretion direct that a yacht shall be measured by extra girths located as deemed necessary to determine the proper after end of "L".

.4 *Formula for AOCG:*

$$AOCG = \frac{GSDA\,(FA - 0 \cdot 375B - 0 \cdot 5GD + 0 \cdot 2BA)}{0 \cdot 0625B + FA - FAI - 0 \cdot 2BAI + 0 \cdot 2BA}$$

.5 *Formula for AOCP:*

$$AOCP = \frac{GSDA\,(FA - VHA - 0 \cdot 018LBGC)}{VHAI - VHA + FA - FAI}$$

Where $(FA - VHA - 0 \cdot 018LBGC)$ is negative, the factor

$$\frac{GSDA}{VHAI - VHA + FA - FAI}$$

shall not be taken as greater than 6·0.

.6 *Formula for AOC:*

$$AOC = 0 \cdot 5\,(AOCP + AOCG)$$

333. *Formula for After Overhang Component Corrected* (AOCC)

If AOC + Y is positive AOCC shall be equal to AOC or 1·25GSDA whichever is the smaller.

If AOC + Y is negative or zero AOCC shall be negative and its absolute value shall be the greater of the absolute values of 0·6AOC or Y.

334. *Formula for Rated Length* (L)

$$L = LBG - FOC - AOCC$$

FOC (Forward Overhand Component) is the amount by which the forward end of L lies abaft FGS. If it lies forward of FGS, FOC will be negative and consequently will be an addition to LBG.

AOCC (After Overhang Component Corrected) is the amount by which the after end of L lies forward of AGS. If it lies abaft of AGS, AOCC will be negative and consequently will be an addition to LBG.

Formulae for Depths

335. *Formulae for Immersed Depths*

The immersed depths at FD and MD stations shall be known as forward depth immersed (FDI), centre midship depth immersed (CMDI), midship depth immersed (MDI) and outer midship depth immersed (OMDI) respectively, and shall be found from the formulae:

$$
\begin{aligned}
FDI\ &= FD\ &&- FFD \\
CMDI &= CMD &&- FMD \\
MDI\ &= MD\ &&- FMD \\
OMDI &= OMD &&- FMD
\end{aligned}
$$

336. *Formula for MDIA*

Midship depth immersed adjusted (MDIA) is found by the following formula:

$$\text{MDIA} = 0.125 \,(3 \times \text{CMDI} + 2 \times \text{MDI} - 2 \times \text{OMDI}) + \frac{(0.5 \times \text{OMDI} \times \text{BWL})}{B}$$

337. *Formula for D*

Rated depth (D) is found by the formula:

$$D = 1.3\text{MDIA} + 0.9\text{FDI} + 0.055 \,(3\,\text{FOC} - \text{AOCC}) + \frac{L + 10 \text{ ft.}}{30}$$

Part IV—Freeboard Correction

401. *The Freeboard Correction* (FC) for inclusion in the measured rating (MR) shall be determined from the following formulae:

402. *Base Freeboard* (FB)
$$\text{FB} = 0.057\text{L} + 1.20 \text{ ft.}$$

403. *Measured Freeboard* (FM)

$$\text{FM} = \frac{1.2\text{FF} + 0.8\text{FA}}{2}$$

404. *Freeboard Correction* (FC)
.1 If FM exceeds FB,   FC = 0.15 (FB − FM).
.2 If FM is less than FB, FC = 0.25 (FB − FM).

Part V—Draft Correction and Movable Appendage Factor

Definitions and Limitations of Keels

501. *Definitions of Keels.* A yacht's keel configuration shall be determined by its characteristics and shall be classified as one of the following.

.1 *Fixed Keel.* A yacht shall be classified as fixed keel when no part of the keel is adjustable when racing so as to alter the yacht's maximum draft.

.2 *Centreboard.* A yacht shall be classified as centreboard when she is fitted with a centreboard(s) which can and may be moved when racing to modify the yacht's total draft. The total weight in air of such boards shall be less than 0.05DSPL.

.3 *Drop Keel.* A yacht shall be classified as drop keel when she is fitted with a board or boards which can and may be moved when racing to modify the yacht's total draft and where the total weight in air of such board(s) is (are) more than 0.05DSPL (see 509).

502. *Limitations of Centreboards and Drop Keels*

.1 The movement of a centreboard or drop keel while racing, other than the secondary movement permitted under 515 below, shall be restricted to one of the following.
  A. Straight extension or retraction as in a dagger board.
  B. Extension about a single fixed pivot.

.2 The longitudinal movement of the centre of gravity of a Drop Keel when it is being raised or lowered (CBLD) shall not exceed 0·06L.

.3 Any centreboard or drop keel which fails for any reason to fulfil the requirements of 502.1 and .2 above shall be capable of being fixed in a single predetermined position and shall be so fixed both for measurement and at all times when racing. A yacht with a centreboard drop keel so fixed shall be classified and measured as a fixed keel yacht for rating purposes.

Measurements of Centreboards

503. In order to determine draft correction (DC), in yachts having a centreboard or drop keel, measurements of any movable keels are required in addition to the hull measurement DM as defined in 324.2.

504. *Centreboard Extension* (CD). CD shall be the maximum extension of the centreboard or drop keel below the low point of DM as defined in 324.2 measured in the vertical plane of the yacht or, if the board is not in the centre plane, measured in the plane of the board. If there is more than one board, the largest extension shall be used.

505. *Centreboard Weight* (WCBA). WCBA shall be the weight of the centreboard or drop keel in air. Where there is more than one board the weight of the additional board shall be recorded as WCBB.

506. *Centreboard Total Weight* (WCBC). WCBC shall be the sum of the weights of all centreboards and drop keels on the yacht.

507. *Centreboard Longitudinal Displacement of Centre of Gravity* (CBLD). CBLD shall be the maximum fore and aft movement of the centre of gravity of any centreboard or drop keel between its fully raised and lowered positions.

Draft Correction Formulae

508. *Base Draft* (DB) shall be determined from the formula:

$$DB = 0 \cdot 146L + 2 \cdot 0 \text{ ft.}$$

509. *Displacement* (DSPL) shall be the yacht's approximate weight as determined from the formula:

$$DSPL = \frac{L \times MDIA \times B}{2} \times 64 \cdot 0$$

510. *Centreboard Proportion* (CBP) shall be determined from the formula:

$$CBP = \frac{WCBC}{DSPL}$$

CBP shall not be taken greater than 0·233.

511. *Depth of Keel Equivalent* (DK) shall be determined from the formula:

$$DK = \frac{CD}{1·45 - 2·80CBP}$$

512. *Rated Draft* (RD) shall be determined from the formula:

$$RD = DM + DK$$

513. *Draft Difference* (DD) shall be determined from the formula:

$$DD = RD - DB$$

514. *Draft Correction* (DC) shall be determined:

(a) Where DD is negative or zero: $DC = 0·04L \left(\dfrac{RD}{DB} - 1·0\right)$

(b) Where DD is positive: $DC = 0·07L \left(\dfrac{RD}{DB} - 1·0\right)$

Note: If WCBC exceeds 0·05DSPL, a Centreboard becomes a Drop Keel, in which case where CBLD exceeds 0·06L, the drop keel must be fixed as required by 502.3 and the yacht re-rated as fixed keel.

Movable Appendages

515. *Movable Appendage.* A yacht having any of the keel configurations defined in 501 may in addition have a movable appendage. A movable appendage is defined as any underwater surface which has some capability for inducing asymmetry in, or altering the underwater configuration of, the yacht. The only exceptions are the yacht's main rudder (provided it only has motion about a single fixed axis) and a single centreboard or drop keel as permitted in 501.2 or 501.3 above.

If any centreboard or drop keel is fitted with any gybing mechanism or if, in any lowered position, the board can move in such a way that the relative transverse movement, at any level, between the leading and trailing edges of the board can exceed 3·5% of fore and aft measurement of the board at that level, the centreboard or drop keel shall also be classed as a movable appendage.

A. Limitations in the permissible movement of any movable appendage are as follows:

(1) No movable appendage is permitted to have fore and aft movement except as part of a centreboard.

(2) If movable appendage weight exceeds 0·05DSPL, the movable appendage may have movement only about an axis passing through its centre of gravity.

Movable Appendage Measurements

516. *Movable Appendage Weight* (MAW). MAW is the weight of the movable appendage in air.

If a movable appendage is fitted to the yacht but is to be locked for measurement and at all times when racing, MAW shall be recorded as zero.

517. *Movable Appendage Centre of Gravity* (MACG). MACG shall define the centre of gravity of a movable appendage. Where movement of the appendage moves its centre of gravity relative to the yacht MACG shall be recorded as 1·0.

Where the axis of movement passes through the centre of gravity of the appendage MACG shall be recorded as zero.

Movable Appendage Formulae

518. *Movable Appendage Factor* (MAF). Any yacht having a movable appendage as defined and permitted in 515 above shall have a MAF of 1·0075. A yacht not having a movable appendage or a yacht having a movable appendage positively locked while racing shall have a MAF of 1·0000.

Part VI—Engine and Propeller Factor

601. *Engine and Propeller Factor* (EPF) results from the application of the following formula:

$$EPF = 1 - (EMF + DF)$$

EPF shall not be taken as less than 0·9600.

The Engine and Propeller factor shall apply only if:

.1 The racing propeller can be demonstrated to be capable of driving the yacht in calm water at a speed of at least $\sqrt{L}$ knots. During the test the wind shall not be abaft the beam.

.2 The propeller is at all times ready for use and shall not be retracted, housed or shielded except by a conventional strut or aperture.

.3 The propeller can be locked or otherwise secured in an easily releasable manner to prevent rotation while racing.

.4 The yacht's engine is an outboard motor complying with 202.2 O, in which case DF shall be taken as zero.

602. *Engine Dry Weight* (EW). EW shall be the engine dry weight in pounds taken from the manufacturer's catalogue. Reverse and reduction gearboxes when bolted to the engine, a single engine mounted generator (dynamo/alternator), and self-starter shall,

if fitted, be included in the engine weight. When the engine is an outboard motor EW shall be the dry weight of the motor less tankage.

603. *Engine Weight Distance* (EWD). EWD shall be the horizontal distance between the centre of the cylinder block of the engine and the midpoint of LBG. When the engine is an outboard motor EWD shall be the horizontal distance from the centre of gravity of the engine when mounted in its stowage to the midpoint of LBG.

604. *Engine Moment* (EM). EM is the product of EW and EWD: that is,

$$EM = EW \times EWD$$

605. *Engine Moment Factor* (EMF). EMF shall be determined according to the formula:

$$EMF = \frac{0 \cdot 1 EM}{L^2 \times B \times D}$$

606. *Propeller Diameter* (PRD). PRD shall be the diameter of the propeller disc.

607. *Propeller Blade Width* (PBW). PBW shall be the greatest width of the propeller blade measured across the driving face of the blade on a chord at right angles to the radius of the blade.

608. *Propeller Size* (PS). PS shall be equal to PRD or 4 × PBW, whichever is the smaller.

609. *Propeller Installation.* The propeller installation shall be classified in accordance with the following rules:

.1 *In Aperture.* To qualify as an "In Aperture" installation, the propeller must be entirely surrounded (in the vertical plane of the shaft line) by the deadwood, skeg and/or rudder. Aperture size shall be determined from the dimensions:

A. *Aperture Height* (APH). APH shall be the maximum height of the aperture opening measured at right angles to the shaft line.
B. *Aperture Widths* (APT) and (APB). APT and APB shall be the maximum widths of the aperture opening measured parallel to the shaft line at distances not less than PRD/3 above and below the shaft line.

When APH is not less than 1·125PRD and neither APT nor APB is less than 0·4PRD, the installation shall qualify as "In Aperture full size".
If the aperture size conditions are not met the installation shall qualify as "In Aperture small".

.2 *Out of Aperture.* Out of Aperture classification shall be determined from the following dimensions:

A. *Exposed Shaft Length* (ESL). ESL shall be the length of the exposed shaft measured from the centre of the propeller (the intersection of the blade axis and shaft) to the point at which the shaft centre line emerges from the hull or appendage. A pipe enclosing the shaft, that is indistinguishable from a shaft except for the fact that it does not rotate, shall not disqualify measurement of the shaft for ESL.

B. *Exposed Shaft Clearance* (ESC). ESC shall be the lesser of either:

    (i) 0·5PRD plus the minimum clearance between the propeller blade and the hull (measured at right angles to the shaft line).

or   (ii) The minimum clearance between the shaft centre line and the hull (measured at right angles to the shaft line) at a distance equal to 1·5PRD from the inboard end of ESL.

Where ESL is not less than 1·5PRD and ESC is not more than 0·75PRD the installation may qualify as "Out of Aperture, Exposed Shaft", provided that in addition the shaft is supported by a strut, positioned adjacent to the propeller hub. The strut shall be measured and shall comply with the following requirements:

C. ST1. The maximum thickness of the strut at any section between the shaft and the hull shall not be less than 0·05PRD. The smallest such dimension found shall be recorded as ST1.

D. ST2. The minimum width of the strut, measured parallel to the shaft, shall not be less than 0·2PRD. The minimum width found shall be recorded as ST2.

E. The maximum width of the strut, measured parallel to the shaft, shall not exceed 0·5PRD. The maximum width found shall be recorded as ST3. *Note:* Struts may be found that are too small according to this formula. In this case they may be enlarged by the addition of tape, fibreglass, micro balloon, or any similar reasonably permanent material.

F. Where the propeller is on the forward end of the shaft, and is abaft the fin keel or any other appendage, the distance from any part of the propeller to any part of the fin keel, or other appendage, shall not be less than PRD.

If any one of the above conditions is not met the installations shall qualify as "Out of Aperture, other".

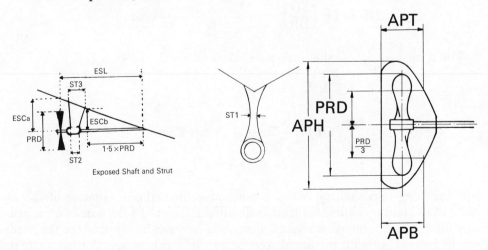

Exposed Shaft and Strut

610. *Propeller Factor* (PF). The Propeller Factor for the appropriate installation and propeller type shall be determined from the table below:

Installation Type	*Folding*	*Propeller Type* *Feathering*	*Solid*
IN APERTURE—FULL SIZE	0·95	0·95	1·05
IN APERTURE—SMALL	0·475	0·475	0·525
OUT OF APERTURE—			
EXPOSED SHAFT	0·85	1·05	2·05
OUT OF APERTURE—OTHER	0·35	0·55	1·05

Solid Propellers. For a propeller to qualify as a solid propeller:

A. Each of the blades must have a normal elliptical shape or such shape as disposes the area of the blade so as to reasonably approximate the same.
B. The blades must have a pitch that gives an angle, measured at any point at or beyond the half radius, of not less than 45° between the shaft line and the face of the blade.

If either of the above conditions is not fulfilled the propeller, for the purposes of determining PF, shall be considered as feathering.

611. *Propeller Drag Factor* (DF). DF shall be calculated from the following formulae.
.1 if PS is not less than 0·03L

$$DF = PF \left(\frac{PD}{DB}\right)^{\frac{1}{4}} \times \frac{PS}{L}$$

The value of $\frac{PS}{L}$ shall not be taken as greater than 0·05

.2 if PS is less than 0·03L

$$DF = PF \left(\frac{PD}{DB}\right)^{\frac{1}{4}} \times \left(\frac{PS^2 \times 60·0}{L^2} - 0·024\right)$$

The term $\frac{PS^2 \times 60·0}{L^2}$ shall never be taken as less than 0·024.

Part VII—Centre of Gravity Factor

Inclining Tests

701. Inclining tests shall be made to determine the righting moment of the yacht. The yacht shall be in measurement trim as detailed in 202.2. In the case of a yacht fitted with any form of centreboard, leeboard, drop keel or movable appendage the inclining tests will be carried out with the board, keel or movable appendage, if it has a capability of vertical movement, fully raised. The yacht shall be inclined as detailed below:

.1 A manometer, to the specification circulated to rating authorities, shall be positioned athwart the yacht where it can be read by the Measurer, who shall be stationed off the yacht.

.2 A pole, normally the spinnaker pole shall be positioned at the BMAX station and suspended outboard to provide an arm for supporting inclining weights. The pole shall be arranged as nearly horizontal as is possible while allowing sufficient clearance to prevent the weights touching the water.

.3 When the pole is rigged, but with no weights attached, the datum on the manometer shall be marked.

.4 Two sets of weights shall be prepared. The weights shall be recorded in pounds when the yacht is measured in feet and in kilograms when the yacht is measured in metres. Weights shall be adjusted to exact pounds or kilograms and no tolerance is intended or implied. If water containers are used as weights the scales used for measurement shall be regularly tested to ensure that they are accurate to within 1%.

.5 The yacht shall be inclined to starboard with each set of weights after which the procedure will be repeated, transferring the pole to the port side. Simultaneous rigging of two poles on opposite sides of the yacht is not permitted.

Inclining Measurements

702. *Pendulum Length* (PL) shall be the length of the manometer from the centre line of the water container to the measurement scale. PL shall be common to all four sets of readings; it shall be recorded in millimetres to one place of decimals and shall not be less than 1500·0.

703. *Weight Distances* (AWD) (BWD) (CWD) (DWD) shall be the lengths of the inclining arms. They shall be the horizontal distances from the centre line of the yacht when upright to the point of attachment of the weights. They shall be measured when the halyard supporting the pole is under load. The weight distances shall be of the order of 0·5BMAX + SPL.

704. *Pendulum Deflections* (APD) (BPD) (CPD) (DPD) shall be the deflections of the gauge on the manometer with each set of weights, from the datum established when the pole only is rigged. They shall be recorded in millimetres and shall be within the limits given in 705 below.

705. *Weights* (AW) (BW) (CW) (DW) shall be the weights used for each inclining. They shall be of suitable magnitude to ensure that the smallest value of PD is not less than 25 mm and the largest PD is not in excess of 0·052PL (78·0 mm when PL = 1500). The larger weights (BW, DW) shall not be less than 1·9 times the smaller weights (AW, CW).

706. *Centreboard Centre of Gravity Drop* (CBDA). CBDA shall be the vertical distance through which the centre of gravity of the centreboard or drop keel can be lowered. When there is more than one board the figure for the additional board shall be recorded as CBDB.

Formulae

707. *Righting Moments at One Degree* (ARM) (BRM) (CRM) *and* (DRM) shall be determined for each set of measurements from the formulae:

$$\text{ARM} = \frac{\text{AW} \times \text{AWD} \times \text{PL} \times 0 \cdot 0175}{\text{APD}}$$

$$\text{BRM} = \frac{\text{BW} \times \text{BWD} \times \text{PL} \times 0 \cdot 0175}{\text{BPD}}$$

similarly for CRM and DRM.

708. *Righting Moment* (RM). RM shall be determined from the following formula:

$$\text{RM} = (\text{ARM} + \text{BRM} + \text{CRM} + \text{DRM}) \times 0 \cdot 25$$

709. *Righting Moment Corrected* (RMC). RMC shall be determined as follows:

.1 For keel yachts: RMC = RM
.2 For centreboard or drop keel yachts:

$$\text{RMC} = \text{RM} + 0 \cdot 0175 \, ((\text{WCBA} \times \text{CBDA}) + (\text{WCBB} \times \text{CBDB}))$$

710. *Tenderness Ratio* (TR). TR shall be determined from the following formula:

$$\text{TR} = \frac{0 \cdot 97 \text{L} \times (\text{BWL})^3}{\text{RMC}}$$

TR shall not be taken as less than 5·15.

711. *Centre of Gravity Factor* (CGF). CGF shall be determined from the following formula:

$$\text{CGF} = \frac{2 \cdot 2}{\text{TR} - 5 \cdot 1} + 0 \cdot 8925$$

CGF shall not be taken as less than 0·9680.

Part VIII—Rig and Sail Area Measurements

Calculation of Sail Area

801. *General.* All sails must be set and trimmed in a manner consistent with the way they are measured. Conflicts will exist between these rules and those of the I.Y.R.U. and National Authorities; in such cases, the I.O.R. rules will govern but when not in conflict, the rules of the I.Y.R.U. or the appropriate National Authority shall be observed.

For yachts measured under this Rule:

.1 Check wires are not required in sails. (Exception to I.Y.R.U. Measurement Rules Section III, 1.(8).)

802. *Miscellaneous Restrictions*. Except as specifically permitted by 812.2, double luffed sails (those with thick or wrap-around luffs, not spinnakers or squaresails), rotating masts, mechanically or permanently bent spars or similar contrivances are excluded for yachts measured under the rule. Mainsails, schooner foresails and mizzens may be reefed at the foot only. Roach, slab or flattening reefs are permitted along the foot only.

.1 *Permanently Bent Spars*. A mast that will straighten when stresses imposed by the rigging are removed does not constitute a permanently bent mast. It could be a requirement for the sail area measurements to be taken with the mast so straightened.

.2 *Mechanically Bent Spars*.

A. Adjustment to the standing rigging between masts and hull while racing does not constitute mechanical bending of spars.

B. Altering the location of the mast at the step or deck while racing would be considered as mechanical bending of the spar and is thus not permitted. This shall, however, not prohibit a natural movement at the deck not exceeding 10% of the greatest fore and aft or transverse dimension of the mast at that point.

.3 *Roach, Slab or Flattening Reefs*. Cunningham holes in mainsails and other sails are permitted.

803. *Determination of MSA*. MSA is the measured sail area determined by applying triangulation to the uncorrected measurements of a single element of the rig.

804. *Determination of RSA*. RSA shall be the rated sail area of any part of the rig determined by applying the corrected dimensions in the formulae as further defined.

805. *Total Rated Sail Area* (RSAT). The RSAT to be used for each rig shall be determined by combining the RSA for each sail or part of the rig in the formulae of 896 to 899. The parts of the rig to be included shall be as below:

.1 For Sloop rig: Mainsail (RSAM) and Foretriangle (RSAF).

.2 For Yawl or Ketch: Mainsail (RSAM), Foretriangle (RSAF) plus Mizzen and Mizzen staysail (YSAC).

A yawl or ketch is a two-masted rig in which the height of the aftermast (IY) is not greater than the height of the forward mast (the greater of I or P + BAD). No distinction between a yawl or ketch is required under these rules.

.3 For Foresail Schooner: Mainsail (RSAM), Foretriangle (RSAF) and Foresail (RSAG), see 873.

A foresail schooner is a two-masted rig in which the height of the after or mainmast (P + BAD) is greater than the height of the foremast (I or PSF + BADS).

.4 For a Schooner or Staysail Ketch: Mainsail (RSAM), Foretriangle (RSAF) and Area between the Masts (RSAB), see 882.

A schooner or staysail ketch is a rig carrying a variety of unspecified sails between the masts (see 872.2 and .3), irrespective of the height of the masts.

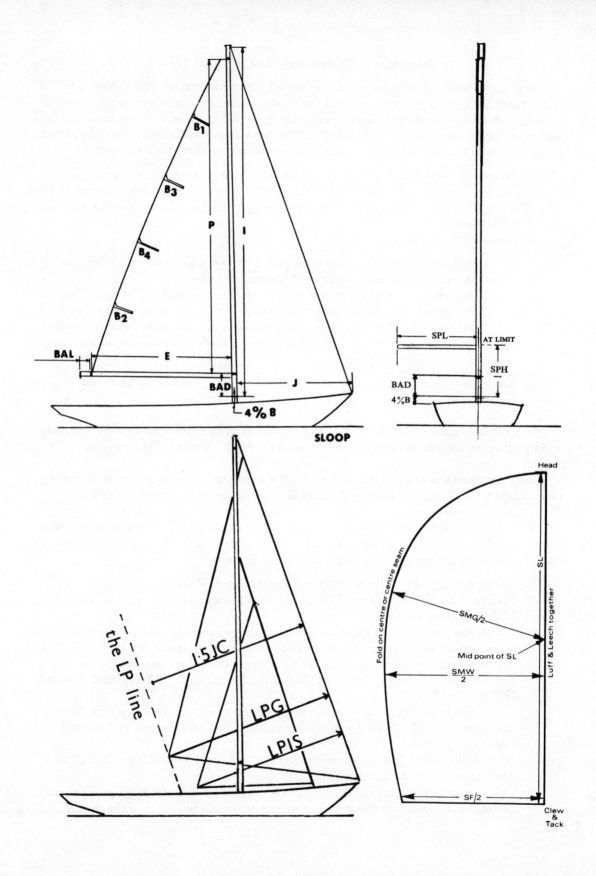

B1

B3

B4

P

I

B2

BAL

E

BAD

J

4% B

SLOOP

SPL

AT LIMIT

SPH

BAD

4%B

Head

1.5JC

the LP line

LPG

LPIS

SL

Fold on centre or centre seam

SMG/2

Mid point of SL

Luff & Leech together

SMW
2

SF/2

Clew
& Tack

806. *Height of Deck*

.1 The height of deck used as a datum for sail area measurements shall be taken at 4% of B above the sheer line abreast the mast.

.2 Where FBI + 0·04B exceeds FS (see 328.7 and .8) the difference shall be added to the measurements of I, BAD and SPH at the time flotation measurements are taken.

Foretriangle

807. *Base of Foretriangle* (J). J shall be the actual foretriangle base measured horizontally from the foreside of the mast at the deck to the centre line of the foremost stay on which headsails are set (the centre line of the luff if the foremost headsail is to be set flying) extended if necessary to intersect the top of the rail, including rail cap or its extension or bowsprit if used, or to the centre line of the deck, should this be above the rail or rail cap.

808. *Spinnaker Pole Length* (SPL). SPL shall be the length of the spinnaker pole when in its fitting on the mast and set in a horizontal position athwartships, measured from the centre line of the yacht to the extreme outboard end of the pole and any fittings used when a spinnaker is set.

809. *Height of Foretriangle* (I). I shall be the foretriangle height measured along the foreside of the mast from the main deck (as defined in 806) to either:

.1 The highest of the following three points:

    A. The intersection of the centre line of the highest stay used for headsails, with the fair line of the foreside of the mast or topmast (projected if necessary).

    B. The centre of the highest eye bolt or eye used for headsail or spinnaker halyard block. A spinnaker halyard block may be set forward enough to permit a clear lead, without measurement penalty.

    C. The intersection of the foreside of the mast or topmast with the highest strop used for headsail or spinnaker halyard.

or .2 As determined under the 1957 R.O.R.C. Rule, Section V, para. (11), as reprinted in 1968. This method may at the owner's option be applied to yachts holding R.O.R.C. Rule certificates valid during any part of 1969 or earlier. This option shall be withdrawn as from January 1st, 1974.

810. *Height of Spinnaker Pole* (SPH). SPH shall be the maximum height on the mast of the inboard end of the spinnaker pole above the main deck (as defined in 806). It shall be measured to the centre line of the pole when set at the highest point on its track or to the underside of a painted measurement band on the mast. Where a measurement band is used as the upper end of SPH the centre line of the pole at the mast may not be carried above this height except when actually gybing. (For penalty for excessive length of SPH, see 829.2.)

811. *Headsails*

.1 In these rules the word headsail is defined as a sail set in the foretriangle. It can be either a spinnaker or a jib.

.2 *Distinction between Spinnakers and Jibs.* A sail shall not be measured as a spinnaker unless the midgirth is 75% or more of the foot length and the sail is symmetrical about a line joining the head to the centre of the foot. No jib may have a midgirth measured between the midpoints of luff and leech more than 50% of the foot length. Thus headsails with midgirths between 50% and 75% shall not be allowed.

Definition of Jibs

812 .1 A jib is defined as any sail, other than a spinnaker, that is to be set in the foretriangle. In any jib the midgirth, measured between midpoints of luff and leech, shall not exceed 50% of the foot length nor shall the length of any intermediate girth exceed a value similarly proportionate to its distance from the head of the sail.

.2 Notwithstanding the restrictions of 802, a yacht may use:

A. A double luff jib that wraps around the forestay and/or

B. A luff groove device provided that such luff groove device is of constant section throughout its length and is either essentially circular in section or is free to rotate without restraint. A permitted luff groove device shall be measured for FSP (see 814).

.3 Jibs may be sheeted from only one point on the sail except in the process of reefing the sail. (Thus quadri-lateral or similar sails or sails in which the sailcloth does not extend to the cringle at each corner are excluded.)

Measurement of Jibs

813. *Longest Perpendicular of Jibs* (LPG)

.1 Jibs shall be measured on the perpendicular from the luff (outside edge of the sail and/or luff rope) to clew (intersection of the lines of the foot and leech). A wrap around jib shall be measured on the perpendicular from the line of junction of the wrap around parts to the clew.

.2 LPG shall be the largest such dimension found on the jibs carried on the yacht.

814. *Forestay Perpendicular* (FSP)

FSP shall be the larger of either:

.1 Twice the maximum dimension, measured at right angles to the longitudinal axis, of a luff groove device.

or .2 The largest dimension of the doubled portion of a wrap around jib measured at right angles to the luff line when opened out.

815. *Longest Perpendicular of Inner Jib* (LPIS). LPIS shall be the greatest distance between the clew of any jib and the foremost headstay, measured perpendicular to the

stay, which occurs because of tacking such jib inside another headsail. This dimension is required only where the dimension LP (see 827) is to be established by a jib which is so set.

Limitations on Jibs

816 .1 No clewboards may be used in jibs.

.2 No headboards may be used in jibs.

.3 Battens may be used in jibs only if:

    A. Their length is not more than 0·08J.

    B. Their forward end is forward of the centre line of the mast supporting their halyard.

    C. The number of battens is limited to four, which must be arranged with approximately equal spacing between head and clew.

.4 The distance, measured on the surface of the sail, between the midpoint of the foot and the midpoint of the luff shall not exceed 0·55 of the length of the leech.

Definition of Spinnakers

817. For measurement as a spinnaker a sail must have the following characteristics.

.1 Luff and leech must be of equal length.

.2 The sail must be symmetrical about a line joining the head to the centre of the foot.

.3 The midgirth (see 823) shall not be less than 75% of the foot length (see 822).

Measurement of Spinnakers

818. Spinnakers shall be measured with such tension as will remove all wrinkles across the line of measurement. The Measurer shall sign the sail indicating the date of measurement, and the maximum length of luff and leech and maximum width, and his approval with respect to all other requirements. These measurements shall apply during the unaltered life of the sail.

819. *Spinnaker Headboard* (HBS). HBS shall be the maximum width of a spinnaker headboard.

820. *Spinnaker Maximum Width* (SMW). SMW shall be spinnaker maximum width, whether at the foot or across the body of the sail, measured between points on the luff and leech equidistant from the head.

821. *Spinnaker Luff or Leech* (SL). SL shall be the greatest length of spinnaker luff and leech measured around the edges of the sail.

822. *Spinnaker Foot Length* (SF). SF shall be the distance from tack to clew measured in the shortest path on the surface of the sail.

823. *Spinnaker Midgirth Length* (SMG). SMG shall be the distance between the mid-points of luff and leech measured in the shortest path on the surface of the sail.

824. For calculation of RSAF the dimensions of HBS, SMW and SL shall be the largest of such dimensions to be found on any of the spinnakers carried on the yacht.

Limitations of Spinnakers

825 .1 Spinnakers shall be sheeted from only one point on the sail.

.2 Battens shall not be used in spinnakers.

.3 Luff and leech (SL) shall be of equal length and shall not without penalty exceed LL (for penalty see 829.1).

.4 Maximum width (SMW) shall be limited. If SMW exceeds 1·8J or 1·8SPL, JC will be increased (see 826).

.5 The headboard (HBS) shall be limited to 0·05JC. For penalty for wider headboard see 829.3.

.6 Adjustable leech lines are not permitted in spinnakers.

Foretriangle Formulae

826. *Determination of JC.* JC shall be the corrected base of the foretriangle taken as the greatest of the three measurements, J, SPL, or SMW divided by 1·80.

827. *Determination of LP.* LP shall be taken as the greatest of:

$$\text{LPG} + \text{FSP, or } 1\cdot5\text{JC, or LPIS}$$

Note: The dimension of LP shall establish the LP line (see 832.1 B).

828. *Determination of Luff Limit of Spinnaker* (LL). LL shall be $0\cdot95 \sqrt{I^2 + JC^2}$.

829. *Determination of IC.* IC shall be the corrected foretriangle height. It shall be determined by adding to I any of the penalties incurred in .1, .2 or .3 below:

.1 If SL exceeds LL twice the difference shall be added to I.

.2 If SPH exceeds 0·25I the difference shall be added to I.

.3 If HBS exceeds 0·05JC any excess shall be multiplied by

$$\frac{1\cdot8 \times \text{SL}}{\text{SMW}} \text{ and added to I.}$$

830. *Determination of RSAF.* RSAF shall be the rated sail area of the foretriangle determined by the formula:

$$\text{RSAF} = 0\cdot5\text{IC} \times \text{JC}\left[1 + 1\cdot1\left(\frac{\text{LP} - \text{JC}}{\text{LP}}\right)\right] + 0\cdot125\text{JC (IC} - 2\text{JC)}$$

The quantity 0·125JC (IC − 2JC) shall be discarded if negative.

Where there is no provision for setting sails in the foretriangle, RSAF shall be zero.

831. *Determination of SPIN.* SPIN shall be the rated spinnaker area determined by the formula:

$$SPIN = 1 \cdot 01 JC \times (LL \text{ or } SL \text{ whichever is the greater})$$

Restrictions on Setting and Sheeting of Headsails

832. *Jibs*
.1 *Tack Points of Jibs.*

A. No jib may be set under a spinnaker nor inside another jib tacked in such a position that, if the sail were trimmed flat along a parallel to the centre line of the yacht, its clew would fall abaft the LP line (see B below).

B. The LP line is defined as a line abaft and parallel to the foremost headstay and separated from it by the dimension of LP declared in the Rating Certificate (see 827). The foremost headstay is defined as the line joining the upper measurement point of I and the forward measurement point of J (not JC).

C. No jib may be set under or abaft another headsail and so tacked that, if trimmed along a parallel to the centre line of the yacht, more than 50% of its area would fall abaft the foreside of the mast.

D. No combination of jib-luff and tack pennant may be set, whether hanked on to a stay or set flying, the combined length of which, as set, cannot be fully stretched when hoisted on the highest jib halyard and tacked at the forward measurement point of J.

.2 *Sheeting of Jibs.* Jibs may be sheeted to any part of the rail or deck, but no higher than 0·05B above the deck or to the main boom, within the measurement limits (see 836.2), and to the spinnaker pole when the pole is set on the opposite side from the main boom but may not be sheeted to any other spar or outrigger.

.3 No jib may be set in conjunction with any other headsail so as by any means to simulate a double clewed or double luffed jib. (For example, no two jibs may be carried simultaneously in a luff groove device.)

833. *Spinnakers*
.1 *Setting of Spinnakers.*

A. The spinnaker tack must be carried close to the spinnaker pole. The spinnaker shall not be carried without the spinnaker pole except when gybing.

B. Spinnaker Pole. The outboard end of the spinnaker pole shall be used only on the windward side of the yacht (i.e. that opposite to the main boom). A spinnaker pole shall only be used with its inboard end attached to the mast (foremast if there is more than one mast).

C. Notwithstanding failure to meet the definition and limitation of a spinnaker (see 817), a bona fide jib (see 812) otherwise permitted and for which the yacht has been measured may be used as a spare spinnaker, having no other, or as a heavy weather running sail. Such a sail may be set with either its tack or clew to the spinnaker pole.

.2 *Sheeting of Spinnakers.*

    A. A spinnaker may be sheeted to any part of the rail or deck or to the main boom, within the measurement limits (see 836), but to no other spar or outrigger.

    B. Struts, spools or similar devices used solely for the purpose of keeping the spinnaker guy away from the windward main or foremast shrouds are permitted but are not to be used for any other purpose.

834. *Squaresail.* A yacht may carry a squaresail, square topsail and raffee instead of a spinnaker. The total measured area (MSA) of these sails may not exceed the rated foretriangle area (RSAF) nor may the total length of their yard or yards exceed SPL.

835. *Heavy Weather Running Sails.* When neither the mainsail nor the spinnaker are set two spinnaker poles, or one spinnaker pole and the main boom, may be used simultaneously without violating 833.1 B, 832.2 or 832.3 and two jibs may be set and sheeted to the poles or boom. Neither jib shall be of larger area than the largest jib for which the yacht is measured.

Mainsail

836. *Foot of Mainsail*

.1 *Foot of Mainsail* (E). E shall be the length measured along the boom, of the foot of the mainsail taken from the after side of mast (or the fair extension of the base of the track), to extreme aftermost position to which the sail can be extended. If this latter point is inside of boom end, it shall be located by the inner edge of a one inch measurement band around the boom.

.2 *Sheeting Limit* (BAL). BAL shall be the distance from the outer measurement point of E to a contrasting measurement band denoting the limit on the boom beyond which no lead for the sheeting of headsails shall be attached. In the absence of such a band BAL shall be measured to the boom end.

.3 *Determination of EC.* EC shall be the corrected length of the foot of the mainsail obtained by adding to E any amount by which BAL exceeds 0·50 ft.

    A. For loose footed mainsail, see paragraph 895.2.

Jib Headed Mainsail

837. *Mainsail Hoist* (P). P shall be the measured length of the hoist of a jib headed mainsail. It is the distance along the afterside of the mainmast from the highest level to which the head of the sail may be set to the lowest position of the tack. The highest point shall be taken as the top of the highest sheave used for the main halyard, or to the lower edge of a one inch measurement band (see 846.2). The lowest position of the foot shall normally be the fair extension of the top of the boom track or boom if there is no track.

.1 If a sliding gooseneck is used, measurement is to be made with the boom at the extreme bottom of the slide unless the lowest sailing position of the foot of the sail (boom or boom track) is marked by the upper edge of a one inch measurement band around the mast. The top of the boom (or track) shall not be carried below this point when the mainsail is set, except when actually putting in or shaking out a reef in the mainsail.

.2 In the event that the tack of the sail is carried below the boom, its lowest position shall be marked by the upper edge of one inch measurement band around the mast from which the low point of P shall be measured.

.3 If rake of mast exceeds 15%, P shall be taken as the vertical height. Percent of rake shall be determined by taking the horizontal distance on deck between plumb bob or equivalent suspended freely from masthead, and dividing this distance by the height of masthead from deck measured along after side of mast.

838. *Boom above Deck* (BAD). BAD shall be the distance between the low point used in the determination of P, and the main deck at the mast, see 806. This shall not without penalty be taken as more than $0.05P + 4.0$ ft. For penalty see 846.1.

839. *Mainsail Headboard* (HB). HB shall be the maximum fore and aft dimension from the luff of the mainsail, projected if necessary, to the extreme aft edge of the leech measured across the widest part of the headboard. Notwithstanding I.Y.R.U. Sail Measurement instructions any stiffening used to extend the leech beyond a reasonable roach shall be added to HB. For penalty see 846.3.

840. *Batten Leech Penalty* (BLP). BLP shall be the distance, measured along the leech of the mainsail, from the lower outer corner of the headboard to the centre line of the top batten pocket. For penalty see 848.1.

841. *Boom Depth* (BD). BD shall be the maximum depth of the main boom. For penalty see 846.4.

Gaff Mainsail

842. *Hoist* (H). H is the measured length of the hoist for a gaff mainsail. It shall be the distance along the after side of the mast from the lower edge of one inch measurement band around the mast, above which mark the upper inner edge of the throat cringle of the mainsail shall not be hoisted, to the upper side of the boom or measurement band, denoting the lowest point of the tack, as defined in 837. BAD for gaff mainsails shall not without penalty exceed $0.05 (H + 0.6G) + 4.0$ ft. and any excess shall be included in HC.

843. *Gaff* (G). G is the measured length of the head of the mainsail along the gaff. It is the distance from the afterside of mast to outboard point of gaff, determined in a manner similar to that for outboard end of main boom in paragraph 836 above.

844. *Determination of MSAT*. MSAT shall be the area of the topsail calculated from the measurement of the three sides. Taking the height from the upper point of the mainsail hoist to the highest point to which the topsail may be set, including sprit if any; the length of gaff (G) to which it is sheeted, plus extension of club if any; and the length of leech measured from the sail when stretched taut.

845. *Batten Lengths* (BL1), (BL2), (BL3), (BL4), (BL5)

.1 BL1 shall be the maximum length of the top batten.

.2 BL2 shall be the maximum length of the bottom batten.

.3 BL3 and BL4 shall be the lengths of the two shortest intermediate battens.

.4 BL5 shall be the sum of the lengths of the fifth and subsequent battens in the mainsail.

.5 The number of battens in any mainsail, mizzen or foresail in a schooner shall without penalty be limited to four, except that, when the foot of the sail exceeds 40 ft., five battens may be used. Batten spacings shall be approximately equal between the head of the sail (junction of leech and headboard) and clew. For penalties see 848.

Mainsail Formulae

846. *Determination of PC.* PC is the corrected length of P calculated by adding to P the value of any of the penalties defined below and batten penalties defined in 848.

.1 *Boom Above Deck Penalty.* If BAD exceeds $0 \cdot 05P + 4 \cdot 0$ ft. the excess shall be added to P in computing PC.

.2 *Mainsail Head Penalty.* If P + BAD is less than $0 \cdot 96I$, the difference shall be added to P in computing PC.

.3 *Headboard Penalty.* If HB is greater than the larger of $0 \cdot 04E$ or $0 \cdot 5$ ft. the excess shall be multiplied by P/E and added to P in computing PC.

.4 *Boom Depth Penalty.* If BD exceeds $0 \cdot 05E$ the excess shall be added to P in computing PC.

847. *Determination of HC.* HC is the corrected length of the hoist of a gaff mainsail determined by increasing H by any of the following penalties:

> Boom depth penalty, see 846.
> Boom above deck penalty, see 842.
> Batten penalty, see 848.4.

848. *Batten Penalties*

.1 Should the distance between the centre line of the top batten and the lower outer edge of the headboard, measured along the leech (BLP), be less than $0 \cdot 2P$, the deficit shall be added to the measured length of the top batten (BL1).

.2 The length of the battens shall not without penalty exceed:

> Upper and lower battens: $0 \cdot 10E + 1$ ft.
> Intermediate battens: $0 \cdot 12E + 1$ ft.

In the case of any excess length, the whole of the top batten excess plus one-sixth of the total excess length of the remaining battens shall be multiplied by P/E and added to P in computing PC.

.3 In the event of the number of battens being in excess of those allowed, the total length of the longest excess intermediate battens shall be multiplied by P/E and added to P in computing PC of jib headed sails.

.4 For gaff sails, one-sixth of the total excess of all battens shall be added to H in computing HC. In the case of additional batten or battens, the whole excess shall be added to HC.

.5 The rules for mainsail batten penalties above are applicable also to mizzens and foresails of schooners by substitution of the equivalent dimensions for those sails.

849. *Determination of RSAM.* RSAM shall be the rated sail area of the mainsail determined by the appropriate formula:

.1 For jib-headed mainsail:

$$RSAM = 0.35 \, (EC \times PC) + 0.2EC \, (PC - 2E).$$

The quantity $0.2EC \, (PC - 2E)$ shall be discarded if negative.

.2 For gaff-headed mainsail:

$$RSAM = 0.35 \, (HC \times EC) + 0.35G \, \sqrt{HC^2 + EC^2} + 0.2EC \, (HC - 2E) + 0.6MSAT.$$

The quantity $0.2EC \, (HC - 2E)$ shall be discarded if negative.

850. *Minimum Rated Sail Area of Mainsail.* A yacht must be rated with a mainsail. If RSAM calculated as above is less than $0.094 \, (IC)^2$, RSAM shall be taken as $0.094 \, (IC)^2$. For schooners, the minimum RSAM is $0.094 \, (IS + BADX)^2$.

Limitations of Mainsails

851. *Mainsails*

.1 *Loose-footed Mainsails.* These are permitted only when they are the regular mainsail normally used for the boat in question. Under these conditions, when a loose-footed mainsail is used, it is not permissible to carry on board a second mainsail that is not loose-footed, nor is it permissible to shift back and forth between a loose-footed and a secured foot mainsail for various races; rather the selection must be made regarding mainsail type at the time the measurement certificate is issued. A loose-footed mainsail shall only be sheeted from a single clew.

.2 *Light-weight Mainsails.* These are not permitted to be carried on board with the expectation of improved performance, as for varying weather conditions or points of sailing, but rather a second mainsail can only be carried on board as a bona fide spare for emergency replacement.

.3 *Storm Trysails.* These, as distinguished from loose-footed mainsails, must be materially smaller than a normal close reefed mainsail and of a strength consistent with their intended purpose, viz. use in extremely severe weather.

Mizzen (Yawl and Ketch) including Mizzen Staysails and Spinnaker-type Mizzen Staysails

852. *Foot of Mizzen*

.1 *Foot of Mizzen* (EY). EY is the measured length of the foot of the mizzen sail. The method by which this is measured shall follow that used for the foot of the mainsail.

.2 *Sheeting Limits* (BALY). BALY is the distance from the outer measurement point of EY to any bale on the mizzen boom provided for the lead of any mizzen staysail sheet.

.3 *Determination of EYC*. EYC is the corrected length of the foot of the mizzen sail. EYC is obtained by adding any amount by which BALY exceeds 0·50 ft. to the greater of EY or

$$\frac{0\cdot85E}{P} \times PY.$$

Jib Headed Mizzen

853. *Mizzen Hoist* (PY). PY is the measured length of the hoist of a jib headed mizzen sail. The method by which this is measured shall follow that used for the hoist of the mainsail (see 837).

854. *Boom Above Deck* (BADY). BADY shall be the distance between the low point used in the determination of PY, and the main deck at the mast. This shall not without penalty be taken as more than 0·05PY + 4·0 ft. Any excess shall be included in PYC.

855. *Mizzen Headboard* (HBY). HBY shall be the maximum fore and aft dimension from the luff of the mizzen, projected if necessary, to the extreme aft edge of the leech measured across the widest part of the headboard.

856. *Batten Leech Penalty* (BLPY). BLPY shall be the distance, measured along the leech of the mizzen sail, from the lower outer corner of the headboard to the centre line of the top batten pocket.

857. *Mizzen Boom Depth* (BDY). BDY shall be the maximum depth of the mizzen boom.

858. *Height of Mizzen Mast* (IY). IY is the height measured along the foreside of the mizzen mast from the deck as defined in 806.1 to the higher of:

      A. The centre of the highest eyebolt or eye used for a mizzen staysail; or
      B. The intersection of the foreside of the mast with the highest strop used for the halyard of a mizzen staysail.

Gaff Mizzen

859. *Determination of HY*. HY is the measured length of the hoist of a gaff mizzen sail. The method by which this is determined shall follow that used for a gaff mainsail (paragraph 842). BADY shall not without penalty be taken as more than 0·05 (HY + 0·6GY) + 4·0 ft. above deck (see 806.1). Any excess shall be included in HYC.

860. *Determination of GY*. GY is the measured length of the mizzen sail along the gaff from the mast to the furthest point of extension determined as in the case of the main boom covered in paragraph 836.1.

861. *Mizzen Batten Lengths* (BY1), (BY2), (BY3), (BY4), (BY5)

.1 BY1 shall be the maximum length of the top batten.

.2 BY2 shall be the maximum length of the bottom batten.

.3 BY3 and BY4 shall be the lengths of the two shortest intermediate battens.

.4 BY5 shall be the sum of the lengths of the fifth and subsequent battens in the mizzen sail.

.5 The number of battens in any mizzen shall without penalty be limited to four.

Mizzen Formulae

862. *Determination of PYC.* PYC is the corrected length of the hoist of the jib headed mizzen sail, determined by increasing PY by any mizzen penalties. Mizzen penalties will be calculated by the same rules as the mainsail penalties (see 846 and 848).

863. *Determination of HYC.* HYC is the corrected length of the hoist of a gaff mizzen sails, determined by increasing HY by any of the following penalties:

> Boom depth penalty, see 846.4.
> Boom above deck penalty, see 854.
> Batten penalty, see 848.

864. *Determination of RSAY.* RSAY shall be the rated sail areas of the mizzen sail determined by the appropriate formula providing simple triangular area:

.1 For jib-headed mizzens:

$$RSAY = \frac{EYC \times PYC}{2}$$

.2 For gaff-headed mizzens:

$$RSAY = 0\cdot5 \ (HYC \times EYC) + 0\cdot5 GY \ \sqrt{HYC^2 + EYC^2}$$

Mizzen Staysail

865. *Distance between Masts* (EB). EB is the distance at deck level between the after side of the mainmast or fair projection of the base of the track to the foreside of the mizzen mast.

866. *Mizzen Staysail Foot* (YSF). YSF is the distance measured along the edge of the foot of the mizzen staysail from tack to clew. For measurement purposes, the foot shall be taken as the shortest side.

867. *Mizzen Staysail Depth* (YSD). YSD is the shortest distance that can be measured across the mizzen staysail from head to foot. For measurement purposes the head shall be taken as the junction of the two longest sides.

868. *Mizzen Staysail Midgirth* (YSMG). YSMG is the distance measured on the surface of the sail between the midpoints of the two longest sides.

869. *Determination of RSAK.* RSAK shall be the mizzen staysail rated area determined by the formula:

$$RSAK = YSD \times \left(\frac{YSF + YSMG}{3}\right) \times 0.30\,\frac{EB}{E}$$

870. *Determination of YSAC.* YSAC shall be the combined area of the mizzen and mizzen staysail and shall be the larger of RSAY or RSAK.

This YSAC and RSAM shall be further combined to become RSAC (see 887).

Sheeting of Mizzen Staysails

871. *Mizzen Staysail on Yawl or Ketch*
.1 *Sheet Leads.* Mizzen staysails may be sheeted to the rail or hull, and to the mizzen boom within the measurement limits (whether or not the mizzen is set) but they may not be sheeted to any other spar or outrigger.
.2 Mizzen staysails must be three-cornered (head, tack and clew). The tack or tack pennant must be secured abaft the point of intersection of the afterside of the mainmast with the main deck and also must be secured directly to and no higher than the rail cap, deck or cabin top (includes dog house top).
.3 There are no restrictions on the number of mizzen staysails on board but not more than one may be set at the same time.
.4 No mizzen staysail may be carried on a yawl or ketch whose mizzen is set on a permanent backstay in lieu of a mizzen mast.

Schooners and Staysail Ketches

872. *Classification of Rigs.* Under this section rigs shall be classified under one of three categories:

.1 *Foresail Schooners.* These comprise schooners that carry only a jib-headed or gaff foresail between the masts. A gaff foresail may also carry a gaff topsail.
.2 *Staysail Schooners.* These comprise schooners carrying any other variety of sails between the masts.
.3 *Staysail Ketches.* These are ketches or yawls that carry sails other than a jib-headed or gaff mainsail, with or without a gaff topsail, plus mizzen staysails between the masts. These shall be rated in all respects as staysail schooners irrespective of the relative height of the masts.

Foresail Schooner Measurements

873. The foresail of a foresail schooner shall be subject to the same restrictions, and be measured in the same manner, as the mainsail of a sloop using the symbols listed below:

.1 Foot of Foresail (EF).
.2 Sheeting Limit (BALF).
.3 Corrected Length of Foot (EFC).

Jib-headed Foresail

.4 Hoist (PSF) (PSFC shall be the corrected value).

.5 Boom above Deck (BADS).

.6 Headboard (HBF).

.7 Batten Leach Penalty (BLPS).

.8 Boom Depth (BDF).

Gaff Foresail

.9 Hoist (HF) (HFC shall be the corrected value).

.10 Gaff (GF).

.11 Fore Topsail Area (MSATF).

Batten Lengths

.12 Batten Lengths (BS1 to BS5).

Foresail Schooner Formulae

874. *Determination of RSAG.* RSAG shall be the rated sail area of the foresail of a schooner determined by the appropriate formula:

.1 *For Jib-headed Foresail*

$$RSAG = 0.35 \, (EFC \times PSFC) + 0.2EFC \, (PSFC - 2EF)$$

The quantity $0.2EFC \, (PSFC - 2EF)$ shall be discarded if negative.

.2 *For Gaff Foresails*

$$RSAG = 0.35 \, (HFC \times EFC) + 0.35GF \, \sqrt{HFC^2 + EFC^2} + 0.6MSATF + 0.2EFC \, (HFC - 2EF)$$

The quantity $0.2EFC \, (HFC - 2EF)$ shall be discarded if negative.

RSAG shall not be taken as less than $0.094 \, (IC^2)$.

Schooner and Staysail Ketch
Area between Masts Measurements

875. *Distance between Masts* (EB). EB shall be the horizontal distance at deck level from the afterside of the foremast to the foreside of the mainmast.

876. *Sail Overlap* (OF). OF shall be the horizontal distance of the maximum overlap abaft the foreside of the mainmast of the clew of any sail set between the masts. It shall be measured as if the sail were trimmed flat along a parallel to the centre line of the yacht.

877. *Foresail Foot Height above Deck* (BADS). BADS shall be the distance above the main deck at the foremast (806) of the lowest level of the foot of any sail set between the masts. Its upper end shall be marked by the upper edge of a painted measurement band on the foremast.

878. *Height of Foremast Hoist* (PSF). PSF shall be the distance measured along the afterside of the foremast used in the determination of area between the masts.

.1 The upper measurement point shall be the higher of the following, used for sails aft of the mast:

    A. The top of the highest sheave in the mast.

    B. The highest eyebolt (centre of eye) or pennant of a halyard block.

.2 The lower measurement point shall be the upper limit of BADS.

879. *Foresail Foot Height* (BADX). BADX shall be the distance above the main deck at the mainmast of the lowest level of any sail set between the masts. Its upper limit shall be at the same height as the upper limit of BADS.

880. *Mainmast Height of Hoist* (IS). IS shall be the distance measured along the fore-side of the mainmast used in the determination of area between the masts.

.1 The upper measurement point shall be the higher of the following used for sails forward of the mast:

    A. The top of the highest sheave in the mast.

    B. The highest eyebolt (centre of eye) or pennant of a halyard block.

.2 The lower point of measurement shall be the upper limit of BADX.

Area between Masts Formulae

881. *Determination of EBC.* EBC shall be the corrected distance between the masts determined from the formula:

$$EBC = EB + 0.5OF$$

882. *Determination of RSAB.* RSAB shall be the rated sail area of sails set between the masts in schooners or staysail ketches determined from the formula:

$$RSAB = 0.35EBC \ (PSF + IS)$$
RSAB shall not be taken as less than $0.094 \ (IC^2)$.

883. The mainsail of any schooner or staysail ketch shall be the sail set abaft the after mast. It shall be measured in all respects as the mainsail of a sloop to determine RSAM except that for schooners and staysail ketches rated using RSAB the minimum rated sail area of the mainsail shall not be taken as less than $0.094 \ (IS + BADX)^2$.

Limitations on Sails between the Masts

884. A foresail schooner rated on RSAG shall set no sails between the masts other than the foresail for which she was measured.

885. In a schooner or a staysail ketch rated on RSAB the following limitations shall apply to all sails set between the masts:

.1 Sails shall be sheeted from only one point on the sail and double clewed sails are not permitted.

.2 Loose-footed sails set between the masts may be sheeted to any part of the rail or deck or to the main boom, but to no other spar or outrigger.

.3 When the mainsail is not set the MSA of any sail set between the masts shall not exceed the total of the measured areas of the mainsail and the area between the masts.

.4 No part of any sail set between the masts shall extend below the level of the upper limits of BADX and BADS.

.5 No sail set between the masts shall be tacked forward of the foremast nor shall it extend abaft the mainmast unless it has been measured to determine OF.

.6 Where sails are set on booms between the mast such booms must be permanent and self tacking.

Rating of Unusual Sails

886. *Rules for rating unusual sails not dealt with elsewhere in this Rule are given below.*

.1 The rated area of a quadrilateral mainsail (other than a gaff sail) or other unusual mainsail shall be determined from the formula:

$$RSAM = 0.75MSA + 0.2EC\,(PC - 2E)$$

.2 Mainsails, mizzens or foresails as in 873 which are set without booms shall be measured for EC, EYC or EFC. The measurement shall be the maximum measurement (at right angles to the luff) of the sail when new. The Measurer shall sign the sail and mark the dimensions.

.3 Main backstay sails (Mules) shall have 50% of their MSA, as determined by measurement of the sail when new, added to the mainsail area RSAM, corrected if necessary for minimum size under 850, to arrive at the final RSAM for the rig.

.4 Gaff Mainsails. If the gaff peaks higher than 70 degrees above the horizontal, mainsail RSA shall be calculated as for a jib-headed mainsail using the formula $P = H + G$.

Combined and Total Sail Areas

887. *Determination of RSAC.* RSAC shall be the combined rated sail area of all sails set abaft the masts in any yacht having two masts. RSAC shall be determined from the formula below:

.1 Yawl or ketch having mainsail and mizzen staysail:

$$RSAC = RSAM + \frac{YSAC^2}{RSAM + YSAC}$$

.2 Foresail schooner:

$$RSAC = RSAM + \frac{RSAG^2}{RSAM + RSAG}$$

.3 Schooner or staysail ketch:

$$RSAC = RSAM + \frac{RSAB^2}{RSAM + RSAB}$$

888. *Determination of Sail Area Total Correction* (SATC)
.1 For single-masted yachts:

$$SATC = 0 \cdot 1 \ (RSAF - 1 \cdot 43RSAM)$$

.2 For two-masted yachts:

$$SATC = 0 \cdot 1 \ (RSAF - 1 \cdot 43RSAC)$$

889. *Determination of Total Rated Sail Area* (RSAT)
.1 For single-masted yachts:

$$RSAT = RSAF + RSAM + SATC$$

.2 For two-masted yachts:

$$RSAT = RSAF + RSAC + SATC$$

890. *Determination of Rated Sail Area Low Limit* (RSAL)
.1 For yawls and ketches rated for YSAC:

$$RSAL = 0 \cdot 8 \left(RSAY + \frac{(YSMG + YSF) \times YSD}{3 \cdot 0} \right)$$

.2 For yachts rated for RSAB or RSAG:

$$RSAL = RSAM + 0 \cdot 4IS \ (EB + OF)$$

.3 For single masted yachts RSAL = RSAT.

891. *Determination of Square Root of Sail Area* ($\sqrt{S}$)
$\sqrt{S}$ shall be the square root of whichever is the greater of RSAT, SPIN or RSAL.

Part IX—Metric Equivalents

901. All measurements except dimensions of sails shall be in metres to three places of decimals. Weights shall be in kilograms to the nearest half unit. Constants and formulae tabulated below shall be used in place of those in the body of the rule when metric measurement is used.

Paragraph

103.2   For 7·0 ft., use 2·133 m.

337   Formula for D: For $\dfrac{L + 10}{30}$ use $\dfrac{L + 3 \cdot 048}{30}$

402   Formula for FB: For 1·20 ft., use 0·366 m.

508   Formula for DB: For 2·0 ft., use 0·610 m.

509   Formula for DSPL: For 64·0, use 1025·8

605   Formula for EMF: Use $EMF = \dfrac{0 \cdot 006243\,EM}{L^2 \times B \times D}$

710   Formula for TR: Use $TR = 16 \cdot 018 \left(\dfrac{0 \cdot 97L \times (BWL)^3}{RMC} \right)$

Sail Areas

836.3	For 0·50 ft., use 0·152 m.	BAL, EC
838	For 4·0 ft., use 1·219 m.	BAD, PC
842	For 4·0 ft., use 1·219 m.	BAD, HC
852.3	For 0·50 ft., use 0·152 m.	BALY, EYC
854	For 4·0 ft., use 1·219 m.	BADY, PYC
859	For 4·0 ft., use 1·219 m.	BADY, HYC
846.1	For 4·0 ft., use 1·219 m.	PC
846.3	For 0·5 ft., use 0·152 m.	HB
848.2	For 0·10E + 1 ft., use 0·10E + 0·305 m.	Battens
	For 0·12E + 1 ft., use 0·12E + 0·305 m.	Battens

Part X—Standard Hull Dimensions

1001. Where a number of yachts of the same class are built in GRP using the same moulds it is desirable that their hull measurements are standardized, in the interest of uniformity and economy in measurement.

1002. The Administrative rules for standardization of hull dimensions are given below.

   .1 The first yachts of a class shall be measured completely in the normal manner.

   .2 When a number of yachts, between four and ten, have been measured and a consistency of measurement has been indicated from the figures of at least two measurers, the class should be standardized on a national standard. This National Standard shall only be used for measurement of yachts owned in the country of its adoption.

   .3 As soon as a National Standard has been produced details of the standard and the data on which it was produced shall be sent to the Chief Measurer to the O.R.C.

   .4 On receipt of a National Standard the Chief Measurer shall call for data on yachts of the class measured in other countries and when he is satisfied with the consistency of the measurements he shall combine the data and issue an O.R.C. International Standard.

   .5 When a standard has been issued all yachts built to the class shall be re-rated on the standard hull dimensions.

   .6 It is of vital importance that a standard applies only to yachts of a class built by the same hull moulder off the same mould. The standards shall therefore be referred to by their official Standard Number and not by builders class names. Careful policing by National Measurement Authorities is necessary to ensure that any modification to the production hulls that modify the standard hull dimensions are detected, and that a fresh standard is produced for these yachts.

1003. *Technical Rules for Production of Hull Standards*

.1 In the interest of uniformity it is necessary that the hull standards be produced by a computer program that is the same through the world. The program will be made available to National Authorities by the Chief Measurer upon request.

.2 The following dimensions shall be standardized:

> A. LBG, FGO, AGO. (Changes in the stemhead fitting or in the stern cut-off could affect LOA, FGO, AGO and Y on a particular yacht. Where these changes are found they shall be modified for the yacht but the remainder of the standard figures shall be used.)
>
> B. BA, BAI, VHA, VHAI, BHA, BHAI, GSDA, BF, BFI, GSDF, B, BMAX, SBMAX.
>
> C. FA, FAI, FMD, OMD, CMD, MD, FFD, FD, FFI, FF.
>
> D. DM, PD at the flotation of the standard sheer line, SDM, SPD. (The standard detail shall include PDT and FPD (see 325) so that these figures may be altered for a particular yacht having a non-standard installation while retaining the remainder of the standard.)

1004. *Measurement of Yachts to Standard Hull Dimensions*

The measurement of yachts to which a hull standard applies shall be conducted as below:

.1 Check that LOA agrees with standard figure. If it does locate FGS and AGS from FGO, AGO. If it does not, locate FGS and AGS from fore or aft end of LOA. Check positions by reference to BF and BA and modify FGO, AGO, Y, SDM, SPD, SBMAX as necessary.

.2 Check that propeller installation is standard and measure PDT, PRD, PBW, and strut and shaft or aperture dimensions as applicable.

.3 Measure all sail area dimensions.

.4 Carry out inclining test with the yacht in measurement trim (see 202.2).

.5 Measure BWL at BMAX station or at 0·25BMAX forward and aft as required by the hull standard.

.6 Measure FFM and FAM (see 329).

.7 Measure FBI and FS (for adjustment of I, SPH and BAD).

1005. *Calculation of Rating for Standard Yachts and Yachts previously measured*

.1 The computer program shall make adjustments to the Standard Freeboards, PD, and DM of Standard yachts (or the original Freeboards, PD, and DM of yachts previously measured) as detailed below:

.2 All the Standard Freeboards shall be entered on the Computer Input Sheet, and also the Standard or original DM and PD. The figure for PD shall be modified by its difference from Standard if the installation is not as Standard. (In the formulae in .3 these dimensions are denoted by the suffix "S".)

.3 The Standard (or original) freeboards shall be modified in the computer to Measurement Freeboards by the formulae:

$$SINK = FFS - FFM$$
$$TRIM = FAM - (FAS - SINK)$$
$$FF = FFS - SINK$$
$$FFI = FFIS - SINK + TRIM \frac{(GSDF)}{LBG}$$
$$FFD = FFDS - SINK + 0 \cdot 25 \; TRIM$$
$$FMD = FMDS - SINK + 0 \cdot 5 \; TRIM$$
$$FAI = FAIS - SINK + TRIM \frac{(LBG - GSDA)}{LBG}$$
$$FA = FAS - SINK + TRIM$$
$$DM = SINK + DMS - TRIM \frac{(SDM - FGO)}{LBG}$$
$$PD = SINK + PDS - TRIM \frac{(SPD - FGO)}{LBG}$$

.4 The corrected figures from the formulae in .3 above shall be output on page 1 of the Rating Certificate. The input figures (Standard or original) shall be printed on page 2 of the Certificate so that the input can be checked.

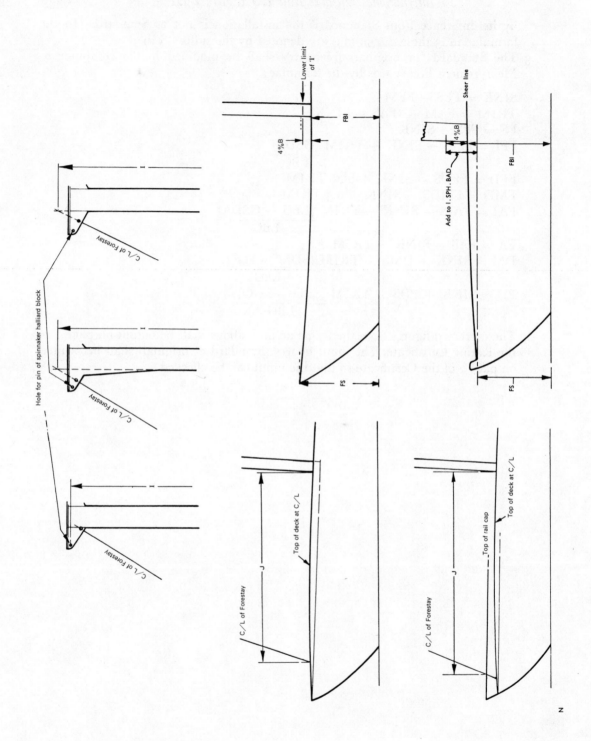

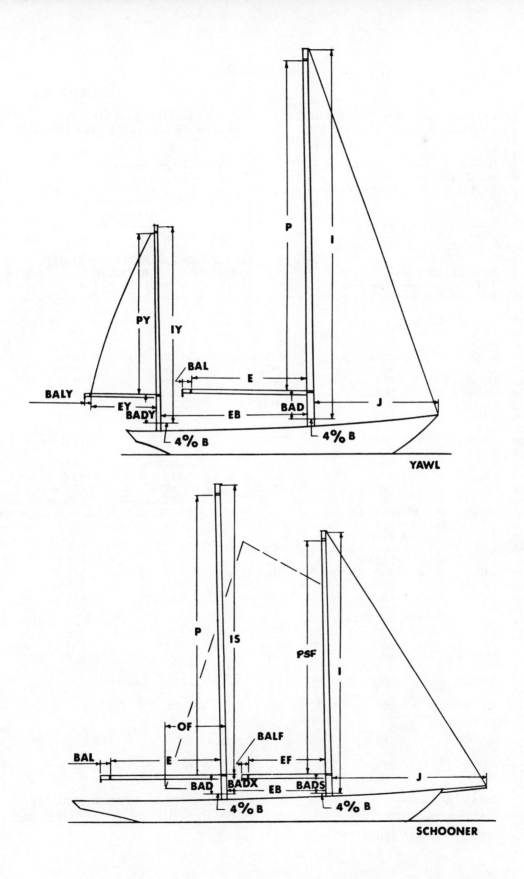

APPENDIX 1

```
 1  INTERNATIONAL OFFSHORE RULE        RATING CERTIFICATE NO...................
 2  MARK III AMEND TO MAY 73           MEASUREMENTS IN METRES AND KGS
 3
 4                                     x   x   x   x   x   x   x   x   x   x
 5  CLASS        ————————              x     YACHT ————————————           x
 6  DESIGNER ————————                  x     SAIL NO. ————————            x
 7  BUILDER  ———————— YEAR ————————    x                                  x
 8                                     x     OWNER ————————               x
 9                                     x                                  x
10  RIG      ————————                  x           ————————————————       x
11  KEEL     ————————                  x           ————————————————       x
12           ————————                  x   x   x   x   x   x   x   x   x   x
13                                     LOCATIONS FROM STEM/WEIGHT
14  PROPELLER                          ANCHORS        BALLAST        RAFTS
15  TYPE        ————————               1 ——— / ———    1 ——— / ———    1
16  INSTALLED   ————————————           2 ——— / ———    2 ——— / ———    2
17              ————————————           3 ——— / ———    3 ——— / ———    3
18  — — —HULL — — — — — — — — —
```

```
19  LOA    ———  BMAX  ———   FF  ————      AW  ————   APD
20  FGO         B           FFI           BW         BPD
21  AGO         BWL         FFD           CW         CPD
22  LBG         BF          FMD           DW         DPD
23  GSDA        BFI         FAI           AWD        PL
24  GSDF        BAI         FA            BWD        SBMAX
25  FD          BA          VHAI          CWD        SPD
26  CMD         GD          VHA           DWD        SDM
27  MD          Y           BHAI          MAW1       MAW2
28  OMD         DM          BHA           MACG1      MACG2
28.5 GDFI
29  EW          EWD         PD            PRD        PBW
30  ESL         ESC         ST1           ST2        ST3
31  CD    ———   WCBA  ———   WCBB          CBDA       CBDB
32                                        CBLDA ———  CBLDB ———
33  — — — FORETRIANGLE — — — — — — — MAINSAIL — — —
34  I      ———  SPL   ———   P   ———       HB   ———   PC
35  J           SPH         E             BL1        IC
36  LPG         SL          BAD           BL2        JC
37  LPIS        SMW         BAL           BL3        EC
38  FSP         SMG         BD            BL4        MX SL
39  FS          SF                        BL5        MXSMW
40  FBI   ———   HBS   ———                 BLP  ———   MX LP ———
41
42  — — — MIZZEN — — — — — —
43  IY     ———  PY    ———   BY1 ———       HBY        PYC
44  EB          EY          BY2 ———       BLPY       EYC
45  YSD         BADY        BY3           S1
46  YSF         BALY        BY4           S2
47  YSMG  ———   BDY   ———   BY5 ———       S3   ———
48
49  x   x   x   x   x   x   x   x   x   x   x   x   x   x   x   x   x   x
50
51  L     ———   S     ———         x   x   x   x   x   x   x   x   x   x
52  B           DC                x   RATING ———— FEET                x
53  D           FC                x   x   x   x   x   x   x   x   x   x
54  GCF         MR                x   RATING ———— METRES              x
55  EPF         R     ———         x   x   x   x   x   x   x   x   x   x
56  MAF   ————
57  MEASURER  ————————            I CERTIFY THAT I UNDERSTAND MY
58  MEASURED ———— EXPIRES ————    RESPONSIBILITIES AS COVERED IN THE
59                                IOR RULE:
60  NATL'    AUTHORITY            OWNER
```

APPENDIX I. Alternative lines for page 1 of the Rating Certificate.

line	**If measurements in feet and lbs.**				
2	MARK III AMEND TO MAY 73		MEASUREMENTS IN FEET AND LBS		
	If standard hull				
3			STANDARD HULL NO.———————		
	If no engine and propeller				
29 & 30	DELETE TEXT.				
	If propeller in aperture				
30	APH	APB	APT		
	If no centreboard, nor drop keel				
31 & 32	DELETE TEXT				
	If gaff-headed mainsail				
34	I	SPL	H	G	HC
	If yacht is single-masted				
42 thru 48	DELETE TEXT				
	If gaff-headed mizzen				
43	IY	HY	BY1	GY	HYC
	If schooner with jib-headed foresail				
42	— — —SCHOONER FORESAIL — — — — — — — — — — — —				
43	IS	PSF	BS1	HBF	PSFC
44	EB	EF	BS2	BLPS	EBC
45	OF	BADS	BS3	S1	
46	EBC	BALF	BS4	S2	
47	BADX	BDF	BS5	S3	
	If schooner with gaff-headed foresail				
42	— — —SCHOONER FORESAIL — — — — — — — — — — — —				
43	IS	HF	BS1	GF	HFC
44	EB	EF	BS2		EBC
45	OF	BADS	BS3	S1	
46	EBC	BALF	BS4	S2	
47	BADX	BDF	BS5	S3	

APPENDIX II. Page 2 of the Rating Certificate. The layout of page 2 of the Rating Certificate shall be at the option of the National Authority issuing the Certificate, but shall contain the information listed below. It may in addition contain other information which they wish to record.

Hull Factors

FOC	AOCP	AOCG	AOC	AOCC
FDI	CMDI	MDI	OMDI	MDIA
FB	FM	DB	DSPL	CBP
DK	RD	DD	EMF	PS
PF	DF	RM	RMC	TR
L	EPF	BSC	BBS	
RSBS1	RSBS2	RSBS3	RSBS4	RSBS5
ARM	BRM	CRM	DRM	RSBS6

If the hull freeboards on page 1 are computer calculated the original input data below shall be included.

FF	FFI	FFD	FMD	FAI
FA	PD	DM		

Foretriangle Factors
RSAF, SL Penalty, SPH Penalty, HBS Penalty

Mainsail Factors
RSAM   RSAM Minimum
HB Penalty, BLP Penalty, Batten Penalty
BD Penalty, BAD Penalty, I over P Penalty

Sail Area Factors
RSAC   SATC   SPIN   RSAT   RSAL

Mizzen Factors
RSAY   RSAK   YSAC
HBY Penalty, BLPY Penalty, Batten Penalty
BDY Penalty, BADY Penalty, IY over PY Penalty

Schooner Foresail Factors
RSAB or RSAG
HBF Penalty, BLPS Penalty, Batten Penalty
BADS Penalty, BDF Penalty, I over PSF Penalty

APPENDIX TEN

BY COMMANDER SIR DAVID MACKWORTH, Bt., R.N.

Working the I.O.R. Rule with a Mini-computer

In outline the I.O.R. Mk. III rule:

$$MR = 0{\cdot}13 \times \frac{L\sqrt{S}}{\sqrt{B \times D}} + 0{\cdot}25L + 0{\cdot}2\sqrt{S} + DC + FC$$

is the same as the old R.O.R.C. rule:

$$MR = 0{\cdot}15 \times \frac{L\sqrt{S}}{\sqrt{B \times D}} + 0{\cdot}2L + 0{\cdot}2\sqrt{S}$$

but it has been extended and modified in detail in an attempt to overcome the defects which had become apparent in the R.O.R.C. rule and to benefit from the best features of the C.C.A. rule.

This extension and modification comprises, *inter alia*, a number of additional hull measurements and a more complicated set of formulae within the framework of the basic rule. For example the formula for the After Overhang Component (AOC) which determines the after end of "L", the effective sailing length, formerly in the R.O.R.C. rule:

$$GSDA\left[\frac{FA - 0{\cdot}25B}{0{\cdot}0625B + ASFD}\right]$$

has been further developed and amplified in the I.O.R. Mk. III rule to take into account both the depth and beam of the hull at the measurement station, and becomes the awe-inspiring formula:

$$0{\cdot}5\left[\frac{GSDA\,(FA - VHA - 0{\cdot}018LBGC)}{VHAI - VHA + FA - FAI} + \frac{GSDA\,(FA - 0{\cdot}375B - 0{\cdot}5GD + 0{\cdot}2BA)}{0{\cdot}0625B + FA - FAI - 0{\cdot}2BAI + 0{\cdot}2BA}\right]$$

This complication has made the computations required to arrive at a yacht's rating from the measured parameters so lengthy, and complex in detail, that they cannot be tackled readily with logarithm tables or a desk calculator, and the chance of error for anyone other than a trained computer, or one who has reason to carry out these calculations constantly, is unacceptably high. In addition they are extremely time consuming; a situation which presents a particular difficulty to the naval architect designing to the I.O.R. rule.

Granted that, in an ideal world, the naval architect has only to design a "good" yacht with an "efficient" sail plan and he can rely on the rule to rate the yacht fairly; but let him tell that to the eventual owner, particularly if the rating measures out six inches higher than an apparently faster rival!

In the real world the designer must work with one eye on the rule, and this means calculating and recalculating the rating to check the effect of every design change. Further, in the case of a fixed handicap "Ton" yacht he must take every precaution to ensure that when completed and actually measured the yacht is given the intended rating.

The rating authorities, the R.O.R.C. for Europe and the C.C.A. for America, have chosen the obvious solution and official ratings are now calculated on large general-purpose computers for which suitable programs have been written.

Unfortunately, this is not a great deal of help to the designer. Turn-round time for rating computations is a matter of days or weeks and this is unacceptable to the trial-and-error technique which is the designer's only practicable approach at the present time.

One solution to this problem lies in the use of one of the mini-computers, which have been developed to fill the gap between the desk calculator, which must be instructed directly to carry out each step in a computation and whose memory, or storage capacity, is limited to the quantities actually being worked upon, and the big computer costing hundreds of thousands of pounds and many orders more powerful than is necessary to perform the *relatively* simple calculations required for the I.O.R. rule.

The big snag to the big computer lies in the lengthy effective turn-round time and its inflexibility. One cannot keep such a machine on one's desk or even in the next room, ready to try out new ideas as they come along, and in general one must accept turn-round times of a week or more. Granted, there are technical ways round this problem with "on-line" working and "remote terminals", but these are a very long way from practicable economics for a yacht designer in this country or, it would seem, in the U.S.A.

Even accepting or overcoming, by some means, the turn-round delays, there remains the problem of inflexibility. Even if a designer were able to devote the time necessary to become an efficient big-computer programmer and write his own programs this is not a realistic solution.

The task of writing an I.O.R. Rule program for a big computer is far too lengthy and expensive in time, that is both the programmer's time and time spent on the computer in de-bugging the program and subjecting it to full tests.

The mini-computer, on the other hand, can quite literally sit on the designer's desk or drawing board, or perhaps beside it, and programming is simple enough to be undertaken by anyone with sufficient mathematics to design a yacht, and with no more instruction than the maker's handbook.

Both in the U.S.A. and in this country, one of the earliest, simplest and cheapest machines, the Olivetti 101, is being used for this purpose. There are several others equally suitable, but the Olivetti 101 is perfectly adequate to the task.

The writer has some experience with this mini-computer and the illustrations which follow have been worked on an Olivetti 101. It will therefore be convenient at this point to describe the practical side of computing an I.O.R. rating with this machine.

The first requirement is a set of instructions or program, which will tell the machine the arithmetical steps, the value of the various coefficients, and the several logical decisions in the proper sequence necessary to work out a rating. This must be prepared and checked against the rule with great care. The process is tedious, but once done, the care exercised is, in effect, stored with the program, which is itself stored on a simple magnetic card or series of cards. This same care will be re-exercised automatically by the machine every time the program is used.

In practical terms the rating is worked in two steps. The first step is to determine the value of $\sqrt{S}$, and to do this the relevant parameters (measurements) are set out in the following form, which shows a typical example:

I.O.R. Mark III

SAIL PLAN

Ref No
YACHT
Date
Run Nos

J	10·400			Min Mnsl		
SPL	11·200			RSAMC		
SMW	20·200			SATC		
JC				RSAT		
1·5JC				"S"		
LPG	16·800			Total area		
FSP	0·400			Root "S"		
LPIS	0·000			Hull factor{ "A" / "B" }		
I	29·600					
SPH	7·400			Rating		
LL						
SL	30·000					
IC						
SPIN						
Spin area						
RSAF						
Hdsl area						
E	9·000					
EC	9·000					
PC	26·700					
RSAM						
Mnsl area						

Hull factors

Rating is given by: A × Root "S" + B
Factors "A" and "B" are taken from the corresponding Hull computations

Areas

Spinnaker taken as: $\dfrac{SMW \times SL}{1 \cdot 2}$

Headsail taken as: $\dfrac{LPG \times \sqrt{J^2 + I^2}}{2}$

Mainsail taken as: $\dfrac{PC \times EC}{2}$

Total area taken as Mainsail plus Headsail

Figure of merit

The quantity $\dfrac{\text{Total area}}{\text{RSAT}}$ is calculated as a "figure of merit" for comparison purposes. Since Main and Headsail areas are given equal weight, it should be treated with discretion.

The computer is given its instructions, or program, by inserting the magnetic card into the machine. When this has been done, the parameters are entered in the sequence shown on the form via a set of numerical keys. As the parameters are entered and the various intermediate quantities listed on the form computed, they are printed out sequentially with the entered data on a paper roll, for transfer to the form which, when completed will look like this:

I.O.R. Mark III

SAIL PLAN

Ref. No
YACHT
Date
Run Nos

J	10·400			Min Mnsl	82·359040		
SPL	11·200			RSAMC	99·765000		
SMW	20·200			SATC	9·695820		
JC	11·222222			RSAT	349·082970		
1·5JC	16·833333			"S"	349·082970		
LPG	16·800			Total area	383·690541		
FSP	0·400			Root "S"	18·683762		
LPIS	0·000			Hull factor{"A"/"B"			
I	29·600			Rating			
SPH	7·400						
LL	30·073138						
SL	30·000						
IC	29·600000						
SPIN	340·862304						
Spin area	504·999990						
RSAF	239·622150						
Hdsl area	263·540541						
E	9·000						
EC	9·000						
PC	26·700						
RSAM	99·765000						
Mnsl area	120·150000						

Hull factors
Rating is given by: A × Root "S" + B
Factors "A" and "B" are taken from the corresponding Hull computations

Areas

Spinnaker taken as: $\dfrac{SMW \times SL}{1 \cdot 2}$

Headsail taken as: $\dfrac{LPG \times \sqrt{J^2 + I^2}}{2}$

Mainsail taken as: $\dfrac{PC \times EC}{2}$

Total area taken as Mainsail plus Headsail

Figure of merit

The quantity $\dfrac{\text{Total area}}{\text{RSAT}}$ is calculated as a "figure of merit" for comparison purposes. Since Main and Headsail areas are given equal weight, it should be treated with discretion.

It will be noted that the "print-out" contains rather more information than the Official R.O.R.C. Rating Certificate "print-out". This additional information is readily computed at the same time, or as a part of the rating calculation, and the quantities have been selected as being helpful to the designer in assessing his design in relation to the rating rule. With experience other useful quantities may suggest themselves.

The final computed figure, the value of $\sqrt{S}$, or more probably a series of values of $\sqrt{S}$ derived from different Sail Plan configurations, is entered on the Hull Measurement form together with the other Hull Measurements. The form is shown below with measurements entered:

I.O.R. Mark III Hull

Ref. No.
YACHT
Date
Run Nos.

VHA	1·680			FB			
VHAI	1·940			FM			
LBG	25·490			FC			
GD	0·420			DSPL			
GSDA	1·110			WCBA	0·000		
B	7·840			WCBB	0·000		
FA	2·280			CD	0·000		
FAI	2·280			DM	4·630		
BA	4·620			RD			
BAI	5·310			DC			
AOC				DB			
Y	1·080			Root S	18·683762		
AOCC				MR			
BF	1·660			PD	1·01		
BFI	2·570			PS	0·92		
FF	2·940			PF	0·85		
FFI	2·840			DF			
GSDF	1·080			EW	62·000		
FOC				EWD	4·15		
L				EMF			
FMD	2·610			EPF			
CMD	3·700			RMC	287·000		
MD	3·520			TR			
OMD	2·430			CGF			
BWL	7·120			MAF	1·000		
FFD	2·750			Rating			
FD	3·210			Hull factor {"A" / "B"}			
D							

and on completion of the computation:

I.O.R. Mark III Hull

Ref. No
YACHT
Date
Run Nos.

VHA	1·680			FB	2·577329		
VHAI	1·940			FM	2·676000		
LBG	25·490			FC	−0·014800		
GD	0·420			DSPL	3634·376128		
GSDA	1·110			WCBA	0·000		
B	7·840			WCBB	0·000		
FA	2·280			CD	0·000		
FAI	2·280			DM	4·630		
BA	4·620			RD	4·630000		
BAI	5·310			DC	−0·156997		
AOC	0·368229			DB	5·527897		
Y	1·080			Root S	18·683762		
AOCC	0·368229			MR	22·943092		
BF	1·660			PD	1·01		
BFI	2·570			PS	0·92		
FF	2·940			PF	0·85		
FFI	2·840			DF	0·013833		
GSDF	1·080			EW	62·000		
FOC	0·958091			EWD	4·15		
L	24·163680			EMF	0·002275		
FMD	2·610			EPF	0·983892		
CMD	3·700			RMC	287·000		
MD	3·520			TR	29·477652		
OMD	2·430			CGF	0·982746		
BWL	7·120			MAF	1·0000		
FFD	2·750			Rating	22·184019		
FD	3·210			Hull factor {"A" / "B"}	0·883605 / 5·674943		
D	2·469987						

Again, the print-out contains more intermediate quantities, of interest to the designer, than the R.O.R.C. print-out.

The foregoing straightforward calculation of ratings, and other intermediate and associated quantities, is clearly a useful service in itself. But such is the versatility of the mini-computer that it has been readily possible to write one or two auxiliary programs to deal with special points without the labour and risk of error inherent in hand computing.

One of these auxiliary programs computes the value of $\sqrt{S}$ required to give a fixed rating on a particular set of hull measurements. This is of great value when designing to a fixed rating.

Another auxiliary program examines the effect of changes of trim and flotation. These can be large and thus direction of operation is not always self evident.

Quite apart from this type of service to the designer, the use of a mini-computer facilitates the task of "interpreting" the Rule.

Perhaps the best example lies in the After Overhang Component (AOC), which plays such a major part in determining the theoretical sailing length "L". Under the R.O.R.C. rule the formula for AOC could be interpreted in terms of the geometric concept from which it was derived. Perhaps this may be possible in the case of the I.O.R. Mk III Rule, but such direct interpretation is beyond the wit of this writer. Inability to interpret the formula in such a manner makes it difficult to comprehend in advance the effect which changes in the configuration of a yacht's stern may have on her rating, by any process of visualisation. On the other hand, the designer can learn a good deal from the computer's facility to work and re-work the same computation, varying individual parameters or combinations of parameters in a controlled manner.

To illustrate this method, we may take two very different yachts of comparable size, *Quiver IV* designed to the R.O.R.C. Rule and *Bay Bea II* designed to the C.C.A. rule. The two portions of the Hull computer forms which are shown below have been made out from the Rating Certificates of these two yachts and cover the part of the computation employed to compute the value of AOC, the After Overhang Component. It will be seen that for each yacht the same set of parameters have been entered seven times in seven separate columns. The same, that is, except that in each of columns 2–7 one parameter or combination of parameters has been varied. Column 1 contains the Rating Certificate values. In columns 2 and 3, the two parameters concerned with the Beam at the After Girth Station, BA and BAI, have been first increased by 10 per cent and then reduced by 10 per cent from the Rating Certificate value. In columns 4 and 5, the same treatment has been applied to the Freeboards at the After Girth Stations, FA and FAI. Finally, in columns 6 and 7, the Rated Beam, B, has been varied in a similar manner plus and minus 10 per cent from the Rating Certificate value.

Hull Measurements

Form A

(Card 1 Key V)	(1)	(2)	(3)	(4)	(5)	(6)	(7)
VHA	2·61	2·61	2·61	2·61	2·61	2·61	2·61
VHAI	3·31	3·31	3·31	3·31	3·31	3·31	3·31
LBG	38·51	38·51	38·51	38·61	38·51	38·51	38·51
GD	0·00	0·00	0·00	0·00	0·00	0·00	0·00
GSDA	1·52	1·52	1·52	1·52	1·52	1·52	1·52
B	12·000	12·000	12·000	12·000	12·000	13·200	10·800
LBGC	38·510	38·510	38·510	38·510	38·510	38·510	38·510
FA	3·19	3·19	3·19	3·509	2·871	3·19	3·19
FAI	3·17	3·17	3·17	3·487	2·853	3·17	3·17
BA	6·46	7·106	5·814	6·46	6·46	6·46	6·46
BAI	7·11	7·821	6·399	7·11	7·11	7·11	7·11

(Card 2 Key W)							
Y	2·80	2·80	2·80	2·80	2·80	2·80	2·80
AOC	−0·316	−0·1289	−0·4963	0·4063	−1·0433	−0·8876	0·4066

(Card 3 Key Y)							
AOCC	−0·316	−0·1289	−0·4963	0·4063	−1·0433	−0·8876	0·4066
BF							
BFI							
FF							

Bay Bea II

Hull Measurements

Form A

(Card 1 Key V)	(1)	(2)	(3)	(4)	(5)	(6)	(7)
VHA	2·48	2·48	2·48	2·48	2·48	2·48	2·48
VHAI	2·95	2·95	2·95	2·95	2·95	2·95	2·95
LBG	42·85	42·85	42·85	42·85	42·85	42·85	42·85
GD	0·00	0·00	0·00	0·00	0·00	0·00	0·00
GSDA	1·75	1·75	1·75	1·75	1·75	1·75	1·75
B	11·900	11·900	11·900	11·900	11·900	13·090	10·710
LBGC	42·850	42·850	42·850	42·850	42·850	42·850	42·850
FA	3·71	3·71	3·71	4·081	3·399	3·71	3·71
FAI	3·68	3·68	3·68	4·048	3·312	3·68	3·68
BA	5·90	6·49	5·31	5·90	5·90	5·90	5·90
BAI	6·84	7·524	6·156	6·84	6·84	6·84	6·84

(Card 2 Key W)							
Y	2·77	2·77	2·77	2·77	2·77	2·77	2·77
AOC	1·0484	1·2925	0·8198	2·2209	−0·1368	0·2524	2·0763

(Card 3 Key Y)							
AOCC	1·0484	1·2925	0·8198	2·1875	−0·1368	0·2524	2·0763
BF							
BFI							
FF							

Only space prevents this being applied to the other parameters, but the example should be sufficient to make the method clear. The same treatment has been applied to both yachts with their widely differing computed values of AOC and the results are illustrated graphically below.

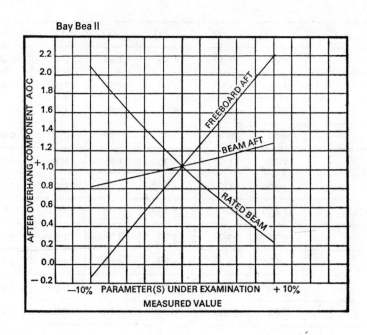

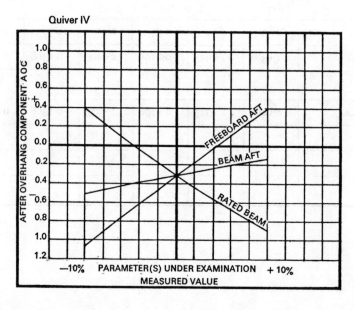

Apart from demonstrating very clearly the direct effect of the changes, an effect which can reasonably be treated as linear over this range and reduced proportionately for smaller change, it also demonstrates that *Bay Bea II*, with a much larger and more advantageous value of AOC, is also much more sensitive to changes in all the parameters examined. AOCC has been included in the computation and in the case of *Bay Bea II* demonstrates the "cut-off" when it reaches the limiting high value of 2·1875 equal to 1·25 GSDA.

When it comes to sail plans the formulae are less complicated, with a smaller number of parameters. This makes it possible by slight rearrangement of the equations to demonstrate the more important relationships graphically. For instance, suppose, instead of considering simply the Rated Area of the Fore Triangle (RSAF), we examine the ratio of the actual area of the largest genoa which, for convenience, we will call G. Area and RSAF, in the form G. Area/RSAF; and if instead of IC, JC and LPG we enter the aspect ratio of the Fore Triangle, IC/JC, and the Overlap Ratio, LPG/JC. It now becomes a simple matter to derive an equation linking these parameters and we can readily set the computer to work to calculate a sufficient number of points to form the set of curves which are shown in the next diagram. I would mention in passing that because the actual calculation is simple and the number of parameters small it was possible to set the computer to work in what one might call an auto-repetitive mode, varying one parameter a prescribed amount at the end of each computation and then repeating the process automatically This is a great convenience when plotting curves.

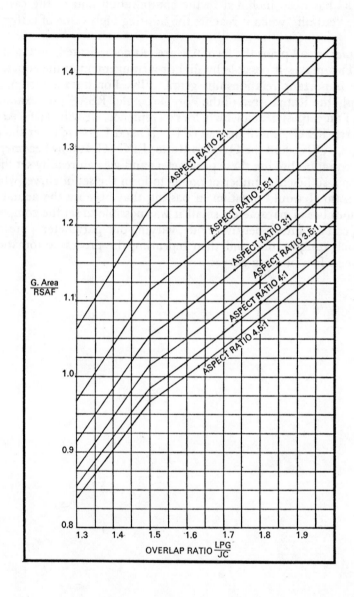

Values of G. Area/RSAF can be read off on the left hand vertical scale against values of Overlap Ratio, LPG/JC, on the bottom scale for a range of values of Aspect Ratio IC/JC. The sharp kink, or break point, in the curves represents the point where LPG becomes in effect fixed at 1·5JC. Looking at these curves must stimulate the thought that fixed break points such as this could, perhaps with advantage, be replaced by slightly modified formulae giving almost the same effect but with a continuous smooth curve and thereby avoiding the frequent tendency for every designer to go for break point.

A similar graph connecting the ratio Mainsail Area/RSAM and the Mainsail Aspect Ratio, PC/EC, is equally readily computed and is reproduced below:

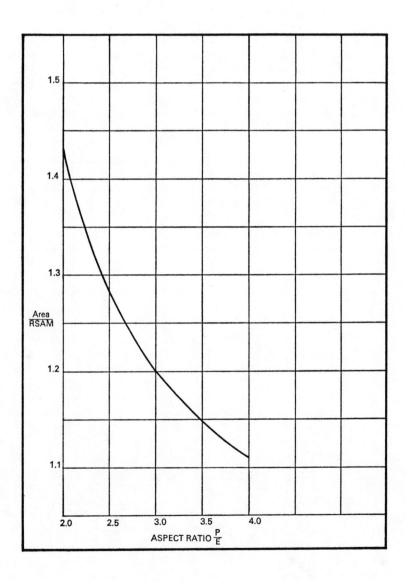

Clearly the foregoing are no more than examples of one approach to the study of the I.O.R. Mk III rule; an approach based on the use of a mini-computer.

Space does not allow, and it is not the purpose here to attempt a detailed examination of the new rule. That it is very appreciably more complex than the R.O.R.C. rule, or any other rating rule which has preceded it, is not in doubt. On the other hand, the value of this complexity, based, as it appears to be, largely on empiricism, remains to be proved. What is certain is that it presents an additional problem to yacht designers, to which the foregoing attempts to suggest a solution.

INDEX OF SUBJECTS

INDEX OF NAMES

135.⁰⁰